CHAUCER: THE CRITICAL HERITAGE

VOLUME I 1385-1837

THE CRITICAL HERITAGE SERIES

GENERAL EDITOR: B. C. SOUTHAM, M.A., B. LITT. (OXON.)
Formerly Department of English, Westfield College, University of London

For a list of books in the series see the back end paper

CHAUCER

THE CRITICAL HERITAGE

VOLUME I 1385-1837

Edited by
DEREK BREWER
Emmanuel College, Cambridge

ROUTLEDGE & KEGAN PAUL
LONDON, HENLEY AND BOSTON

First published in 1978
by Routledge & Kegan Paul Ltd
39 Store Street,
London WC1E 7DD,
Broadway House,
Newtown Road,
Henley-on-Thames,
Oxon RG9 1EN and
9 Park Street,
Boston, Mass. 02108, USA
Printed in Great Britain by
Redwood Burn Ltd
Trowbridge & Esher
© Derek Brewer 1978

British Library Cataloguing in Publication Data

Chaucer, the critical heritage.—(The Critical
heritage series).
1. Chaucer, Geoffrey—Criticism and
interpretation—Addresses, essays, lectures
I. Brewer, Derek Stanley II. Series
821'.1   PR1924   78-40016

ISBN 0 7100 8497 8

General Editor's Preface

The reception given to a writer by his contemporaries and near-contemporaries is evidence of considerable value to the student of literature. On one side we learn a great deal about the state of criticism at large and in particular about the development of critical attitudes towards a single writer; at the same time, through private comments in letters, journals or marginalia, we gain an insight upon the tastes and literary thought of individual readers of the period. Evidence of this kind helps us to understand the writer's historical situation, the nature of his immediate reading-public, and his response to these pressures.

The separate volumes in the *Critical Heritage Series* present a record of this early criticism. Clearly, for many of the highly productive and lengthily reviewed nineteenth- and twentieth-century writers, there exists an enormous body of material; and in these cases the volume editors have made a selection of the most important views, significant for their intrinsic critical worth or for their representative quality—perhaps even registering incomprehension!

For earlier writers, notably pre-eighteenth century, the materials are much scarcer and the historical period has been extended, sometimes far beyond the writer's lifetime, in order to show the inception and growth of critical views which were initially slow to appear.

In each volume the documents are headed by an Introduction, discussing the material assembled and relating the early stages of the author's reception to what we have come to identify as the critical tradition. The volumes will make available much material which would otherwise be difficult of access and it is hoped that the modern reader will be thereby helped towards an informed understanding of the ways in which literature has been read and judged.

B.C.S.

For Helena

Contents

CONTENTS

CONTENTS

x

The late Dr. *Johnson* being asked his opinion of the expediency of Mr. Derrick's republishing an old book, with his usual bluntness replied,—'Why, Sir, if you *must* print, it had better be some other person's nonsense than your own.' And yet, if one *must* print, how shall an undiscriminating editor know what to rescue from oblivion?

F. G. Waldron, Advertisement to
'The Loves of Troilus and Cresseid
       ... with a commentary by Sir Francis Kinaston', 1796

It was Augustine, I believe, who invoked in jest or in earnest a curse on those who had anticipated him in the utterance of his ideas. . . .

A. C. Swinburne, 'Miscellanies', 1886, p. 123

Introduction

The heritage of criticism of Chaucer is a body of writing
unique in English literature. No other author has been
commented on in English so regularly and extensively over
so long a period. The literary observations and discus-
sions threaded together by their reference to Chaucer constitute a unique index to the course of English criticism
and literary theory. Some well-known critical texts take
on a fresh importance when seen in connection with Chaucer, while other less-known comments reveal an unexpected
significance.

All the later major poets, and almost all distinguished
English and American men of letters up to the first third
of the twentieth century have made at least passing allusion to Chaucer. But it is not the purpose of the present
volumes to collect such allusions, a task already superbly,
though inevitably selectively, performed by Miss
Spurgeon.(1) Nor is it their purpose to reprint the very
many modernisations, translations and imitations made over
the centuries, which imply various critical views, but
views that are more explicit elsewhere and whose bulk
would have required impracticably vast volumes for relatively small critical return. The aim of the present volumes is to give a copious selection, including all the
significant passages, of all the 'critical' writings on
Chaucer from his own day up to 1933. That date has been
chosen, as the Introduction to Volume 2 more fully
explains, as marking roughly the end of the tradition of
the generally cultivated amateur critic and reader, who
shared, usually unconsciously, the general tradition of
Neoclassical, Romantic and Victorian premises about literature, with their social implications. This general tradition, as will be shown more fully below, began about

1

the middle of the sixteenth century in England and became
dominant with Dryden.

The first volume of these extracts covers the period
which begins from Chaucer's lifetime (when rhetorical
principles of thinking about poetry prevailed), continues
through the Neoclassical and Romantic periods (which begin
towards the end of the sixteenth century), and concludes
at 1837 on the brink of the Victorian period, where, however, there is no major break. The second volume covers
the subsequent hundred years. The range of both volumes
is thus slightly greater than that of Miss Spurgeon's
monumental work, and of a somewhat different orientation,
as more fully explained in the Bibliographical Note. The
aim has been to trace critical opinions and attitudes.
Many extracts are necessarily the same as in Miss Spurgeon's work, but a few references have been added, a good
many have been extended, and very many have been dropped
from her list in the earlier centuries, while nineteenth-
century contributions have been much increased.

II

Chaucer's genius was recognised as outstanding even in his
own day. Leaving aside the probable intention of honour-
ing him by burial in Westminster Abbey, then normally re-
served for royalty, what other English author has been so
heartily praised by a *French* contemporary (No. 1)? It is
worth glancing for comparison at the reputations of Chaucer's English contemporaries. Apart from Chaucer, only
Lydgate and Gower attracted comment in the fifteenth and
sixteenth centuries, and they were often noticed mainly
because of their association with Chaucer. From the seventeenth century until the middle of the twentieth Lydgate
has been practically forgotten except, notably, by the
poet Gray (No. 81). During the same period Gower slum-
bered on without being awakened even by Gray, though
modern taste now places him above Lydgate and in a few
respects not too far below Chaucer. Langland's 'Piers
Plowman', widely read at the end of the fourteenth century and in the fifteenth, was for some reason not printed
by Caxton, who was otherwise so assiduous to preserve late
medieval English culture. 'Piers Plowman' was at last
printed, probably for religious rather than literary reasons, in 1550, but only from the middle of the twentieth
century has it been given the attention its greatness
deserves. The 'Gawain'-poet, as great a poet as Chaucer,
though very different, survived from the fourteenth century in only one small MS., was unknown till the nine-

teenth century, and hardly discussed till the 1950s.
Chaucer alone, from his own day onwards, has been accepted
as a major English poet, and, understandably though erro-
neously, has very often been taken as the founding father
of English literature, and the first refiner of our language. His work has been present as a general, much-
enjoyed, if often little understood, possession of the
English literary mind, solidly 'there', since his own
lifetime.

III

The tradition of commenting in reference to Chaucer is
thus the only tradition of critical commentary in English
that exists continuously from before the end of the sixteenth century, and it immediately reveals the remarkable
change and innovation that began to take place around
1600 in England in the premises, expectations and theories
held about literature. The change may be described as the
change from Gothic to Neoclassical concepts of literature.
We are immediately in a difficulty here, because we owe
most, if not all, of our ideas about what literature is,
or should be, and the very idea of literary criticism and
theory itself, to Neoclassicism; more strictly, to Humanism, i.e. the study of *literae humaniores,* 'the more
humane writings'. In our era it was Humanism, and especially the Humanist scholars of Italy and France in the fifteenth and sixteenth centuries, who established the nature
and importance of literature.(2) Almost everything that
it seems natural for normal twentieth-century liberal educated Westerners to say about literature, for example that
it represents 'reality', is 'educative', and in some way
'improving', and almost all our artistic criteria, derive
specifically from Humanism. Naturally, not all Humanistic
concepts were entirely original. Most were rooted in some
aspect of medieval literature, in particular, medieval
Latin literature, which itself was largely a product of
the official ecclesiastical tradition, as well as heir to
the prestige of ancient Roman literary culture. But even
medieval Latin *literature* (in the sense of avowed verbal
fictions) was not always highly thought of, especially as
scholasticism became dominant from the beginning of the
thirteenth century, and the vernacular was for long a poor
relation of Latin.(3) One of the great achievements of
literary Humanism, reflected in the course of the criticism of Chaucer, was to raise the status of the vernacular, as of literature itself - a dual achievement to
which, in England, Chaucer's own works also contributed.

But the very diversity of attitudes to Chaucer's works in
the latter part of the sixteenth century reveals some of
the dilemmas of Humanistic, or more conveniently named
Neoclassical criticism, when confronted with a substantial
body of vernacular literature composed with no regard for
Neoclassical rules. The difficulty is not that Neoclassical rules were broken (though they constantly were), but
that in the earlier tradition fundamental attitudes towards, and within, literature, were different. It is convenient to sum up the pre-Neoclassical attitudes as 'rhetorical', typical of all sorts of traditional literature,
including so-called 'oral literature'. The English seg-
ment of traditional literature which is represented by
Chaucer's work is most conveniently called English Gothic
literature, by analogy with the contemporary easily recog-
nisable Gothic style in the visual and plastic arts, and
like that style extending roughly from about 1200 to about
the end of the sixteenth century.(4)
    'Rhetoric' is a wide and confusing term. It is partly
a technical term, and largely, since about 1700, a term of
abuse.(5) Like the old soldier, it's dead but it won't
lie down. The concept and practice of rhetoric are un-
avoidable in language and above all in literature but they
may well be misconceived, distorted or disregarded. The
history of rhetoric has been well traced in general,(6)
and the criticism of Chaucer, amongst much other evidence,
gives specific examples of its use or absence as a critical premise. As a technical term 'rhetoric' may refer to
the various treatises written from Classical Antiquity onwards, which in the Middle Ages degenerated into lists of
verbal devices, with little (though still some) attention
paid to underlying structural principle. It is easy to
see how these, and even their sixteenth-century successors, came to be despised. Yet they offer a clue to a
most important and until recently neglected aspect of
language, its *intrinsic* vitality, its creative autonomy.
Language, by elaboration, by choice of purely verbal resource, independent of external control, can be conceived
as in itself a work of art. How this can be involves difficult questions of the relation of the universe of discourse to non-linguistic universes, and these cannot be
examined here. Neoclassicism introduced a literalism of
discourse, which denied its creative autonomy, subduing
language (as far as it could) to a narrowly descriptive
function. Since such literal description was plainly inadequate to convey personal feeling, Romanticism emphasised the expressive element through the speaker's or
writer's own *self*-description. Accuracy and sincerity
thus became important criteria. Of course these have

their places in traditional pre-Neoclassical writing,
since most writing is a multiple-level activity, but accuracy and sincerity are only part of a general creative
linguistic effort which allows other effects too, such as
word-play, hyperbole, proverbial (not personal) wisdom.
This *general* creative linguistic effort is what is denoted
by a 'rhetorical', that is, traditional, way of writing.
Failure to understand this underlies much modern misunder-
standing of the Bible, Shakespeare, Chaucer. Our misun-
derstanding may be partly excused by the lack of literary
conceptualisation characteristic of traditional writers,
and found even in the writers of technical rhetorical
treatises, who were mostly men with a practical concern to
teach the tricks of the trade. They were teaching how to
generate verbal structures: 'creative writing', in fact.
The treatises themselves were never intended as manuals of
criticism or of the theory of literature, and hardly enter
into the history of the criticism of Chaucer (though cf.
Brathwait, No. 55). The notions about literature and language that underlie the treatises on rhetoric do however
underlie critical commentary up to the middle of the sixteenth century, when Neoclassical ideas begin to enter.
If we are sympathetic to these rhetorical, traditional and
Gothic premises about literature we can learn a good deal
about Chaucer's poetry, English poetry and criticism, and
the nature of literature itself.

The very first comment on Chaucer, by the contemporary
French poet, Deschamps, emphasises Chaucer's variety. The
warmest praise, if reiteration is any guide, is for Chaucer as a translator, and though there may be some French
conceit in this, it accords well with the general medieval
and indeed traditional sense, as implicit in medieval rhetoric, that a poet's greatness consists in his ability
specifically to find *words* for matter which is already
provided. Deschamps' praise of Chaucer *as a man* goes far
beyond this, even taking hyperbole into account. Learned,
scientific, good, practical, not too talkative: we are
told that these were Chaucer's personal characteristics,
though seen in his writing as well. As a *poet,* Chaucer is
compared with Ovid, the master of pathos, of love, of
comedy and witty verbal elaboration. The comparison is
profoundly apt, but never significantly realised in the
full Neoclassical period even though Dryden sees it, as
well as one or two others (Nos 66, 77, 99a). Though both
Chaucer and Ovid are extraordinarily creative and both in
various ways may be said to teach, neither laid claim to
the poet's sublime superiority of wisdom and morality over
historian and philosopher, let alone over the non-writing
part of humanity, which the noble Neoclassical ideal of

Sidney and Milton asserted.

The comments of Usk (No. 2), and of others in the early
period, do however refer to Chaucer's serious and nourish-
ing subject-matter, the 'fructuous entendement' (No.
7), that 'sentence', which the Gothic poet is certainly
required to provide, as for example by the Host of the
Tabard. But the Host also wants 'solas' or 'mirth'. The
Gothic poet besides his learning should provide variety;
'some sad stories, some merry', as the very Gothic Skelton
remarks (No. 19).

The fullest near-contemporary criticism of Chaucer is
by Lydgate, who very frequently comments on, alludes to,
and imitates Chaucer. Lydgate is not writing criticism
in our sense, for reasons already explained, but from his
remarks emerges an account of Chaucer's poetry that deserves attention. After Chaucer's personal genius and
primacy as a poet, which Lydgate is rightly never tired of
praising, Chaucer's quality as a 'noble rethor' is for
Lydgate most significant. Lydgate emphasises the richness
of Chaucer's language, 'the gold dewdrops of rhetoric so
fine' (No. 4c, cf. 4b), his 'sugared' style, (the same
word that Francis Meres used to praise his own contemporary Shakespeare's Sonnets). Lydgate seems to register
something of Chaucer's realism of style, by his reference
to 'Word for word, with every circumstance' (No. 4 e) but
the concept of 'flowers of rhetoric and eloquence' (No.
4 d) is essentially that of the creative power of language, which rhetorical theory implies, and not the imitative dependence on some external factor which dominated
views of poetry from the seventeenth to the twentieth century, and which is characteristic of Neoclassical and Romantic views. Rhetorical theory, although it accepts the
creative autonomy and thus elaboration of language, does
not deny the validity of subject-matter, and Lydgate emphasises both the fullness of Chaucer's subject-matter
and, especially, its variety: fictions, 'historial'
things, morality, disport, comedy, tragedy and ribaldry
(No. 4 e). Lydgate gives an account of many of Chaucer's
works, but describes him as being particularly without a
peer in his power to tell stories (No. 4 g). The status
of poets, says Lydgate (owing something to Boccaccio here
in his 'Chapitle' on poets (No. 4 g)), is to be maintained
by princes, and he is pleased that Chaucer in his life
attained a 'virtuous sufficiency', but no claim is made
for the poet's supremacy as a man in society, for all his
learning. Thus the outline of Chaucer the poet emerges,
as one rich in linguistic resource, of a traditional kind,
but in English an innovator; a story-teller, capable of
telling many different kinds of stories, and interested

in writing many different kinds of works; learned, wise,
prudent, modest, dependent, and genial even to the extent
of being apparently uncritical. It seems a very satisfactory account, granted its broad outline, both of Chaucer
himself, and of the Gothic ideal of a poet. The notion
in Lydgate's 'Chapitle' of the poet as a man leading a
quiet life, needing the support of wine and his prince,
may not fully correspond to the facts of Chaucer's life
as we know or guess them, but it corresponds quite closely
(apart from the detail about wine) with the way Chaucer
presents himself, and also of course with Lydgate's own
life. It will not be the only occasion when the 'critic'
(if the term may be used so early as Lydgate) of Chaucer
is found to describe himself. Such self-description does
not necessarily invalidate the criticism. It is of the
nature of great poets that they mirror many readers of
different kinds; they are spokesmen for all or for many
of us. The Gothic poet, in his variety and his activa-
tion of many different strands of tradition, from morality
to ribaldry, is especially to be conceived of as a spokesman for a culture, rather than its priest, prophet, or unacknowledged legislator.

Subsequent comments by other men in the fifteenth century fill in the picture of the rhetorical Gothic poet,
with further emphasis on 'morality', e.g. by Scogan (No.
5), while Walton (No. 6) appears to mention Chaucer the
'flower of rhetoric' and 'excellent poet' in order impli-
citly to contrast him with Gower's 'morality' and to condemn his use of pagan morality.

Chaucer's social setting and possible contemporary
references are reflected in Shirley's gossipy remarks (No.
9), while on the other side Henryson (No. 11) is percep-
tively aware of the fictional inventiveness of Chaucer.
A sense emerges from such contrasts, not only of the
critic's own interests and of the poet's multiplicity, but
also of the way that Chaucer's poetry spans the range between pure fiction and actual historicity: it is not a
self-enclosed fictional mirror set against a true 'reality', any more than it is simply documentary. Hence
arises an ambivalence of ontological status very characteristic of Gothic poetry, and perhaps represented by the
mingled collection of books once owned by Sir John Paston
II (No. 12).

After Lydgate, Caxton (No. 14) is Chaucer's most copious commentator, reiterating the same general characteristics of rich language and pregnant meaning. The elaboration of rhetoric is seen not as empty flourishes, but
as the delightful conveyance of solid nourishment, so
that the translation of Boethius's 'Consolation of

Philosophy' ranks as high among the poet's achievements
as the great poems. But Caxton also does full justice to
the variety of 'The Canterbury Tales', and displays a
laudable anxiety - which seems not to have extended to his
actual practice - to get the text accurate.(7) Hawes (No.
18) once again strikes familiar notes, employing the
useful word 'sententious' (specifically of 'The House of
Fame') which describes that rhetorical Gothic rich verbalisation of an accepted tradition characteristic of so much
of the poetry of Chaucer as of Shakespeare, but which was
rejected by Neoclassical theory and practice.

There are some aspects of Gothic poetry which are
easily assimilated to Neoclassicism: moralising is one;
another is 'realism'. Realism, which is certainly present
in Chaucer's poetry, is touched lightly on by Lydgate, as
already noted, and occasionally picked up elsewhere, as
in the anonymous comment of c. 1477 (No. 13).

Humour is traditionally related to realism through
satire, as in Chaucer's poetry itself, but though it is
clear enough that Lydgate, for example, greatly appreciated Chaucer's humour, it is not much commented on in the
fifteenth and early sixteenth centuries. Skelton (No.
19), for all his New Learning a very Gothic poet, responds
to it most vigorously, as we might expect from his own
works.

Skelton also seems to be the first to feel the need to
defend Chaucer's language; and the passage of time, making
Chaucer 'an ancient', for good and bad, begins to be felt.
Furthermore, the sixteenth century sees the steady rise of
the tide of Humanism. Gavin Douglas condemns Chaucer's
'lakar' (faulty) style (No. 20) in translating Virgil in
an insufficiently Virgilian way - a true enough judgment,
if somewhat beside the point. Sir Brian Tuke, in his
dedication (No. 22) to Thynne's edition of 'The Workes of
Geffray Chaucer', on the other hand, reveals how the Humanist inspiration received from the great literary
achievements of Classical Antiquity could lead not only
to veneration of Chaucer and a higher valuation of the importance of literature in itself, but also to the practical achievements of scholarship and the first edition of
the complete works of Chaucer by Thynne in 1532. Scholarship is a product of Neoclassicism rather than of the mul-
tiple, fluid, casual, Gothic spirit. But Tuke is also the
first to express a characteristic Humanist, anti-medieval,
surprise that so good a poet as Chaucer could exist as it
were against the cultural climate, in so barbarous a time
'when all good letters were laid asleep throughout the
world'. Sidney echoes this in a memorable phrase (No.
43).

In England Humanism also often drew strength and moral
conviction from the immense zeal of Protestant reform,
though the case of Erasmus shows that Humanism need not
necessarily go with Protestantism. At first Protestant
zeal took over one aspect of medieval Latin official culture in comdemning literature for being fiction, and fiction for being in itself reprehensible; and contrasted
Chaucer's works (especially 'The Canterbury Tales') un-
favourably with the Bible (Nos 21, 23, 31). But the literary perception of Ascham, severe moralist though he was,
marks a more subtle appreciation, and an assimilation of
Chaucer's works to the status of the Classics. The literary prominence of the men of St John's College, Cambridge,
around the end of the sixteenth century, with their numerous comments on Chaucer, may reflect the influence of
Ascham, or at least of his type of Humanism. In the later
seventeenth century and the eighteenth the Protestant interest in Chaucer lapsed, as he was seen primarily as a
humorist, to return with vigour in the nineteenth century
(cf. No. 99).(8)

Humanism was the main force that transformed Chaucer
criticism by introducing those Neoclassical concepts of
literature and of the superior status of the poet that
help to disclose, as well as to develop, a new feeling,
beginning in the sixteenth century, about our experience
of the world, and of the relation of language (and hence
literature) to the world. Although there are important
adumbrations, the significant text in English is Sidney's
'An Apology', where the reference to Chaucer is significantly brief (No. 43). Sidney's genius creamed off the
long labours of many brilliant European scholars and
critics, to offer England for the first time in English a
coherent theory of literature.(9) 'An Apology' is only
casually and incidentally 'criticism'. But 'criticism' is
often taken to be Sidney's principal aim, and in consequence 'An Apology' has been often misunderstood, and
undervalued, by readers looking primarily for critical
'insights', rather than a theory of literature. Nevertheless, some of Sidney's critical 'insights', or judgments,
usefully point to the nature of what he was looking for
in literature. Of these judgments his remarks on drama
are the most striking, for there, as is well known, he
categorically condemns that current English drama, developed from medieval sources, that Shakespeare was to write
- the English language's supreme achievement. Why should
Sidney have been so wrong?

The reason is that he was applying the wrong literary
principles, or at least principles different from those
hitherto accepted. Perhaps Sidney, had he lived to see

or read Shakespeare's mature work, might have recognised
his genius as an empirical fact, as did Ben Jonson; but
again like Jonson, he might well have reiterated his criticisms. Sidney's Neoclassical doctrine required in the
drama obedience to the celebrated pseudo-Aristotelian
three unities of time, place and action. Well-known as
these are, their underlying significance is often not
recognised. It consists in the attempt to make the presentation of the events of the play apparently identical
with the way things appear to happen in life, but in a
self-enclosed, self-consistent, completed fiction. Thus
a fundamentally mimetic theory of literature is being invoked by Sidney for the first time in the vernacular English tradition. Ben Jonson's implicit criticisms of
Shakespeare in the various Prologues to his plays apply
the same theory. Jonson explains that his own plays do
not cover a person's lifetime, i.e. they do not represent
time symbolically, nor violate time-keeping; as with time,
so other aspects of 'reality', such as war, are not, he
boasts, given purely token or symbolic, verbal, representation: 'three rusty swords,/And help of some few foot-
and-halfe-foote-words' (Prologue to 'Every Man in his
Humour', with which Neoclassical Jonson begins his collected 'Works' (1640).) Gothic Shakespeare never bothered
to collect and publish his own plays. The status of the
poet (and Jonson calls himself poet, not playwright) is
claimed to be different. Jonson specifically claims an
authoritative, edifying and improving function for himself
as poet. To quote Sidney again, the 'poet's nobleness'
(ed. cit., p. 104) can never, by definition, create mock-
ery, indecency, or the grotesque; that is, such abuse as
infects the fancy with unworthy objects (p. 125) or as,
'in the comical part of our tragedy', the 'scurrility,
unworthy of any chaste ears' (p. 136). Thus the Neoclassical true poet will never be in such a position that he
will need to 'revoke' as Chaucer did, in the name of the
official culture, the larger proportion of his works. The
Neoclassical poet is not only better than other men, he is
more learned: 'of all sciences (I speak still of human,
and according to the human conceits) is our poet the monarch' (p. 113). There is here a glance at the supremacy
of religious truth, but Sidney effectively assumes an
identity of interest and conviction between poet and theologian or preacher, for 'ever-praiseworthy Poesy is full
of virtue-breeding delightfulness' (p. 141).
   Yet 'Poesy is an art of imitation' (p. 101), and Sidney's whole theory, like that of the great European scholars on whom he drew, is based on this premise. Thus in
the Neoclassical view poetry is by definition both

imitative of life and morally improving. The poet is a
monarch of realistic representation, of learning, and of
morality, whose very humour has no need of laughter (which
'hath only a scornful tickling' (*ed. cit.*, p. 136)). It
is hard to fit Chaucer, or Shakespeare, into such a frame.
Yet so powerful and seductive is the Neoclassical doctrine
that Dr Jonson in the eighteenth century, whose empirical
contemplation of Shakespeare forced him to reject the
doctrine of the necessity of the three unities in a play,
because Shakespeare who violated them was so successful,
was still impelled to maintain (No. 79) that the graces
of a play are 'to copy Nature and instruct life'; that is,
the aim is to be 'realistic' and didactic at the same time.
Such an aim is often self-contradictory, for Nature is by
no means always edifying. Yet Neoclassicism is irremedi-
ably committed to an essentially didactic view of literature, which involves also the superiority of poetry, as
Sidney claims, over history and philosophy, and the superiority of the poet over everyone else. 'A good book is
the life-blood of a master-spirit', says Milton who also
maintains the (alas) extraordinary notion that good poets
are *ipso facto* good men. Both Samuel Johnson and Shelley
describe poets, in Shelley's famous final phrase in his
'Defence', as 'the unacknowledged legislators of mankind'.
It is not surprising that Shelley has nothing to say of
Chaucer. Neoclassical subsumes Romantic in this as in
several other matters. The poet is no ordinary man, he is
'a curious universal scholar', as Gabriel Harvey was to
call him, simultaneously a law-giver, priest and prophet;
vates, as even so early as 1556 Chaucer was described on
his tomb (cf. Foxe, No. 36).

Thus Chaucer in the sixteenth century can only be represented as a moral teacher, by those who approve of him
(and not all do), by emphasising his moral elements and
disregarding both his 'mirth' and his modesty, in contrast
with the less unified, more miscellaneous, Gothic view, in
accordance with which Chaucer, Langland, Gower, the
'Pearl'-poet, Deschamps, Machaut, Boccaccio, Dante, all
present themselves in their own poems as ignorant, and
sometimes foolish or absurd learners. Those who disapp-
rove of Chaucer in the sixteenth century can, on the other
hand, like Harington (No. 49) or the early Protestants,
condemn him for his undignified or unedifying aspects, his
modesty and 'mirth', which is to disregard the equally
Gothic traditional moralising and morality also fully present in Chaucer's work, and frequently noted in the sixteenth century.

Sidney resolves his Neoclassical dilemma between 'following Nature' and 'instructing life' by stipulating that

the poet must create a 'second Nature', a golden Nature,
different from the tarnished brass of ordinary experience; and the poet himself must be a 'better teacher than
Aquinas', as Milton was to call Spenser, not just a genius
with words. Indeed, words tend to become suspect or unim-
portant, in the seventeenth century, and regarded as mere
labels to things; often misleading labels.

This last point, about the status of words, introduces
the final element in the critical developments of the
seventeenth century, which owed much to the influence of
Bacon. There was a shift in the general sense of the
relationship of 'words' to 'things'. It is clear that the
development of scientific empiricism, the 'mechanical
philosophy', accompanied or helped to cause, or was partly
caused by, a distrust of the intangible, irremediable
vagueness of language.(10) The metaphorical nature of
language was attacked, for example, by Hobbes. Sprat's
famous account in his 'History of the Royal Society',
1667, of the Royal Society's ideal of a 'close, naked and
natural way of speaking', by which, as in primitive times,
men might deliver 'so many *things*, almost in an equal
number of words', represented a determined down-grading
of language as itself autonomous and creative (No. 61).
Instead of thinking of language as taking its proper
origin and validity from the mind, as being a communication between minds, language was thought of as validated
by its correspondence with 'external', 'objective' reality, which comes to be thought of increasingly as primarily material.(11) The demand was for language to
reject metaphor and abstraction and to become more literalistic. This is essentially a 'mimetic' theory of language, which obviously chimed with the mimetic or natur-
alistic basis of more specifically Neoclassical literary
principle. As with Neoclassical 'naturalism', linguistic
'realism', or literalism, was at that time limited by
certain social, moral and religious constraints, by the
conservatism which preserved older ways of thought and
feeling, and by the ordinary human situation. The importance of the change, however, may be measured by the fact
that in the twentieth century we often retain the didactic naturalism in literature and in behaviour that is
derived from Neoclassical theory, even though we have cast
off the traditional restraints.(12)

However, in Sidney and in the seventeenth century,
traditional moral and social constraints accompanied literary theory. When combined with the desire for edifica-
tion and for consistency in literary works they led to
the notion of 'decorum' (which, as Milton says, 'is the
grand masterpiece'), meaning an avoidance of the

undignified Gothic mixture of different tones and of different kinds of material or attitude in the same work of art, such as allowed, in Shakespeare, comic scenes in tragedies; or, in Chaucer, a tasteless mixture of the indecent with the devout, the flippant with the serious, 'sad stories with some merry'. Neoclassical literary criticism is firmly based on a theory of the clearly separate *genres* of literature, to which it is very hard to adapt the actual practice of Chaucer and other Gothic writers (or indeed of much literature of other periods, though that is a different question).(13) In England we may see the clash between Gothic and Neoclassical principle played out before our eyes around 1600 by the juxtaposition and contrast between Shakespeare, our last and greatest Gothic writer, and Ben Jonson, our first great Neoclassical writer.

IV

What now of Chaucer? The purest Neoclassical critics who 'rode al of the newe jet' avoid or condemn him. Sidney is lukewarm; and Ben Jonson though citing him in his grammar is not influenced by him and hardly mentions him critically, in contrast to Shakespeare who frequently echoes him (though, as a true Gothic writer, Shakespeare does not practise formal literary criticism). Rymer, our most extreme Neoclassical critic, has no good to say of Chaucer (No. 64), nor has Addison (No. 65). Cowley could not read him (cf. No. 66). Samuel Johnson, our greatest Neoclassical critic, is evidently unsympathetic (No. 79). Chaucer's mixture of *genres*, his fantasy in so many poems, his humour, satire, irony, his touches of the grotesque, his lack of decorum, the hyperbolical or at least non-mimetic nature of so much of his language, his strangeness because of the passage of time, his refusal of the role of poetic *vates*, all make him unsympathetic to the immediate requirements of Neoclassicism. Hence the pause in appreciation of Chaucer in the seventeenth century (though it is somewhat over-emphasised by Miss Spurgeon). One must recognise here the increasing difficulty of Chaucer's language, commented on with increasing frequency, and resulting in Kynaston's Latin translation (cf. No. 59) and Sidnam's (?) English modernisation of about 1630 (cf. No. 57), each of 'Troilus and Criseyde'. But 'The Canterbury Tales' apparently gave less trouble (or seemed, as usual, more worth it), and Chaucer continued to be read. An edition, with the conscious antiquarian appeal of blackletter (i.e. Gothic) type (very mannered and

beautiful), was published in 1687, though the interval
between that and Speght's last edition of 1602 was the
longest between any editions of Chaucer. Old-fashioned
people, or people with traditional tastes (which usually
includes the majority of the reading public), courtiers
like Wentworth, Earl of Strafford, or at a lower social
level, Pepys (No. 60), and Cambridge men in general, all
continued to enjoy him. The strong vein of Gothicism in
Milton (a Cambridge man, who had for many years intended
to write his epic on the Gothic subject of King Arthur)
rejoices in the romance element in Chaucer, as we know
from the allusion in 'L'Allegro'. Dryden too (No. 66),
who was yet another Cambridge man, appreciated the romance, 'The Knight's Tale'; but it is highly significant
that he transposed appreciation of it into the terms of
epic, or heroic poem, which, as W.P. Ker showed many
years ago in his Introduction to Dryden's 'Essays' (1926),
was one of the most characteristic, as it was the most
valued, of genres acknowledged by early Neoclassical criticism. Dryden's praise and his translation of 'The
Knight's Tale' in 'The Fables' ensured that it was frequently commented on in the next century, but as epic,
which is in some respects an anti-type of romance.
     Yet when considering Chaucer's sustained appeal one
may feel that the relish for Chaucer in the latter part
of the seventeenth century felt by dirty-minded courtiers
like Mennes (cf. No. 60), as revealed in his imitations
of Chaucer reprinted with his own scatological effusions,
is coarser and far narrower than the pleasure felt by
earlier courtiers like Wyatt (No. 26). The advent of a
new realism, Neoclassical and 'scientific' rather than
Gothic, reinforced the Gothic alliance between laughter,
satire, and gross realism, which is of course genuinely
present in Chaucer, but broke the vital link between
these and the more idealising styles and works. One
cannot help feeling that this new coarse realism in
Dryden and Pope, with their new marked vein of scatological or sexual grossness, over-emphasised some elements
of Chaucer's work, for the sake of finding a mirror to
itself, even though Dryden felt he could not publish a
translation of 'The Wife of Bath's Prologue' because of
its indecency.
     However that may be, a new sense of Chaucer's own
realism develops in the appreciation and criticism of
Chaucer's work in the late seventeenth and the eighteenth
century. Great verbal art has by definition an ability
to answer historically inappropriate questions, to meet
demands different from those of its own age. Chaucer's
supreme realisation of the variety inherent in fourteenth

century English empiricism paradoxically made some elements of his work very readily available to Neoclassical
assumptions, especially if other elements in his work were
ignored. Dryden, responding perhaps to something of
Chaucer's own Gothic casualness, stepped with majestic
ease across the gulf between Neoclassical and Gothic to
seize on Chaucer's realism and make it compatible with
Neoclassical premises. Henceforth, that Chaucer follows
'Nature', especially as a comic, and has a command of
pathos, are the dominant notes of the criticism. His
reputation for 'epic' after a while fades, and he is
further assimilated to the novelist, and especially the
dramatist.
     There were some important changes in the Romantic
period, and in the nineteenth century, which will be discussed in the Introduction to the second volume; but
here it may be worth briefly noticing how persistent is
the notion of Neoclassical realism, of the emphasis on
the derivativeness of word from thing, throughout both
the eighteenth and the nineteenth centuries, Neoclassical
and Romantic. For Samuel Johnson, great lexicographer,
in his Preface to his 'Dictionary' (1755), 'words are the
daughters of earth' and 'things are the sons of heaven',
which has an anti-feminist bias in favour of male things.
Blake (No. 90) emphasises the importance of character,
and can say that names alter, but things do not. Hazlitt
(No. 95) remarks that Chaucer describes as if giving
evidence on oath. Lowell (Vol. 2, No. 17) thinks that
for Chaucer what is important is 'the thing in itself',
not the description: 'names alter, things never do' -
consciously or not echoing Blake. Arnold (Vol. 2, No.
24) speaks of Chaucer's 'large, free, sound representation
of things'. Arnold is particularly interesting because
his general notions of poetry as 'a criticism of life',
of the need for a poet 'to know life and the world before
dealing with them in poetry', and of the critical power
'to see the object as in itself it really is',(14) are
all extensions of the Neoclassical division between objective experience and the subjective mind, between 'real
things' and their dependent verbalisation. Arnold cannot
bring himself to admit Chaucer's absolute greatness as a
writer because he wants more than great writing; he wants
great writing arising out of and concerned with the
subject-matter of serious moral, indeed religious, exaltation. Arnold recognises that this is sometimes present
in Chaucer, as it is much more fully in Dante; but even
in Dante, and especially in Chaucer, seriousness is mixed
with such variety, indecorum, and 'modesty' that the
vatic demand often receives a check, as if the same man

should appear as both priest and clown. A flexibility of
response, a humour, on the part of a reader is required,
which Neoclassical and Romantic principles hardly allow
for. It is significant that Arnold barely notices the
existence of Dickens, his great contemporary, who of all
nineteenth-century writers, with his fantasy-realism, his
hyperbolical manner and style, his pathos and his laughter, his closeness to the popular mind and remoteness from
Neoclassicism, is closest to Chaucer in genius and temperament. Bagehot (Vol. 2, No. 10), more worldly, does
better here.

Once the Neoclassical and Romantic emphasis on 'realism'
is recognised as part of a characteristic outlook, the
question how far Chaucer's own work can legitimately be
said to be 'realistic' would take us further afield than
an introductory essay on the history of the criticism of
Chaucer should extend.(15)

Another important Neoclassical literary concept had a
remarkably delayed action in the criticism of Chaucer.
This is the concept expressed in the curious term 'poetic
justice', implying that kind of justice, too rarely met
with in real life, which imposes appropriate punishment
'to fit the crime'. W.S. Gilbert's Mikado expressed the
notion most vividly in the wider world in 1885. Chaucer
criticism soon followed on, most clearly with the work
of W.M. Hart (Vol. 2, No. 32) at the beginning of the
twentieth century, and since then 'poetic justice' has
been the most hardworked of all inappropriate concepts
that have been applied to Chaucer's popular comic tales,
or *fabliaux*. It is a characteristic Neoclassical concept
and emerges in the early eighteenth century.(16) The
main use of the term in relation to Chaucer has, however,
been in the twentieth century.

V

Neoclassical principles never so seized hold of the English literary mind as, for example, they seem to have
occupied the French in the seventeenth and eighteenth
centuries. There are several reasons. One is the presence of some inherent self-contradiction, as briefly
discussed above, in the principles themselves; another is
the existence of Shakespeare and, to a lesser extent, of
Chaucer. The work of Shakespeare, our greatest Gothic
writer, is self-evidently almost totally recalcitrant
to Neoclassical principles, while any critical principles
which deny Shakespeare his greatness stand self-condemned.
The classic confrontation between Shakespeare and

Neoclassical critical theory is Samuel Johnson's 'Preface
to Shakespeare'. Shakespeare is not even as realistic as
Chaucer, and cannot, as a dramatist, be treated as selectively as the poet, though Johnson does significantly,
like most eighteenth-century critics of Chaucer, respond
most easily to Shakespeare's comedy and realism.
   The presence of Shakespeare and Chaucer kept the English literary mind to some extent open to Gothic romance
and humour, even with such sturdy Neoclassics as Milton
and Pope. Then as early as 1760 the great stirrings of
Romanticism, in England as in Europe, led to a more sympathetic interest in the past and the beginning of the
historical imagination that sees the past as different
from the present. The works of Hurd (No. 82) and Thomas
Warton (No. 83) are very important in this respect in the
English context. Yet though Chaucer benefits from the
new sensibility, Romantic literary principles are sufficiently a natural development of Neoclassical principles, at least as they focus on Chaucer, for the changes
in the critical appreciation of Chaucer among Romantic
writers not to be so great as one might have expected.

VI

The deeper changes significantly begun in the seventeenth
century affected the value put on the various parts of
Chaucer's works. 'The Canterbury Tales', and especially
'The General Prologue' and 'The Wife of Bath's Prologue',
had always been appreciated. Lydgate's imitation of
Chaucer's 'Prologue to the Canterbury Tales' in the Prologue to his own 'Thebes'; the several early references
to the Wife of Bath, besides Chaucer's own references;
perhaps the proverbial phrase 'a Canterbury tale'; Caxton's printings and comments; Skelton's appreciation of
the mixture of 'some sad stories, some merry': all testify
to knowledge of and pleasure in 'The Canterbury Tales' in
the fifteenth and sixteenth centuries. Yet up to the end
of the seventeenth century the highest praise of specific
works is for 'Troilus and Criseyde', commended by Sidney's
aristocratic taste, chosen for modernisation by Sidnam
(No. 57), and for translation into Latin by Kynaston.
The general effect of the changes in the seventeenth century, on which Dryden sets his seal, is that 'The Canterbury Tales' comes to the fore. 'Troilus and Criseyde'
has since 1700 been relatively neglected until well into
the twentieth century. We may take the opportunity here
to notice that the didactic element in Gothic literature
found some expression in the non-fictional 'Parson's

Tale', which in Chaucer, as in at least part of his source,
reflects the characteristically Puritanical tones of the
devout layman, rather than the subtleties, so much more
liberal in effect, of the professional theologian. But
apart from Ascham no critic refers to 'The Parson's Tale',
and even Ascham's knowledge is doubtful (No. 29).

VII

The changes in the seventeenth century displaced rhetoric
as a central Humanistic activity. It may be objected
against this that Neoclassical critics used and even revived rhetoric in the sixteenth century, and that rhetoric
was still flourishing in the eighteenth century. One
might add too that some form of rhetoric is inherent in
almost all human communication. Granted that these objections have force, it still seems that traditional rhetoric
conceived as a primary mental activity manipulating speech
for various purposes, received its death-blow in the
seventeenth century, though it was an unconscionably long
time dying. Even in the Middle Ages rhetoric was frequently concerned merely with stylistic adornment. But,
to recapitulate the essential nature of rhetoric, the
characteristic praise of Chaucer by Lydgate, Hoccleve, or
Dunbar (Nos 4, 7, 17), reveals their inner sense, however
little consciously realised, of the importance of rhetoric
as a mode of knowledge and creative perception, using language as a mental tool. Chaucer, they continually say,
refined and extended language, as well as adorning it.
There is an underlying sense in the early period that
Chaucer *created* meaning; not that he 'imitated' it in
words. By contrast, from Dryden onwards the tendency is
quite different. When critics say that Chaucer 'followed
Nature' they imply a theory of literature that can only
attribute an at best 'second-hand reality' (if the expression may be permitted) to words. A necessary corollary is that the more literalistic the use of words, the
better; the less literalistic (i.e. by using pun, hyperbole, sententiousness, mixed metaphor - which are in
fact the common coin of most common speech and traditional
literature) the worse.(17) Such an attitude is still frequently met with in criticism as late as the second half
of the twentieth century. Literalism is totally opposed
to rhetoric. Rhetoric was not, can never be, completely
destroyed, but in England it was progressively weakened
until it was finally discredited by Romanticism.
    The fictionality of the subject-matter of literature is
necessarily emphasised by literalism, since the subject-

matter so vividly and (in intention) concretely focused
is confessedly non-existent. Literature has often been
thought to 'mirror' life, but in the eighteenth century
the image takes on a new precision.(18) In consequence,
works of art were felt to be enclosed fictions which
'imitated' life by 'mirroring' it in convincing detail.
This amounts to an 'illusionist' theory of art.(19)
Such at least may be deduced from the apparently increasing awareness in the eighteenth century of Chaucer's work
as a fiction, filled with convincing illusionist detail,
of which the verses published in 1740 by Astrophil (No.
77) are the earliest clear example after Dryden. A work
of fiction is then necessarily conceived as concerned with
self-subsistent dramatic characters. The general inspiration of all this, which leads to the novelistic and dramatic concept of Chaucer, is that Neoclassical movement of
which for our present purposes Dryden is the head. It of
course genuinely responds to something in Chaucer which
is not in most, if any, of his contemporaries, and it
still flourishes in the latter part of the twentieth century. A tiny but vivid example of the difference of
feeling about Chaucer's dramatic realism as initiated in
the seventeenth century and developed in the eighteenth
and later centuries may be found in regard to 'The Wife
of Bath's Prologue', III, 585-6, a couple of lines where
we have to modern eyes a literalistic, or illusionist,
imitation of the Wife forgetting for a moment what she
was going to say. The lines provide an excellently dramatic touch, but for the old-fashioned literary amateur
Brathwait (No. 55), writing in 1616 (though published much
later), it is a delightful piece of rhetoric, an example
of the figure 'Epanodos' (in Latin *Regressio*). Literalistic and rhetorical interpretations need not be mutually
exclusive, but they approach the poetry in very different
ways.

VIII

There is another more practical and limited aspect of
language which in the history of the criticism of Chaucer
naturally calls for comment: that is, the problem of in-
telligibility of language, which is often connected by
critics with such stylistic qualities as simplicity or
purity or elaboration. Again the seventeenth century
marks a watershed. Chaucer as the 'first finder of our
fair language' (No. 7) has already been noticed, but it
is worth emphasising how often his early admirers remarked upon his brilliant new complexity of vocabulary -

'fresh anamalit terms celical' - even as late as Dunbar
(No. 17). Poets in particular responded to the improvement of the language as an instrument. But already early
in the sixteenth century Skelton the Englishman (as opposed to the more intellectual Scots?) has to tell his English audience that Chaucer's terms are not *really* dark
(No. 19). By 1546 Peter Ashton (No. 30) (one of two Cambridge men of this name), who wrote 'A Short Treatise vpon
the Turkes Chronicles', finds Chaucer's words 'almost out
of use'. Both Ashton, and Betham who wrote in 1543 (No.
28), are chiefly concerned with the problem of writing
plain English, which seems to have been a Cambridge obses-
sion in the mid-sixteenth century, (cf. Wilson, No. 32);
but whereas Ashton condemns, Betham recommends Chaucer as
a model. Betham was an Oxford man who became a fellow of
Peterhouse, Cambridge, 1540-7, and one of the Ashtons was
also a fellow of Peterhouse, 1543-53. Perhaps they were
members of that Peterhouse group which Speght (No. 53)
refers to, which may well have had a great influence on
Chaucer criticism, and on knowledge of Chaucer. However
that may be, the signs of the increasing remoteness and
difficulty of Chaucer's language multiply, even though he
continues to be sturdily exalted by some Cambridge men, as
for instance, Spenser. Paradoxically the difficulty of
Chaucer's language made it seem all the more 'natural' and
'native', original, of ancient stock, not adulterated like
the modern tongue with newfangled 'inkhorn' terms which
all true Cambridge men abhor. In fact Chaucer's language
was full of French and Latin neologisms which were exactly
what the sixteenth century called 'inkhorn terms'. There
is, however, one difference. It seems likely that many of
Chaucer's new, more polished and elaborate words, came
from courtly *speech*.(20) They do not smell of the lamp
and the inkpot. By the end of the sixteenth century Spenser's 'well of English undefiled' (No. 41b) needed, in
Speght's edition, a glossary of his 'hard works
explained'. As already noted, translation by Kynaston
(cf. No. 59) and modernisation by Sidnam (cf. No. 57)
were attempted in the 1630s. By the end of the seventeenth century it seems that Chaucer's text had really become quite difficult, though the first edition of Dryden's
'Fables' (1700) contained an Appendix with the original
texts of Chaucer; and nearly half of a cross-section of
later seventeenth-century gentlemen's private libraries
owned a copy of Chaucer's 'Works'.(21) Throughout the
eighteenth century we are liable to hear how hard Chaucer
is to read, and modernisations increase in number. But
from Coleridge onwards (No. 96) a more energetic attitude
develops, though with exceptions, and with still more
modernisations.

IX

Along with his language Chaucer's metre offered a problem,
not entirely settled even today. The fifteenth- and early
sixteenth-century writers occasionally remark upon the delightful ease of his metre, (e.g. Lydgate, No. 4, Metham,
No. 8), but the briefest acquaintance with manuscripts
themselves (either direct or through the Chaucer Society
transcripts), or with sixteenth-century editions, or facsimiles, demonstrates clearly, especially when comparisons
between copies are made, how careless Gothic scribes and
printers were in omission or addition of words that ruin
the metre. The complaint of one of Caxton's customers
(No. 14c), about the variations of Caxton's edition from a
manuscript, assures us that some early readers were as
sharp as those at any other time in these matters, and
were as concerned to get the text right as we know Chaucer
himself was, from his poem to Adam Scriveyn and his anxious reference at the end of 'Troilus' (V, 1793-9). But
readers must have been used to many mistakes. George Gascoigne seems to be the first to make much comment on
metre. His remarks (No. 37), and even more Puttenham's
a little later (No. 47), about 'riding rhyme' suggest
that, as we might guess, Chaucer's metre, especially in
'The Canterbury Tales', had to be read as joggling along,
though Gascoigne has a strong sense of some underlying
regularity, and there is perhaps a difference recognised
between 'The Canterbury Tales' and 'Troilus'. A true
sense of Chaucer's metre could not begin to be re-
established until the need was realised usually to sound
the final -e when it represents an earlier fuller inflexion, and more accurate texts were available. The much
maligned Urry, or rather, the 1721 edition begun by him
and known under his name, made a not unintelligent,
though very unscholarly, attempt to recover the metre, as
Gray notes (No. 81), and the Urry edition deserves a
credit which it has been usually denied for this intention. Gray himself has some remarkably percipient things
to say about metre as about many other matters. He is a
rare example of a fine poet whose critical remarks are
not merely a projection of his own designs, and whose
scholarship is as good as his poetry. His remarks on
Chaucer's metre are not particularly original (cf. Morell,
No. 74), but they sum up the matter exactly, including
the use or not of final -e as required, and one can only
lament that his Commonplace Books have remained so long
unpublished, and are even now available only in a partial
and (except, I hope, in the present quotation) very inaccurate transcript. Warton insists on the harmony of

Chaucer's versification (No. 83e), and by the early nineteenth century most intelligent readers recognised, as
Hazlitt did (No. 95), that the pronunciation, when required, of final -e was the secret of understanding Chaucer's versification, though Nott (No. 94) disputes this.
Controversy continued at a usually more scholarly level
in the nineteenth century.

X

An important element in the historic changes in English
society in the sixteenth century had been the decision of
the gentry to send their sons to one or other of the two
universities, which up till then had been more like professional seminaries and research institutes. Thus the
universities took on a broader educational concern, and
under Humanist interest rhetoric was intensively studied,
at least at Cambridge, and there was much more interest in
literature. From Wyatt onwards it is a rare English poet
(though this interestingly includes Shakespeare) who has
not attended a university, usually, until the late nineteenth century, Cambridge. The fanciful biography of
Chaucer which was developed in the sixteenth century (No.
24), itself a product of Humanist interests, followed
this trend and made sure of Chaucer's education by sending him to *both* universities. Cambridge men tended to
show more interest in Chaucer than Oxford men, although
there are one or two exceptions. Much, no doubt, stems
from the group of Chaucer enthusiasts at Peterhouse in
the mid-century already noted. It seems, too, that Cambridge was more interested in rhetoric than was Oxford:
Thomas Wilson (No. 32) and Gabriel Harvey (No. 45) are
obvious names of distinguished rhetoricians, but there
were others, like Peacham (No. 56); sixteenth-century
Oxford has no-one similar. (In the late nineteenth century, the situation changes.)

XI

In the matter of texts, Cambridge in the late sixteenth
century seems to have led the way with the editions of
Speght, 1598 and 1602, the latter reprinted in 1687 (see
note on the editions). After Urry's bad start, Oxford
developed a textual tradition that triumphed with Tyrwhitt
(No. 84). In the seventeenth and eighteenth centuries
Oxford men usually seem to have had more difficulty with
the language and to have insisted more on the 'barbarism'
of the past.

XII

Chaucer was himself close to the courtly centre of power
and prestige in his own day, and was always a courtiers'
poet, until the late seventeenth century, when the English
Gothic court tradition, with much else that had some organic connection with Chaucer's own time, finally ended.
In the eighteenth century Chaucer changes in appearance
from courtier to man-of-the-world, as Warton calls him
(No. 83a), and indeed a gentleman (cf. No. 85) like so
many of his admirers. In the seventeenth century Chaucer
was less admired by men of letters (like Cowley) perhaps
because men of letters were less easily absorbed into the
courtier's circle than in the eighteenth century they were
absorbed into the world of polite society.
    In the eighteenth century the topics of Chaucer's hum-
our and his decency are necessarily re-handled in the
light of what is felt to be his realism. His humour had
always been enjoyed as an integral part of his Gothic
multiplicity. Lydgate refers to his comedies, Skelton to
his merry tales. By the end of the sixteenth century the
indecency that a fourteenth-century monk could easily
stomach was being questioned by so coarse a feeder as
Harington (No. 49), but Harington is looking for excuses
for himself. By the latter part of the seventeenth century
it seems clear that the grossness of Mennes (or of his
collaborator, the Rev. James Smith) was felt to correspond
with a vein of Chaucer. Pope, in a comic pastiche of
Chaucer's language, in his 'Imitations of English Authors'
said to have been written in youth, is more gross than
Chaucer ever was. Chaucer's Gothic indecency tends to be
an aspect of the grotesque, both realistic and humorous,
asserting the existence of the physical world in absurd
but related contrast to the mental. It has already been
argued that this relationship begins to break down in the
seventeenth century under a doctrine that considers that
literature ought to be a literalistic imitation which instructs life, since that doctrine indicates that literature has a direct effect on life. Immoral literature, or,
what is not the same thing, literature about immorality,
may thus seem to encourage immorality in life, whereas
Gothic humour is more of a conscious invocation of 'the
world-upside-down', grotesque fantasy, parody, satire and
release by laughter. However, much of the response to
literary indecency also depends on the general social climate of permissiveness, and on the nature of the critic,
so that in Chaucer's case the problem whether he encou-
rages indecency is variously treated in later centuries
without much discernible pattern. Only in the latter part

of the twentieth century, as we might guess, have Chaucer's bawdy comic poems been elevated to the position of
central importance in his work and poetic message - the
'world upside-down' now assumed to be a true imitation of
the world right-side-up.

XIII

Romanticism introduces some important new developments.
The notable figures are Gray (No. 81), Hurd (No. 82), and
Coleridge (No. 96). Gray has a combination of historical
sense, with calm, clear, critical scholarship, and with a
practitioner's feeling for literary problems, that must
be rare in any age. Hurd by a fine imaginative sympathy,
though primarily in relation to Spenser, discovers, or re-
discovers, something of the nature of the contrast between
on one side Gothic form and Gothic fantasy, and on the
other Neoclassical literalism. Hurd's discovery was
allied with the new Romantic historical imagination and
feeling for the glamour of medievalism. He is subtle in
literary perception, but devotes relatively little space
to Chaucer. Perhaps Spenser's veneer of Neoclassicism
over his own fundamentally Gothic genius made his work
more immediately appealing to Hurd's taste than Chaucer.
Furthermore, Chaucer was unlucky in having written on the
further side of the phonetic watershed, the 'great English vowel-shift' that divides our earlier from our later
language in the fifteenth century, and which along with
lexical changes puts Spenser and Shakespeare, for all
their Gothic quality, on our apparently sunny side of the
slope, and fourteenth-century writers in relative obscurity on the other. Coleridge (No 96) takes up the concepts of the Gothic, and of the marvellous in Chaucer,
and Campbell in 1819 (No. 97) finds some pleasure in romance, of which, naturally, there are traces later in the
century; but the leading ideas of Chaucer criticism in
the nineteenth century change less from eighteenth-century
ideas than one would expect, impressive as the criticism
is. Romantic theories of the imagination, or of metaphor,
pass Chaucer by, which illustrates a certain limitation in
them, founded, as they would seem to be, for all their
apparent revolt, on Neoclassical principles. Hazlitt's
lecture on poetry is a fine and fiery statement of
poetry's imaginative glory, placed on an inherently realistic basis which is fairly obviously Neoclassical in
origin, with Romantic colouring, but his theory has very
little effect on his actual criticism of Chaucer (No. 95),
as is so often the case.

Neoclassical concepts of poetry find little place for narrative. Even the novel is presumably thought to take its narrative flow from the temporal sequence of event that it ostensibly imitates. The climax of this neglect comes in the explicit contempt of early twentieth-century criticism for 'story-telling'. Romanticism here makes little change. Hurd's famous reference in 'The Letters of Chivalry and Romance' (1762), from which extract No. 82 is taken, to 'the world of fine fabling' that we have lost, shows some feeling for the non-naturalistic nature of narrative, but he loses it in Neoclassical condemnation of the extravagances of chivalric romance to 'men of sense', and in equally Neoclassical praise of the comedy of 'Sir Thopas'. Crabbe (No. 92) makes a valuable claim for the poetry of narrative, in his admirable critical Preface, but he is using Chaucer as a stalking-horse for his own more sombre interests, and he too neglects Chaucer's Gothic fantasy and non-naturalistic narratives, thus remaining within the stream of eighteenth-century literalism.

XIV

A different development of Romanticism already briefly touched on, began, however, to reverse a characteristic Neoclassical attitude. From the early Humanistic comment of Sir Brian Tuke (No. 22) and throughout the seventeenth and eighteenth centuries there are pitying or condescending or contemptuous references to the remote barbarism of Chaucer's times. The Romantic Revival, on the other hand, glamorised the Middle Ages. It was perhaps this glamorisation that enabled readers to reverse the Neoclassical trend and imagine the historical and more especially the medieval past with sympathetic appreciation. Hurd's vigorous assertion, Romantic in inspiration, of the value of Gothic form (No. 82), and the labours of Thomas Warton (No. 83), Tyrwhitt (No. 84), together with the general movement of the times, allowed Godwin (No. 87) to make an important attempt to describe Chaucer's historical culture in its own terms, whatever his own failings in historical method and scholarship. The works of Chaucer are thus felt to provide an introduction to the culture of his own period; and, indeed, as the 'Blackwood's' reviewer of 1819 (No. 98) perceived, the very existence of Chaucer's works, since art is to some extent historically conditioned, reflects very favourably on the state of culture in his own time. The following passage (No. 99), perhaps by Henry Southern, carries this further by

relating Chaucer to 'the national mind', and develops a
curious reversal of Sidney's exaltation of the poet above
historian or philosopher, by making it Chaucer's special
supremacy to be an instructive historian of the highest
order. Yet here we may still find the fundamental Neoclassical principles of 'imitation' and 'instruction', and
Chaucer is still presented as a dramatist *avant la lettre,*
and still essentially a comic writer. Nevertheless the
reversal of Neoclassical social and cultural elitism implicit in the idea that Chaucer was responsive to the
whole of his society is carried a little further by
Southey's emphasis in 1831 (No. 101) on Chaucer's reten-
tion of 'popular' elements, and by an anonymous reviewer
in 1837 (No. 102) who more explicitly relates Chaucer to
the common people, though still as 'a gentleman'. This
last is a perceptive general account of Chaucer's social
situation within the context of nineteenth-century knowledge, followed by an equally perceptive account of Chaucer's variety, though still on the basis of the drama.

XV

Another Romantic note concerns Chaucer's style. There
has already been occasion to note how Chaucer's earliest,
rhetorical, critics in the fifteenth century praised the
elaboration of his diction, (e.g. Nos 4, 7, 17), and how
in the sixteenth century there was controversy over whether it was 'plain' and 'pure', or 'dark' (e.g. Nos 19,
28, 30, 32, 41b). In the eighteenth century comment on
Chaucer's language is more liable to be in terms of its
difficulty for historical linguistic, not stylistic,
reasons. Romantic writers make much less ado (e.g. Coleridge, No. 96) and there begins a corresponding emphasis
on Chaucer's simplicity of style. Southey in 1831 (No.
101) makes this plain, while in 1837 the same unknown reviewer (No. 102) who related Chaucer to the whole English
people (in contrast to the Norman conquerors) also found
his voice that of the 'literary spirit of the English
people, vigorous, simple and truthful'. 'Truthfulness'
must be regarded, from a literary point of view, rather
as a Neoclassical than a Gothic characteristic, and we
see in its conjunction with 'simple' how easily this
aspect of Neoclassical literalism leads on to Romantic
simplicity, and both into an expressive personal 'sincerity' as the criterion of literary merit. (From this
line too, springs in part the later concept of Chaucer's
'childlikeness', so strong in the late nineteenth century,
see Vol. 2). Although there is some truth in the notion

of the plainness of Chaucer's style, the recognition of
it is weakened by the failure to identify those particular
passages, and their purposes, where plainness is used.
The discovery of plainness must at least in part be attributed to the new desire for plainness in the diction of
poetry of many Romantic writers, most notably Southey's
friend Wordsworth.

XVI

The intelligent and sensitive anonymous author of passage
No. 102 also seems to be the first to introduce loud and
clear that special note of strong, patriotic, virtuous
self-confidence in Englishry that is so marked a characteristic of nineteenth-century England, though not un-
accompanied by self-criticism. There is an unconscious
echo of sixteenth-century English self-confidence, but the
nineteenth century, as Volume 2 shows, is fully independent.

XVII

The present volume closes with an extensive, but still
only representative, selection of extracts from the book
by John Hippisley, whose comments on Chaucer gather up
many of the themes of the previous century, and express
them as they continue to be expressed, with local variation, throughout the nineteenth century. Thus Chaucer's
as a dramatist, his comedy, the truth and simplicity of
a primitive age, are mentioned. Hippisley is one of the
earliest to refer to Chaucer's naivety, though he does it
hesitantly. Thus he looks both forward and backward.
One innovation deserves special mention. Hippisley appears to be the first to attempt a regular account of the
history of Chaucer criticism, thus making a new, articulated use of the comments on Chaucer that editors had gath-
ered in their volumes from Speght in 1598 onwards. This
new historical perspective is part of the earlier historical sympathy generated by Romanticism, but extends and
intellectualises it, and was destined to have important
effects in literary and cultural history and criticism.
It enables the critic to distinguish on other than grounds
of mere taste and preference between the various works of
an author, and thus to work towards a more consciously
systematic and rationalised account of an author's
achievement. We see this beginning in Hippisley's comments on Chaucer's various works.

Hippisley's criticism therefore, substantial as it is, offers a convenient place for a pause in the story of the criticism of Chaucer's work. He gathers up much previous comment, and points forward to much more which, though continuing in unbroken succession, also steadily introduces new considerations, which will be the subject of the second volume.

Notes

1 C.F.E. Spurgeon, 'Five Hundred Years of Chaucer Criticism and Allusion', 3 vols, Cambridge University Press, 1925.
2 O.P. Kristeller, 'Renaissance Thought: the Classical Scholastic and Humanist Strains', Harper & Row (Torchbooks), New York, 1961; B. Weinberg, 'A History of Literary Criticism in the Italian Renaissance', 2 vols, Chicago University Press, 1961; Sir Philip Sidney, 'An Apology for Poetry', ed. G. Shepherd, formerly Nelson now Manchester University Press, 1965.
3 E.R. Curtius, 'European Literature and the Latin Middle Ages', trans. W.R. Trask, Routledge & Kegan Paul, 1953.
4 Derek Brewer, Gothic Chaucer, 'Writers and their Background: Geoffrey Chaucer', ed. Derek Brewer, Bell, 1974, 1-32; 'Chaucer', 3rd (supplemented) edition, 1974.
5 Derek Brewer, Some Observations on the Development of Literalism and Verbal Criticism, 'Poetica' 2 (Sanseido, Tokyo) 1974, pp. 71-95.
6 W.S. Howell, 'Logic and Rhetoric in England 1500-1700', Princeton University Press, 1956. Cf. also R.C. Alston and J.L. Rozier, Rhetoric and Style: A Bibliographical Guide, 'Leeds Studies in English', New Series, I (1967), pp. 137-62.
7 Cf. N.F. Blake, Caxton and Chaucer, 'Leeds Studies in English', New Series, I (1967), pp. 19-36.
8 Sir William Vaughan in 'The Golden Fleece', 1626, made a series of references to 'The Plowman's Tale'; cf. A. Wawn, 'English Language Notes', X (1972), pp. 15-20.
9 Sir Philip Sidney, 'An Apology for Poetry', above, n. 2. I owe much to the Introduction of this edition, as to Professor Shepherd personally.
10 See Brewer, 'Literalism', above n. 5.
11 R.F. Jones, 'The Triumph of the English Language', Blandford, 1953, pp. 293-323; R.F. Jones and others, 'The Seventeenth Century', Stanford University Press, 1961, pp. 143-60.

12 E.g., D.H. Lawrence.

13 On the historical theory of *genre* see Shepherd's
    learned note and further references, 'An Apology', *ed.
    cit.* p. 163.

14 The Study of Poetry, 'Essays in Criticism', Second
    Series, 1888; The Function of Criticism at the Present
    Time, 'Essays in Criticism', First Series, 1865.

15 For some further discussion see Derek Brewer, 'Towards
    a Chaucerian Poetic', British Academy Sir Israel Gol-
    lancz Memorial Lecture, Oxford University Press, 1974.

16 M.A. Quinlan, 'Poetic Justice in the Drama', Notre
    Dame, 1912; C.C. Greene, 'The Neoclassic Theory of
    Tragedy in England during the Eighteenth Century',
    Cambridge, Mass., 1934.

17 For detailed evidence of these attitudes in the eight-
    eenth-century criticism of Shakespeare and Milton, see
    Brewer, 'Literalism', above, n.5.

18 M.H. Abrams, 'The Mirror and the Lamp', 1953, Oxford
    University Press, 1960, p. 69. Abrams goes on to
    argue a reversal of this attitude in the work of Cole-
    ridge, who substituted 'a projective and creative mind
    and, consonantly, an expressive and creative theory of
    art' (such as I have attributed to the essential rhet-
    orical tradition). Without disputing Abrams' impres-
    sive work it must nevertheless be said that no such
    Coleridgean change appears in the history of the
    actual criticism of Chaucer.

19 Naturally such a sweeping generalisation will meet
    with certain exceptions. One of the most apparent,
    however, only confirms the trend. Sterne's 'Tristram
    Shandy' plays jokes on the reader by violations and
    variations of literalistic, illusionist, detail.
    Sterne can only exploit the mysterious no-man's-land
    between fiction and actuality because earlier thought
    (especially Locke) and the practice of the novel (that
    quintessentially Neoclassical genre) had made the two
    opposing forces so distinct, as well as so closely
    related. The vagueness of the distinction between
    fiction and actuality in English Gothic literature in
    general, not Chaucer alone, as illustrated for example
    by the presence of the real author in his own fiction-
    al poem, is such that we are constantly puzzled to
    conceptualise the difference between 'art' and 'life'
    in English Gothic literature.

20 Derek Brewer, Chaucer and the English and European
    Traditions, in 'Chaucer and Chaucerians', ed. Derek
    Brewer, Nelson, 1966, pp. 25-7.

21 R. Ashcraft, John Locke's Library, 'Cambridge Biblio-
    graphical Society', V (1969), pp. 47-60.

Bibliographical note

The general aim of the two volumes is to present a copious
selection of the criticism of Chaucer in English from his
own day until 1933. Though necessarily selective, I
believe nothing of significance has been omitted. The two
volumes divide conveniently almost in mid-nineteenth
century.

Speght was the first editor to include 'the judgments
and reports of some learned men, of this worthy and famous
Poet' ('Workes', 1598, c.i. a). Urry collected more such
'Testimonies'. Hippisley, with an extract from whose
work this first volume concludes, appears to be the first
to attempt an articulated account of the course of such
comments. The process culminates in the great collection
made by Miss C.F.E. Spurgeon, 'Five Hundred Years of Chaucer Criticism and Allusion', 3 vols, Cambridge, 1925
(reprinted 1961), whose entries reprint in full or in selected extracts the comments she lists. Further references
to other criticisms and allusions have been made in the
bibliographies by D.D. Griffith, 'Bibliography of Chaucer
1908-1953', Seattle, 1955; and W.R. Crawford, 'Bibliography of Chaucer, 1954-63', Seattle, 1967. The present work
has added a few more comments not previously noted elsewhere, but this has not been a principal object. W.L. Alderson and A.C. Henderson, 'Chaucer and Augustan Scholarship', Berkeley, 1970, is a detailed study of one aspect
of the reception of Chaucer, with new bibliographical information. The work by A. Miskimin, 'The Renaissance
Chaucer', Yale University Press, 1975, appeared too late
to be used.

The present work has an orientation different from that
of Miss Spurgeon. Her intention was, especially in the
earlier period, to collect as far as possible every reference, however repetitious, and whether literary or not,
while for the nineteenth century she was forced to be very

selective. The present collection has a more specifically
critical orientation. There could be no question of re-
printing the great number of adaptations or textual reminiscences, for their bulk is great and their critical
interest minimal. Nor have simple allusions, references,
nor quotations, been recorded, except in rare instances
where they have further, representative, interest. The
number of references to Chaucer listed in the fifteenth
and sixteenth centuries has consequently been much reduced, though some new ones have been added. The actual
number of references, allusions, etc. from subsequent centuries is also somewhat reduced: for example, Scott's
numerous allusions to Chaucer find no place in this collection because they are of little critical interest, and
such as they have, arising out of their mere number, is
adequately represented by Miss Spurgeon. Keats read,
enjoyed and imitated Chaucer; he exulted in the possession
of a copy of Speght's edition of 1598 (wrongly dated
1596; letter of 31 July 1819 to Dilke), but once again,
his brief comments are of no special Chaucerian interest
as criticism and have not been included. In contrast,
many of the passages reprinted in the present volumes are
in themselves more extensive than the extracts printed by
Miss Spurgeon, in order to help the passages to be seen as
autonomous critical units, and at least to suggest their
own premises. The nineteenth-century passages in particular are more extensive than those reprinted by Miss Spurgeon, and differ considerably in material and emphasis.
Nevertheless Miss Spurgeon's work has naturally offered a
most valuable guideline even when I have departed from it,
and it cannot be replaced.

In many cases, especially before the nineteenth century, I have perforce reprinted mostly the same text as
that of Miss Spurgeon, but I have in almost every case
gone back to the originals and have often reprinted a more
extensive passage. In only a very few cases over the
whole work has a first edition or a manuscript not been
used as a base. I only hope I have been as accurate as
Miss Spurgeon, but even her texts have a few minor errors
which I have corrected, and in some cases, most notably
that of Gray, I have been able to give a text more accurate than any at present current.

The texts have been presented with the minimum of editorial interference. The original spelling and punctuation have been retained but marginal comments and footnotes, except where necessary for understanding, have been
removed. In some modern scholarly essays in Volume 2 a
large selection of footnotes has necessarily been retained. I have not attempted to alter the mode of

reference to Chaucer's text in any period, variable as it
is. The source of each comment has been given as briefly
as possible in the headnote to the comment, except where
it is more conveniently noted with the extracts themselves. All the comments by one single writer are grouped
together even when separated in time. The headnotes aim
to give such information about the writer, where it is
available, as may enable him to be 'placed', for his comment to be better understood. Some main aspect of the
comment is also usually touched on, partly, but not
always, with reference to the principal points of the
Introduction, without, of course, any pretence to completeness. The main sources of biographical details are
those monuments of self-effacing scholarship, 'The Dictionary of National Biography'; A.B. Emden, 'A Biographical Register of the University of Cambridge to 1500', and
his equivalent three volumes for Oxford; J. Foster,
'Alumni Oxonienses'; J. and J.A. Venn, 'Alumni Cantabri-
gienses'; 'Who Was Who 1871-1916'; 'Who's Who' for subsequent years; 'The Dictionary of American Biography'; 'Who
Was Who in America'.

The principal editions of Chaucer's 'Works' up to 1933

A. MANUSCRIPTS

Chaucer died in 1400. Manuscripts of his works, or at
least of his later works, circulated for reading during
his lifetime, as we may deduce from his little poem to
Adam, his scribe, from 'Lenvoy de Chaucer a Bukton', and
from Deschamps' poem (No. 1); but all the manuscripts we
now have were written in the fifteenth century. In number
they vary from the eighty-odd complete or fragmentary
copies of 'The Canterbury Tales' through the twenty-odd
complete or fragmentary copies of 'Troilus and Criseyde'
to the unique copy of 'Adam Scriveyn'. Some are splendid
compilations fit for a king, others are solid bookshop
products, some others (of short poems) are copies by
interested amateurs. The shorter poems are sometimes
placed in small groups, but no manuscript aims to put together the complete Works - the very concept did not
exist.

B. EARLY PRINTS

Caxton first printed 'The Canterbury Tales' about 1478,
and reprinted it about 1484. Wynkyn de Worde and Pynson,
his successors, reprinted it again. Similarly Caxton and
his successors reprinted separately a number of other
works by Chaucer. Copies of these editions are now excee-
dingly rare.

C. FURTHER EDITIONS

(1) 1532, 'The Workes of Geoffrey Chaucer', etc., folio
blackletter, edited by W. Thynne, printed by T. Godfray.

This contains most of Chaucer's genuine works, together
with the non-Chaucerian verse 'Testament of Cressida', the
prose 'Testament of Love', and other spurious poems. It
is in effect a collection of Chaucer and Chaucerian works,
and resembles in appearance one of the great fifteenth-
century manuscript volumes. It contains the Preface by
Sir Brian Tuke (see No. 22) and other prefatory matter,
all of which was continued in the later booksellers'
reprints.
    Thynne (d. 1546), educated at Oxford, became an offi-
cial in the king's household, and in 1526 chief clerk of
the kitchen. He sought assiduously for texts of Chaucer,
and the 1532 edition is the first edition with claims to
completeness. He presumably recognised that several items
were not by Chaucer, though many careless readers attributed them to him. For a list, see Leland, c. 1540 (No.
24). The dedication of his edition was written by Sir
Brian Tuke (cf. No. 22). Thynne wrote nothing on Chaucer
that has survived but is noted here for the sake of his
edition, the foundation of all subsequent editions until
that begun by Urry, published 1721 (cf. No. 71 and below,
item 8). 'A Short Title Catalogue of Books Printed 1475-
1640', The Bibliographical Society, 5068.
(2) 1542, 'The workes of Geoffrey Chaucer', etc., folio,
blackletter. Two issues, imprints by W. Bonham and John
Reynes. Contents are as in Thynne, save that 'The Plowman's Tale' is added after 'The Canterbury Tales'.
'Short Title Catalogue', 5069, 5070.
(3) c. 1550, 'The workes of Geoffrey Chaucer', etc., folio,
blackletter; published by W. Bonham, R. Kele, T. Petit,
R. Toye. Except for the differing printers' names there
is no difference between these issues. Contents are as
in Thynne, save that 'The Plowman's Tale' is now incorporated within 'The Canterbury Tales', immediately preceding 'The Parson's Tale'. 'Short Title Catalogue', 5071-
4.
(4) 1561, folio, blackletter. Edited by John Stowe, printed by Ihon Kyngston for Ihon Wight. There are two
issues: (a) 'The workes of Geoffrey Chaucer', etc., which
has a series of woodcuts illustrating 'The General Prologue' and is much the rarer of the two, only five copies
being known to me; (b) 'The woorkes', etc., which has no
woodcuts in 'The General Prologue'. John Stowe (c. 1525-
1605), whose education is unknown, was a citizen of London
and son of a tallow-chandler. Stowe himself was a tai-
lor but also a most diligent antiquary, now famous for his
'Survey of London', 1598; his first production, however,
was this edition of Chaucer. He was a collector of manuscripts, some of which are now the treasured possessions

of great libraries, though Stowe himself was very poor in
later life. One, presumably, of his manuscripts was the
large collection of verse which is now R.3.19 of Trinity
College, Cambridge, and from which, it is thought, came
the many mediocre pieces of fifteenth-century verse, 'a
heap of rubbish' in Tyrwhitt's words, which were added to
Chaucer's verse in this edition. But a number of the
additions were authentic poems by Chaucer, and others,
such as Lydgate's 'Story of Thebes', intend no deception.
The volume maintains its character as 'Chaucer and Chaucerian'. 'Short Title Catalogue', (a) 5075, (b) 5076.
(5) 1598, 'The Workes of our Antient and Learned English
Poet Geffrey Chaucer', folio, blackletter, edited by T.
Speght, imprints by G. Bishop, A. Islip for B. Norton, and
A. Islip for T. Wight. (See Nos 51, 53.) Hetherington
points out that Speght disclaims responsibility for the
edition, already nearly complete before he learnt of it.
It is essentially a bookseller's reprint of the 1561
edition, having been entered at Stationers' Hall in 1592
and 1594, to which Speght contributed the Life and Notes.
Stowe made some hitherto unprinted material available to
him. In this edition were first printed the spurious
'Chaucer's Dream', now known as 'Isle of Ladies', and
'The Flower and the Leaf'.
    Although Speght's editing was slight in that he paid
no attention to the text, apart from 'The General Prologue' to 'The Canterbury Tales', the prefatory and ex-
planatory matter make the volume different in kind from
the straightforward unadorned reprints made earlier in
the century in which Chaucer is presented as a 'contemporary'. Chaucer has here become 'ancient and learned'.
Among other additions Speght initiates the process, of
which the present book is the latest example, of printing
a selection of comments on Chaucer's poems, briefly quoting Thynne, Ascham, Spenser, Camden and Sidney's commendations. Chaucer has become a classic - an idea which, with
its veneration for literary achievement, is itself Neoclassical, not Gothic. 'Short Title Catalogue', 5077-9.
(6) 1602, 'The Workes of . . . Geffrey Chaucer', folio,
blackletter, edited by T. Speght, imprints by Adam Islip
and G. Bishop. See No. 53. This edition is re-set, more
fully punctuated, and with frequent marginal fists inserted to mark 'sentences and proverbs'. Chaucer's 'A.B.C.'
is here printed for the first time, and 'Iacke Upland'
added. Speght benefited from the 'Animadversions' of
William Thynne, who is thanked. See Nos 51, 53.
'Short Title Catalogue', 5080-1.
(7) 1687, 'The Works of . . . Jeffrey Chaucer', folio.
Reset in handsome, rather mannered blackletter. Not all

the errata of the 1602 edition are corrected. The period
between this and the preceding edition is the longest between any editions. This edition is essentially a reprint
of the 1602 edition, with spurious brief conclusions to
the 'Cook's' and 'Squire's Tales' added. The spelling
Jeffrey is distinctive, and used for the first time. The
blackletter style was antiquated and this must have been
one of the last large books printed in such type.
J. Harefinch was responsible. See the valuable study by
W.L. Alderson and A.C. Henderson, *Chaucer and Augustan
Scholarship,* University of California Publications: English Studies 35: 1970.
(8) 1721, 'The Works of Geoffrey Chaucer', edited by John
Urry and others, folio. (Cf. No. 71). This large handsome volume continues the process of presenting Chaucer
as an 'ancient'. As in editions of the Latin Classics,
pride of place is given to a large engraving of the editor,
Urry (who died before completing his work), and an engraving of Chaucer follows on the next leaf. The prefatory
matter is rewritten and increased. The Glossary is much
improved. Chaucer's 'Retracciouns' to 'The Canterbury
Tales' are printed for the first time.
   John Urry (1666-1715), born in Dublin of Scottish parents, graduated B.A. from Christ CHurch, Oxford, and was
also elected Student (i.e. fellow) in 1686. He was persuaded by Bishop Atterbury to publish an edition of Chaucer largely because his Scotch-Irish accent was considered an advantage. Notwithstanding the claims on the
title-page to have consulted manuscripts, his edition
mended Chaucer's metre (sadly mangled in the earlier
printed editions) quite arbitrarily without due regard to
the manuscripts, and has been universally condemned since
Tyrwhitt's scathing remarks in his edition of 'The Canterbury Tales, (No. 84). But his principles were not so
foolish. The British Library copy of the edition contains the agreement to publish by Bernard Lintot of 26
August 1715, which provides for 1000 copies to be sold at
£1 10s. 0d. and 250 more on large paper at £2 10s. 0d.
But Urry died very soon after this agreement was made, and
ultimately the edition was completed by Timothy Thomas,
helped by W. Thomas, presumably his brother, who contributed together a sensible Preface and useful Glossary
(mainly William's). The Life was written mainly by John
Dart (No. 71). The spurious tales of 'Gamelyn' and
'Beryn', not before printed, were added. The copy in
the British Library is annotated in manuscript by Timothy
Thomas (1694-1751), a Welsh clergyman, who graduated B.A.
from Christ Church in 1716. Of William little is known.
See Alderson and Henderson, above, item 7.

(9) 1737, 'The Canterbury Tales of Chaucer', edited by the
Reverend Thomas Morell. This comprises only 'The General
Prologue', and 'The Knight's Tale', but prints them in a
Middle English text, with variant readings, notes and references, together with modernised versions by Dryden and
others. Morell used some thirteen manuscripts and his
edition is the first to do what Urry's claimed to do,
namely attempt a scientifically constructed text. See
Alderson and Henderson, above, item 7; and Nos 73, 74.
(10) 1775, 'The Canterbury Tales of Chaucer', edited by
T. Tyrwhitt, 5 vols, 1775-8. The fifth volume, containing
the Glossary, appeared in 1778. See No. 84. Tyrwhitt's
textual method was still unsystematic, but nevertheless an advance on all previous editors. He was also
the first editor not merely to refrain from adding further
works to Chaucer's credit or discredit, but to make an
attempt, largely successful, to sort the genuine works
from the spurious, which he did by the criterion of style.
(11) 'The Works of Chaucer' in John Bell's 'The Poets of
Great Britain Complete from Chaucer to Churchill', Vols
24mo, 1782-3. Chaucer's works appear in Vols 1-14, with
text from Tyrwhitt supplemented by Urry, like numerous
other booksellers' reprints of the next few decades.
(12) 1845, 'The Works of Chaucer' in Pickering's Aldine
Poets, 6 vols, 1845. This edition has the memoir by Sir
Harris Nicolas. For the first time the life is scientifically examined, but the text is not greatly improved.
(13) 1894, 'The Complete Works of Geoffrey Chaucer',
edited by W.W. Skeat, The Clarendon Press, Oxford, 6
vols. A supplementary Vol. VII, 'Chaucerian and Other
Pieces', containing most of pieces formerly attributed
in error to Chaucer, appeared in 1897. The second edition, 1899, is that current. Skeat's text is eclectic,
but his command of Middle English and his textual intuition were outstanding. The edition as a whole is out of
date, but the Glossary in especial is still valuable, and
the whole is a fine work of humane scholarship.
(14) [1933], 'The Complete Works of Chaucer', edited by
F.N. Robinson, Oxford University Press, 1 vol. A new
text, and in the Notes a remarkably full reference to current scholarship; weak Glossary.

These brief comments on some editions have been com-
piled from E.P. Hammond, 'Chaucer: A Bibliographical
Manual', 1908; J.R. Hetherington, 'Chaucer 1532-1602;
Notes and Facsimile Texts', published by the author,
Vernon House, 26 Vernon Road, Birmingham 16; W.L. Alder-
son and A.C. Henderson, 'Chaucer and Augustan Scholarship',
University of California Publications: English Studies,

35, University of California Press, 1970; and from personal observation. A facsimile of the 1532 edition, based on the British Library copy, was edited by W.W. Skeat, 1912. Another facsimile (based on the copy in Clare College Library, Cambridge, formerly owned by Sir Brian Tuke himself), and supplemented with facsimiles of the material added in the editions of 1542, 1561, 1598, and 1602 was published by The Scolar Press, Menston, Yorkshire, 1969, edited by Derek Brewer.

Comments

1. EUSTACHE DESCHAMPS, GREAT OVID

c. 1385

Deschamps (1340?-1410?), Chaucer's exact contemporary, was a notable and enormously productive French court poet. His relations with Chaucer are known only through the following poem. Although Deschamps composed some invectives against the English he obviously valued Chaucer's work highly, and the Clifford referred to, l. 29, a distinguished English soldier in the French wars, was presumably a friend. The variety of Chaucer's genius is praised in a set of comparisons with the authors of Rome (as well as with Socrates), very different from those the Humanists would invoke. The comparison with Ovid is particularly apt, and relatively unusual. The poem exists in only one carelessly copied MS, Paris, Bibliothèque Nationale, No. 840 fonds français, f.lxiia and b; printed in Deschamps, 'Oeuvres', ed. le Marquis de Saint-Hilaire and G. Raynaud, Société des Anciens Textes Français, 11 vols, Paris (1878-1904), II, 138-9, and T.A. Jenkins, 'MLN' 33 (1918), 268-87, with translation and notes. The poem is intensely artificial and rather difficult. The present translation is the editor's.

                    AUTRE BALADE

O Socratès plains de philosophie,
Seneque en meurs, Auglius en pratique,
Ovides grans en ta poëterie,
Briés en parler, saiges en rethorique,
Aigles treshaulz, qui par ta theorique   5
Enlumines le regne d'Eneas,
L'Isle aux Geans, ceuls de Bruth, et qu'i as
Semé les fleurs et planté le rosier
Aux ignorans de la langue Pandras,
Grant translateur, noble Geoffrey Chaucier;   10

Tu es d'Amours mondains Dieux en Albie:
Et de la Rose, en la terre Angelique
Qui, d'Angela saxonne, est puis flourie
Angleterre, d'elle ce nom s'applique
Le derrenier en l'ethimologique,   15
En bon anglès le Livre translatas;
Et un vergier, où du plant demandas
De ceuls qui font pour eulx auctorisier,
A ja long temps que tu edifias,
Grand translateur, noble Geffroy Chaucier.   20

A toy pour ce de la fontaine Helye
Requier avoir un buvraige autentique,
Dont la doys est du tout en ta baillie,
Pour rafrener d'elle ma soif ethique,
Qui en Gaule seray paralitique   25
Jusques a ce que tu m'abuveras.
Eustaces sui, qui de mon plant aras:
Mais pran en gré les euvres d'escolier
Que par Clifford de moy avoir pourras,
Grand translateur, noble Gieffroy Chaucier.   30

                    L'ENVOY

Poete hault, loënge d'escuîrie,
En ton jardin ne seroie qu'ortie:
Considère ce que j'ay dit premier -
Ton noble plant, ta douce melodie;
Mais, pour sçavoir, de rescripre te prie,   35
Grant translateur, noble Geffroy Chaucier.

Notes

line 2 MS. et anglux

line 13 MS. et puis
line 25 MS. Qui men
line 31 MS. destruye (?)

TRANSLATION

O Socrates, full of philosophy, Seneca for morality, for
practical life an Aulus Gellius,(1) a great Ovid in your
poetry; brief in speech, wise in the art of writing,
lofty eagle, who by your science enlighten the kingdom of
Aeneas, the island of Giants, of Brutus,(2) who have sown
there the flowers(3) and planted the rose-tree(4) for
those who are ignorant of French; great translator, noble
Geoffrey Chaucer.

You are the god of earthly love in Albion; and in the
Angelic land,(5) (which from the Saxon lady Angela has
flowered into Angle-land - from her this name is now applied as the last in the series of names) you translate the
Book of the Rose; and long since you have set up an orch-
ard, for which you have asked plants from those who
make(6) in order to be authorities;(7) great translator,
noble Geoffrey Chaucer.

From you therefore, I have sought an authentic drink
from the fountain of Helicon(8) whose stream is entirely
under your control, to quench from it my feverish
thirst;(9) I, who will be paralysed in Gaul until you
give me drink. I am Eustace;(10) you shall have some of
my plants;(11) accept graciously the schoolboy works which
you will receive from me by Clifford;(12) great translator, noble Geoffrey Chaucer.

THE ENVOY

High poet, glory of the esquires,(13) in your garden I
should be only a nettle: bear in mind what I said first
of your noble plants, your sweet music; for me to realise
this, I pray you reply; great translator, noble Geoffrey
Chaucer.

Notes

1 Aulus Gellius; Roman writer of the miscellaneous
   'Noctes Atticae', fl. c. 130 AD, well known in the
   Middle Ages as a lawyer and a literary man, who, like
   Chaucer (cf. 'The House of Fame', 643-64) had to do his
   literary work at night.

  2 Brutus; grandson of Aeneas, and legendary founder of
     Britain, which he conquered from giants.
  3 I.e., flowers of poetry.
  4 I.e., translated 'Le Roman de la Rose'.
  5 I.e., England.
  6 Makers, i.e., poets.
  7 I.e., authors of repute.
  8 Helicon, mountain of the Muses.
  9 Or, 'ethic thirst', i.e., thirst for philosophy.
 10 Eustace was Deschamps' own Christian name, but there
     is also a punning allusion to St Eustace, a type of
     humility.
 11 I.e. his verses, which one assumes Chaucer has asked
     him to send.
 12 Sir Lewis Clifford, soldier, courtier, Lollard, friend
     of Chaucer.
 13 The esquires were the general body of minor courtiers
     and administrative officers of the court. Chaucer was
     an esquire for many years.

  2. THOMAS USK, LOVE PRAISES THE PHILOSOPHICAL POET

  c. 1387

  Usk (d. 1388) was a City of London official who became
  embroiled in factional intrigues and was brutally behead-
  ed. His 'Testament of Love' is a long prose treatise
  imitative of Chaucer's translation of Boethius' 'De Consolatione philosophiae'. No manuscript survives. It was
  first printed by Thynne in Chaucer's 'Workes', 1532,
  (from which this text is taken, fol. CCCLlXb), and edited
  by W.W. Skeat, 'Chaucerian and Other Pieces', 1897. In
  the 'Testament' Usk praises Chaucer in the following quotation, but the treatise was nevertheless frequently attributed to Chaucer, and is the source of the biographical
  nonsense about his imprisonment and betrayal of his
  friends (which Usk confesses to), and which was accepted
  as part of Chaucer's life till the nineteenth century.

[The author asks how God's foreknowledge may be reconciled
with free will.]

(Quod Loue) I shal tel the / this lesson to lerne myne
owne trewe seruaunt / the noble philosophical poete / in
Englissh / whiche euermore hym besyeth and trauayleth
right sore / my name to encrease / wherefore al that
wyllen me good / owe to do him worshyp & reuerence bothe /
trewly his better ne his pere in schole of my rules coude
I neuer fynde: he (quod she) in a treatise that he made
of my seruant Troylus / hath this mater touched / and at
the ful this questyon assoyled. Certaynly his noble
sayenges can I not amende: In goodnes of gentyl manlyche
speche / without any maner of nycite of starieres [sic;
read storiers] ymagynacion in wytte and in good reason of
sentence he passeth al other makers. In the boke of
Troylus / the answere to thy questyon mayste thou lerne.

3.   JOHN GOWER, VENUS SENDS GREETINGS

c. 1390

Gower (*c*. 1340-1408), gentleman and poet, wrote long
poems in Latin and in French, and also 'Confessio Amantis' in English, of which the first version, finished
about 1390, contains the greeting from Venus quoted.
Later versions omit this greeting, more probably because
of a rearrangement of the MS. to admit other matter than
as the result of a quarrel. Text in 'Works', ed. G.C.
Macaulay, III (1901), p. 466; Book VIII, 2941-57.

And gret wel Chaucer whan ӡe mete,
As mi disciple and mi poete:
ffor in þe floures of his ӡouþe
In sondri wise, as he wel couþe,
Of Ditees and of songes glade,
The whiche he for mi sake made,
The lond fulfild is oueral:
Wherof to him in special
Aboue alle oþre I am most holde.
fforþi now in hise daies olde

Thou schalt him telle þis message,
That he vpon his latere age,
To sette an ende of alle his werk,
As he which is myn owne clerk,
Do make his testament of loue,
As þou hast do þi schrifte aboue,
So þat mi Court it mai recorde.

4. JOHN LYDGATE, THE GOTHIC POET

c. 1400-39

John Lydgate (?1370-?1451), monk of Bury St Edmunds monas-
tery, was a prolific writer of all kinds of verse, including the dramatic and satiric, only excluding indecent
fabliaux. He wrote for noble patrons, and for merchants,
for court and city; he composed religious and secular
verse, in high and low styles. In his variety, and in his
modesty, if not in genius, he exemplifies the Gothic poet.
He is also the most tediously verbose of English poets.
Nevertheless he knows Chaucer's works well and has important things to say about them. He knows best 'The Parliament of Fowls', 'Troilus' and 'The Knight's Tale' (cf. D.
Pearsall, 'John Lydgate', Routledge & Kegan Paul, 1970,
p. 64), but perhaps his favourite poem is 'The Legend of
Good Women', whose Gothic femininity may have counterbal-
anced his monkish antifeminism. But he several times
refers to the Wife of Bath. He makes numerous passing
allusions to, or echoes phrases from, practically all
Chaucer's works, not all recorded here. The extracts that
follow comprise, however, all Lydgate's substantial and
significant comments. He emphasises Chaucer's great fame
(on which chronicles and political sources are silent).
He claims that Chaucer was the first to make English a
rich and flexible instrument (in which there may be more
truth than used to be allowed). He emphasises Chaucer's
rhetorical ability, his gay style, 'sugrid mouth,' 'the
golde dewe dropes of speche and eloquence' which reflect
both his linguistic and his rhetorical power - the flowers
of rhetoric that first illumined our rude English tongue.
Implicit in this is the notion that the poet, though a
'noble Rethor' must also please, and depend for a living
on a patron, and in his 'Chapitle of the governance of

Poetis' (g: 'Fall of Princes', III, 3837ff.) he is glad to
note that prudent Chaucer found virtuous 'suffisance'.
The poet should be a good man, like any other man, and
Lydgate praises his 'wise, prudent' master, Chaucer, for
his wisdom and science, for writing devoutly, and for his
wise saws; but he sees him as a teacher only of the craft
of poetry, to poets, not to lead mankind as a whole
higher. Lydgate recognises Chaucer's variety - his desport, morality, knighthood, love, *gentillesse*, perfect
holiness, ribaldry to make laughter - and in the Prologue
to 'The Seige of Thebes', where Lydgate enumerates the
variety, he does his best to indulge in a Chaucerian
humour. Lydgate's own frequent self-depreciation no
doubt expresses a genuine and attractive personal modesty
- so copious a writer had much to be modest about - but it
is also the characteristic stance of the Gothic poet and
reflects Chaucer's own (though so much more subtle) self-
depreciatory attitude. Lydgate's sense of the lameness
and 'rudeness' of his own metre and his request to the
reader to 'favour' it suggest that he was sharply conscious, as well he might be, of Chaucer's superior smoothness. It seems unlikely, to judge from the end of section
(c), that Lydgate had ever actually met Chaucer.
    All quotations from material published by the Early
English Text Society are made by permission of the Council
of the EETS.

(a) 'The Flower of Courtesy', *c*. 1400, ed. W. Thynne,
1532, fol. cclxxxiiiib, stanzas 34-5 (cf. 'Chaucerian and
Other Pieces', ed. W.W. Skeat, 1897).

(34)

Euer as I can supprise in myn herte
Alway with feare betwyxt drede and shame
Leste oute of lose, any worde asterte
In this metre, to make it seme lame,
Chaucer is deed that had suche a name
Of fayre makyng that [was] without wene
Fayrest in our tonge, as the Laurer grene.

(35)

We may assay forto countrefete
His gay style but it wyl not be;
The welle is drie, with the lycoure swete
Bothe of Clye and of Caliope.

(b) 'The Life of Our Lady', *c*. 1410, ed. J. Lauritis,
R. Klinefelter and V. Gallagher, 'Dusquesne Studies,
Philological Series', No 2, Pittsburg, 1961.

And eke my maister Chauser is ygrave   1628
The noble Rethor, poete of Brytayne
That worthy was the laurer to haue   1630
Of poetrye, and the palme atteyne
That made firste, to distille and rayne
The golde dewe dropes of speche and eloquence
Into our tunge, thurgh his excellence

And fonde the floures, firste of Retoryke
Our Rude speche, only to enlumyne
That in our tunge, was neuere noon hym like
For as the sonne, dothe in hevyn shyne
In mydday spere, dovne to vs by lyne
In whose presence, no ster may a pere   1640
Right so his dytes withoutyn eny pere
Euery makyng withe his light disteyne
In sothefastnesse, who so takethe hede
Wherefore no wondre, thof my hert pleyne
Vpon his dethe, and for sorowe blede
For want of hym, nowe in my grete nede
That shulde alas, conveye and directe
And with his supporte, amende eke and corecte

The wronge traces, of my rude penne
There as I erre, and goo not lyne Right   1650
But for that he, ne may not me kenne
I can no more, but with all my myght
With all myne hert, and myne Inwarde sight
Pray for hym, that liethe nowe in his cheste
To god above, to yeve his saule goode reste

(c) 'Troy Book', 1412-20, ed. H. Bergen, Early English
Text Society (EETS), ES 97, 103, 106, 126 (1906-20).

And ouermore to tellen of Cryseyde   II 4677
Mi penne stumbleþ for longe or he deyde
My maister Chaucer dide his dilligence
To discryve þe gret excellence
Of hir bewte and þat so maisterly
To take on me it were but hiʒe foly
In any wise to adde more þer-to;
For wel I wot, anoon as I haue do,
þat I in soth no þanke disserue may,   4685
Because þat he in writyng was so gay....

Gret cause haue I & mater to compleyne   4694
On Antropos & vp-on hir envie,
þat brak þe þrede & made for to dye
Noble Galfride, poete of Breteyne,
Amonge oure englisch þat made first to reyne
þe gold dewe-dropis of rethorik so fyne,
Oure rude langage only tenlwmyne.   4700
To God I pray, þat he his soule haue,
After whos help of nede I most[e] crave,
And seke his boke þat is left be-hynde
Som goodly worde þer-in for to fynde,   4704
To sette amonge þe crokid lynys rude
Whiche I do write; as, by similitude,
þe ruby stant, so royal of renoun,
With-Inne a ryng of copur or latoun,   4708
So stant þe makyng of hym, dout[e]les,
Among oure bokis of englische per[e]les:
þei arn ethe knowe, þei ben so excellent;
þer is no makyng to his equipolent;   4712
We do but halt, who-so takeþ hede,
þat medle of makyng, with-outen any drede.
Whan we wolde his stile counterfet,
We may al day oure colour grynde & bete,   4716
Tempre our aʒour and vermyloun:
But al I holde but presumpcioun
It folweþ nat, þerfore I lette be.
And first of al I wil excuse me   4720
And procede as I haue be-gonne,
And þoruʒ his fauour certeyn, ʒif I konne,
Of Troye boke for to make an ende;
And þer I lefte ageyn I wil now wende,   4724
Vn-to Cryseyde, and þouʒ to my socour
Of rethorik þat I haue no flour
Nor hewes riche, stonys no perre...
ʒet for al þat, now I wil not leue...   4730

And Chaucer now allas is nat alyue   III 550
Me to reforme or to be my rede
For lak of whom slouʒer is my spede
þe noble Rethor that alle dide excelle;
For in makyng he drank of þe welle
Vndir Pernaso þat þe Musis kepe
On whiche hil I myʒt neuer slepe

[Of the Woe of Troylus & Cressid.]
It wolde me ful longe occupie   III 4192
Of euery þinge to make mencioun
And tarie me in my translacioun
ʒif I shulde in her wo procede

But me semeth þat it is no nede
Sith my maister chauncer her-a-forn
In þis mater so wel hath hym born
In his boke of Troylus and Cryseyde
Whiche he made longe or þat he deyde   4200

[Summarises the story]

þe hool story Chauncer kan ȝow telle   4234
ȝif þat ȝe liste no man bet alyue
Nor þe processe halfe so wel discryue,
For he owre englishe gilt with his sawes
Rude and boistous firste be olde dawes
þat was ful fer from al perfeccioun
And but of litel reputacioun   4540
Til þat he cam & þoruȝ his poetrie
Gan oure tonge firste to magnifie
And adourne it with his elloquence
To whom honour laude & reuerence
þoruȝ-oute þis londe ȝoue be & songe
So þat þe laurer of oure englishe tonge
Be to hym ȝoue for his excellence
Riȝt a[s] whilom by ful hiȝe sentence
Perpetuelly for a memorial
Of Columpna by the cardynal   4550
To Petrak fraunceis was ȝouen in Ytaille
þat þe report neuere after faille
Nor þe honour dirked of his name
To be registred in þe house of fame
Amonge oþer in þe hiȝeste sete
My maister Galfride as for chefe poete
þat euere was ȝit in oure langage
þe name of whom shal passen in noon age
But euer ylyche with-oute eclipsinge shyne.
And for my part I wil neuer fyne   4560
So as I can hym to magnifie
In my writynge pleinly til I dye,
And god I praye his soule bring in Ioie.

For he þat was gronde of wel seying   V 3519
In al hys lyf hyndred no makyng
My maister Chaucer þat founde ful many spot
Hym liste not pinche nor gruche at euery blot
Nor meue hym silf to perturbe his reste
I haue herde telle but seide alweie þe best
Suffring goodly of his gentilnes
Ful many þing enbracid with rudnes
And ȝif I shal shortly hym discryve
Was neuer noon to þis day alyue

To reckne alle boþe ȝonge & olde
þat worþi was his ynkhorn for to holde   3530
And in þis lond ȝif þer any be
In borwe or toun village or cite
þat konnyng haþ his tracis for to swe
Wher he go brood or be shet in mwe
To hym I make a direccioun
Of þis boke to han inspeccioun.

(d) 'The Serpent of Division', c. 1420, printed 1520,
1559, whence this text, Sig. D5b-D6; ed. H.N. MacCracken,
1911; the Preface.

So that touchinge the vengeable maner of hys [Julius
Caesar's] pyteous murder I may conclude with him that
was floure of Poetes in our Englishe tounge / and the
first that euer enlumined our language with floures of
Rhetorique and Eloquence, I meane my maister Chaucer,
which compendiouslie wrote the death of this mightie
Emperour, saying in this wise, as foloweth hereafter in
these lines of metre.

    With bodkins was Cezar Iulius,
    Murdred at Rome by Brutus Crassus
    when many a region he had broght lov
    Lo who mai trust fortune ani throw

    Thus by writing of my wise prudent maister tofore
said: the frowarde and the contrarious Lady Dame Fortune,
spareth neyther Emperour nor king to plunge him downe
sodeynly fro the highest prik of her vnstable wheele.

(e) 'The Siege of Thebes', 1420-2, Prologue, ed. A.
Erdmann and E. Ekwall, EETS, ES 108, 125 (1911, 1920).

            Incipit Prologus
Whan briȝte phebus / passëd was þe ram
Myd of Aprille / and in-to bolë cam,
And Satourn) old / with his frosty face
In virgyne taken had his place,   4
Malencolik / and slowgñ of mocioun,
And was also / in thoposicioun
Of lucina / the monë moyst and pale,
That many Shour / fro heuene made avale;   8
whan Aurora / was in þe morowe red,
And Iubiter / in the Crabbës Hed
Hath take his paleys / and his mansioun;

The lusty tyme / and Ioly fressh Sesoun   12
whan that Flora / the noble myghty quene,
The soyl hath clad / in newë tendre grene,
With her flourës / craftyly ymeynt,
Braunch and bough / wiþ red and whit depeynt,   16
Fletinge þe bawme / on hillis and on valys:
The tyme in soth / whan Canterbury talys
Complet and told / at many sondry stage
Of estatis // in the pilgrimage,   20
Euerich man / lik to his degrè,
Some of desport / some of moralitè,
Some of knyghthode / loue and gentillesse,
And some also of parfit holynesse,   24
And some also in soth / of Ribaudye
To makë laughter' / in þe companye,
(Ech admitted / for non wold other greve)
Lich as the Cook / þe millere and the Reve   28
Aquytte hem-silf / shortly to conclude,
Boystously / in her teermës Rude,
whan þei hadde / wel dronken of the bolle,
And ek also / with his pyllëd nolle   32
The pardowner / beerdlees al his Chyn,
Glasy-Eyed / and face of Cherubyn,
Tellyng a tale / to angre with the frere,
As opynly // the storie kan ʒow lere,   36
word for word / with euery circumstaunce,
Echon ywrite / and put in remembraunce
By hym þat was / ʒif I shal not feyne,
Floure of Poetes / thorghout al breteyne,   40
Which sothly haddë / most of excellence
In rethorike / and in eloquence
(Rede his making' / who list the trouthë fynde)
Which neuer shal / appallen in my mynde,   44
But alwey fressh / ben in my memorye:
To whom be ʒoue / pris / honure / and glorye
Of wel seyinge / first in oure language,
Chief Registrer / of þis pilgrimage,   48
Al þat was tolde / forʒeting' noght at al,
Feyned talis / nor þing' Historial,
With many prouerbe / diuers and vnkouth,
Be rehersaile / of his Sugrid mouth,   52
Of eche thyng' / keping' in substaunce
The sentence hool / with-outë variance,
Voyding' the Chaf / sothly for to seyn,
Enlumynyng' / þe trewe piked greyn   56
Be crafty writinge / of his sawes swete,
Fro the tyme / that thei deden mete
First the pylgrimes / sothly euerichon,
At the Tabbard / assembled on be on,   60

And fro suthwerk / shortly forto seye,
To Canterbury / ridyng' on her weie,
Tellynge a tale / as I reherce can,
Lich as the hoste / assigned euery man,   64
None so hardy / his biddyng' disobeye.
    And this while / that the pilgrymes leye
Att Canterbury / wel loggẽd on and all,
I nott in soth / what I may it call,   68
Hap / or fortune / in Conclusioun,
That me byfil / to entren into toun,
The holy seynt / pleynly to visite
Aftere siknesse / my vowes to aquyte,   72
In a Cope of blak / and nott of grene,
On a palfrey / slender / long' / and lene,
wiþ rusty brydel / mad natt for þe sale,
My man to-forn / with a voidë male....   76

(f) 'The Pilgrimage of the Life of Man', 1426-8, ed. F.J.
Furnivall and K.B. Locock, EETS, ES 77, 83, 92 (1899-
1904).

And touchynge the translacioun   19751
Off thys noble Orysoun,
Whylom (yiff I shal nat feyne)
The noble poete off Breteyne,
My mayster Chaucer, in hys tyme,
Afftter the Frenche he dyde yt ryme,
Word by word, as in substaunce,
Ryght as yt ys ymad in Fraunce,
fful devoutly, in sentence,
In worshepe, and in reuerence   19760
Off that noble hevenly quene,
Bothe moder and a mayde clene.
    And sythe, he dyde yt vndertake,
ffor to translate yt ffor hyr sake,
I pray thys [Quene] that ys the beste,
ffor to brynge hys soule at reste,
That he may, thorgh hir prayere,
Aboue the sterrys bryht and clere,
Off hyr mercy and hyr grace
Apere afforn hyr sonys fface,   19770
Wyth seyntys euere, for A memórye,
Eternally to regne in glorye.
    And ffor memoyre off that poete,
Wyth al hys rethorykes swete,
That was the ffyrste in any age
That amendede our langage;
Therfore, as I am bounde off dette,

In thys book I wyl hym sette,
And ympen thys Oryson
Affter hys translacion,   19780
My purpos to determyne,
That yt shal énlwmyne
Thys lytyl book, Rud off makyng,
Wyth som clause off hys wrytyng.
   And as he made thys Orysoun
Off ful devout entencioun,
And by maner off a prayere,
Ryht so I wyl yt settyn here,
That men may knowe and pleynly se
Off Our lady the .A. b. c....   19790

[Chaucer's 'ABC' follows.]

(g) 'The Fall of Princes', 1431-9, ed. H. Bergen, EETS,
ES 121-4 (1918-19).

                        (Prologue)

And theih my stile nakid be and bare,   229
In rethorik myn auctour for to sue,
Yit fro the trouthe shal I nat remue,

But on the substance bi good leiser abide   232
Afftir myn auctour lik as I may atteyne,
And for my part sette eloquence aside,
And in this book bewepen and compleyne
Thassaut off Fortune, froward and sodeyne,   236
How she on pryncis hath kid her variaunce
And off her malice the dedli mortal chaunce.

But, o allas! who shal be my muse,
Or onto whom shal I for helpe calle?   240
Calliope my callyng will refuse,
And on Pernaso here worthi sustren alle;
Thei will ther sugre tempre with no galle,
For ther suetnesse & lusti fressh syngyng   244
Ful ferr discordith fro materis compleynyng.

My maistir Chaucer, with his fresh comedies,
Is ded, allas, cheeff poete off Breteyne,
That whilom made ful pitous tragedies;   248
The fall of pryncis he dede also compleyne,
As he that was of makyng souereyne,
Whom al this land sholde off riht preferre,
Sithe off oure language he was the lodesterre....   252

And semblabli as I ha[ue] told toforn,   274
My maistir Chaucer dede his besynesse,
And in his daies hath so weel hym born,   276
Out off our tunge tauoiden al reudnesse,
And to refourme it with colours of suetnesse;
Wherfore lat us yiue hym laude & glory
And putte his name with poetis in memory.   280

Off whos labour to make mencioun,
Wherthoruh off riht he sholde comendid be,
In youthe he made a translacioun
Off a book which callid is Trophe   284
In Lumbard tunge, as men may reede & see,
And in our vulgar, longe or that he deide,
Gaff it the name off Troilus & Cresseide.

Which for to reede louers hem delite,   288
Thei ha[ue] theryn so gret deuocioun.
And this poete, hymsilff also to quite,
Off Boeces book, The Consolacioun,
Maad in his tyme an hool translacioun.   292
And to his sone, that callid was Lowis,
He made a tretis, ful noble & off gret pris,

Vpon thastlabre in ful notable fourme,
Sette hem in ordre with ther dyuysiouns,   296
Mennys wittis tapplien and confourme,
To vndirstonde be ful expert resouns
Be domefieng off sundry mansiouns,
The roote out-souht at the ascendent,   300
Toforn or he gaff any iugement.

He wrot also ful many day agone,
Dante in Inglissh, hymsilff so doth expresse,
The pitous story off Ceix and Alcione,   304
And the deth eek of Blaunche the Duchesse,
And notabli dede his bisynesse,
Bi gret auys his wittis to dispose,
To translate the Romaunce off the Rose.   308

Thus in vertu he sette al his entent,
Idilnesse and vicis for to fle;
Off Foulis also he wrot the Parlement,
Theryn remembryng of roial Eglis thre,   312
How in ther chois thei felte aduersite,
Tofor Nature profred the bataile,
Ech for his parti, yiff it wolde auaile.

He dede also his dilligence & peyne   316
In our vulgar to translate and endite
Origen vpon the Maudeleyne,
And off the Leoun a book he dede write;
Off Anneleyda and of fals Arcite   320
He made a compleynt, doolful & pitous,
And off the broche which that Vulcanus

At Thebes wrouhte, ful dyuers of nature,
Ouide writith, who theroff hadde a siht,   324
For hih desir he shulde nat endure
But he it hadde, neuer be glad nor liht;
And yiff he hadde it onys in his myht,
Lich as my maistir seith and writ in deede,   328
It to conserue he sholde ay lyue in dreede.

This poete wrot, at request off the queen,
A legende off parfit hoolynesse,
Off Goode Women to fynde out nynteen   332
That dede excelle in bounte and fairnesse;
But for his labour and [his] bisynesse
Was inportable his wittis to encoumbre,
In al this world to fynde so gret a noumbre.   336

He made the book off Cantirburi Talis,
Whan the pilgrymis rood on pilgrymage
Thoruhout Kent bi hillis and bi valis,
And alle the stories told in ther passage,   340
Enditid hem ful weel in our language:
Summe off knyhthod, summe off gentilesse,
And summe off loue & summe off parfitnesse,

And summe also off gret moralite,   344
Summe off disport, includynge gret sentence.
In prose he wrot the Tale off Melibe,
And off his wiff, that callid was Prudence,
And off Grisildis parfit pacience,   348
And how the Monk off stories newe & olde
Pitous tragedies be the weie tolde.

This said poete, my maistir in his daies,
Maad and compiled ful many a fressh dite,   352
Compleyntis, baladis, roundelis, virelaies
Ful delectable to heryn and to see,
For which men sholde, off riht and equite,
Sithe he off Inglissh in makyng was the beste,   356
Preie onto God to yiue his soule good reste.

Book I

[After mentioning the fifty daughters of Danaus]

But yiff ye list han cleer inspeccioun   1781
Off this story vpon eueri side,
Redith the legende of martirs off Cupide,
Which that Chaucer, in ordre as thei stood,   1784
Compiled off women that were callid good.

Touchyng the story off kyng Pandioun,
And off his goodli faire douhtren tweyne,
How Thereus, fals off condicioun,   1788
Hem to deceyue dede his besi peyne,
Thei bothe namyd, off beute souereyne,
Goodli Progne and yong[e] Philomene,
Bothe innocentis and off entent ful cleene.   1792

Ther pitous fate in open to expresse,
It were to me but a presumpcioun,
Sithe that Chaucer dede his besynesse
In his legende, as maad is mencioun,   1796
Ther martirdam and ther passioun,
For to reherse hem dede his besy peyne,
As cheef poete callid off Breteyne.

Off goode women a book he dede write,   1800
The noumbre compleet fully off nynteene;
And there the story he pleynli dede endite
Off Tereus, off Progne & Philomeene,
Where ye may seen ther legende, thus I meene,   1804
Doth hem worshepe & foorth ther liff doth shewe
For a cleer merour, because ther be so fewe.

I will passe ouer and speke off hem no more,
And onto Cadmus foorth my stile dresse -   1808
Yit in my writyng it greueth me sore,
Touchyng off women off feith or stabilnesse, -
Blessid be God, - I fynde noon excesse;
And for ther been so fewe, as thynkith me,   1812
The goode sholde been had in mor deynte.

Book II

Touchyng Lucrece, exaumple off wifli trouthe,   974
How yonge Tarquyn hir falsli dede oppresse,
And afftir that, which was to gret a routhe,
How she hirsilff[e] slouh for heuynesse,
It nedith nat rehersyn the processe,

Sithe that Chaucer, cheeff poete off Bretayne,
Wrot off hir liff a legende souerayne.   980

Rehersyng ther among[es] other thynges
Ech circumstaunce and ech occasioun:
Whi Romeyns exilid first ther kynges,
Neuer to regnen afftir in ther toun,   984
As olde cronycles make mencioun,
Remembryng also thunkyndli gret outrage
Bi Eneas doon to Dido off Cartage.

Eek othir stories which he wrot his lyue   988
Ful notabli with eueri circumstaunce,
And ther fatis dede pitousli descryue,
Lik as thei fill put hem in remembraunce,
Wherfore yiff I sholde my penne auaunce,   992
Afftir his makyng to putte hem in memorie,
Men wolde deeme it presumpcioun & veynglorie.

For as a sterre in presence off the sunne
Lesith his fresshnesse and his cleer[e] liht,   996
So my reudnesse vnder skies dunne
Dareth ful lowe and hath lost his siht,
To be compared ageyn the bemys briht
Off this poete; wherfore it were but veyn   1000
Thyng seid be hym to write it newe ageyn.

    [How Lucrece / oppressid bi Tarquin slouh hirsilf.]

But at Lucrece stynte I will a while,
It were pite hir story for to hide,
Or slouthe the penne of my reud[e] stile,   1004
But for hir sake alle materis set a-side.
Also my lord bad I sholde abide,
By good auys at leiser to translate
The doolful processe off hir pitous fate.   1008

                    Book III

        A chapitle of þe gouernance of Poetis.

To descryue the disposicioun   3837
Of al poetis be old ordynaunce, -
Thei shold be quieet fro worldli mocioun,
And it sequestre out of ther remembraunce,   3840
Fare compotent vnto ther sustenaunce,
Drynk wyn among to quike ther diligence,
Support of princis to fynde hem ther dispence.

For thei that lakke lond & pocessioun,   3844
And can of lucre no maner cheuisaunce,
Ther coffres void, ther purs turnid up-so-doun,
And wante vitaille to fynde hem in substaunce,
Ther corage dullith, thei faile contenaunce, -   3848
What mihte beste ther sorwes recompence?
Support of princis to fynde hem ther dispence.

Lordis in erthe ha[ue] domynacioun;
Men of the cherche of gold haue habundaunce;   3852
The kniht get good[e] thoruh his hih renoun;
Marchauntis with wynnyng ha[ue] souereyn aqueyntaunce:
But [poor] poetis (God sheeld hem fro myschaunce!)
May now-adaies for ther impotence,   3856
For lakke of support go begge ther dispence.

Daunt in Itaille, Virgile in Rome toun,
Petrak in Florence hadde al his plesaunce,
And prudent Chaucer in Brutis Albioun   3860
Lik his desir fond vertuous suffisance,
Fredam of lordshepe weied in ther ballaunce,
Because thei flourede in wisdam and science,
Support of princis fond hem ther dispence.   3864

O welle of fredam, enclyne thyn eris doun,
And of thi bounte yiue sum attendaunce,
To heere of merci my supplicacioun,
In releuyng of myn hertis greuaunce;   3868
Oppressid with pouert, & kan no purueiaunce,
Sauff to resort to thi magnificence,
Onli be support to fynde me my dispence!

        [How Malleus Duk of Cartage for oppressioun
                tirannye was hewen in to pecys.]

Whan Bochas hadde rehersid of poetis,   3872
Ther straunge studie & ther soleyn writynqis,
And ther desirs of solitarie seetis,
In plesaunt placis to make ther duellyngis,
Beside ryuers & holsum welle spryngis,   3876
Which accomplisshed, he gan his penne auaunce,
Pryncis off Affrik to putte in remembraunce.

                        Book VI

The pitous deth & the hatful caas   3618
Of gret Antonye and Cleopatras.

The tragedie of these ilke tweyne
For me as now shal be set aside,
Cause Chauceer, cheef poete of Breteyne,
Seyng ther hertis koude nat deuyde,
In his book, the Legende of Cupide,   3624
Remembryng ther, as oon thei dide endure,
So wer thei buryed in oon sepulture.

Thyng onys said be labour of Chauceer
Wer presumpcioun me to make ageyn,   3628
Whos makyng was so notable & enteer,
Riht compendious and notable in certeyn.
Which to reherse the labour wer but veyn,
Bochas remembryng how Cleopatras   3632
Caused Antonye that he destroied was.

Book VIII

Myn auctour heer no lenger list s[o]iourne   666
Of these emperours the fallis for to write,
But in al haste he doth his stile tourne
To Zenobia hir stori for to endite.
But for Chauceer dide hym so weel aquite
In his tragedies hir pitous fall tentrete,
I will passe ouer, rehersyng but the grete.   672

In his book of Cauntirbury Talis
This souereyn poete of Brutis Albioun,
Thoruh pilgrymys told be hillis & be valis,
Wher of Zenobia is maad mencioun,   676
Of hir noblesse and of hir hih renoun,
In a tragedie compendiousli told all,
Hir marcial prowesse & hir pitous fall.

Epilogue

To alle thoo that shal this book be-holde,   3394
I them be-seke to haue compassyoun,
And ther-with-al I prey hem that they wolde   3396
Favoure the metre and do correccyoun;
Off gold nor asewr I hadde no foysoun,
Nor othir colours this processe tenlvmyne,
Sauff whyte and blak; and they but dully shyne.   3400

I nevir was aqueynted with Virgyle,
Nor with [the] sugryd dytees of Omer,
Nor Dares Frygius with his goldene style,

Nor with Ovyde, in poetrye moost entieer,   3404
Nor with the souereyn balladys of Chauceer,
Which among alle that euere wer rad or songe,
Excellyd al othir in our Englyssh tounge.

I can nat been a iuge in this mateer,   3408
As I conceyve folwyng my fantasye,
In moral mateer ful notable was Goweer,
And so was Stroode in his philosophye,
In parfyt lyvyng, which passith poysye,   3412
Richard Hermyte, contemplatyff of sentence,
Drowh in Ynglyssh the Prykke of Conscience.

As the gold-tressyd bryght[e] somyr sonne
Passith othir sterrys with his beemys clere,   3416
And as Lvcyna chaseth skyes donne,
The frosty nyghtes whan Esperus doth appere,
Ryght so my mayster had[de] nevir pere, -
I mene Chauceer - in stooryes that he tolde;   3420
And he also wrot tragedyes olde.

The Fal of Prynces gan pitously compleyne,
As Petrark did, and also Iohn Bochas;
Laureat Frraunceys, poetys bothe tweyne,   3424
Toold how prynces for ther greet trespace
Wer ovirthrowe, rehersyng al the caas,
As Chauceer did[e] in the Monkys Tale.
But I that stonde lowe doun in the vale,   3428

So greet a book in Ynglyssh to translate,
Did it be constreynt and no presumpcioun.
Born in a vyllage which callyd is Lydgate,
Be old[e] tyme a famous castel toun;   3432
In Danys tyme it was bete doun,
Tyme whan Seynt Edmond, martir, mayde and kyng,
Was slayn at Oxne, be recoord of wrytyng.

5.   HENRY SCOGAN, MORAL CHAUCER

c. 1407

Henry Scogan (1361?-1407) is presumed to be the friend and
literary disciple to whom was addressed the jesting

'Lenvoy de Chaucer a Scogan'. He was a courtier who became
tutor to the sons of King Henry IV - more evidence of that
monarch's interest in learning (cf. K.B. MacFarlane,
'Lancastrian Kings and Lollard Knights', 1972). Scogan
sent a poem, which he says is written in his own hand, to
the princes. In this he describes himself as their
'fader', i.e. tutor. The heading of one MS, (Ashmole 59)
written by John Shirley (cf. No. 9) says obscurely that
the poem was 'at a souper of feorthe merchande in the
Vyntre in London at the hous of Lowys Johan' - perhaps a
London business-dinner of merchants and nobility, indica-
tive of the general quality of Chaucer's audience. The
poem recommends virtue to the princes and finally quotes
the whole of Chaucer's 'Gentillesse'. Henry V was, it
seems, an apt pupil. Scogan speaks of Chaucer as his
'master', presumably in poetry, but this is the only poem
known to be by Scogan. References are to 'The Wife of
Bath's Tale'. The text is from W.W. Skeat, 'Chaucerian
and Other Pieces', 1897, pp. 239-41.

My mayster Chaucer, god his soule have!   65
That in his langage was so curious,
He sayde, the fader whiche is deed and grave,
Biquath nothing his vertue with his hous
Unto his sone; therfore laborious
Ought ye to be, beseching god, of grace,   70
To yeve you might for to be vertuous,
Through which ye might have part of his fayr place....

Thus 'by your eldres may ye nothing clayme,'   97
As that my mayster Chaucer sayth expresse,
'But temporel thing, that man may hurte and mayme';
Than is god stocke of vertuous noblesse;   100
And sith that he is lord of blessednesse,
And made us alle, and for us alle deyde,
Folowe his vertue with ful besinesse,
And of this thing herke how my mayster seyde: -

The firste stok, fader of gentilesse, (etc.)   105

6. JOHN WALTON, OLDE POYSEES CLERK

1410

Walton was a Canon of the Augustinian Abbey at Oseney,
Oxford, at the end of the fourteenth century. His translation of Boethius' 'De Consolatione Philosophiae' was
made in 1410 and exists in nineteen MSS. In his 'Preface
of the Translator' he addresses his patron who commissioned the work. He proclaims his own insufficiency and
remarks on Chaucer's superiority as rhetorical poet in
true Gothic manner, but although he reveals a good knowledge of Chaucer's poetry, and of his translation of
Boethius, the passage in fact condemns Chaucer's secular
and classicising subject-matter. The audience of this
apparently popular work was 'every lord or lady, what ye
be/Or clerk þat liketh for to rede þis' (Stanza 31, ed.
M. Science, EETS, OS 170, 1927). Text after E.P. Hammond,
'Fifteenth Century Prose and Verse', 1927, based on
British Museum MS Royal 18 Axiii.

---

(5)

To chaucer þat is floure of rethoryk	33
In englisshe tong & excellent poete	
This wot I wel no þing may I do lyk	35
þogh so þat I of makynge entyrmete	
And gower þat so craftily doþ trete	
As in his book of moralite	
þogh I to þeym in makyng am vnmete	
ȝit most I schewe it forth þat is in me.	40

(6)

Noght lyketh me to labour ne to muse	
Vppon þese olde poysees derk	
ffor crystes feith suche þing schuld refuse,	
Witnes vppon Ierom þe holy clerk,	
Hit schold not ben a cristenmannes werk	45
Tho fals goddes names to renewe	
ffor he þat haþ reseyued cristes merk	
If he do so to crist he is vntrewe.	

(7)

Of þo þar crist in heuene blis schall,	
Suche manere werkes schold ben set on side,	50

ffor certaynly it nedeþ noght at all
To [whette] now þe dartes of cupide
Ne for to bidde þat Venus be oure gide
So þat we may oure foule lustes wynne,
On aunter lest þe same on vs betide
As dede þe same venus for hyre synne.

                    (8)
And certayn I haue tasted wonder lyte
As of þe welles of calliope
No wonder þough I sympilly endite
Yet will I not vnto tessiphone   60
Ne to allecto ne to megare
Besechin after craft of eloquence
But pray þat god of his benignyte
My spirit enspire wiþ his influence.

7.   THOMAS HOCCLEVE, THE DISCIPLE'S COMMEMORATION

1412

Thomas Hoccleve (*c*.1368-*c*.1430) was for many years Clerk
to the Privy Seal (i.e. a civil servant) on the fringes of
the court, and something of a poet.   In his poem 'The
Regement of Princes' he repeats the usual praise of
Chaucer's eloquence and rich meaning, but also commis-
sions a portrait.   The present quotation is taken from
the early fifteenth-century British Museum MS. Harleian
4866, f.34, f.36, f.37, f.37b, f.87, which has the portrait of Chaucer referred to in the last stanza.   Cf.
'Works', Part III, ed. F.J. Furnivall, EETS, Extra Series,
72 (1897).

              [An aged man addresses the poet:]

What schal I calle the What is thi name?
hoccleue fadir myn men clepen me....
thou were aqueynted with Caucher pardee
God haue his soule best of any Wyght....

O maister deere / and fadir reuerent
Mi maister Chaucer flour of eloquence

Mirour of fructuous entendement
O vniuersal fadir in science
Allas that thou thyn excellent prudence
In thi bed mortel mightist naght by qwethe
What eiled deth / allas Whi wolde he sle the
O deth thou didest naght harme singuleer
In slaghtere of him / but al this land it smertith
But nathelees / yit hast thou no power
His name sle / his hy vertu astertith
Vnslayn fro the / Which ay vs lyfly hertyth
With bookes of his ornat endytyng
That is to al this land enlumynyng

Hast thou nat eeke my maister Gower slayn....

Mi dere maistir / god his soule quyte
And fadir Chaucer fayn Wolde han me taght
But I was dul, and lerned life or naght

Allas my worthi maister honorable
This landes verray tresor and richesse
Deth by thi deth / hath harme irreparable
Vnto vs doon / hir vengeable duresse
Despoiled hath this land of the swetnesse
Of rethorik for vnto Tullius
Was neuer man so lyk amonges vs

Also who was hier in philosophie
To Aristotle / in our tonge but thow
The steppes of virgile in poesie
Thow filwedist eeke men wot wel ynow...

The firste fyndere of oure faire langage
Hath seyde in caas semblable & othir mo
So hyly wel that it is my dotage
For to expresse or touche any of thoo
Alasse my fadir fro the worlde is goo
My worthi maister Chaucer hym I mene
Be thou aduoket for hym heuenes quene

As thou wel knowest o blissid virgyne
With louyng hert and hye deuocioun
In thyne honour he wroot ful manye a lyne
O now thine helpe & thi promocioun
To god thi sone make a mocioun
How he thi seruaunt was mayden marie
And lat his loue floure and fructifie

Al thogh his lyfe be queynt the resemblaunce
Of him hath in me so fressh lyflynesse
That to putte othir men in remembraunce
Of his persone I haue heere his lyknesse
Do make to this ende in sothfastnesse
That thei that haue of him lest thought & mynde
By this peynture may ageyn him fynde

8. JOHN METHAM, CHAUCER'S EASE

1448-9

Metham studied philosophy at Cambridge. Not very learned,
he knew Chaucer's 'Troilus', at least, which influenced
his poem 'Amoryus and Cleopes', from which the quotation
is taken ('The Works of John Metham', ed. H. Craig,
EETS, Original Series, 132, (1916 for 1906), p. 80,
2170-2, 2189-91). His comment on Chaucer's 'great style'
is commonplace; not so his sense of natural speech in
rhyme.

And yff I the trwthe schuld here wryght   2170
As gret a style I schuld make in euery degre
As Chauncerys off qwene Eleyne, or Cresseyd, doht
                          endyght....

My mastyr Chauncerys, I mene, that longe dyd endure   2189
In practyk off rymyng: qwerffore proffoundely
With many prouerbys hys bokys he rymyd naturally.

9.   JOHN SHIRLEY, GOSSIP. CHAUCER WROTE FOR ALL THOSE THAT BE GENTLE OF BIRTH OR OF CONDITIONS

c.1450

John Shirley, about whom little is known, lived to around

ninety and died in London in 1456. At the end of his life
he owned four shops and it has been assumed from this and
certain manuscript evidence that he transcribed, compiled
and hired out copies of books of literary interest -
London's first lending library and, perhaps, one of the
earliest of publishing firms. A number of manuscripts
are known to be in his hand and others are clearly copied
from his versions (E.P. Hammond, 'English Verse between
Chaucer and Surrey', 1927). Shirley is distinguished by
gossipy headings to a few poems clearly meant as advert-
isements, and by very inaccurate texts. There is no reason to believe that the gossip is any more accurate than
the texts, but it reflects an authentic interest that must
have been contemporary with Chaucer's inner circle, since
it is clear that at least 'The General Prologue' to 'The
Canterbury Tales' reflects on some known living persons.
Shirley is valuable and unique in establishing a sense of
the social setting of the poetry. It is unfortunate that
Shirley's gossip is so unauthentic in detail. Extract (a)
is from Shirley's own manuscript, now Trinity College,
Cambridge, R. 3. 20, and constitutes the heading to
'Anelida', the opening and closing remarks to 'The Complaint of Mars' (pp. 106, 130, 139), and a final remark
to 'The Complaint of Venus' (p. 142). (Cf. A. Brusendorff,
'The Chaucer Tradition', 1925, pp. 263-4.) Extract (b) is
his introduction to 'The Knight's Tale', a MS. not in his
hand, but deriving from him, British Museum MS. Harleian
7333, f. 37. Extract (c) is from one of the two tables of
contents he wrote and testifies once again to Chaucer's
fame. It is from British Museum MS. Adds. 16165, f. 2(a).
It is thought that he wrote when elderly, but the date
1450 is purely notional.

(a)

Take þe heed sirs I prey yowe of þis compleynt of
Anelyda Qweene of Cartage Roote of trouthe and stedfastnesse þat pytously compleyneþe Upon þe varyance of daun
Arcyte lord borne of þe blood Royal of Thebes. englisshed
by Geffrey Chaucier In the best wyse and moost Rethoricy-
ous þe mooste vnkou eþ metre. coloures and Rymes þ^t euer
was sayde. tofore þis day - redeþe and preveþe þe
sooþe....
    Loo yee louers gladeþe and comforteþe you . of þally-
aunce etrayted bytwene þe hardy and furyous Mars . þe god
of armes and Venus þe double goddesse of loue made by

Geffrey Chaucier . at þe comandement of þe renoumed and
excellent prynce my lord þe duc John of Lancastere.

þus eondeþe here þis complaint whiche some men sayne
was made . by my lady of york doughter to þe kyng of
Spaygne and my lord of huntyngdon . some tyme duc of
Excestre and filowyng begynneþe . a balade translated out
of frenshe . in to englisshe by Chaucier Geffrey þe
frenshe made sir Otes de Grauntsomme . knight.   Savosyen.

Hit is sayde pat Graunsomme made þis last balade for
Venus resembled to my lady of york . aunswering þe com-
playnt of Mars....

(b)

O yee so noble and worthi pryncis and princesse, oþer
estatis or degrees, what-euer yee beo, þat haue disposic-
ione or plesaunce to rede or here þe stories of old tymis
passed, to kepe yow frome ydelnesse and slowthe, in esch-
euing oþer folies þat might be cause of more harome filowyng, vowcheth sauf, I be-seche yowe to fynde yowe occu-
pacioun in þe reding here of þe tales of Caunterburye
wiche beon compilid in þis boke filowing First foundid,
ymagenid and made boþe for disporte and leornyng of all
þoo that beon gentile of birthe or of condicions by þe
laureal and moste famous poete þat euer was to-fore him
as in þemvelisshing of oure rude moders englisshe tonge,
clepid Chaucyer a Gaufrede of whos soule god for his
mercy have pitee of his grace.   Amen.

(c)
þE PROLOGE OF þE KALUNDARE OF þIS LITTLE BOOKE

Boicius in prose
Of Nichodeme
þe *maistre of þe game*
þe *dreme for lovers*
þe *Ruyle of preestis*
þe *compleynt of a lover*
þe *compleynt of anelida*
Item xii oþer litel balades
  complaintes & roundelles

   If, þat you list / for to entende /
Of þis booke / to here legende /
Suche as is / right vertuous /
Of maner of mirthe nought vicious /
As wryten haue / þees olde clerkes /

þat beon appreued / in alle hir werkis /
By oure eldres / here to fore
Remembraunce / ellys were forlore /
  Wher fore / dere sirs / I you beseche
þat ye disdeyne not / with my speche /   10
ffor affter þe symplesse / of my witt /
So as feblesse / wolde suffice hit /
þis litell booke / with myn hande /
wryten I haue / ye shul vnderstande /
And sought þe copie / in many a place /
To haue þe more thank / of youre grace /
  And doon hit bynde / In þis volume /
þat boþe þe gret / and þe comune /
May þer on looke / and eke hit reede
þeyres beo þe thanke / and þe meede   20
þat first hit studyed / and owt founde
Nowe beon þey dolven / deep in þe grounde /
Beseche I god / he gyf hem grace /
In hevens blisse / to haue a place /
  And for to put hit / in youre mynde /
ffirst þus by ordre / shul ye fynde /
Of Boece / þe hole translacyoun /
And Phylosofyes / consolacyoun /
Laboured by Geffrey Chaucier
Whiche in oure wolgare / hade neuer his pere /
Of eloquencyale retorryke /
In Englisshe / was neuer noon him lyke /
Gyff him þe prys and seyþe þer hoo /
For neuer knewe ye / suche na moo /

10. GEORGE ASHBY, EMBELYSSHING OURE ENGLISSHE

c. 1470

___

After forty years as writer of the signet, possibly to
Alice, Duchess of Suffolk and granddaughter of Chaucer,
Ashby (c. 1390-1475) wrote his earliest extant poem in
that literary academy of the fifteenth century, a prison,
c. 1463. His only other extant work consists in two verse
treatises directed to the education of Henry VI's son
Edward, murdered in 1471. In one of them, 'Active Policy
of a Prince', Ashby declares that he is nearly eighty, and
prefaces his advice with the following prologue, in the

sole surviving MS. Cambridge University Library, Mm. IV,
42. Ashby is presumed to have been, like Scogan, a royal
tutor, and continues the line of Chaucer's courtier/civil
servant followers. (Cf. 'George Ashby Poems', ed. M.
Bateson, EETS, ES LXXVI, 1899.)

---

(1)

Maisters Gower, Chauncer & Lydgate,
  Primier poetes of this nacion,
Embelysshing oure englisshe tendure algate
  Firste finders to oure consolacion
  Off fresshe douce englisshe and formacion
    Of newe balades, not vsed before
    By whome we all may haue lernyng and lore.

(2)

Alas! saufe goddes wille & his plesaunce,
  That euer ye shulde dye & chaunge this lyffe,
Vntyl tyme / that by youre wise pourueunce
  Ye had lafte to vs / sum remembratife
  Of a personne, lerned & Inuentif,
    Disposed aftur youre condicion,
    Of fresshe makyng to oure Instruccion.

(3)

But sithe we all / be dedly and mortal,
  And no man may eschewe this egression,
I beseche almyghty god eternal
  To pardon you all / youre transgression
  That ye may dwelle in heuenly mansion
    In recompense of many a scripture
    That ye haue englisshede without lesure.

(4)

So I George Asshby not comparison
  Making to youre excellent enditing
With right humble prayer & orison,
  Pray god that by you I may haue lernyng,
  And as a blynde man in the wey blondryng
    As I can I shall now lerne and practise
    Not as a maister but as a p[r]entise.

11.   ROBERT HENRYSON, WHO KNOWS IF ALL THAT WORTHY CHAUCER
WROTE WAS TRUE?

c. 1475

Henryson was probably a schoolmaster and notary public in
Dunfermline, Scotland, born perhaps before 1440 and dead
by 1505 (cf. his 'Testament of Cresseid', ed. D. Fox,
1968). By far the earliest text surviving of the 'Testament' is that printed by Thynne in his edition of Chaucer's 'Works', 1532, f.CCXIX et seq., from which this
extract is taken. It immediately follows Chaucer's 'Troilus' and was probably a last-minute insertion by the
printer. Notwithstanding the poet's remarks in the
extract quoted, the poem was sometimes attributed to Chaucer, and was best known in this form, as reprinted in many
subsequent editions. Henryson has a poet's consciousness
of the beauty of Chaucer's verse, with an unusual and
drily humorous sense of the inventiveness, the fictional
quality, notwithstanding appeals to authority, which both
poets deploy.

I made the fyre and beaked me about   [Stanza 6]
Than toke A drinke my spirites to conforte
And armed me wel fro the colde therout
To cutte the wynter nyght and make it shorte
I toke a queare / and left al other sporte
Written by worthy Chaucer glorious
Of fayre Creseyde / and lusty Troylus

And there I founde....   [Stanza 7]
[Summarises Diomede's seduction of Criseyde]

Of his [Troilus's] distresse me nedeth nat
                                reherse   [Stanza 9]
For worthy Chaucer in that same boke
In goodly termes / and in ioly verse
Compyled hath his cares who wyl loke
To breke my slepe another queare I toke
In whiche I founde the fatal desteny
Of fayre Creseyde / whiche ended wretchedly

Who wot if al that Chaucer wrate was trewe   [Stanza 10]
Nor I wotte nat if this narration
Be authorysed / or forged of the newe

Of some poete by his inuention
Made to reporte the lamentation
And woful ende of this lusty Creseyde
And what distresse she was in or she deyde

12. INVENTORY OF SIR JOHN PASTON II

1475-9

Sir John was a member of the Norfolk landed family famous
through the preservation of their letters. The inventory
(now British Museum MS. Add. 43491, f.26, an autograph in
the hand of Sir John) is on a narrow strip of paper whose
right-hand edge has decayed (shown here by . . .). The
present text is taken, with the correction of a minor mis-
print, from *The Paston Letters*, ed. J. Gairdner, 1900,
Vol. 1, p. 300. See also *The Paston Letters and Papers of
the Fifteenth Century*, ed. N. Davis, 1971, pp. 516-18, and
Plate VII. Sir John, 1442-79, was a courtier, traveller,
soldier, at various times MP and JP. His list of books in
English may be taken as an index of the tastes of the
landed gentry of the second half of the fifteenth century,
though he was perhaps unusually literate. There are Arthurian and other romances, devotional works, books of
heraldry, a chronicle, a statute book, a number of poems
by Lydgate and others, and the Chaucer items noted below.
'The Parliament of Fowls' appears twice in anthology-type
collections with poems by Lydgate and also, probably, 'The
Legend of Good Women'. There is no 'Canterbury Tales'.
'Troilus and Criseyde' appears to have been a valuable
book but unfortunately the price is unreadable, as the
book was to John Paston when borrowed by the man whose
name begins 'Bra', who nefariously lent it to Dame Wyngfelde 'where I saw it'. None of the books mentioned can
be detected among surviving MSS.

---

*The Inventory off Englysshe Boks off John . . . . . . made
the v. daye of Novembre, anno regni Regis E. iiij . . . .
    I. A boke had off myn ostesse at the George . . . . off
the Dethe off Arthr begynyng at Cassab[elaun, Guy Earl of]
Warwyk, Kyng Ri. Cur de Lyon, a Cronic[le] . . . . . to
to Edwarde the iij., prec.*

2. Item, a Boke of Troylus whyche William Bra . . . . .
hath hadde neer x. yer, and lent it to Dame . . . .
Wyngfelde, and *ibi ego vidi;* valet . . . . .
   3. Item, a blak Boke with *the Legende off Lad[ies, la
Belle Dame] saunce Mercye, the Parlement off Byrd[es, the
Temple of] Glasse, Palatyse and Scitacus, the Me[ditations
of . . . .] the Greene Knyght; valet, -*
   4. Item, a Boke in preente off the Pleye off the [Chess].
   5. Item, a Boke lent Midelton, and therin is *Bele
Da[me sans] Mercy the Parlement of Byrds, Balade . . . . .
. off Guy and Colbronde, off the Goos th . . . . . , the
Dysputson bytwyen Hope and Dyspeyr, ... Marchaunts,
the Lyffe of Seynt Cry[stofer].*

13.   UNKNOWN, WORD AND THING

c. 1477

A 'Book of Curtesye', one of several circulating in the
fifteenth century, contains an old man's advice to a boy.
It is an educational treatise on forming manners, character, etc. In advice on reading the author comments on the
brevity of Chaucer, and his vividness, whereby word and
matter seem identified - perhaps an early perception of a
kind of 'concreteness,' though the word *thing* (= Latin
res) has a wide range of meaning, not primarily material-
istic. The text follows that printed by Caxton, *c.* 1477-8,
ed. F.J. Furnivall, 'Caxton's Book of Curtesye', EETS,
ES III, 1868, (a) pp. 33ff., (b) pp. 41ff.

(a)

[45]

Excersise your self also in redynge	309
Of bookes enornede with eloquence	
Ther shal ye fynde / bothe plesir & lernynge	311
So that ye may / in euery good presence	
Somwhat fynde / as in sentence	
That shal acorde / the tyme to ocupy	
That ye not nede / to stonden ydelly	315

[46]

It is fayr / for to be comynycatyf
In maters vnto purpose acordynge
So that a wyght seme excersyf   318
For trusteth wel / it is a tedyous thynge
For to here a chylde / multeplye talkyng
Yf it be not to the purpose applyede
Ande also with / goodly termys alyede   322

[47]

Redeth gower in his wrytynge moralle
That auncyent fader of memorye
Redeth his bookes / callede confessionalle   325
With many another vertuous trayttye
Ful of sentence / set ful fructuosly
That hym to rede / shal gyue you corage
He is so ful of fruyt. sentence and langage   329

[48]

O fader and founder of ornate eloquence
That enlumened hast alle our bretayne
To soone we loste / thy laureate scyence   332
O lusty lyquour / of that fulsom fontayne
O cursid deth / why hast thou þᵗ poete slayne
I mene fader chaucer / maister galfryde
Alas the whyle / that euer he from vs dyde   336

[49]

Redith his werkis / ful of plesaunce
Clere in sentence / in langage excellent
Briefly to wryte / suche was his suffysañce   339
What euer to saye / he toke in his entente
His langage was so fayr and pertynente
It semeth vnto mannys heerynge
Not only the worde / but verely the thynge   343

[50]

Redeth my chylde / redeth his bookes alle
Refuseth none / thy ben expedyente
Sentence or langage / or bothe fynde ye shalle   346
Ful delectable / for that good fader mente
Of al his purpose / and his hole entente
How to plese in euery audyence
And in our tunge / was welle of eloquence   350

(b)

[58]

Loo my childe / these faders auncyente   400
Repen the feldes fresshe of fulsomnes
The flours fresh they gadred vp & hente
Of siluer langage / the grete riches
Who wil it haue my lityl childe doutles
Muste of hem begge / ther is no more to saye
For of our tunge / they were both lok & kaye   406

[59]

Ther can noman now her werkis disteyne
The enbamed tunge / and aureate sentence
Men gete it now / by cantelmele & gleyne   409
Here and there by besy diligence
And fayne wold reche / her craft of eloquence
And by the gleyne / it is ful oft sene
In whos felde / the gleyners haue bene   413

[60]

And vnto me / age hath bode good morowe
I am not able clenly / for to gleyne
Nature is fayn of craft / her eyen to borowe   416
Me lacketh clerenes / of myn eyen tweyne
Begge I maye / gleyne I can not certeyne
Therfore þ^t werck / I wil playnly remytte
To folkis yong / more passyng clere of witte   420

[61]

Seche ye therfore / and in caas ye fynde
Such gleynors fressh as haue som apparence
Of fayr langage / yet take hem & vnbynde   423
And preue ye / what they be in existence
Coloured in langage / sauerly in sentence
And doubte not my childe / withoute drede
It wil prouffite to see suche thingis & red[e]   427

[62]

Yet eft sones my childe / lete vs resorte
To thentente of yur first matere
Degressed somwhat / for we wold reporte   430
And reuiue the laude of hem that were
Famous in our langage / these faders dere
Whos sowles in blysse / god eternel auaunce
That lysten so our langage to enhaunce   434

14. WILLIAM CAXTON, HIGH AND QUICK SENTENCE

1478, 1483, 1484

After a long career as a successful businessman in the
Low Countries, Caxton (1422?-91) returned home in 1476 to
become England's first printer. He printed works commissioned by noble patrons, and also works that in pleasing
him would please others. Perhaps his greatest service was
in printing almost all the major works of vernacular English medieval literary culture, though he regrettably
omitted Langland. He often contributed prologues and epi-
logues to his editions, expressive of shrewd appreciation.
The following examples are: (a) the 'Epilogue' to Chaucer's translation of Boethius, 1478; (b) the 'Epilogue' to
'The House of Fame', 1483; (c) the 'Prohemye', to 'The
Canterbury Tales', 2nd edition, 1484; cf. edition by W.J.B.
Crotch, EETS, Ordinary Series 176 (1927). For the Epitaph referred to at the end of (a) see next, No. 15.

(a)

Thus endeth this boke whiche is named the boke of Consolacion of philosophie whiche that Boecius made for his com-
forte and consolacion he beyng in exile for the comyne and
publick wele hauyng grete heuynes & thoughtes and in maner
of despayr / Rehercing in the sayde boke howe Philosophie
appiered to him shewyng the mutabilite of this transitorie lyfe / and also enformyng howe fortune and happe
shold bee vnderstonden / with the predestynacion and pre-
science of God as moche as maye and ys possible to bee
knowen naturelly / as a fore ys sayd in this sayd boke /
Whiche Boecius was an excellente auctour of dyuerce
bookes craftely and curiously maad in prose and metre /
And also had translated dyuerce bookes oute of Greke into
latyne / and had ben senatour of that noble & famous cite
Rome. And also his two sones Senatours for their prudence
& wisedom. And for as moche as he withstode to his power
the tyrannye of theodorik thenne Emperour / & wold haue
defended the sayde cite & Senate from his wicked hondes /
wherupon he was conuict & putte in prison / in whiche
prisone he made this forsaide boke of consolacion for his
singular comfort, and for as moche as the stile of it / is
harde & difficile to be vnderstonde of simple persones

Therfore the worshipful fader & first foundeur & enbelis-
ssher of ornate eloquence in our englissh. I mene / Maister Geffrey Chaucer hath translated this sayd werke oute
of latyn in to oure vsual and moder tonge. Folowyng the
latyn as neygh as is possible to be vnderstande.
wherein in myne oppynyon he hath deservid a perpetuell
lawde and thanke of al this noble Royame of Englond / And
in especiall of them that shall rede & vnderstande it.
For in the sayd boke they may see what this transitorie &
mutable worlde is And wherto euery mann liuyng in hit /
ought to entende. Thenne for as moche as this sayd boke
so translated is rare & not spred ne knowen as it is
digne and worthy. For the erudicion and lernyng of suche
as ben Ignoraunt & not knowyng of it / Atte requeste of a
singuler frende & gossib of myne. I william Caxton haue
done my debuoir & payne tenprynte it in fourme as is here
afore made / In hopyng that it shal prouffite moche peple
to the wele & helth of their soules / & for to lerne to
haue and kepe the better pacience in aduersitees / And
furthermore I desire & requi. re you that of your charite
ye wold praye for the soule of the sayd worshipful mann
Geffrey Chaucer / first translatour of this sayde boke
into englissh & enbelissher in making the sayd langage
ornate & fayr. whiche shal endure perpetuelly. and therfore he ought eternelly to be remembrid. of whom the body
and corps lieth buried in thabbay of Westmestre beside
london to fore the chapele of seynte benet. by whos sepulture is wreton on a table hongyng on a pylere his Epit-
aphye maad by a poete laureat. wherof the copye foloweth
&c.

(b)

I fynde nomore of this werke to fore sayd / For as fer as
I can vnderstonde / This noble man Gefferey Chaucer fynys-
shyd at the sayd conclusion of the metyng of lesyng and
sothsawe / where as yet they ben chekked and maye not
departe / whyche werke as me semeth is craftyly made /
and dygne to be wreton & knowen / For he towchyth in it
ryght grete wysedom & subtyll vnderstondyng / And so in
alle hys werkys he excellyth in myn oppynyon alle other
wryters in our Englyssh / For he wrytteth no voyde wordes /
but alle hys mater is ful of hye and quycke sentence /
to whom ought to be gyuen laude and preysyng for hys noble
makyng and wrytyng / For of hym alle other haue borowed
syth and taken / in alle theyr wel sayeng and wrytyng /
And I humbly beseche & praye yow / emonge your prayers to
remembre hys soule / on whyche and on alle crysten soulis
I beseche almyghty god to haue mercy Amen

(c)

Grete thankes lawde and honour / ought to be gyuen vnto
the clerkes / poetes / and historiographs that haue wreton
many noble bokes of wysedom of the lyues / passions / &
myracles of holy sayntes of hystoryes / of noble and famous Actes / and faittes / And of the cronycles sith the
begynnyng of the creacion of the world / vnto thys present
tyme / by whyche we ben dayly enformed / and have know-
leche of many thynges / of whom we shold not haue knowen /
yf they had not left to vs theyr monumentis wreton /
Emong whom and inespecial to fore alle other we ought to
gyue a synguler laude vnto that noble & grete philosopher
Gefferey chaucer the whiche for his ornate wrytyng in our
tongue may wel haue the name of a laureate poete / For to
fore that he by hys labour enbelysshyd / ornated / and
made faire our englisshe / in thys Royame was had rude
speche & Incongrue / as yet it appiereth by olde bookes /
whyche at thys day ought not to haue place ne be compared
emong ne to hys beauteuous volumes / and aournate writ-
ynges / of whom he made many bokes and treatyces of many
a noble historye as wel in metre as in ryme and prose /
and them so craftyly made / that he comprehended hys
maters in short / quyck and hye sentences / eschewyng
prolyxyte / castyng away the chaf of superfluyte / and
shewyng the pyked grayn of sentence / vtteryd by crafty
and sugred eloquence / of whom emonge all other of hys
bokes / I purpose temprynte by the grace of god the book
of the tales of cauntyrburye / in whiche I fynde many a
noble hystorye / of euery astate and degre / Fyrst reher-
cyng the condicions / and tharraye of eche of them as properly as possyble is to be sayd / And after theyr tales
whyche ben of noblesse / wysedom / gentylesse / Myrthe /
and also of veray holynesse and vertue / wherin he fynys-
shyth thys sayd booke / whyche book I haue dylygently
ouersen and duly examyned to thende that it be made
acordyng vnto his owen makyng / For I fynde many of the
sayd bookes / whyche wryters haue abrydgyd it and many
thynges left out / And in somme place haue sette certayn
versys / that he neuer made ne sette in hys booke / of
whyche bookes so incorrecte was one brought to me vj yere
passyd / whyche I supposed had ben veray true & correcte /
And accordyng to the same I dyde do enprynte a certayn
nombre of them / whyche anon were sold to many and dyuerse
gentyl men / of whome one gentylman cam to me / and said
that this book was not accordyng in many places vnto the
book that Gefferey chaucer had made / To whom I answerd
that I had made it accordyng to my copye / and by me was
nothyng added ne mynusshyd / Thenne he sayd he knewe a

book whyche hys fader had and moche louyd / that was very
trewe / and accordyng vnto hys owen first book by hym
made / and sayd more yf I wold enprynte it agayn he wold
gete me the same book for a copye / how be it he wyst wel /
that hys fader wold not gladly departe fro it / To whom I
said / in caas that he coude gete me suche a book trewe
and correcte / yet I wold ones endeuoyre me to enprynte
it agayn / for to satysfye thauctour / where as to fore by
ygnouraunce I erryd in hurtyng and dyffamyng his book in
dyuerce places in settyng in somme thynges that he neuer
sayd ne made / and leuyng out many thynges that he made
whyche ben requysite to be sette in it / And thus we fyll
at accord / And he ful gentylly gate of hys fader the
said book / and delyuerd it to me / by whiche I haue
corrected my book / as here after alle alonge by thayde
of almyghty god shal folowe / whom I humbly beseche to
gyue me grace and ayde to achyeue / and accomplysshe / to
hys lawde honour and glorye / and that alle ye that shal
in thys book rede or heere / wyll of your charyte emong
your dedes of mercy / remembre the sowle of the sayd
Gefferey chaucer first auctour / and maker of thys book /
And also that alle we that shal see and rede therin / may
so take and vnderstonde the good and vertuous tales / that
it may so prouffyte / vnto the helthe of our sowles / that
after thys short and transitorye lyf we may come to euer-
lastyng lyf in heuen / Amen

15.   STEPHEN SURIGO, CHAUCER'S EPITAPH

1479

───

Stefano de Surigone, an Italian Humanist scholar, belonged
to the order of the Humiliates, and is described by Caxton
as a licentiate of Milan University. A poet laureate, he
taught Latin Eloquence at Oxford (1454-*c*.1471?), as well
as teaching at various times in other universities abroad.
He wrote a Latin Elegy on Chaucer, which was included in
Caxton's edition of Chaucer's Boethius, and reprinted
throughout the sixteenth century. It is in a strained,
elaborate style, and a literal translation is given here.
The final paragraph, enclosed in square brackets, was
probably added by Caxton himself. Cf. N.F. Blake, Caxton
and Chaucer, 'Leeds Studies in English', I (1967),

pp. 19-36. (Biographical detail from 'Biographical and
Bibliographical Dictionary of the Italian Humanists in
Italy, 1300-1800', ed. M.E. Cosenza, Boston, Mass., 6
vols, 1962.)

Epitaphium Galfridi Chaucer. per poetam laureatum
Stephanum surigonum Mediolanensem in decretis licenciatum

Pyerides muse, si possunt numina fletus
  Fundere . diuinas atque rigare genas,
Galfridi vatis chaucer crudelia fata
  Plangite . sit lacrimis abstinuisse nephas
Vos coluit viuens . at vos celebrate sepultum
  Reddatur merito gracia digna viro
Grande decus vobis . est docti musa maronis
  Qua didicit melius lingua latina loqui
Grande nouumque decus Chaucer . famamque parauit
  Heu quantum fuerat prisca britanna rudis
Reddidit insignem maternis versibus . vt iam
  Aurea splendescat . ferrea facta prius
Hunc latuisse virum nil . si tot opuscula vertes
  Dixeris . egregiis que decorata modis
Socratis ingenium . vel fontes philosophie
  Quitquid & archani dogmata sacra ferunt
Et quascunque velis tenuit dignissimus artes
  Hic vates . paruo conditus hoc tumulo
Ah laudis quantum preclara britannia perdis
  Dum rapuit tantum mors odiosa virum
Crudeles parce . crudelia fila sorores
  Non tamen extincto corpore . fama perit
Viuet ineternum . viuent dum scripta poete
  Viuant eterno tot monimenta die
Si qua bonos tangit pietas . si carmine dignus
  Carmina qui cecinit tot cumulata modis
Hec sibi marmoreo scribantur verba sepulchro
  Hec maneat laudis sarcina summa sue
Galfridus Chaucer vates : et fama poesis
  Materne . hac sacra sum tumulatus humo

Post obitum Caxton voluit te viuere cura
  Willelmi. Chaucer clare poeta tuj
Nam tua non solum compressit opuscula formis
  Has quoque sed laudes . iussit hic esse tuas

Translation

Epitaph of Geoffrey Chaucer by the laureate poet Stephen
Surigo of Milan, licensed (doctor) by decree at Milan.

(Translated by R.G.G. Coleman, Fellow of Emmanuel College,
Cambridge.)

Pierian Muses, if heavenly powers can pour forth tears and
moisten their divine cheeks, lament the cruel fate of the
bard Geoffrey Chaucer. Let it be a crime to refrain from
weeping. He worshipped you in his lifetime, but [I bid
you] honour him now that he is buried. Let a worthy
reward be paid to a deserving man. The Muse [or Music]
of learned Maro is a great honour to you, the Muse through
whose agency the Latin tongue learned to speak better. A
great new honour and fame has Chaucer provided for you.
By the verses [that he composed] in his [British] mother
tongue he made it [as] illustrious as, alas, it had once
been uncouth,(1) so that now it takes on a golden splendour where formerly it was iron.
   One will affirm that there was nothing in which this
man was not distinguished (2) if he turns the pages of so
many works which [are] embellished with excellent measures.
The genius of Socrates or the springs of philosophy, and
all the secrets which holy doctrine contains and all the
arts that you could wish for - these were in the possession of this most worthy bard [who is] buried in this tiny
grave.
   Ah, how much renown you lose, famed Britannia, now that
hateful death has snatched away so great a man! Cruel
[are the] Fates, cruel their threads, O Sisters!(3) Yet
even when the body is dead fame does not perish. It will
live forever, as long as the poets' writings live. May
all these monuments live in everlasting day. If the good
are touched by any piety and if the man who sang songs
amassed in so many measures is [himself] worthy of a
song,(4) let these words as spoken on his own behalf, be
inscribed upon his marble tomb, let this remain the crown-
ing burden to his own praise:
   'I, Geoffrey Chaucer the bard, glory of my native
   poesy, am buried in this sacred ground.'
[It was the eager wish (5) of your admirer William Caxton
that you should live, illustrious poet Chaucer. For not
only has he printed your works but he has also ordered
this eulogy of you to be here.]

Notes

1 Construing: quantum prisca Britanna [lingua] (cf.
   lingua Latina above) fuerat rudis, [tantum] insignem
   reddidit maternis versibus.
2 Taking *dixeris* as addressed to the reader. *Hunc
   latuisse virum nil* is difficult. I have rendered it as
   if it were classical, viz. 'this man lay hidden in
   nothing'; but the unclassical meaning 'nothing was
   hidden from this man' might be better in the context.
3 Taking *sorores* as vocative, addressed to the Muses, and
   parce = Parcae.
4 The punctuation from *fama perit* to *cumulata modis* is
   very uncertain. I have assumed:
       perit. Viuet in eternum, uiuent ... poete. Viuant
       ...... die. Si qua ... pietas, si carmine ...
       modis, hec ...
5 Construing *cura* as subject to *volvit* and *Caxton* as
   genitive with *Wilhelmi..tuj*. The alternative 'Caxton
   wished you to live by the care of your William' seems
   less satisfactory.

16. JOHN PARMENTER'S WILL

1479

He was licensed BCL by 1454; was rector of several pari-
shes; and from at least 1464 to 1481 was Commissary-
General of the Archbishop of Canterbury. He died in
1485. His will made in 1479 leaves 'vnum librum vocatum
Canterbury tales'. He also owned the large folio volume,
a 'Biblia Sacra', now Cambridge University Library, Dd.
1.6. He represents the professional, clerical and
legal element in Chaucer's fifteenth-century readership.

---

17.   WILLIAM DUNBAR, GOLDEN ELOQUENCE

*c.*1503

Dunbar (*c.*1465-*c.*1530) versatile Scots poet, courtier, and probably graduate of St Andrews University, praises Chaucer for his 'bright, fresh, enamelled terms' in 'The Goldyn Targe', 253-61 (ed. J. Small, 'Poems', II, p. 10, Scottish Text Society, X, 1893).

O reverend Chaucere, rose of rethoris all,
As in oure tong ane flour imperiall
That raise in Britane ewir, quho redis rycht,
Thou beris of makaris the tryumph riall;
Thy fresch anamalit termes celicall
This mater coud illumynit haue full brycht:
Was thou noucht of oure Inglisch all the lycht,
Surmounting ewiry tong terrestriall
Alls fer as Mayes morow dois mydnycht?

O morall Gower, and Ludgate laureate,
Your sugurit lippis and tongis aureate,
Bene to oure eris cause of grete delyte;
Your angel mouthis most mellifluate
Our rude langage has clere illumynate,
And faire our-gilt oure speche, that imperfyte
Stude, or your goldyn pennis schupe to wryte;
This Ile before was bare, and desolate
Off rethorike, or lusty fresch endyte.

18.   STEPHEN HAWES, VIRTUOUS, OR GLAD AND MERRY

1506

Possibly educated at Oxford, Hawes, who was perhaps a Suffolk gentleman, became groom of the chamber to Henry VII, and was poet and playwright. 'The Pastime of Pleasure', ed. W.E. Mead, EETS, OS 173, 1928 (whence this text, cap. XIV, pp. 54-6, 1310..71) shows a courtier's knowledge of

the range and variety of Chaucer's work as already available in print.

O pensyfe herte / in the stormy pery   1310
Mercury northwest / thou mayst se appere
After tempest / to glad thyne emyspery
Hoyse vp thy sayle / for thou muste drawe nere
Towarde the ende / of thy purpos so clere
Remembre the / of the trace and daunce   1315
Of poetes olde / with all thy purueyaunce

As morall gower / whose sentencyous dewe
Adowne reflayreth / with fayre golden beames
And after Chaucers / all abrode doth shewe
Our vyces to clense / his depared stremes   1320
Kyndlynge our hertes / with the fyry leames
Of morall vertue / as is probable
In all his bokes / so swete and prouffytable

The boke of fame / whiche is sentencyous
He drewe hymselfe / on his owne inuencyon   1325
And than the tragydyes / so pyteous
Of the nyntene ladyes / was his translacyon
And vpon his ymagynacyon
He made also / the tales of Caunterbury
Some vertuous / and some glade and mery   1330

And of Troylus / the pytous dolour
For his lady Cresyde / full of doublenesse
He dyde bewayle / full well the langoure
Of all his loue / and grete vnhappynesse
And many other bokes doubtles   1335
He dyde compyle / whose goodly name
In prynted bokes / doth remayne in fame

And after hym / my mayster Lydgate . . .

Were not these thre / gretely to commende
Whiche them applyed suche bokes to contryue
Whose famous draughtes no man can amende
The synne of slothe they dyde frome them dryue
After theyr dethe for to abyde on lyue
In worthy fame by many a nacyon   1370
Theyr bokes / theyr actes do make relacyon

19.   JOHN SKELTON, SOME SAD STORYES, SOME MERY

*c.*1507

John Skelton (1460-1529) was educated at Cambridge (perhaps Peterhouse) and at Oxford, took Holy Orders, acquired
a somewhat disreputable character, and wrote many poems,
devotional, satirical, delicate and ranting, many in the
characteristic metre of the extract below. He received
laureation at Cambridge, 1492-3, and though he attacked
Wolsey was patronised as poet by Henry VII and various
nobles. In his long poem 'The Garland of Laurell' (ed.
A. Dyce, 'Poetical Works', 1843, Vol. I), which shows the
influence of 'The House of Fame', Skelton begins the sixteenth-century tradition of introducing Chaucer and Gower
as persons speaking in the poem, but nothing of critical
interest ensues. Skelton's important remarks on Chaucer,
referring to his language, and emphasising his variety and
humour, occur in 'Phillip Sparrowe' (ed. Dyce, 'Works', I,
pp. 69-75), in which a young girl is speaking, lamenting
the death of her sparrow.

An epytaphe I wold haue   605
For Phyllyppes graue:
But for I am a mayde,
Tymerous, halfe afrayde,
That neuer yet asayde
Of Elyconys well,   610
Where the Muses dwell;
Though I can rede and spell,
Recounte, reporte, and tell
Of the Tales of Caunterbury,
Some sad storyes, some mery;
As Palamon and Arcet,
Duke Theseus, and Partelet;
And of the Wyfe of Bath,
That worketh moch scath
Whan her tale is tolde   620
Amonge huswyues bolde,
How she controlde
Her husbandes as she wolde,
And them to despyse
In the homylyest wyse,
Brynge other wyues in thought
Their husbandes to set at nought:

And though that rede haue I
Of Gawen and syr Guy....

And though I can expounde   672
Of Hector of Troye,
That was all theyr ioye,
Whom Achylles slew,
Wherfore all Troy dyd rew;
And of the loue so hote
That made Troylus to dote
Vpon fayre Cressyde,
And what they wrote and sayd,   680
And of theyr wanton wylles
Pandaer bare the bylles
From one to the other;
His maisters loue to further,
Somtyme a presyous thyng,
An ouche, or els a ryng;
From her to hym agayn
Somtyme a pretty chayn,
Or a bracelet of her here,
Prayd Troylus for to were   690
That token for her sake;
How hartely he dyd it take,
And moche therof dyd make;
And all that was in vayne,
For she dyd but fayne;
The story telleth playne,
He coulde not optayne,
Though his father were a kyng,
Yet there was a thyng
That made the male to wryng;   700
She made hym to syng
The song of louers lay;
Musyng nyght and day,
Mournyng all alone,
Comfort had he none,
For she was quyte gone;
Thus in conclusyon,
She brought him in abusyon;
In ernest and in game
She was moch to blame;   710
Disparaged is her fame,
And blemysshed is her name,
In maner half with shame;
Troylus also hath lost
On her moch loue and cost,
And now must kys the post;
Pandara, that went betwene,

Hath won nothing, I wene,
But lyght for somer grene;
Yet for a speciall laud   720
He is named Troylus baud,
Of that name he is sure
Whyles the world shall dure....

I am but a yong mayd,   770
And cannot in effect
My style as yet direct
With Englysh wordes elect:
Our naturall tong is rude,
And hard to be enneude
With pullysshed termes lusty;
Our language is so rusty,
So cankered, and so full
Of frowardes, and so dull,
That if I wolde apply   780
To wryte ornatly,
I wot not where to fynd
Termes to serue my mynde.
    Gowers Englysh is olde,
And of no value told;
His mater is worth gold,
And worthy to be enrold.
    In Chauser I am sped,
His tales I haue red:
His mater is delectable,   790
Solacious, and commendable;
His Englysh well alowed,
So as it is enprowed,
For as it is enployd,
There is no Englysh voyd,
At those dayes moch commended,
And now men wold haue amended
His Englysh, whereat they barke,
And mar all they warke:
Chaucer, that famus clerke,   800
His termes were not darke,
But plesaunt, easy, and playne;
No worde he wrote in vayne.
    Also Johnn Lydgate
Wryteth after an hyer rate;
It is dyffuse to fynde
The sentence of his mynde,
Yet wryteth he in his kynd,
No man that can amend
Those maters that he hath pende;   810
Yet some men fynde a faute,
And say he wryteth to haute.

20.   GAVIN DOUGLAS, VENERABILL CHAUSER, ALL WOMANIS FREND

1513

Gavin Douglas (1474?-1522) bishop, politician and poet,
son of an earl, was educated at St Andrews University.
Although he praises Chaucer for his eloquence and the
beauty of his verse, he condemns in 'The House of Fame'
what is in effect the usual sentimentally feminist medieval reading of Virgil, and gives a more genuinely classical interpretation as it arises from his consideration of
the problem of translation, in the Prologue to Book I of
his translation of the 'Aeneid: Eneados', 1513; ed. D.F.C.
Coldwell, Vol. II, Scottish Text Society, 339-46, 405-18,
445-9.

Thoght venerabill Chauser, principal poet but peir,
Hevynly trumpat, orlege and reguler,   340
In eloquens balmy, cundyt and dyall,
Mylky fontane, cleir.strand and royss ryall,
Of fresch endyte, throu Albion iland braid,
In hys legend of notabill ladeis said
That he couth follow word by word Virgill,   345
Wisar than I may faill in lakar stile....

I say nocht this of Chauser for offens,   405
Bot till excuss my lewyt insufficiens,
For as he standis beneth Virgill in gre,
Vndir hym alsfer I grant my self to be.
And netheless into sum place, quha kend it,
My mastir Chauser gretly Virgill offendit.   410
All thoch I be tobald hym to repreif,
He was fer baldar, certis, by hys leif,
Sayand he followit Virgillis lantern toforn,
Quhou Eneas to Dydo was forsworn.
Was he forsworn? Than Eneas was fals -   415
That he admittis and callys hym traytour als.
Thus wenyng allane Ene to haue reprevit,
He hass gretly the prynce of poetis grevit,...

Bot sikkyrly of resson me behufis   445
Excuss Chauser fra all maner repruffis
In lovyng of thir ladeis lylly quhite
He set on Virgill and Eneas this wyte,
For he was evir (God wait) all womanis frend.

21.   WILLIAM TYNDALE, TO CORRUPT THE MINDS OF YOUTH

1528

William Tyndale (d.1536) translator of the Bible, Protestant martyr, was educated at Magdalen Hall, Oxford, and
wrote many books, besides his Biblical translation.   In
'The Obedience of a Christen Man', Preface, fol.xx he
attacks secular reading.

Fynally that this thretenynge and forbiddynge the laye
people to reade the scripture is not for love of youre
soules (which they care for as ye foxe doeth for ye
gysse) is evidente & clerer then the sonne / in as moch as
they permitte & sofre you to reade Robyn hode & bevise of
hampton / hercules / hector and troylus with a tousande
histories & fables of love & wantones & of rybaudry as
fylthy as herte can thinke / to corrupte ye myndes of
youth with all / clene contrary to the doctrine of christ
& of his apostles.

22.   SIR BRIAN TUKE, POETS PURIFY THE DIALECT OF THE TRIBE

1531

Tuke (d.1545), whose education is unknown, became secre-
tary to King Henry VIII and was known as a patron of
learning.   A friend of Thynne's, he wrote the dedication
of Thynne's 'Chaucer' to the king while at Greenwich,
waiting for the tide, as he notes in his own copy of
Thynne's 'Chaucer' now at Clare College, Cambridge.   Tuke
comments on the fundamental importance of language in
human affairs, and how great poets and orators have perfected the original 'rudeness and barbarity of speech',
first in antiquity, then in the European vernaculars, and
then continues as follows.

And verayly / lyke as all these and the rest haue ben thus
vigilant & studyous to meliorate or amende their langages:
so hath there nat lacked amonges vs Englissh men / whiche
haue right well and notably endeuoyred and employed them
selues / to the beautifyeng and bettryng of thenglysh
tonge. Amonges whom, moost excellent prynce / my moost
redoubted and gracious soueraygne lorde / I your most
humble vassall / subiecte and seruaunt Wylliam Thynne /
chefe clerke of your kechyn / moued by a certayne inclyn-
acion & zele / whiche I haue to here of any thyng soundyng
to the laude and honour of this your noble realme / haue
taken great delectacyon / as the tymes and laysers might
suffre / to rede and here the bokes of that noble & famous
clerke Geffray Chaucer / in whose workes is so manyfest
comprobacion of his excellent lernyng in all kyndes of
doctrynes and sciences / suche frutefulnesse in wordes /
wel accordynge to the mater and purpose / so swete and
plesaunt sentences / suche perfectyon in metre / the composycion so adapted / suche fresshnesse of inuencion /
compendyousnesse in narration / suche sensyble and open
style / lackyng neither maieste ne mediocrite couenable in
disposycion / and suche sharpnesse or quycknesse in conclusyon / that it is moche to be marueyled / howe in his
tyme / whan doutlesse all good letters were layde a slepe
throughout the worlde / as the thynge whiche either by
the disposycion & influence of the bodies aboue / or by
other ordynaunce of god / semed lyke and was in daunger
to haue vtterly perysshed / suche an excellent poete in
our tonge / shulde as it were (nature repugnyng) spryng
and aryse. For though it had ben in Demosthenes or Hom-
erus tymes / whan all lernyng and excellency of sciences
florisshed amonges the Grekes / or in the season that
Cicero prince of eloquence amonges latyns lyued / yet had
it ben a thyng right rare & straunge, and worthy perpet-
uall laude / that any clerke by lernyng or wytte coulde
than haue framed a tonge before so rude and imperfite /
to suche a swete ornature & composycion / lykely if he had
lyued in these dayes / being good letters so restored and
reuyued as they be / if he were nat empeched by the enuy
of suche as may tollerate nothyng / whiche to vnderstonde
their capacite doth nat extende / to haue brought it vnto
a full and fynall perfection. Wherfore, gracious souerayne lorde / takynge suche delyte and pleasure in the
workes of this noble clerke (as is afore mencioned) I haue
of a longe season moche vsed to rede and visyte the same:
and as bokes of dyuers imprintes came vnto my handes / I
easely and without grete study / might and haue deprehen-
ded in them many errours / falsyties / and deprauacions /
whiche euydently appered by the contrarietees and

alteracions founde by collacion of the one with the
other / wherby I was moued and styred to make dilygent
sertch where I might fynde or recouer any trewe copies or
exemplaries of the sayd bookes / whervnto in processe of
tyme / nat without coste and payne I attayned / and nat
onely vnto such as seme to be very trewe copies of those
workes of Geffray Chaucer / whiche before had ben put it
printe / but also to dyuers other neuer tyll nowe imprinted / but remaynyng almost vnknowen and in oblyuion /
whervpon lamentyng with my selfe / the neglygence of the
people / that haue ben in this realme who doutlesse were
very remysse in the settyng forthe or auauncement either
of the histories therof / to the great hynderaunce of the
renoume of such noble princes and valyant conquerours &
capitayns as haue ben in the same / or also of the workes
or memory of the famous and excellent clerkes in all
kyndes of scyences that haue florisshed therin / Of
whiche bothe sortes it hath pleased god as highly to
nobilytate this yle as any other regyon of christendome:
I thought it in maner appertenant vnto my dewtie / and
that of very honesty and loue to my countrey I ought no
lesse to do / than to put my helpyng ha[n]de to the rest-
auracion and bringynge agayne to lyght of the said
workes / after the trewe copies and exemplaries aforesaid. And deuisyng with my selfe / who of all other were
most worthy / to whom a thyng so excellent and notable
shulde be dedicate / whiche to my conceite semeth for the
admiracion / noueltie / and strangnesse that it myght be
reputed to be of in the tyme of the authour / in comparison / as a pure and fyne tryed precious or polyced iewell
out of a rude or indigest masse or mater / none coulde to
my thynkyng occurre / that syns / or in the tyme of Chaucer / was or is suffycient / but onely your maieste
royall / whiche by discrecyon and iugement / as moost
absolute in wysedome and all kyndes of doctryne / coulde
& of his innate clemence and goodnesse wolde adde or
gyue any authorite hervnto.
   For this cause most excellent and in all vertues most
prestant prince / I as humbly prostrate before your
kyngly estate / lowly supply and beseche the same / that
it wol vouchsafe to take in good parte my poore studye
and desyrous mynde / in reducynge vnto lyght this so precious and necessary an ornament of the tonge of this your
realme / ouer pytous to haue ben in any poynt lost / fal-
sifyed / or neglected: So that vnder the shylde of your
most royall protectyon and defence, it may go forthe in
publyke / & preuayle ouer those that wolde blemysshe /
deface/ and in many thynges clerely abolyssh the laude /
renoume / and glorie hertofore compared / and

meritoriously adquired by dyuers princes / and other of
this said most noble yle / whervnto nat onely straungers,
vnder prestexte of highe lernyng & knowlege of their
malycious and peruers myndes / but also some of your owne
subiectes / blynded in foly & ignorance / do with great
study contende.

23. SIR THOMAS ELYOT, A DISCORD

1533

Thomas Elyot (1490?-1546), diplomat and Humanist, notable
for 'The Boke called the Gouernour', 1531, and other
books, was educated at home but became a familiar friend
of such noted Humanists as Sir Thomas More and Roger
Ascham. He was no Protestant but in 'Pasquill the
Playne', 1533, which is a dialogue, Pasquill takes as
severe a line as Tyndale (No. 21) - or the aged Chaucer
himself. Sig. A iiib (after Spurgeon).

Pasquill [to Gnato] what a gods name haue ye a booke in
youre hand? A good feloweshyp wherof is it? Let me se
Nouum stestamentum [sic]....But what is this in youre
bosom? An other booke....Let se, what is here? Troylus
& Chreseid? Lorde what discord is bytwene these two
bokes.

24. JOHN LELAND, A LIFE FOR CHAUCER

*c.*1540

Leland (*c.*1500-52), graduate of Christ's College, Cambridge, was employed for six years by the King in historical researches throughout England. He became insane and
his 'Commentarie de Scriptoribus Britannicis' was first
printed, ed. A. Hall, Oxford, 1709. Even in manuscript

it was the principal source of biographies till the nineteenth century, being used by Bale, Pits, and Speght.
T. Lounsbury showed the account to be practically worth-
less. Lounsbury's translation, 'Studies in Chaucer',
1892, Vol. I, pp. 133-42, is printed here.

Geoffrey Chaucer, a youth of noble birth and highest promise, studied at Oxford University with all the earnestness of those who have applied themselves most diligently
to learning. The nearness of that institution was in a
measure the motive that induced him to resort thither; for
I am led by certain reasons to believe that Oxfordshire or
Berkshire was his native county. He left the university
an acute logician, a delightful orator, an elegant poet, a
profound philosopher, and an able mathematician. The last
he became through the instructions of John Some, and of
Nicolas, a Carmelite friar of Lynn, two men very profi-
cient in mathematics, whom he names in his treatise on the
'Astrolabe.' Moreover, he left the university a devout
theologian. I have certainly made use of strong language;
but whoever has turned over his books with a curious hand
will have no hesitation in declaring me a reporter who can
be trusted. Nevertheless, I shall frankly admit that
while he so applied himself at Oxford, he also pursued
his studies elsewhere, and by long devotion to learning
added many things to the knowledge he had there accumulated. It is a settled fact that about the last years of
Richard II., to whom he was personally not unknown, he
resided in France. There he acquired for himself great
glory by his assiduous practice of literary composition.
He gained more than glory. He imbibed at that time
through this same practice the charm, the humor, the
delightfulness, the wit, in fine all the graces of the
French speech, and imbibed them to such a degree as is
hardly to be believed. Praise of this sort followed
Geoffrey upon his return to England, as if it were an
inseparable attendant upon his excellence. Rejoicing,
therefore, in successes of this kind, he resorted regularly to the London tribunals and the inns of court
occupied by the lawyers who were there engaged in interpreting the laws of their country. This perhaps he had
done before he visited France.

In those times the most celebrated man among the advo-
cates was John Gower, whose life we have already written.
He was a man of reverend age and was taking wonderful
pains to polish the English tongue. No sooner had he
perceived and proved the genius and worth of Chaucer than

he made of him an intimate friend, took him to his em-
brace, looked upon him as one of his noblest delights - in
short, honored him almost as if he were some divinity.
Let this not rest upon my authority. Gower himself, in
his work which bears the title of 'Amantis,' makes abundantly evident how high was his estimation of Chaucer. In
addition to praise most intelligently bestowed, he calls
him a distinguished poet, and constitutes him a sort of
Aristarchus for his own labors. Behold for thyself, O
reader, a most beauteous contest of virtue! For as Gower,
a man claiming little for himself, modestly submitted what
he had done to the judgment of Chaucer, so in turn Chaucer
referred the 'Loves of Troilus' to the criticisms of Gower
and Strode. Who this Strode was I have thus far been
unable to learn from any author. But though he is mentioned by no one else, I remember to have read creditable
things of a certain Strode, an alumnus of the college of
Merton at Oxford, as one most learned in poetry. He is
enrolled in the catalogue of Merton College in the last
years of Edward III. So much is evident from the lines of
Chaucer that he had been a student of philosophy. Add at
this point that just as Chaucer was at the same time an
admirer and an imitator of Gower, so Scogan, a man given
to all sorts of jocoseness and wit, whose monument stands
in Westminster Abbey, was likewise an admirer and imitator
of Chaucer. But, on the other hand, by how much the disciple Chaucer was greater than the master Gower, by so
much was Scogan inferior to Chaucer.
   Now, indeed, the order of our discourse demands that we
show clearly what aim Geoffrey had in view in his studies.
Assuredly it was a peculiar one. It was to render the
English speech as polished as possible in all respects.
He had observed that in this very matter Gower had made
excellent progress. Therefore he thought that no stone
should be left unturned by himself in order to reach the
farthest goal of success. And since poetry had always
pleased him above everything else, he devoted himself to
it with ardor, he cultivated it religiously. It seemed
to him that through its agency it was most easy to lay
open the path to the very heights of expression. For
poetry is of such a nature that it not only admits of
figures, of graces of style, of ornaments of speech, of
richness of language, and of whatever is attractive and
delightful; it even demands these as of right belonging
to itself. Add to this that he called in to take part in
his work the Italians and the French who wrote in their
own tongues very many things with purity, beauty, and
elegance. So great a thing is it to have renowned leaders to follow. About that time Petrarch flourished with

fame in Italy, and by his labors the common speech of
that land was brought to such a point of refinement that
it vied with Latin itself for the palm of eloquence. A
certain Alain also polished the French tongue in an infinite variety of ways. Each of these two - for I omit
many others of greatest note who did the same things -
added a spur to the efforts of Chaucer, who was sufficiently inclined of himself to press forward. It was under
favorable auspices, therefore, that he applied himself
to the work he had undertaken. Sometimes he turned into
the speech of his native land works composed carefully,
ornately, and eloquently in the French tongue. Sometimes
he translated Latin verse into English, but with learning,
with skill, with harmony. Sometimes he committed to
writings destined to survive many original things which
equalled the happiest success of the Latins. Sometimes he
strove with all his power to instruct the reader, and
again took pains as sedulously to give him pleasure. Nor
did he cease from his labors until he had carried our
language to that height of purity, of eloquence, of con-
ciseness and beauty, that it can justly be reckoned among
the thoroughly polished languages of the world. Therefore it is that in my book of 'Epigrams' I soar in the
following verses to his glory.
     [At this point Leland breaks out into verse. He in-
serts in his narrative three Latin poems, which abound in
praise of the poet, but which naturally do not convey
much information even of the kind that he has already
given. The first of them is to the effect that as Florence celebrates Dante, and the whole of Italy Petrarch,
so all England venerates Chaucer as the one who before
any one else gave beauty to his native tongue. In the
second he compares him to Homer and Virgil, and says that
while happy ages gave birth to these two, it was the fate
of the English poet to be born in a rude and turbulent
time. Had he lived in an age when the Muses flourished,
it is hinted that he would have equalled or excelled the
greatest of the past. Then follows the third poem, which
consists of some hendecasyllabics which Leland tells us
he had composed some years before at the request of
Thomas Berthelet, a most painstaking and learned printer.
In this he renews the statement of Chaucer's services to
his native tongue, likens him to Hesperus among the lesser stars, and ends by enjoining the youth of Britain to
scatter with joyful hand - presumably upon his tomb,
though that is not mentioned - the fragrant rose and the
more delicate violet, and bestow upon their poet the ivy
crown. He then returns to his subject with a slight apology for the display he had made of his own literary
powers.]

But now [he goes on] we have served up to you enough
of our trifles. It is not a man of his quality who can
obtain his due praises from the commendation of any muse
of mine. Oh, at the hands of an impartial judge how much
more speedily will he gain just applause from his own
works. I would, therefore, that our tongue were familiar
to the Latin poets. Then easily I say, easily would they
come into my opinion. But since I am wishing for what
can hardly happen, I should like them to be prevailed
upon so far as to have in this matter some faith in me as
a lover of Latin literature. Under that encouragement I
shall not feel it a burden to give the titles of his productions in Latin. In this way they may be able, as it
is said in the proverb, to form some judgment of the lion
from his claws.

And yet before I undertake that which I have just
now promised, it will not be foreign to my purpose to
speak publicly of William Caxton, a man who was lacking
neither in diligence nor learning. He, as is well known,
was the first to practise the art of printing at London.
The works of Chaucer, so far as he could gain possession
of them by buying or begging, he collected in one volume. Nevertheless, our Berthelet has surpassed this edition of Caxton through the exertions of William Thynne.
The latter employed much labor, zeal, and care in searching diligently for ancient copies, and added many things
to the first edition. Nor in this matter, moreover, was
lacking Brian Tuke, a most intimate friend of my own,
and gifted with wonderful skill in the use of the English
tongue. He for the sake of his own glory has contributed
to the last edition an elevated, excellent, and polished
preface. I shall therefore follow the copy printed a few
years since and add the promised table of contents:

Fabulae Cantianae xxiv. (The Canterbury Tales.)
Two of these are written in prose. But the Tale of Piers
    Plowman, which by the common consent of the learned is
    attributed to Chaucer as its true author, has been
    suppressed in each edition, because it vigorously in-
    veighed against the bad morals of the priests.
De Arte Amandi, alias Romaunce of the Rose.
Amores Troili et Chrysidis, lib. 5. (Troilus and Cres-
    sida.)
Testamentum Chrysidis, et ejusdem lamentatio. (The Tes-
    tament of Cressida and her Complaint.)
Amores Heroidum. (The Legend of Good Women.)
De Consolatione Philosophiae, soluta oratione. (Boe-
    thius's Consolation of Philosophy, in prose.)
Somnium Chauceri. (The Death of Blanche the Duchess.)

Chorus Avium. (The Parliament of Fowls.)
Flos Humanitatis. (The Flower of Courtesy.)
   This book is rejected by many as spurious.
De Pietate mortua, et ejus Sepultura. (The Complaint of
   the Death of Pity.)
Chorus Heroidum. (The Assembly of Ladies.)
De Astralabio ad Ludovicum filium suum, prosa. (A Trea-
   tise on the Astrolabe, addressed to his son Lewis, in
   prose.)
Querela Equitis cogn. Nigri. (The Complaint of the Black
   Knight.)
Encomium Mulierum. (A Praise of Women.)
De Fama, lib. 3. (The House of Fame.)
Testamentum Amoris, lib. 3. (The Testament of Love.)
Threni Magdalenae. (The Lamentation of Mary Magdalen.)
De Remedio Amoris. (The Remedy of Love.)
Querelae Martis et Veneris. (The Complaints of Mars and of
   Venus.)
Epistola Cupidinis. (The Letter of Cupid.)
Cantiones. (Minor Poems.)

Thus far as regards the titles of his works which at the
present day are read everywhere. Yet besides those which
I myself have recounted, he states in the prologue prefixed to the 'Legend of Good Women' that he had written a
little book on the Death of the Duchess Blanche, and that
he had moreover translated a short treatise of Origen
about Magdalen. This, provided Origen ever wrote any such
thing at all, I take to be the same as the 'Lamentation of
Magdalen,' which I have mentioned in the list given above.
   Perhaps at this point some will expect me to make an
end of speaking, but I still have a few things to say
which will greatly commend Chaucer to posterity. For just
as he was well known to Richard of Bordeaux, the English
monarch, and dear to him on account of his virtues, so
also for the same reasons he was highly valued by Henry
IV. and by his son, the triumphant victor over the French.
In addition to this, all the nobility of England looked
upon him as the consummate example of high-wrought expression. It added, moreover, to his repute that he had a
sister who was married to William Pole - unless I mistake
the name - Duke of Suffolk, and passed her life in great
splendor at Ewelme. There, also, at the will of God, she
afterwards passed away, and there, as I have somewhere
heard, she was buried.
   In the midst of these events Chaucer reached the period
of gray hairs, and found his disease to be old age itself.
This continued to oppress him more and more, and while he
was attending to his affairs in London he died. He was

buried in Westminster Abbey, in the south aisle of the
church dedicated to St. Peter. He left Lewis as the heir
of his fortunes, whatever they were, and especially of his
villa at Woodstock, adjoining the palace of the king. Some
time after William Caxton caused this distich to be inscribed upon his monument:
    Galfridus Chaucer vates, et fama poesis
    Maternae, hac sacra sum tumulatus humo.
These two lines were taken from a certain elegy which Stephen Surigon of Milan, a celebrated poet of his time,
wrote at the request of William Caxton. It is therefore a
pleasure to repeat on this occasion the whole of the elegy,
for it is terse, flowing, and sonorous. For in this way
Chaucer, who was great in himself, will seem greater by
the noble tribute paid him by a foreign writer....

[See above, Surigo, 1478, No. 15.]

    You have now, O most courteous reader, the elegiac
lines inscribed on a snow-white tablet which Surigon
affixed to the Westminster column adjoining the tomb of
Chaucer. May my persuasion and their attractiveness dispose you, whoever you are, to read them often for the sake
of our poet.

25.   UNKNOWN, CHAUCER WROTE MUCH TO DO US GOOD

*c.*1540

The following anonymous verses are from BM Harleian MS.
4826, fol. 139. The main text of the MS. is Hoccleve's
'De Regimine Principum', written in a fifteenth-century
hand. The page here contains the lines in which Hoccleve
refers to Chaucer and says he has commissioned the accompanying portrait (cf. above, No. 7), but in this text the
portrait has been cut out. To judge from the fragment
remaining, the portrait, which extended down the whole
right-hand margin of the page, some ten or eleven inches
long (three times the length of the half-length portrait
accompanying the same verses in the earlier Harleian MS.
4866), was in a fairly coarse style, showing Chaucer
standing on a green patch, wearing a knee-length gown of
dark colour, facing right, without any background. All

readers will echo the sentiments expressed by the infuri-
ated sixteenth-century reader.

Off worthy Chaucer
here the pickture stood
That much did wryght
and all to doe vs good

Summe ffuryous ffoole
Have Cutt the same in twayne
His deed doe shewe
He bare a barren Brayne.

26.   SIR THOMAS WYATT, NOBLE SCORN

c.1540

Sir Thomas Wyatt (1503?-42), poet, diplomat, courtier,
soldier, lover, educated at St John's College, Cambridge,
knew Chaucer's works well. His poems were first published
in Tottel's 'Miscellany', 1557. In 'Of the Courtiers life
written to Iohn Poins' he comments sarcastically on those
who scorn noble tales such as Chaucer's 'Knight's Tale'
(a: Sig. L. iii.b); in 'How to vse the court' he comments
ironically on those who will do anything for money, thereby paying an unusual compliment to Pandarus (b: Sig.
M.i.).

(a)

I am not he that can...
Praise syr Topas for a noble tale,
And scorne the story that the knight tolde.

(b)

In this also se thou be not idle:
Thy nece, thy cosyn, thy sister, or thy daughter,
If she bee faire: if handsome be her middle:

If thy better hath her loue besought her:
Auaunce his cause, and he shall helpe thy nede,
It is but loue, turne it to a laughter.
But ware I say, so gold thee helpe and spede:
That in this case thou be not so vnwise,
As Pandar was in such a like dede.
For he the fole of conscience was so nice:
That he no gaine would haue for all his payne.

27.   AN ACTE

1542-3

An Acte for thaduauncement of true Religion and for thab-
olisshment of the contrarie. Statute 34 and 35 Henry VIII,
chap. i, section v. (Statutes of the Realm, vol. iii,
1817, p. 895.) The statute provides for the utter abolish-
ment, etc., of forbidden books but excludes from prohibi-
tion religious books, histories, biographies, literature,
including Chaucer's works.

Provided allso that all bokes in Englishe printed before
the yere of our Lorde a thousande fyve hundred and fourtie
intytled the Kings Hieghnes proclamacions iniunctions,
translacions of the Pater noster, the Aue Maria and the
Crede, the psalters prymers prayer statutes and lawes of
the Realme, Cronycles Canterburye tales, Chaucers bokes
Gowers bokes and stories of mennes lieues, shall not be
comprehended in the prohibicion of this acte....

28.   PETER BETHAM, PLAIN ENGLISH

1543

Betham graduated BA at Oxford, 1536, then came to Cambridge where he took his BA, 1538-9. He was fellow of

Peterhouse, 1540-7, and shows the interest in translation
and pure English, together with knowledge of Chaucer, that
characterised that college in the mid-century. In the
Prefatory Epistle to his translation 'The preceptes of
Warre' he condemns inkhorn terms: his translators ought to
use usual English terms; and continues (Sig. A vii) as
follows.

Yet lette no man thyncke, that I doo damne wll vsuall
termes borowed of other tounges, whan I doo well knowe
that one tounge is interlaced with an other. But nowe to
be shorte, I take them beste englyshe men, which folowe
Chaucer, and other olde wryters, in whyche studye the
nobles and gentle men of Englande, are worthye to be
praysed, whan they endeavoure to brynge agayne to his owne
clennes oure englysshe tounge, & playnelye to speake wyth
our owne termes, as our others dyd before vs, which men I
coulde reherce by name, but that I shulde be thought to
flatter. The dead I maye well prayse.
    Wyate was a worthye floure of our tounge....

29. ROGER ASCHAM, CHAUCER OUR ENGLISII HOMER

1545, 1552, 1563

Roger Ascham (1515-68), educated at St John's College,
Cambridge, tutor to Queen Elizabeth I, famous Puritan and
Humanist, condemned the 'Morte Darthur' as stories of
'open manslaughter and bold bawdry' ('The Scholemaster'),
yet loved Chaucer (who also sneered at Arthurian tales),
and regarded him as a valuable moralist. Chaucer's
'Parson's Tale' is rarely quoted with such relish, though
unfortunately it does not contain the vivid image that
Ascham thought he found in it; but Ascham apparently knew
other tales too. He well perceives the subtlety of Chaucer's representations of mind and feeling, characteristically comparing them with the Greek classics.
    To call Chaucer our English Homer was fresh and high
praise by one of the earliest of English Greek scholars,
and shows Chaucer being assimilated to the notion of a
'classic' author. The comparison with Homer became a mid-
sixteenth-century commonplace, though B. Goog in 1565

substituted the more primitive 'olde Ennius'. The present
extracts are first, from 'Toxophilus', (a) from Sig. E
i b; (b) Sig. E ii b; (c) Sig. E iv; and (d) from 'A
Report...of the affaires and state of Germany', written
1552, published c.1570, Sig. A iiii. Extract (e), from
'The Scholemaster', published posthumously in 1570, Sig. R
iiii b et seq. shows the beginning of a Neoclassical critical sense.

(a)

The Nource of dise and cardes, is werisom Ydlenesse,
enemy of vertue, ye drowner of youthe, that tarieth in it,
and as Chauser doth saye verie well in the Parsons tale,
the greene path waye to hel, hauinge this thing appropriat
vnto it, that where as other vices haue some cloke of hon-
estie, onely ydlenes can neyther do wel, nor yet thinke
wel.

(b)

Whose horriblenes [Gaming] is so large, that it passed the
eloquence of our *Englishe Homer*, to compasse it: yet because I euer thought hys sayinges to haue as muche authoritie, as eyther *Sophocles* or *Euripides* in Greke, therefore gladly do I remembre these verses of hys. [Not from
Thynne's text, 1532]

> Hasardry is Very mother of lesinges
> And of deceyte and cursed sweringes
> Blasphemie of Chist [sic], manslaughter, and waste also,
> Of catel of tyme, of other thynges mo.

(c)

Cursed sweryng, blasphemie of Christe, These halfe verses
Chaucer in an other place, more at large doth well set
out, and verye liuely expresse, sayinge.

> Ey by goddes precious hert and his nayles
> And by the blood of Christe, that is in Hales,

(d)

Diligence also must be vsed [by an Historian] in kepyng
truly the order of tyme: and describyng lyuely, both the
site of places and nature of persons not onely for the
outward shape of the body: but also for the inward disposition of the mynde, as *Thucidides* doth in many places very
trimly, and *Homer* euerywhere, and that alwayes most excellently, which obseruation is chiefly to be marked in hym.
And our *Chaucer* doth the same, very praise worthely: marke
hym well and conferre hym with any other that writeth of
in our tyme in their proudest toung, whosoeuer lyst.

(e)

Some that make *Chaucer* in Englishe and *Petrarch* in *Italian*,
their Gods in verses, and yet be not able to make true
difference, what is a fault, and what is a just prayse, in
those two worthie wittes, will moch mislike this my writyng. But such men be euen like followers of *Chaucer* and
Petrarke as one here in England did folow Syr *Tho*. *More*:
who, being most vnlike vnto him, in wit and learning,
neuertheles in wearing his gowne awrye vpon the one shoul-
der, as Syr *Tho*. *More* was wont to doe, would needes be
counted like vnto hym.

30.   PETER ASHTON, CHAUCER'S WORDS OUT OF USE

1546

There were two Peter Ashtons of about this date: the
elder (d. 1548), BA Cambridge 1515-16, Fellow of Christ's
1523-8, lawyer and medical man; and a younger, BA Cambridge 1539-40, MA from Peterhouse 1543, Fellow of Peterhouse, 1543-53. Either may be the translator of P. Jovius
(or Giovo), 'A Short treatise vpon the Turkes Chronicles',
1546, in the 'Epistle Dedicatory' of which he, like
Betham, requires plain English.

For truly, throwghe out al this simple and rude translation, I studied rather to vse the most playn and famylier

english speche, then ether Chaucers wordes (which by reason
of antiquitie be almost out of vse) or else ink horne
termes (as they call them), whiche the common people, for
lacke of latin, do not vnderstand.

31.   EDMUND BECKE, THE BIBLE VERSUS CANTERBURY TALES

1549

Little is known of Becke, who supervised a reprint published in 1549 of T. Matthew's Bible of 1537. In the Prefatory Letter which appears to have been his principal
contribution he contrasts the Bible with 'Canterbury
Tales', which may or may not be a specific reference to
Chaucer, but which certainly would have included his
works. The contrast between Bible and Chaucer is a commonplace of the first half of the sixteenth century.

If all magistrates & the nobilitie, wolde wel wey with
them selfs the inestimable dignitie, & incomparable goodnes of Gods boke,...and wolde also as willingly vouchsafe
to suffurate & spare an houre or ii in a day, from theyr
worldly busines, emploing it about the reading of this
boke, as they haue bene vsed to do in Cronicles & Canterbury tales, then should they also abandone...all blas-
phemyes, swearing, carding, dysing....Oh what a florishing
commune wealth should your grace injoy & haue.

32.   THOMAS WILSON, THE FINE COURTIER WIL TALKE NOTHYNG BUT CHAUCER

1553

Dr Thomas Wilson (1525?-81), educated at King's College,
Cambridge, writer and statesman, wrote a very influential
'Arte of Rhetorique', first published in 1553 and several

times reprinted in the sixteenth century. He makes a
famous plea for plainness of speech, against professional,
foreign, or fashionably old-fashioned jargon, with a re-
vealing aside about the continuing fashionableness of
Chaucer at Court. The extract is from the 1553 edition,
fol. f.86a and b.

Plaines what it is

Emong al other lessons, this should first be learned, that
we neuer affect any straunge ynkehorne termes, but so
speake as is commonly receiued: neither sekyng to be ouer
fine, nor yet liuyng ouer carelesse, vsing our speache as
most men do, & ordryng our wittes, as the fewest haue doen.
Some seke so farre for outlandishe Englishe, that thei
forget altogether their mothers language. And I dare
swere this, if some of their mothers were aliue, thei were
not able to tell, what thei say, & yet these fine Englishe
clerkes, wil saie thei speake in their mother tongue, if
a man should charge them for counterfeityng the kynges
English. Some farre iorneid ientlemen at their returne
home, like as thei loue to go in forrein apparell, so thei
wil pouder their talke with ouersea language. He that
cometh lately out of France, wil talke Frenche English, &
neuer blushe at the matter. Another choppes in with
Angleso Italiano: the Lawyer wil store his stomack with
the pratyng of Pedlers. The Auditour in makyng his
accompt and rekenyng, cometh in with sise sould, and cater
denere, for vi.s. iiij.d. The fine Courtier wil talke
nothyng but Chaucer. The misticall wise menne, and Poeti-
call Clerkes, will speake nothyng but quaint prouerbes,
and blynd allegories, delityng muche in their awne dark-
nesse, especially, when none can tell what thei dooe saie.

33. ROBERT BRAHAM, DIVINE CHAUCER LIVED IN A BARBAROUS AGE

1555

About Braham (fl. 1555) nothing is known. In his address

to the reader in his edition of 'The Aunment historie...
of warres betwixte the Grecians and the Troyans' by John
Lydgate, 1555, he comments on the difficulties of the
thankless task of editing old writers, and criticises
Caxton's editing. Sidney (No. 43) appears to share his
feelings. In his complaints Braham sounds like an Oxford
man. After discussing the historians of the Trojan war he
continues (Sig * B la and b) as follows.

And so by these degrees, hath bene at the laste by y^e
diligence of John Lydgate a moncke of Burye, brought into
our englyshe tonge: and dygested as maye appere, in verse
whoes trauayle as well in other his doynges as in this
hathe wythout doubte so muche preuayled in this our vul-
gare language, that hauynge his prayse dewe to his deser-
uynges, may worthyly be numbred amongest those that haue
chefelye deserued of our tunge. As the verye perfect disciple and imitator of the great Chaucer, ye onelye glorye
and beauty of the same. Neuertheles, lyke wyse as it
hapned ye same Chaucer to lease ye prayse of that tyme
wherin he wrote beyng then when in dede al good letters
were almost aslepe, so farre was the grosenesse and barba-
rousnesse of that age from the vnderstandinge of so deuyne
a wryter.

34.   WALTER STEVINS, WITTIE CHAUCER

*c.*1555

Nothing is known of Walter Stevins, who gives his name as
the writer in the Dedication of BM MS. Sloane 261 (of
Chaucer's 'Astrolabe') to Edward Earl of Devonshire, identified as he who bore that title 1553-6 by A.E. Brae (ed.),
'The Treatise on the Astrolabe', 1870. Stevins describes
how he corrected his MS. exemplar (probably Sloane 314),
and is a rare example of one who appreciated the value of
Chaucer's scientific work. Text from Sloane 261, ff. 3-4,
30b: cf. Spurgeon, I, pp. 92-3.

To the reader

When I happenyd to looke vpon the conclusions of the
astrolabie compiled by Geffray Chawcer, and fownde the
same corrupte and false in so many and sondrie places,
that I dowbtede whether the rudenes of the worke weare
not a gretter sclaunder to the authour, then trowble and
offence to the readers; I dyd not a lytell marvell if a
booke showlde come oute of his handes so imperfite and indigest; whose other workes weare not onely reckenyd for
the best that euer weare sette fowrth in oure english
tonge: but also weare taken for a manifest argumente of
his singuler witte, and generalitie in all kindes of knowledge. Howebeit when I called to remembrance that in
his proheme he promised to sette fowrth this worke in fyve
partes, wherof weare never extante but these two first
partes onely, it made me to belyue that either the worke was
never fynisshed of the authoure, or els to haue ben corrupted sens by some other meanes; or what other thinge
might be the cause therof I wiste not. Never the lesse
vnderstandinge that the woorke, which before lay as neglected, to the profite of no man and discourage of many,
mighte be tourned to the commoditie of as manye as her-
after showlde happen to travayle in that parte of knowledge: I thowght it a thinge worth my laboure if I cowlde
sette it in better order and frame. which thinge howe I
haue done it, let be theire indifferente iudgemente,
which heretofore haue readen thother settinge forth; or
lyst to compare this and that together wherin I confesse
that besydes the amendinge of verie many wordes I haue
displaced some conclusions, and in some places wheare the
sentences weare imperfite, I haue supplied and filled
them, as necessitie required. - As for some conclusions I
haue altered them, and some haue I cleane put oute for
vtterlye false and vntrue: as namelye the conclusion of
direction and retrogradaconn of planetes: and the conclusions to knowe the longitudes of sterres, whether thei be
determinate or indeterminate in the astrolabie. The conclusion, to knowe with what degree of the zodiacke any
planet ascendeth on the horizonte whether his latitude be
north or sowth; as the meanynge of the same conclusion was
most hardest by reason of the imparfitenes therof; so in
practise I fownde him most false, as he shall fynde that
lyst to take the lyke paines. Notwithstandinge this haue
I doone, not challenginge for my selffe, but renuncynge
and leauinge to worthie Chawcer his due praise for this
worke. which if it had come parfite vnto oure handes (no
dowbte) woolde have merited wonderfull praise. As for me
if I haue done any thinge therin it shall suffice if the

louers of wittie Chawcer do accepte my good will and
entente.

                                                    Vale.

[Vpon the first degree of Aries] Albeit y^t in Chaucers
tyme vpon the .12. day of march the sonne entred into the
bedde of Aries: yet in our tyme y^u shalt finde that the
sonne entreth therin the .10. day of the same moneth.

35.   BARNABY GOOGE, OLDE ENNIUS

1565

Barnaby Googe (1540-94), gentleman, translator and poet,
was educated at both Christ's College, Cambridge, and New
College, Oxford, without acquiring a degree, perhaps because he was already busy translating 'The First thre
Bokes of the most Christian poet, Marcellus Palingenius,
called the Zodyake of Lyfe', 1560. The third enlarged
edition of 1565 with a new Preface indicates, by the comparison with Ennius, the progressive sense of Chaucer's
remoteness; Sig (‡) 3b.

What pleasure and profite the dilligent reading of vertuous Poets doth minister to the Godly and Christian minde,
so euidently and playnely hath alwayes appeared, that I
neede not to bestowe any time about the declaring hereof.

[Cites Holy Scripture as divine poetry originally in verse
and equal in literary merit with the poetry of the Greeks
and Romans, and asks the 'louing and frendly reader' to]

be not so straight of iudgement as I know a number to be
that can not abyde to reade anye thing written in Englishe
verse, which nowe is so plenteously enriched wyth a numbre
of eloquent writers, that in my fansy it is lyttle inferiour to the pleasaunt verses of the auncient Romaines. For
since the time of our excellente countreyman Sir Geffray
Chaucer who liueth in like estimation with vs as did olde
Ennius wyth the Latines. There hath flourished in England
so fine and filed phrases, and so good & pleasant Poets as
may counteruayle the doings of *Virgill, Ouid, Horace, Iuue-
nal*, etc.

36. JOHN FOXE, INDUSTRIOUS AND FRUITFULLY OCCUPIED IN
LIBERAL STUDIES

1570

Foxe (1516-87), Protestant reformer and martyrologist, was
educated at Magdalen College, Oxford, and led a turbulent
life, partly in exile. The success of his 'Ecclesiasticall history contayning the Actes and Monumentes of
thynges passed in euery Kynges tyme in this Realme', 1563,
led to an enlarged edition, in two huge folios, in 1570,
where his notices of Chaucer appear. It was reprinted
many times. His view of Chaucer's Protestant virtue is
mainly, but not entirely, based on the mistaken attribu-
tion to Chaucer of 'Jack Upland', first published with
Chaucer's 'Works' in 1602, but printed separately before,
c.1536. Text from Vol. I, Sig. ▮iiij; p. 341; II,
pp. 965-6.

(A Protestation to the whole Church of England.)

To discend now somewhat lower in drawing out the des-
cent of the Church. What a multitude here commeth of
faithful witnesses in the time of *Ioh. Wickleffe,* as
Ocliffe, Wickleffe. an. 1376. *W. Thorpe, White, Puruey,
Patshall, Payne, Gower, Chauser, Gascoyne, William Swyn-
derby, Walter Brute, Roger Dexter, William Sautry* about
the year 1400. *Iohn Badley,* an 1410. *Nicholas Tayler,
Rich. Wagstaffe, Mich. Scriuener, W. Smith, Iohn Henry,
W. Parchmenar, Roger Goldsmith,* with an Ancresse called
Mathilde in the Citie of Leicester, Lord *Cobham,* Syr *Roger
Acton* Knight, *Iohn Beuerlay* preacher, *Iohn Ilus, Hierome* of
Prage Scholemaster, with a number of faithfull Bohemians
and Thaborites not to be told with whom I might also
adioyne *Laurentius Valla,* and *Ioannes Picus* the learned
Earle of Mirandula. But what do I stand upon recitall of
names, which almost are infinite....
For so much as mention is here made of these superstitious sects of Fryers, and such other beggerly religions,
it shall not seme much impartinent, being moued by the
occasion hereof...to annexe...a certayne other auncient
treatise compiled by Geoffray Chawcer by the way of a
Dialogue or questions moued in the person of a certaine
uplandish and simple ploughman of the countrey. Which

treatise for the same, ye autor intituled Jack vp land....

   Moreouer to these two [Linacre & Pace], I thought it not
out of season to couple also some mention of Geffray Chaucer, and Iohn Gower: Whiche although beyng much discrepant
from these in course of yeares, yet may seme not vnworthy
to bee matched with these forenamed persons in commendation
of their studie and learnyng....

   Likewise, as touchyng the tyme of Chaucer, by hys owne
workes in the end of his first booke of Troylus and Creseide it is manifest, that he and Gower were both of one
tyme, althoughe it seemeth that Gower was a great deale his
auncient: both notably learned, as the barbarous rudenes of
that tyme did geue: both great frendes together, and both in
like kind of studie together occupied, so endeuoryng themselues, and employing their tyme, that they excelling many
other in study and exercise of good letters, did passe
forth their lyues here right worshipfully & godly, to the
worthy fame and commendation of their name.   Chaucers
woorkes bee all printed in one volume, and therfore knowen
to all men.   This I meruell, to see the idle life of y^e
priestes and clergy men of that tyme, seyng these lay persons shewed themselues in these kynde of liberall studies
so industrious & fruitfully occupied: but muche more I
meruell to consider this, how that the Bishoppes condemnyng and abolishyng al maner of Englishe bookes and treatises, which might bryng the people to any light of knowledge, did yet authorise the woorkes of Chaucer to remayne
still & to be occupied: Who (no doubt) saw in Religion as
much almost, as euen we do now, and vttereth in hys workes
no lesse, and semeth to bee a right Wicleuian, or els was
neuer any, and that all his workes almost, if they be
throughly aduised, will testifie (albeit it bee done in
myrth, & couertly) & especially the latter ende of his
third booke of the Testament of loue: for there purely he
toucheth the highest matter, that is the Communion.
Wherin, excepte a man be altogether blynde, he may espye
him at the full.   Althoughe in the same booke (as in all
other he vseth to do) vnder shadowes couertly, as vnder a
visoure, he suborneth truth, in such sorte, as both priuely
she may profite the godly minded, and yet not be espyed of
the craftye aduersarie: And therefore the Byshops, belike,
takyng hys workes but for iestes and toyes, in condemnyng
other bookes, yet permitted his bookes to be read.   So it
pleased God to blinde then the eyes of them, for the more
commoditie of his people, to the entent that through the
readyng of his treatises, some fruite might redounde
therof to his Churche, as no doubt, it did to many: As also
I am partlye informed of certeine, whiche knewe the parties, which to them reported, that by readyng of Chausers

workes, they were brought to the true knowledge of Religion. And not vnlike to be true. For to omitte other
partes of his volume, whereof some are more fabulous then
other, what tale can bee more playnely tolde, then the
talke of the ploughman? or what finger can pointe out more
directly the Pope with his Prelates to be Antichrist, then
doth the poore Pellycan reasonyng agaynst the gredy Grif-
fon? Under whiche *Hypotyposis* or Poesie, who is so blind
that seeth not by the Pellicane, the doctrine of Christ,
and of the Lollardes to bee defended agaynst the Churche
of Rome? Or who is so impudent that can denye that to be
true, which the Pellicane there affirmeth in describyng
the presumptuous pride of that pretensed Church? Agayne
what egge can be more lyke, or figge vnto an other, then
ye words, properties, and conditions of that rauenyng
Griphe resembleth the true Image, that is, the nature &
qualities of that which we call the Churche of Rome, in
euery point and degre? and therfore no great maruell, if
that narration was exempted out of the copies of Chaucers
workes: whiche notwithstandyng now is restored agayne, and
is extant, for euery man to read that is disposed.

This Geffray Chauser being borne (as is thought) in
Oxfordshire, & dwellyng in Wodstocke, lyeth buried in the
Churche of the minster of S. Peter at Westminster, in an
Ile on the South side of the sayd Churche, not far from
the doore leading to the cloyster, and vpon his graue
stone first were written these ii old verses

    Galfridus Chauser vates et fama poesis
    Maternae, hac sacra sum tumulatus humo.

Afterward, about the yeare of our Lord 1556. one M.
Brickam, bestowyng more cost vppon his tumbe, did adde
therunto these verses folowyng....

[This inscription, no longer extant, describes Chaucer
as 'Anglorum vates ter maximus olim', 'Once the thrice-
great poet of the English'.]

37. GEORGE GASCOIGNE, RIDING RHYME

1575

Gascoigne (1525?-1577), educated at Trinity College,

Cambridge, was member of Parliament, soldier, poet, playwright, translator. He reveals a Cantabrigian warmth of
feeling for 'our father Chaucer'. As a practising poet he
echoes some earlier remarks both on the need for 'fine
invention' and for technical ability in versification. He
is notable for writing the first English technical discussion of verse as an appendix, 'Certayne Notes of Instruction...', to 'The Posies of George Gascoigne Esquire',
1575. Text from Sig. Tii, Sig. Tiiib and Sig. Vii b.

The first and most necessarie poynt that euer I founde
meete to be considered in making of a delectable poeme is
this, to grounde it upon some fine invention. For it is
not inough to roll in pleasant woordes nor yet to thunder
in *Rym, Ram, Ruff*, by letter (quoth my master *Chaucer*) nor
yet to abound in apt vocables, or epythetes....Also our
father *Chaucer* hath vsed the same libertie in feete and
measures that the Latinists do vse: and who so euer do
peruse and well consider his workes, he shall finde that
although his lines are not alwayes of one selfe same number of Syllables, yet beyng redde by one that hath vnder-
standing, the longest verse and that which hath most Syllables in it, will fall (to the eare) correspondent vnto
that whiche hath fewest syllables in it: and like wise
that whiche hath in it fewest syllables, shalbe founde
yet to consist of woordes that haue suche naturall sounde,
as may seeme equall in length to a verse which hath many
moe sillables of lighter accentes...
    [I had forgotten a notable kinde of ryme, called
ryding rime, and that is suche as our Mayster and Father
Chaucer vsed in his Canterburie tales, and in diuers other
delectable and light enterprises.

38.   UNKNOWN, CLASSIC AND HEAVENLY

*c.*1575

A poem discovered among love poems by Professor R.H.
Robbins in a Bodleian MS., Douce 290, f. 94, written in
the second half of the sixteenth century, attests Chaucer's status as a classic, or rather Neoclassic, whose

genius, fame and virtue are equally great and all alike
recognised in earth and heaven. Text from the MS, but cf.
'The Chaucer Review', II (1968), pp. 136-7.

Thy dearest dearlinges death oh howe,
  canst thow (O Brytayne) brooke,
wher is thy springe of learninge nowe,
  Syth fates thy Tullie tooke.   4

Brytayne put one thy wailinge weedes.
  byd thow adue to mearth,
Seinge wormes, wher learninge was, now fe[eds]
  within the dankishe earth.   8

You spytefull fates, how durst you tuitch
  his fatal twyne with kniffe,
Your envyous rancour ay is such,
  to spoile the good of liffe.   12

Tho you ecclipse his mortall daies,
  that to your will were bound,
You can not dym his splendent prayes
  that in the heavens doe sounde.   16

Brute blowes in Trvmp of lastinge fame
  his glittringe laudes well woonn
as phoebus rayes doth shyne, his name
  aboute the world doth roonn.   20

oute of his bones nowe putryfyed,
  his ffame doth dailie sproote,
his blased brute in Realmes doth ryde
  that first from him tooke roote.   24

His prayes the world scarce comprehen[d]
  his fame so thicklie raignes.
The earner, that those lavdes furth send,
  in slender tombe contaynes.   28

Wherone thees verses gravd in gould   f. 94v
  in marble shuld be sett,
Least that in earth his cyndred mould
  thou Brytayne shuld forgett.   32

Heere Geffrey Chaucers carcasse lyes,
  whylom of greate renoune;
his earned prayes, his roome supplyes,
  nowe Death hath prest him doune;   36

Brytayne his famous corps retaynes,
  his freshe fame beares record.
his soule (god send) in heauen Remaynes,
  whith the euerlyuing Lorde.   40

Alyue he learning did encrease,
  that wailes his Destenye,
And chaunging liffe, his soule doth please,
  The supreme god one hye.   44

A pierles poet he lyued one earth,
  and subiect yet to fate,
his soule a heauenlie poet in mearth
  Lyues, whith coelestiall state.   48

39. MEREDITH HANMER, GOOD DECORUM OBSERVED

1576

Educated at Corpus Christi College, Oxford, Hanmer (1543-
1604) became a clergyman and eventually held many Irish
benefices, where he occupied himself with historical research, controversy, and a translation of 'The Auncient
Ecclesiasticall Histories', 1577 (from which the extracts
are taken), which became very popular. Like many religious writers of the sixteenth century he contrasts Chaucer
as a secular author with more religious works, but shows a
balanced sense of the merit of secular writings. The
notion of 'decorum' as a literary merit is Neoclassical,
being first recorded as used by Ascham, in 'The Scholemaster', 1563, of Latin authors. Extract (a) is from the
Dedication, dated 1576, Sig. A iii; (b) is from p. 408.
Chaucer's 'Prophesie' was first printed by Caxton, though
not attributed to Chaucer, and subsequently by Thynne in
the edition of 1532 and in the later sixteenth-century
editions. It became part of the sixteenth-century interest in prophecy. The second quotation is from Chaucer's
poem 'Lak of Stedfastnesse'.

(a)

Many nowe adayes had rather reade the stories of Kinge
Arthur: The monstrous fables of *Garagantua*: the Pallace of
pleasure: the Dial of Princes, where there is much good
matter: the Monke of Burie full of good stories: Pierce
ploweman: the tales of Chaucer where there is excellent
wit, great reading and good decorum obserued, the life of
Marcus Aurelius where there are many good Morall precepts:
the familiar and golden Epistles of *Antonie Gwevarra*
where there is both golden witt & good penning: the pil-
gremage of Princes well penned and Clerckly handeled:
Reinard the Fox: *Beuis* of Hampton: the hundred mery tales:
skoggan:Fortunatus: with many other infortunate treatises
and amorous toies wrytten in Englishe, Latine, Frenche,
Italian, Spanishe, but as for bookes of diuinitie, to edi-
fie the soule, and instructe the inwarde man, it is the
least part of their care, nay they will flatly answere it
belongeth not to theyr calling to occupie their heades
with any such kinde of matters, It is to be wished, if not
all, at leaste wise that some part of the time which is
spente in readinge of suche bookes (althoughe many of them
contayne notable matter) were bestowed in reading of holy
Scripture or other such wrytinges as dispose the mind to
spirituall contemplation.

(b)

But (God be praised for it) we are able to report farre
better of *England*, that there are of the nobilitie, valiant men, vertuous, godly, studious, politicke, zealous, of
auncient houses, and blood neuer stayned. There is hope
the dayes shall neuer be seene when the prophesie of *Chaucer* shall take place where he sayth:

    When fayth fayleth in priestes sawes,
    And Lordes hestes are holden for lawes,
    And robberie is holden purchase,
    And lecherie is holden solace.
    Than shall the land of *Albion*
    Be brought to great confusion.

And to the end our wished desire may take effect, let vs
hearken what exhortation he geueth vnto the chiefe magis-
trate, his wordes are these:

    Prince desire to be honorable,
    Cherishe thy folke and hate extortion,
    Suffer nothing that may be reproueable,

To thine estate done in thy region.
Shewe forth the yarde of castigation.
Dreade God, doe lawe, loue trueth and worthinesse.
And wedde thy folke ayen to stedfastnes.

40.   GEORGE WHETSTONE, SIR CHAUCER'S JESTS

1578

Whetstone (1544?-87?), of unknown education, a dissipated
gentleman, soldier, adventurer and literary hack, among
other productions wrote a bad play, 'The Right excellent
and famous Historye of Promos and Cassandra', 1578, which
shows that for him Chaucer meant bawdy tales. (Text follows Spurgeon, I, 116; 'Promos', Part I, Act I, Sc. 3,
Sig Biii.)

La[mia] . . . .
And can then the force of lawe, or death, thy minde of
    loue bereaue?
In good faith, no: the wight that once hath tast the
    fruits of loue,
Untill hir dying daye will long, Sir *Chaucers* iests to
    proue.

41.   EDMUND SPENSER, DAN CHAUCER, WELL OF ENGLISH
VNDEFILED

1579, 1590-6, 1599(1609)

The poet Spenser (*c*.1552-99), was a sizar at Pembroke
College, Cambridge, where he met Gabriel Harvey (see No.
45). He entered the household of the Earl of Leicester,
and finally held an important civil post in Ireland.
Chaucer is of the greatest significance as a source of
pure English and of inspiration to him in a characteristic

Cambridge way. In Spenser's first important publication,
the pastoral poem, 'The Shepheardes Calendar' (1579) Chaucer figures, not without a debt to Skelton, but in style,
after the artificial manner of classical eclogue, as the
'shepherd' Tityrus in several eclogues, as here, in June
(a lament of love) fol. 24 (a); in 'The Faerie Queene',
work of Spenser's maturity, Book IV, canto 2, stanza
xxxii (edition of 1609) (b); and in his last work 'The
Mutabilitie Cantos', 'The Faerie Queene' Book VII, canto
7, stanza ix, printed posthumously, 1609 (c), Chaucer is
the type of the great English poet, an inspiration and a
model. The reproachful apostrophe to Death goes back to
Hoccleve (No. 7) doubtless via Surigo (No. 15). In Spenser's attitude to Chaucer generally we see the traditional
Gothic and Cambridge loving admiration assimilated to a
fairly superficial Neoclassical model.

(a)

The God of shepheards *Tityrus* is dead,   81
Who taught me homely, as I can, to make.
He, whilst he lived, was the soueraigne head
Of shepheards all, that bene with loue ytake:
Well couth he wayle his Woes, and lightly slake
The flames, which loue within his heart had bredd,
And tell vs mery tales, to keep vs wake,
The while our sheepe about vs safely fedde.

Nowe dead he is, and lyeth wrapt in lead,
(O why should death on hym such outrage showe?)   90
And all hys passing skil with him is fledde,
The fame whereof doth dayly greater growe.
But if on me some little drops would flowe
Of that the spring was in his learned hedde,
I soone would learne these woods, to wayle my woe,
And teache the trees, their trickling teares to shedde.

(b)

(32)
Whylome as antique stories tellen vs,
    Those two [Cambell and Triamond] were foes the fellon-
                                        est on ground,
    And battell made the draddest daungerous,
    That euer shrilling trumpet did resound;

Though now their acts be no where to be found,
As that renowmed Poet them compiled,
With warlike numbers and Heroick sound,
Dan Chaucer, well of English vndefiled,
On Fames eternall beadroll worthie to be filed.

(33)

But wicked *Time* that all good thoughts doth waste,
And workes of noblest wits to nought out-weare,
That famous moniment hath quite defac't,
And robd the world of threasure endlesse deare,
The which mote haue enriched all vs heare.
O cursed Eld! the canker-worme of writs,
How may these rimes (so rude as doth appeare)
Hope to endure, sith workes of heauenly wits
Are quite deuour'd, and brought to nought by little bits?

(34)

Then pardon, O most sacred happy spirit,
That I thy labours lost may thus reviue,
And steale from thee the meed of thy due merit,
That none durst euer whil'st thou wast aliue,
And beeing dead in vaine yet many striue:
Ne dare I like, but through infusion sweet
Of thine owne spirit (which doth in me surviue)
I follow heere the footing of thy feet
That with thy meaning so I may the rather meete.

(c)

So heard it is for any liuing wight,
All her [Dame Nature's] array and vestiments to tell
That old *Dan Geffrey* (in whose gentle spright
The pure well head of Poesie did dwell)
In his *Foules parley* durst not with it mel,
But it transferd to *Alane*, who he thought
Had in his *Plaint of kindes* describ'd it well:
Which who will read set forth so as it ought,
Go seek he out that *Alane* where he may be sought.

42. EDWARD KIRKE, LOADESTARRE OF OUR LANGUAGE

1579

Edward Kirke (1553-1613), friend of Spenser, was like him
a sizar of Pembroke Hall, Cambridge, and also became a
friend of Harvey. Kirke introduced and commented on Spenser's anonymous 'The Shepheardes Calender', 1579, over the
initials E.K., and shared and supported Spenser's respect
for Chaucer, whose work, like that of Lydgate, he knew
well. Extract from the introductory Epistle directed to
Harvey, Sig. §ii, fol.7, fol.2lb, fol.48.

Vncovthe, vnkiste, sayde the olde famous Poete Chaucer:
whom for his excellencie and wonderfull skil in making,
his scholler Lidgate, a worthy scholler of so excellent a
maister, calleth the Loadestarre of our Language: and whom
our Colin clout in his Aeglogue calleth Tityrus the God of
shepheards, comparing hym to the worthiness of the Roman
Tityrus Virgile. Which prouerbe myne owne good friend
Ma. Haruey, as in that good old Poete it serued well Pan-
dares purpose, for the bolstering of his baudy brocage, so
very well taketh place in this our new Poete, who for that
he is vncouthe (as said Chaucer), is vnkist, and vnknown
to most men, is regarded but of few. But I dout not, so
soone as his name shall come into the knowledge of men,
and his worthines be sounded in the tromp of fame, but
that he shall be not onely kiste, but also beloued of all,
embraced of the most, and wondred at of the best.
· · · · · · · · · · · · · · · · · · ·
                          Gride) perced: an olde word
much vsed of Lidgate, but not found (that I know of) in
Chaucer.
[ff.7-7b] [Glosse to Feb.] Heardgromes.) Chaucers verse
almost whole. [The whole line is:-

    "So loytring liue you little heardgroomes."]

Tityrus.) I suppose he meane Chaucer, whose prayse for
pleasaunt tales cannot dye, so long as the memorie of hys
name shal liue, the name of Poetrie shal endure.
· · · · · · · · · · · · · · · · · · ·
There grew) This tale of the Oake and the Brere, he telleth as learned of Chaucer, but it is cleane in another

kind and rather like to Aesopes fables.
[f.216] [Glosse to May.] Chevisaunce) sometime of Chaucer
vsed for gaine: sometime of other for spoyle, or bootie,
or enterprise, and sometime for chiefdome.
[f.48] [Glosse to Nouember.] [Death, overcome by Christ]
is now made (as Chaucer sayth) the grene path way to lyfe.

43.   SIR PHILIP SIDNEY, CHAUCER HAD GREAT WANTS

1581

Sidney (1554-86), soldier, scholar, courtier; hero and
non-pareil of the Elizabethan age, was educated at Christ
Church, Oxford. Unlike Cambridge men he shows little
interest in or affection for Chaucer, and no interest in
contemporary linguistic or religious problems as illustrated by Chaucer, or by works then attributed to him. He
does not include Chaucer in the recommendations of his
'reading list' (printed in 'The Times Literary Supplement', 24 March 1972, pp. 343-4.)
   'An Apologie for Poetrie' has great significance. It
is the first appearance in English of a coherent theory
and justification of literature and literary study. As
such it could only, for historical reasons, be Neoclassical, and derives from the immense European Humanist
achievement in literary studies of the sixteenth century.
(Cf. 'An Apology' ed. G.T. Shepherd, 1965.) The dominant
criteria of Neoclassical taste, i.e. regularity, unity of
plot and tone, realism, moral improvement, high seriousness of the poetic *vates*, were inevitably unfavourable to
Chaucer's Gothic mixtures of grave and gay, of fantasy and
down-to-earth realism, episodic extensiveness, and refusal
as a poet to assert his own superiority over everyone
else. This is most clear when Sidney inevitably condemns
that Gothic drama that Shakespeare was soon to justify so
astonishingly at the very end of its career. The future
of English literature and literary study was to be Neoclassical and Romantic. Small wonder that Sidney, whose
'Apologie' was so prophetic, felt that Chaucer 'had great
wants'.
   Since 'An Apologie' is theory, not practical criticism,
criticism is found only in incidental remarks, which are
penetrating and generous, as we would expect from Sidney.

He reveals a characteristic taste for the noble romances,
'The Knight's Tale' and 'Troilus'.
    The casual reference to Comedies is to 'The Knight's
Tale', I, 886-7, correctly reading,

        I have, God woot, a large field to ere   [plough
        And wayke been the oxen in my plough,   [weak

But sixteenth-century editions available to Sidney read,
after Thynne,

        I haue got wotte/a large felde to ere
        And weked ben the oxen in the plowe.

Perhaps Sidney, by unconscious association with the
'wicked' oxen, mistook, or punned on, *ere* as modern *err*.
(Text from Sig. B ii b, Sig. D iii b, Sig. G iv, Sig. I
iv.)

[Poets came before philosophers and historians.] So among
the Romans were Liuius, Andronicus, and Ennius. So in the
Italian language, the first that made it aspire to be a
Treasure-house of Science, were the Poets *Dante, Boccace,*
and *Petrarch.* So in our English were *Gower* and *Chaucer.*
    After whom, encouraged and delighted with theyr excel-
lent fore-going, others haue followed, to beautifie our
mother tongue, as wel in the same kinde as in other
Arts....
    See whether wisdome and temperance in *Vlisses* and *Dio-*
medes, valure in *Achilles,* friendship in *Nisus,* and *Euri-*
alus, euen to an ignoraunt man, carry not an apparent
shyning: and contrarily, the remorse of conscience in
Oedipus, the soone repenting pride in *Agamemnon,* the
selfe-deuouring crueltie in his Father *Atreus,* the violence of ambition in the two *Theban* brothers, the sowre-
sweetnes of reuenge in *Medaea,* and to fall lower, the
Terentian Gnato, and our *Chaucer's* Pandar, so exprest,
that we nowe vse their names to signifie their trades....
    Thirdly, that it [Poetry] is the Nurse of abuse, in-
fecting vs with many pestilent desires: with a Syrens
sweetnes, drawing the mind to the Serpents tayle of sin-
full fancy. And heerein especially, Comedies giue the
largest field to erre, as *Chaucer* sayth: howe both in
other nations and in ours, before Poets did soften vs, we
were full of courage, giuen to martiall exercises; the
pillers of manlyke liberty and not lulled a sleepe in
shady idlenes with Poets pastimes....

Chaucer, vndoubtedly did excellently in hys *Troylus* and
Cresseid; of whom, truly I know not, whether to meruaile
more, either that he in that mistie time, could see so
clearly, or that wee in this cleare age, walke so stum-
blingly after him. Yet had he great wants, fitte to be
forgiuen, in so reuerent antiquity.

44.   JOHN HIGINS, QUAINT

1585

John Higins produced in 1585 'The Nomenclator or Remem-
brancer of Adrianus Iunius Physician....conteining proper
names and apt termes for all thinges vnder their conuenient Titles...in Latine, Greeke, French and other forrein
tongues: and now in English'. Chaucer is apparently the
only English author mentioned in some six hundred pages -
as it were, the D.H. Lawrence of the time: p. 34, col. b.
(Information by courtesy of Mr J. Sibbald.)

Natura, *Plin.* muliebra, *Eid.* cunnus, *Horat.* [numerous fur-
        ther references and an etymology in Greek] Le con.
        A womans priuie member called of Chaucer a quaint.

45.   GABRIEL HARVEY, EXQUISITE ARTIST AND CURIOUS
UNIVERSAL SCHOLAR

*c.*1585, *c.*1600

Harvey (1545?-1630) was educated at Christ's College,
Cambridge and became a Fellow of Pembroke Hall (later,
College), Cambridge, where he was friendly with Spenser,
then a sizar. For a time he was Public Orator, and hoped,
by his writing and scholarship, to advance himself in the
university and the world; in which ambition he was neither
the first nor last to be disappointed. He bought, read

and annotated books; among a number of references to Chaucer in his marginalia are those in his 'Dionysus Perie-
getes', written c.1585; see 'Gabriel Harvey's Marginalia',
ed. G.C. Moore-Smith, Stratford-upon-Avon, 1913, pp. 160-1,
(a); and those in his copy of Speght's Chaucer, written
c.1598-60, ed. Moore-Smith, pp. 226-7, (b). His comments
emphasise what an intelligent and learned reader appreciated as the main point of each poem, and reflect Harvey's
own interest in science. But Gothic and early Neoclassical taste meet and are reconciled in the pleasure in
variety. The 'new Canterbury Tales' in (b) refers to
'The Cobler of Caunterburie' n.d. (1590).

(a)

The description of Winter, in the Frankleins Tale. In
the beginning of the flowre of Courtesie: made bie Lidgate.
     In the beginning of the assemblie of Ladies. In a
ballad 343.
     The description of the hower of the day: in the Man of
Lawes prologue. In the tale of the Nonnes preist. In
the parsons prologue.
     Notable descriptions, & not anie so artificiall in
Latin, or Greeke.
     Ecce etiam personarum, rerumque Iconismi.
     The artificial description of a cunning man, or Magi-
cian, or Astrologer, in the Franklins tale.
     Two cristall stones artificially sett in the botom of
the fresh well: in the romant of the Rose. 123. The
Natiuitie of Hypermestre: in her Legend.
     Fowre presents of miraculous vertu: An horse, & a
sword: a glasse, & a ring: in the Squiers tale.
     The natiuitie of Oedipus, artificially calculated in the
first part of Lidgats storie of Thebes: bie the cunningest
Astronomers, & Philosophers of Thebes.
     The discouerie of the counterfait Alchymist, in the tale
of the Chanons Yeman.
     Other commend Chawcer, & Lidgate for their witt, plea-
sant veine, varietie of poetical discourse, & all humanitie: I specially note their Astronomie, philosophie, &
other parts of profound or cunning art. Wherein few of
their time were more exactly learned. It is not sufficient for poets, to be superficial humanists: but they
must be exquisite artists, & curious vniuersal schollers.

(b)

[At end of Chaucer's Life:-]
Amongst the sonnes of the Inglish Muses; Gower, Lidgate,
Heywood, Phaer, & a fewe other of famous memorie, ar
meethinkes, good in manie kindes: but aboove all other,
Chawcer in mie conceit, is excellent in euerie veine, &
humour: & none so like him for gallant varietie, both in
matter, & forme, as Sir Philip Sidney: if all the Exercises which he compiled after Astrophil, & Stella, were
consorted in one volume. Works in mie phansie, worthie
to be intituled, the flowers of humanitie. Axiophilus
[i.e. Spenser] in one of his Inglish discourses.
[On *Arguments to euery Tale and Booke'* - on *'Argument to
the Prologues':-*]
Pleasant interteinement of Time, with sociable intercourse of Tales, stories, discourses, & merriments of all
fashions, Gallant varietie of notable veines, & humors in
manie kinds. supra to his loouing frend, concerning his
obseruation of the art of Decorum in his Tales. A fine
discretion in the autor: & a pithie note in the Censor.
utrunque scitum.
[On *'The Knights tale'* - on the words *'deeds of Armes,
and loue of Ladies':-*]
Heroical pageants.
[On *'The Millars tale':-*]
Comical tricks. The Prior disguised like a scull,
shamefully discouered, in the new Canterburie Tales.
[On *'The Reues tale':-*]
Such a reueng vpon Marian of Cherryhynton, bie Sir
Rowland of Peters hostell in Cambridg. In the new Can-
terburie Tales, called The Cobler of Canterburie. A
Tragedie for a Comedie.
Tria grata; Nouitas, Varietas, breuitas.
[On *'The Man of Lawes Tale':-*]
Courtlie practises.
[On *'The Squiers tale':-*]
Heroical, & magical feates.
[On *'The Merchaunts tale':-*]
Comical.
[On *'The Fryars tale'* - on the words *'inuectiue against
the briberie of the spirituall courts':-*]
Ecclesiastical iurisdiction.   J.C.
[On *'The Somners tale':-*]
An od iest in scorne of friars.
[On *'The Clarke of Oxfords tale':-*]
Moral, & pathetical.
[On *'The Frankelins tale'* - on the words *'The scope of
this tale seemeth a contention in curtesie':-*]

A generous Emulation. Magical feates bie the way.
[On *'The Chanons yeomans tale'*:-]
    A chymical discourse, & discouerie of a cunning impos-
tour. One of Axiophilus memorials: with that lost labour
of Aurelius. Two notable discourses of cunning withowt
effect.
[On *'The Shipmans tale'*:-]
    The Smithes tale, in the new Canterburie Tales. A
iealous Cobler, cunningly made a Cuckold. In the Coblers
tale, the Eight orders of Cuckholds. Cuckold Machomita.
Heretick. Lunatick. Patient. Incontinent. Bie consent.
Bie parlament. Innocent.
[On *'Chaucers tale'*:-]
    morall.
[On *'The Monkes tale'* - on the words *'A Tragicall dis-
    course on such as haue fallen from high estate to ex-
    treame miserie'*:-]
    The Mirrour of Magistrates.
[On *'The Manciples tale'*:-]
    No Tales like the Tales of cunning Experiments, or
straung exploits, or queint surprises, or stratagems, or
miracles, or sum such rare singularities.
[On *'The Plowmans tale'*:-]
    Ecclesiastical abuses. For tales of thriftie, husband-
lie, & prosperous courses, none like the reuiued stories
of Jack of Newberie, Dick of Worcester, Tom of Redding,
Will of Salsburie, Georg of Glocester, & diuers such:
who grew passing wealthie & famous bie their trades.
[On *'The Persons tale'*:-]
    Moral, & penitential. The last of his Canterburie
tales, with Lidgates tragical storie of Thebes.
[On *'Troylus and Creseid'*:-]
    A peece of braue, fine, & sweet poetrie. One of Astro-
phils [i.e. Philip Sidney] cordials.
[On *'The Legend of Good women'*:-]
    Heroical, & tragical Legends.
[On *'The Astrolabe'*:-]
    An astronomical discourse.
[On *'The Testament of Love'*:-]
    A philosophical discourse in the veine of Boetius, &
sumtime of Seneca.
[After *'Finis'*:-]
    All notable Legends in one respect, or other: & worthie
to be read, for theire particular invention, or elocution:
& specially for the varietie both of matter, & manner,
that delightes with proffit, & proffittes with delight.
Thowgh I could haue wisshed better choice of sum arguments, and sum subiects of more importance.
[On the text of the poems:-]

['*The Millers tale:-*]
  A student of Astrologie.
['*The Squiers tale*':-]
  The Spring: vt supra jnfra.
  Cunning Compositions bie Natural Magique.
['*The Frankeleins tale*':-]
  A cunning man, & arch-magician.
['*The tale of the Chanons yeman*':-]
  Alchymie.
  The great Alchymist.
['*The tale of the Nonnes priest*':-]
  The spring. The prime of the day.
['*The Plowmans tale*':-]
  The Clergie.
['*The Parsons prologue*':-]
  the description of the howre. ut supra 17.
  Contritio-cordis.
['*The Romant of the Rose*':-]
  Excellent descriptions of Beautie. Richesse. Largesse.

46. WILLIAM WEBBE, PROFITABLE COUNSEL MINGLED WITH
DELIGHT

1586

Webbe (fl.1568-91) was educated at St John's College,
Cambridge (BA 1572-3), and was acquainted with Spenser and
Gabriel Harvey, but little is known of his life beyond his
being a private tutor in Essex. His 'A Discourse of Englishe Poetrie' (1586), of which only two copies survive,
illustrates the critical ideas about English poetry of the
Cambridge of his day, sympathetic to Chaucer's Gothic
variety, but making a valiant attempt to fix him in the
Neoclassical mould. Extracts from 'Elizabethan Critical
Essays', ed. G. Gregory Smith, 1904, Vol. I, (a) 241, (b)
251, (c) 263.

(a)

The first of our English Poets that I haue heard of was

Iohn *Gower*...his freend *Chawcer* who speaketh of him oftentimes in diuers places of hys workes. *Chawcer*, who for
that excellent fame which hee obtayned in his Poetry, was
alwayes accounted the God of English Poets (such a tytle
for honours sake hath been giuen him), was next after if
not equall in time to Gower and hath left many workes,
both for delight and profitable knowledge farre exceeding
any other that as yet euer since hys time directed theyr
studies that way. Though the manner of hys stile may
seeme blunte and course to many fine English eares at
these dayes, yet in trueth, if it be equally pondered, and
with good iudgment aduised, and confirmed with the time
wherein he wrote, a man shall perceiue thereby euen a true
picture or perfect shape of a right Poet. He by his
delightsome vayne so gulled the eares of men with his
deuises, that, although corruption bare such sway in most
matters, that learning and truth might skant bee admitted
to shewe it selfe, yet without controllment myght hee
gyrde at the vices and abuses of all states, and gawle
with very sharpe and eger inuentions, which he did so
learnedly and pleasantly that none therefore would call
him into question. For such was his bolde spyrit, that
what enormities he saw in any he would not spare to pay
them home, eyther in playne words, or els in some prety
and pleasant couert, that the simplest might espy him.
Neere in time vnto him was *Lydgate,* a Poet surely for good
proportion of his verse and meetely currant style, as the
time affoorded, comparable with *Chawcer,* yet more occupied
in supersticious and odde matters then was requesite in so
good a wytte.

(b)

Let thinges that are faigned for pleasures sake haue a
neer resemblance of the truth. This precept may you perceiue to bee most duelie obserued of *Chawcer*: for who
could with more delight prescribe such wholsome counsaile
and sage aduise, where he seemeth onelie to respect the
profitte of his lessons and instructions? or who coulde
with greater wisedome, or more pithie skill, vnfold such
pleasant and delightsome matters of mirth, as though they
respected nothing but the telling of a merry tale? so that
this is the very grounde of right poetrie, to give profitable counsaile, yet so as it must be mingled with delight.

(c)

...For surelie I am of this opinion that the wantonest
Poets of all, in their most laciuious workes wherein they
busied themselues, sought rather by that meanes to withdraw mens mindes (especiallie the best natures) from such
foule vices then to allure them to imbrace such beastly
follies as they detected.

47. RICHARD (?) PUTTENHAM, THE NATURALL OF HIS PLEASANT WIT

1589

'The Arte of English Poesie', 1589, is anonymous, but the
author claims to have been 'a scholler of Oxford' and to
have presented his poems to Queen Elizabeth I. References
in the early seventeenth century suggest that the author's
name was Puttenham. There were two brothers of that name
eligible for the authorship of this important contribution
to early literary criticism, Richard (1520?-1601?), and
George, (d.1590). Recent opinion favours Richard.
Whichever it was, the notion that a love of literature,
and capacity to write, produce moral elevation is denied,
for the conduct of both brothers was deplorable. Although
Puttenham gives an intelligent discussion, his disregard
of the possibility of sounding the final inflexion (usually -e), and failure to recognise the corruption of the
texts, largely invalidate the truth of his nevertheless
influential remarks.

(pp. 49-50) And in her Maiesties time that now is are
sprong vp an other crew of Courtly makers, Noble men and
Gentlemen of her Maiesties owne seruauntes, who haue   written excellently well...But of them all particularly this is
myne opinion, that *Chaucer,* with *Gower, Lidgat* and *Harding* for
their antiquitie ought to haue the first place, and *Chaucer* as the most renowmed of them all, for the much learning appeareth to be in him aboue any of the rest. And
though many of his bookes be but bare translations out of
the Latin and French, yet are they wel handled, as his
bookes of *Troilus* and *Cresseid,* and the Romant of the

Rose, whereof he translated but one halfe, the deuice was
Iohn de Mehunes, a French Poet, the Canterbury Tales were
Chaucers owne inuention as I suppose, and where he sheweth
more the naturall of his pleasant wit, then in any other
of his workes, his similitudes comparisons, and all other
descriptions are such as can not be amended. His meetre
Heroicall of *Troilus* and *Cresseid* is very graue and
stately, keeping the staffe of seuen, and the verse of
ten, his other verses of the Canterbury tales be but
riding ryme, neuerthelesse very well becomming the matter
of that pleasaunt pilgrimage in which euery mans part is
played with much decency....
(p. 62) But our auncient rymers, as *Chaucer, Lydgate,* and
others, vsed these *Cesures* either very seldome, or not at
all, or else very licentiously, and many times made their
meetres (they called them riding ryme) of such vnshapely
wordes as would allow no conuenient *Cesure,* and therefore
did let their rymes runne out at length, and neuer stayd
till they came to the end.

48. THOMAS NASHE, CHAUCER LIUED VNDER THE TIRRANIE OF
IGNORANCE

1589, 1592

Thomas Nashe, pamphleteer and fantasist (1567-1601), was
educated at St John's College, Cambridge. He admired
Spenser and Sidney, hated Gabriel Harvey. Extract (a) is
from his first publication, an address 'To the Gentleman
Students of both Universities', prefaced to Greene's
'Menaphon', 1589, Sig. A.2 (cf. 'Works', ed. R.B. McKerrow,
rev. ed. Oxford, 1957, III, p. 322), where he praises Chaucer like a Cambridge man. Extract (b) is sections from
his pamphlet against Gabriel Harvey, 'Strange Newes of the
intercepting of certaine Letters' published in 1592; Sig.
A.4 (cf. McKerrow, I, 258); Sig. G.3 (ed. cit., I, pp.
298-9); K.1 (ed. cit., I, pp. 316-17). Nashe uses Chaucer's achievement to ridicule Latinate versifying in hexa-
meters, and in connection with the language controversy.

(a)

Tut saies our English Italians, the finest witts our Climate sends foorth, are but drie braind doltes, in comparison of other countries: whome if you interrupt with *redde rationem*, they will tell you of *Petrache, Tasso, Celiano*, with an infinite number of others; to whome if I should oppose *Chaucer, Lidgate, Gower*, with such like, that liued vnder the tirranie of ignorance, I do think their best louers, would bee much discontented, with the collation of contraries, if I should write ouer al their heads, Haile fellow well met. One thing I am sure of, that each of these three, haue vaunted their meeters, with as much admiration in English, as euer the proudest *Ariosto* did his verse in Italian.

(b)

Proceede to cherish thy surpassing carminicall arte of memorie with full cuppes (as thou dost) let Chaucer *bee new scourd against the day of battaile, and* Terence *come but in nowe and then with the snuffe of a sentence, and* Dictum puta, *Weele strike it as dead as a doore naile.*...
The Hexamiter verse I graunt to be a Gentleman of an auncient house (so is many an english begger), yet this Clyme of ours hee cannot thriue in; our speech is too craggy for him to set his plough in, hee goes twitching and hopping in our language like a man running vpon quagmiers, vp the hill in one Syllable and down the dale in another, retaining no part of that stately smooth gate, which he vaunts himselfe with amongst the Greeks and Latins.
Homer and Virgil, two valorous Authors, yet were they neuer knighted; they wrote in Hexameter verses: *Ergo, Chaucer,* and *Spenser* the *Homer* and *Virgil* of England, were farre ouerseene that they wrote not all their Poems in Hexamiter verses also.
In many Countries veluet and Satten is a commoner weare than cloth amongst vs, *Ergo*, wee must leaue wearing of cloth, and goe euerie one in veluet and satten, because other Countries vse so.
The Text will not beare it, good *Gilgilis Hobberdehoy*.
Our english tongue is nothing too good, but too bad *to imitate the Greeke and Latine*....In a verse, when a worde of three sillables cannot thrust in but sidelings, to ioynt him euen, we are oftentimes faine to borrowe some lesser quarry of elocution from the Latine, alwaies retaining this for a principle, that a leake of indesinence

as a leake in a shippe, must needly bee stopt, with what
matter soeuer.

   Chaucers authoritie, I am certaine shalbe alleadgd
against mee for a many of these balductums. Had *Chaucer*
liu'd to this age, I am verily perswaded hee would haue
discarded the tone halfe of the harsher sort of them.

   They were the Oouse which ouerflowing barbarisme, with-
drawne to her Scottish Northren chanell, had left behind
her. Art, like yong grasse in the spring of *Chaucers*
florishing, was glad to peepe vp through any slime of corruption, to be beholding to she car'd not whome for appa-
raile, trauailing in those colde countries. There is no
reason that shee a banisht Queene into this barraine
soile, hauing monarchizd it so long amongst the Greeks
and Romanes, should (although warres furie had humbled her
to some extremitie) still be constrained when she hath
recouerd her state, to weare the robes of aduersitie, iet
it in her old rags, when she is wedded to new prosperitie.

   Vtere moribus praeteritis, saith *Caius Caesar in Aulus
Gellius, loquere verbis praesentibus.*

   Thou art mine enemie, *Gabriell*, and that which is
more, a contemptible vnder-foote enemie, or else I would
teach thy olde *Trewantship* the true vse of words, as also
how more inclinable verse is than prose to dance after
the horrizonant pipe of inueterate antiquitie.

   It is no matter, since thou hast brought godly instruction out of loue with thee, vse thy own destruction,
raigne sole Emperour of inkehornisme, I wish vnto thee all
superabundant increase of the singular gifts of absurdi-
tie, and vaineglory.

49. SIR JOHN HARINGTON, FLAT SCURRILITIE

1591

Harington (1561-1612), courtier, satirist and poet, a
lively, unstable man, was godson of Queen Elizabeth I and
educated at Christ's College, Cambridge. After he had
translated the most indecent passages, with additions, of
Ariosto's 'Orlando Furioso', and circulated them amongst
the Queen's ladies, the Queen punished him by banishment
until he had translated all the rest of the Italian poem.
He published the whole translation in 1591 with 'An

Apologie of Poetrie' prefixed, in which he defends himself
by reference to Chaucer's indecency.

I rather craue pardon then prayse for [Ariosto] in this
point [i.e. indecency]: yet me thinkes I can smile at the
finesse of some that will condemne him [i.e. Ariosto], &
yet not onely allow, but admire our *Chawcer,* who both in
words & sence, incurreth far more the reprehension of flat
scurrilitie, as I could recite many places, not onely in
his millers tale, but in the good wife of Bathes tale, &
many more, in which onely the decorum he keepes, is that
that excuseth it, and maketh it more tolerable. (Sign.
§vii).

50.   ROBERT GREENE (?), POETS WITS ARE FREE

1592

Robert Greene (1560?-92), pamphleteer and dramatist, was
remarked for his profligate life, the length of his hair,
his prolific output and the popularity of his writings.
He was educated at St John's College, Cambridge, notable
for its contribution to English literature in the second
half of the sixteenth century (BA 1578-9), and Clare Hall,
Cambridge (MA 1583).   Several posthumously published pamphlets express repentance for the life he lived and the
works he wrote; among them, though not certainly his, is
'Greene's Vision', 1592, of which only two copies survive.
It is a curious though much more lengthy parallel in certain respects to Chaucer's own 'Retracciouns' to 'The Canterbury Tales' (not printed till 1721).   In it the author
represents himself as visited by 'Chaucer' and 'Gower',
who eventually tell stories ('Chaucer' a *fabliau*-type
comic tale), but their introductory remarks reflect the
important debate between on the one side the serious and
moralising elements in literature, represented by 'Gower'
in Neoclassical guise, and on the other side pure (or im-
pure) entertainment.   The freedom and multiplicity of
literature is argued through 'Chaucer' and with reference
to his works, which are regarded as purely comic, though
there is also an attempt to claim that even low comedy is

improving. But 'Gower' wins the day.
    Text from British Library copy, but cf. 'An Edition of
Greene's Vision' by M.E. McMillan, University Microfilms
Inc., 1961, p. 10 (Sig. B3); p. 14 (Sig. B4b); pp. 17-21
(Sigs C1b-AC3); pp. 23-5 (Sigs C4-C4b); p. 67 (Sigs G4-
G4b).

(Sig. B3) I considered, that wee were borne to profit our
countrie, not onely to pleasure our selues: then the dis-
commodities that grew from my vaine pamphlets, began to
muster in my sight: then I cald to minde, how many idle
fancies I had made to passe the Presse, how I had pestred
Gentlemens eyes and mindes, with the infection of many
fond passions, rather infecting them with the allurements
of some inchanted 'Aconiton', then tempered their thought
with any honest Antidote, which consideration entered thus
farre into my conscience....
    (Sig. B4b) Being in this deepe meditation, lying contem-
plating vpon my bed, I fell a sleepe, where I had not lyne
long in a slumber, but that me thought I was in a faire
medowe, sitting vnder an Oake, viewing the beautie of the
sunne which then shewed himselfe in his pride: as thus I
sat gasing on so gorgeous an obiect, I spied comming
downe the Meade, two ancient men, aged, for their foreheads
were the Calenders of their yeares, and the whitenesse of
their haires bewrayed the number of their dayes, their
pace was answerable to their age, and *In diebus illis*,
hung vpon their garments: their visages were wrinckled,
but well featured, and their countenance conteyned much
grauitie....
    (Sig. C1b) Thou has heere two, whome experience hath
taught many medicines for yong mens maladies, I am sir
Geffrey Chaucer, this *Iohn Gower*, what we can in counsaile, shall be thy comfort, and for secrecie we are no
blabs. Heering sir *Geffrey Chaucer* thus familiar, I tooke
heart at grasse to my selfe, and thought nowe I might haue
my doubt well debated, betweene two such excellent schollers: wherevpon putting of my hat with great reuerence, I
made this replie.
    Graue Lawreats, the tipes of Englands excellence for
Poetry, and the worlds wonders for your wits, all haile,
and happily welcome, for your presence is a salue for my
passions, and the inward greefes that you perceiue by my
outward lookes, are alreadie halfe eased by your comfort-
able promise: I cannot denie but my thoughts are discontent, and my sences in a great maze, which I haue damd vp
a long while, as thinking best to smoother sorrow with

silence, but now I will set fire on the straw, and lay
open my secrets to your selues, that your sweet counsailes
may ease my discontent. So it is, that by profession I am
a scholler, and in wil do affect that which I could neuer
effect in action, for faine would I haue some taste in the
liberall sciences, but *Non licet cuibis adire Corinthum*,
and therefore I content my selfe with a superficiall insight, and only satisfie my desire with the name of a
Scholler, yet as blinde Baiard wil iumpe soonest into the
mire, so haue I ventured afore many my betters, to put my
selfe into the presse, and haue set foorth sundrie bookes
in print of loue & such amourous fancies which some haue
fauoured, as other haue misliked. But now of late there
came foorth a booke called the Cobler of Canterburie, a
merry worke, and made by some madde fellow, conteining plesant tales, a little tainted with scurilitie, such reuer-
end *Chawcer* as your selfe set foorth in your iourney to
Canterbury. At this booke, the grauer and greater sorte
repine, as thinking it not so pleasant to some, as pre-
iudiciall to many, crossing it with such bitter inuec-
tiues, that they condemne the Author almost for an Atheist.
Now learned Lawreat, heere lyes the touch of my passions:
they father the booke vppon me, whereas it is *Incerti
authoris,* and suspitiouslye slaunder me with many harde
reproches, for penning that which neuer came within
the compasse of my Quill....This father *Chawcer* hath made
me enter into consideration of all my former follies, and
to thinke how wantonly I haue spent my youth, in penning
such fond pamphlets, that I am driuen into a dumpe whether
they shall redound to my insuing credit, or my future infamie, or whether I haue doone well or ill, in setting
foorth such amourous trifles, heerein resolue me, and my
discontent is doone.

At this long period of mine, *Chawcer* sat downe &
laught, and then rising vp and leaning his back against a
Tree, he made this merry aunswer. Why *Greene* quoth he,
knowest thou not, that the waters that flow from *Pernassus*
Founte, are not tyed to any particular operation? that
there are nine Muses, amongst whom as there is a *Clio* to
write graue matters, so there is a *Thalis* to endite pleasant conceits, and that *Apollo* hath Baies for them both,
aswell to crowne the one for hir wanton amours, as to
honour the other for her worthy labours: the braine hath
many strings, and the wit many stretches, some tragical
to write, like *Euripedes:* some comicall to pen, like *Terence*: some deepely conceited to set out matters of great
import: others sharpe witted to discouer pleasant fantasies: what if *Cato* set foorth seueare censures, and *Ouid*
amorous Axiomes, were they not both counted for their

faculties excellent? yes, and *Ouid* was commended for his
Salem ingenii, when the other was counted to haue a dull
wit, & a slow memory: if learning were knit in one
string, and could expresse himself but in one vaine, then
should want of variety, bring all into an imperfect Chaos.
But sundry men, sundry conceits, & wits are to be
praised not for the grauity of the matter, but for the
ripenes of the inuention: so that *Martiall, Horace* or any
other, deserue to bee famoused for their Odes and Elegies,
as wel as *Hesiode, Hortensius,* or any other for their
deeper precepts of doctrines. Feare not then what those
Morosie wil murmure, whose dead cinders brook no glowing
sparkes nor care not for the opinion of such as hold none
but Philosophie for a Subiect: I tell thee learning will
haue his due, and let a vipers wit reach his hand to
Apollo, and hee shall sooner haue a branch to eternize his
fame, than the sowrest Satyricall Authour in the worlde.
Wee haue heard of thy worke to be amorous, sententious,
and well written. If thou doubtest blame for thy wantonnes, let my selfe suffice for an instaunce, whose Canterburie tales are broad enough before, and written homely
and pleasantly: yet who hath bin more canonised for his
workes, than Sir *Geffrey Chaucer.* What *Green*? Poets
wits are free, and their words ought to be without
checke: so it was in my time, and therfore resolue thy
selfe, thou hast doone Scholler-like, in setting foorth
thy pamphlets, and shalt haue perpetual fame which is
learnings due for thy endeuour. This saying of *Chawcer*
cheered mee vntill olde *Iohn Gower* rising vp with a sowre
countenance began thus.

Iohn Gower to the Authour.

Well hath *Chawcer* said, that the braine hath sundrie
strings, and the wit diuerse stretches: some bent to pen
graue Poems, other to endite wanton fancies, both honoured
and praised for the height of their capacitie: yet as the
Diamond is more estimated in the Lapidaries shop than the
Topace, and the Rose more valued in the Garden than Gilly-
flowers: So men that write of Morall precepts, or Philoso-
phicall Aphorismes are more highly esteemed, than such as
write Poems of loue, and conceits of fancie....
(Sig. C4) Thou hast applied thy wits ill, & hast sowed
chaffe & shalt reape no haruest. But my maister *Chaucer*
brings in his workes for an instance, that as his, so
thine shalbe famoused: no, it is not a promise to conclude
vpon: for men honor his more for the antiquity of the
verse, the english & prose, than for any deepe loue to
the matter: for proofe marke how they weare out of vse.

Therfore let me tel thee, thy books are baits that allure
youth, Syrens that sing sweetly, and yet destroy with
their notes, faire flowers without smel and good phrases
without any profite.

Without any profite (quoth *Chawcer*) and with that hee
start vp with a frown: no *Gower*, I tell thee, his labours,
as they be amorous, so they be sententious: and serue as
well to suppresse vanity, as they seem to import wantonnes.
Is there no meanes to cure sores, but with Corasiues?
no helpe for vlcers, but sharpe implasters? no salue
against vice, but sowr satyres? Yes, a pleasant vaine,
quips as nie the quicke as a grauer inuectiue, and vnder a
merry fable can *Esope* as wel tant folly, as *Hesiode* correct manners in his Heroicks. I tell thee this man hath
ioyned pleasure with profite, & though his Bee hath a
sting, yet she makes sweet honny. Hath he not discouered
in his workes the follies of loue, the sleights of fancy,
and lightnesse of youth, to be induced to such vanities?
and what more profit can there be to his countrey than
manifest such open mischiefes, as grew from the conceit
of beauty & deceit of women: and all this hath he painted down in his pamphlets. I grant (quoth *Gower*) the
meaning is good, but the method is bad: for by aming at an
inconuenience, he bringeth in a mischiefe: in seeking to
suppresse fond loue, the sweetnes of his discourse allures
youth to loue, like such as taking drink to cool their
thirst, feele the tast so pleasant, that they drinke
while they surfeit. *Ouid* drewe not so many with his
remedie of Loue from loue, as his *Ars Amandi* bred amorous
schollers, nor hath *Greenes* Bookes weaned so many from
vanity, as they haue wedded from [sic] wantonnesse. That is the
reason (quoth *Chawcer*) that youth is more prone vnto euil
than to good, and with the Serpent, sucke honny from the
sweetest sirops, and haue not Poets shadowed waightie
precepts in slender Poems and in pleasant fancies vsed
deepe perswations? who bitte the Curtizans of his time and
the follies of youth more than *Horace*, and yet his Odes
were wanton. Who more inuaied against the manners of men
than *Martiall*, and yet his verse was lasciuious? And had
hee not better (quoth *Gower*) haue discouered his principles in some graue sort as *Hesiode* did or *Pindaris*, than
in such amorous & wanton manner: the lightnesse of the
conceit cracks halfe the credite, and the vanitie of the
pen breeds the lesse beleefe. After *Ouid* had written his
Art of Loue, and set the youth on fire to imbrace fancy,
he could not reclaime them with

  Otia si tollas periere cupidinis arcus.

The thoughts of young men are like Bauins, which once
set on fire, will not out till they be ashes, and therefore doe I infer, that such Pamphlets doe rather preiudice
than profite. Tush (quoth *Chawcer*) all this is but a per-
emptorie selfe conceit in thine owne humour: for I will
shew thee for instance, such sentences as may like the
grauest, please the wisest, and instruct the youngest and
wantonnest, and they be these: first, of the disposition
of women.

[Twenty 'sentences' follow, derived from Greene's own
works. After the 'sentences' first Chaucer then Gower
tells a tale.]

(Sig. G4) Now Sir *Geffrey Chawcer* (quoth *Gower*) how like
you this tale, is it not more full of humanity, then your
vain and scurrulous inuention? and yet affecteth as muche
in the mind of the hearers? are not graue sentences as
forcible, as wanton principles? tush (quoth *Chawcer*) but
these are not plesant, they breed no delight, youth wil
not like of such a long circumstance. Our English Gentlemen are of the mind of the Athenians, that will sooner bee
perswaded by a fable, than an Oration: and induced with a
merrie tale, when they will not be brought to any compasse
with serious circumstances. The more pittie (quoth *Gower*)
that they should bee so fond, as to be subiect to the delight of every leud fancy, when the true badge of a
Gentleman, is learning ioyned with vallour and vertue,
and therefore ought they to read of Martiall Discipline,
not of the slight of *Venus:* and to talke of hard labours,
not to chat of foolish and effeminate amoures.

51.   FRANCIS BEAUMONT, ANCIENT LEARNED MEN IN CAMBRIDGE

1597

Francis Beaumont (*c*.1550-1624) was not the dramatist but
the Master of Charterhouse, who was at Peterhouse, Cambridge, 1565-70, at the same time as Thomas Speght, who
brought out an edition of Chaucer's works, partially
edited by himself, in 1598. Beaumont's letter is part of
the prefatory matter of Speght's edition. It is dated
1597. (See T.W. Baldwin, 'Modern Language Notes', 39

(1924), pp. 504 ff., and E.P. Kuhl, 'The Times Literary
Supplement', 23 September 1926, p. 632.)   Chaucer is
placed among the classics studied in the universities, and
the reference to the Cambridge group is most interesting.

F.B. to his very louing friend, T.S.

I am sorrie that neither the worthinesse of *Chaucers* owne
praise, nor the importunate praiers of diuerse your louing
friendes can yet mooue you to put into print those good
obseruations and collections you haue written of him.   For
as for the obiections, that in our priuate talke you are
wont to say are commonly alledged against him, as first
that many of his wordes (as it were with ouerlong lying)
are growne too hard and vnpleasant, and next that hee is
somewhat too broad in some of his speeches, and that the
worke therefore should be the lesse gratious: these are no
causes, or no sufficient causes to withhold from *Chaucer*
such desert of glorie, as at your pleasure you may bestow
vpon him.   For first to defend him against the first re-
proofe.
    It is well knowne to wise and learned men, that all
languages be either such as are contained in learning, or
such as be vsed amongst men in daily practise: and for the
learned tongues, they hauing *Iure testamentario,* their
legacies set downe by them that be dead, wordes must bee
kept and continued in them in sort as they were left without alteration of the Testators wils in any thing.   But
for usuall languages of common practise, which in choise
of wordes are, and euer will bee subiect vnto chaunge,
neuer standing at one stay, but sometimes casting away
old wordes, sometimes renewing of them, and alwaies
framing of new, no man can so write in them, as that all
his wordes may remaine currant many yeares.   Which thing
Horace rightly noteth, where hee saieth, that words in
common tongues, like vnto fruites, must of necessitie
haue their buddings, their blossomings, their ripenings,
and their fallings: so that it was impossible that either
Chaucer or any man liuing could keep them from falling
after so long a time: And this hath happened amongst the
Latin writers themselues, when the Latine tongue was a
spoken tongue, as ours now is: for diuers of *Statius,*
Ennius, and *Plautus* wordes haue beene long since by later
Latinists reiected.   But yet so pure were *Chaucers* wordes
in his owne daies, as *Lidgate* that learned man calleth
him *The Loadstarre of the English language*: and so good

they are in our daies, as Maister *Spencer,* following the
counsaile of *Tullie in de Oratore,* for reuiuing of antient
wordes, hath adorned his owne stile with that beauty and
grauitie, which *Tully* speakes of: and his much frequenting
of *Chaucers* antient speeches causeth many to allow farre
better of him, then otherwise they would. And furthermore by your interpretation of the most vnusuall words,
that hardnesse and difficultie is made most cleare and
easie: and in the paines and diligence you haue vsed in
collecting his life, mee thinkes you haue bestowed vpon
him more fauorable graces then *Medea* did vpon *Pelias:* for
you haue restored vs *Chaucer* both aliue again and yong
again, and deliuered many of the doubtfull coniectures
they conceiued of him. And therefore though you haue not
made euery thing perfect to your owne mind (for nothing at
one time is both begun and perfected) yet since you haue
opened the way to others, and attempted that which neuer
was begun before you, your endeuours herein cannot bee but
very well accepted, vnlesse of such as are more readie to
find fault, then willing to amend.

Touching the inciuilitie *Chaucer* is charged withall;
What Romane Poet hath lesse offended this way then hee?
Virgil in his *Priapus* is worse by a thousand degrees, and
Ouid in *de Arte amandi,* and *Horace* in manie places as
deepe as the rest: but *Catullus* and *Tibullus* in vncleane
wantonnesse beyond measure passe them all. Neither is
Plautus nor *Terence* free in this behalfe: But these two
last are excused aboue the rest, by their due obseruation of *Decorum,* in giuing to their comicall persons such
manner of speeches as did best fit their dispositions.
And may not the same bee saied for *Chaucer?* How much had
hee swarued from Decorum, if hee had made his Miller, his
Cooke, and his Carpenter, to haue told such honest and
good tales, as hee made his Knight, his Squire, his Lawyer, and his Scholler tell? But shewing the disposition
of these meaner sort of men, hee declareth in their prologues and tales, that their chiefe delight was in vnde-
cent speeches of their owne, and in their false defama-
tions of others, as in these verses appeareth:

Let be thy leud dronken harlotry,
It is a sinne and eke a great folly
To apairen any man, or him defame,
And eke to bring wiues in such blame.

And a little after in excuse of himselfe for vttering
those broad speeches of theirs, he vseth these words:

> *Demeth not for Gods love, that I say*
> *Of evill entent, but that I mote reherce*
> *Her tales all, ben they better or werce,*
> *Or els falsen some of my matere.*

So that no man can imagine in that large compasse of
his, purposing to describe all men liuing in those daies,
how it had been possible for him to haue left vntouched
these filthie delights of the baser sort of people.

And now to compare him with other Poets: His Caunterbury tales containe in them almost the same kind of Argument, that is handled in Comedies: his Stile for the most
part is lowe and like vnto theirs; but herein they differ:
Terence followeth *Plautus*, *Plautus Statius*, *Statius Menander*, and *Menander* other Graecians before him. The ring
they beate is this, and farther they goe not: to shewe the
wantonnesse of some young women: the loosenesse of many
young men: the craftie schoole-poynts of olde bawdes: the
fawning flatterie of clawing Parasites: the miserie of
diuers fonde fathers, who for sauing their money keepe
their sonnes so long vnmarried, till in the ende they
prouide some vnfortunate matches for themselues: and their
notable follie in committing these children of theirs, to
the attendance of their leudest and worst disposed seruing
men. *Chaucers* deuise of his Canterburie Pilgrimage is
meerely his owne, without following the example of any
that euer writ before him. His drift is to touch all
sortes of men, and to discouer all vices of that Age, and
that he doth in such sort, as he neuer failes to hit euery
marke he leuels at.

In his fiue Bookes of *Troylus* and *Creside*, and the
Booke of the praise of good women, and of the mercilesse
Ladie, and that of Blaunch, and of his Dreame (which is in
your handes and was neuer yet imprinted) hee soareth much
higher then he did in the other before: and in his *Troylus*
is so sententious, as there bee fewe staues in that Booke,
which are not concluded with some principall sentence:
most excellently imitating *Homer* and *Virgil,* and borrowing
often of them, and of *Horace* also, and other the rarest
both Oratours and Poets that haue written. Of whome, for
the sweetnesse of his Poetrie may be saide, that which is
reported of *Stesichorus*: and as *Cethegus* was tearmed
Suadae medulla, so may *Chaucer* bee rightly called, The
pith and sinewes of eloquence, and the verie life itselfe
of all mirth and pleasant writing: besides, one gifte hee
hath aboue other Authours, and that is, by the excellencie
of his descriptions to possesse his Readers with a stronger imagination of seeing that done before their eyes,
which they reade, than any other that euer writ in any

tongue. And here I cannot forget to remember vnto you
those auncient learned men of our time in Cambridge, whose
diligence in reading of his workes themselues, and commen-
ding them to others of the younger sorte, did first bring
you and mee in loue with him: and one of them at that time
was and now is (as you knowe) one of the rarest Schollers
of the worlde: The same may bee saide of that worthy man
for learning,your good friend in Oxford, who with many
other of like excellent iudgement haue euer had *Chaucer* in
most high reputation.

     Now (M. *Speght*) tell mee, seeing not onely all Greeke
and Latine Poets haue had their interpretours, and the
most of them translated into our tongue, but the French
also and Italian, as *Guillaume de Saluste seigneur du
Bartas,* that most diuine French poet, *Petrarke,* and
Ariosto, of whome this last instructed by M. *Harrington*
doeth now speake as good English as he did Italian before,
and is withall encreased with many good notes, shall onely
Chaucer our Poet, no lesse worthy than the best of them
amongst all the Poets of the world lie alwaies neglected
and neuer be so well vnderstood of his owne countriemen as
strangers are? Well set your heart at rest, for seeing I
was one of them which first set you in hand with this
worke, and since you haue giuen me of your Copies to vse
priuatly for mine owne pleasure, if you will not put them
abroad your selfe, they shall abroad whether you will or
no. Yet least many inconueniences might happen by this
attempt of mine, and diuers things be set foorth contrarie
vnto your owne liking, let mee once againe entreat you
(as I haue done often heretofore) to yeeld to my iust and
reasonable suit. Wherein you shall not onely satisfie
that conceit which I haue many yeares carried of your
vnfained loue towards me: but pleasure many who daylie
expect your paines herein, and perfourme vnto *Chaucer*
great part of that honour that he most worthely deserueth.
So with my thrise-heartie commendations I bid you farewel.
                    From Leicester the last of Iune,
                    Anno. 1597.

               Your assured and euer louing friend,
                    Francis Beaumont.

52. GEORGE CHAPMAN, NEWE WORDES

1598

The poet Chapman (1559?-1634), educated at either or both
universities, wrote plays, translated Homer, and made the
following comment in his address to the reader in 'Achilles Shield', 1598, Sig. B.2 ('Elizabethan Critical Essays',
ed. G. Gregory Smith, 1904, II, p. 305).

All tongues haue inricht themselues from their originall
...with good neighbourly borrowing...& why may not ours.
    Chaucer (by whom we will needes authorise our true eng-
lish) had more newe wordes for his time then any man
needes to deuise now.

53. THOMAS SPEGHT, IN MOST VNLEARNED TIMES BEING MUCH ESTEEMED

1598, 1602

Speght (fl. 1600) was a sizar of Peterhouse, where, as
Beaumont notes (above No. 51) he was introduced to Chaucer's work. He became a schoolmaster regarded as a para-
gon of his profession, headmaster of the Cathedral Grammar
school (now the King's School) at Ely, and minor canon of
the Cathedral. His edition is not critical either as to
life, text or attributions, but he added a glossary of
hard words. He also added 'The Flower and the Leaf' (universally enjoyed and admired until shown in the mid-
nineteenth century not to be by Chaucer); and the equally
apocryphal 'Chaucer's Dream' (now usually known as 'The
Isle of Ladies'). Francis Thynne, son of William Thynne
who edited the 1532 edition, had been preparing an edition
which on the appearance of Speght's he abandoned. But he
wrote a long detailed critique in the form of a letter,
not published till the nineteenth century (cf. 'Animadversions', etc. by Thynne, ed. F.J. Furnivall, Chaucer Society, 1875), but communicated at least in part to Speght,

who incorporated some of the corrections and additions,
especially in the Glossary, in his new and more careful
edition of 1602, which also added two texts, 'Jack Upland',
printed once before separately 1536 (?), not by Chaucer,
and 'An ABC', which is. The 1598 edition is the first to
incorporate scholarly, or would-be scholarly, matter. The
address to the Readers, and extracts from the Life, Annotations, and the Glossary follow here.

To the Readers.

Some few yeers past, I was requested by certaine Gentlemen
my neere friends, who loued *Chaucer*, as he well deserueth;
to take a little pains in reuiuing the memorie of so rare
a man, as also in doing some reparations on his works,
which they iudged to be much decaied by iniurie of time,
ignorance of writers, and negligence of Printers. For
whose sakes thus much was then by me vndertaken, although
neuer as yet fully finished....As that little which then
was done, was done for those priuat friends, so was it
neuer my mind that it should be published. But so it fell
out of late, that *Chaucers* Works being in the Presse, and
three parts thereof alreadie printed, not only these
friends did by their Letters sollicit me, but certaine
also of the best in the Companie of Stationers hearing of
these Collections, came vnto me, and for better or worse
would haue something done in this Impression. Whose
importunitie hath caused me to commit three faults: first
in publishing that which was neuer purposed nor perfected
for open view: then, in putting diuerse things in the end
of the booke, which els taken in time might haue bene
bestowed in more fit place: lastly, in failing in some of
those eight points, which might more fully haue bene performed, if warning and conuenient leisure had bene giuen.
But seeing it is as it is, I earnestly entreat all friendly Readers, that if they find anie thing amisse they would
lend me their skilfull helpe against some other time, & I
wil thankefully receiue their labors, assuring them that
if God permit, I wil accomplish whatsoeuer may be thought
vnperfect. And if herein I be preuented, those honest
and learned Gentlemen that first set me on worke, haue
promised to succeed mee in these my purposes. But howso-
euer it happen either in mine or their determination, I
earnestly entreat al to accept these my endeuours in best
part, as wel in regard of mine owne well meaning, as for
the desert of our English Poet himselfe: who in most vn-

vnlearned times and greatest ignorance, being much esteemed, cannot in these our daies, wherein Learning and
riper iudgement so much flourisheth, but be had in great
reuerence, vnlesse it bee of such as for want of wit and
learning, were neuer yet able to iudge what wit or Learning meaneth. And so making no doubt of the friendly
acceptance of such as haue taken pains in writing themselues, and hoping wel also of all others, that meane to
employ any labour in reading, I commit our Poet to your
fauourable affection, and yourselues to the protection of
the Almightie.

The Life of Geffrey Chaucer

This famous and learned Poet Geffrey Chaucer Esquire, was
supposed by Leland to haue beene an Oxfordshire or Barke-
shireman borne....But as it is euident by his owne wordes
in the Testament of Loue, hee was borne in the Citie of
London....
     ... the parents of Geffrey Chaucer were meere English,
and he himselfe an Englishman borne. For els how could he
haue come to that perfection in our language, as to be
called, The first illuminer of the English tongue, had
not both he, and his parents before him, been born & bred
among vs. But what their names were or what issue they
had, otherwise then by coniecture before giuen, wee can
not declare.
     Now whether they were Merchants, (for that in places
where they haue dwelled, the Armes of the Merchants of
the Staple haue been seene in the glasse windowes) or
whether they were of other calling, it is not much necessary to search: but wealthy no doubt they were, and of
good account in the common wealth, who brought vp their
Sonne in such sort, that both he was thought fitte for
the Court at home, and to be imployed for matters of
state in forraine countreyes.

His Education

His bringing vp, as *Leland* saieth, was in the Vniuersi-
tie of Oxford, as also of Cambridge, as appeareth by his
owne wordes in his booke entituled 'The Court of
Loue'....
     It seemeth that both these learned men [Chaucer and
Gower] were of the inner Temple: for not many yeeres

since, Master *Buckley* did see a Record in the same house,
where *Geoffrey Chaucer* was fined two shillings for beating
a Franciscane fryer in Fleetstreete.

Thus spending much time in the Vniuersities, Fraunce,
Flaunders, and Innes of Court, he prooued a singular man
in all kind of knowledge.

His Friends

Friends he had in the Court of the best sort: for besides
that he alwaies held in with the Princes, in whose daies
he liued, hee had of the best of the Nobility both lords &
ladies, which fauoured him greatly. But chiefly Iohn of
Gaunt Duke of Lancaster, at whose commandement he made the
Treatise 'of the alliance betwixt Mars and Venus': and also
the booke of the Duchesse. Likewise the lady Isabel
daughter to King Edward the third, and wife to Ingeram De
Guynes, Lord De Coucy: also the lady Margaret daughter to
the same King, maried to Iohn Hastings Earle of Penbrooke,
did greatly loue and fauour Geffrey Chaucer, and hee
againe did as much honour them, but specially the Lady
Margaret, as it may appeare in diuers Treatises by him
written. Others there were of great account, wherof some
for some causes tooke liking of him, and other for his
rare giftes and learning did admire him. And thus hee
liued in honour many yeares both at home and abroad.

Yet it seemeth that he was in some trouble in the daies
of King Richard the second, as it may appeare in the Testament of Loue: where hee doth greatly complaine of his
owne rashnesse in following the multitude, and of their
hatred against him for bewraying their purpose. And in
that complaint which he maketh to his empty purse, I do
find a written copy, which I had of Iohn Stow (whose library hath helped many writers) wherein ten times more is
adioined, then is in print. Where he maketh great lamentation for his wrongfull imprisonment, wishing death to
end his daies: which in my iudgement doth greatly accord
with that in the Testament of Loue....

His Bookes

Chaucer had alwaies an earnest desire to enrich & beautifie our English tongue, which in those daies was verie
rude and barren: and this he did following the example of
Dantes and *Petrarch*, who had done the same for the Italian
tongue; *Alanus* for the French; and *Iohannes Mena* for the
Spanish: neither was Chaucer inferior to any of them in

the performance hereof: And England in this respect is
much beholden to him, as *Leland* well noteth....

Corrections of some faults, and Annotations upon some
places. [sig. Bbbb iii et seq. Two excerpts given here.]

Fol. 28. p. I [Ref. *Merchant's Tale*, IV 1424.] [Sig.
Bbbbiiiib]
They connen so much craft in Wades bote, etc.) Concerning
Wade and his bote called Guingelot, as also his strange
exploits in the same, because the matter is long and fabu-
lous, I passe it ouer.

[Fol. 33. p. 2.] [Sig. Bbbbiiiib.]
Ye know what I meane. etc. An *Aposiopesis* often vsed by
Chaucer: as that, which he is said to haue written with
his Diamond somtime in glassewindowes, expounded by his
man Wat; which was thus:
   A maried man, and yet, qd, Chaucer.
   A merry man, qd. Wat.
   He is a knaue that wrote me that, qd. Chaucer.

[From Glossary, sig. Ttt vi. Edition of 1602]
Iape, (prolog.) Iest, a word by abuse growen odious, and
therefore by a certain curious gentlewoman scraped out in
her Chaucer: whereupon her seruing man writeth thus:
   My mistres cannot be content,
   To take a iest as Chaucer ment,
   But vsing still a womans fashion
   Allowes it in the last translation:
   She cannot with a word dispence,
   Although I know she loues the sence.
   For such an vse the world hath got,
   That words are sinnes, but deeds are not.

54. RICHARD VERSTEGAN, MINGLER OF ENGLISH WITH FRENCH

1605

Verstegan, also known as Richard Rowlands (fl.1565-1620),
antiquary and Roman Catholic controversialist, was educated at Christ Church, Oxford, where he studied Old English.

Among numerous other works he published 'A Restitution of
Decayed Intelligence in Antiquities Concerning the English
Nation', over the initials R.V., Antwerp, 1605. In it, p.
203, he makes a sensible comment on Chaucer's language
that later lexicographers, critics, etc. often refer to.

Some few ages after [the Conquest] came the poet *Geffrey
Chaucer*, who writing his poesies in English, is of some
called the first illuminator of the English toung: of
their opinion I am not (though I reuerence *Chaucer* as an
excellent poet for his tyme). He was indeed a great mingler of English with French, vnto which language by lyke
for that hee was descended of French or rather wallon
race, he caryed a great affection.
    Since the tyme of *Chaucer* more Latin & French, hath bin
mingled with our toung then left out of it.

55. RICHARD BRATHWAIT, AN EXCELLENT EPANODOS

1616

Richard Brathwait (1588?-1673) was educated at Oriel College, Oxford and Pembroke College, Cambridge, was trained
for the law, but lived the rest of his life as a gentleman
in Westmorland, publishing numerous volumes, mostly in
verse. He is said to have served on the Royalist side in
the Civil War. He wrote in 1616 but did not publish till
1665 his discursive 'Comments upon Chaucer's Tales of the
Miller and the Wife of Bath' (ed. C.F.E. Spurgeon, Chaucer Society, 1901, from which the following extracts are
taken). Brathwait's comments are characteristic of perhaps old-fashioned gentry, with his sense of rhetorical
manipulation and anecdotal good humour. Extracts reprinted from Spurgeon (a) p. X, (b) p. 21, (c) pp. 60-1. In
this latter, the quotations from 'The Wife of Bath's Prologue' are modernised and a little careless, corresponding
exactly to no edition.

(a)

[Chaucer speaks:]

The Tales I told, if morally applide,
  How light soe're, or wanton to the show,
  Yet they in very deed were nothing so;
For were the marke they aym'd at but descride,
Even in these dayes they would be verifide;
    And like Sybillas Oracles esteem'd,
    Worth worlds of wealth, how light soe're they seem'd.

Witness my *Miller*, and my *Carpenter*,
  The amorous stories of my *Wife of Bath*,
  Which such variety of humours hath;
My *Priour*, *Manciple*, and *Almoner*,
My subtile *Sumner*, and the *Messenger*;
    All which though moulded in another age,
    Have rais'd new subjects both for *Presse* and *Stage*.

Yet note these times disrelishing my tongue,
  Whose Idioms-distaste by nicer men
  Hath made me mince it like a Citizen!
Which Chaucer holds a manifest wrong,
To force him leave what he had used so long:
    Yea, he dislikes this polishing of art,
    Which may refine the Core, but spoiles the heart.

But yet in serious sadnesse I impute
  This to no fate or destiny of mine,
  But to the barraine Brain-wormes of this time;
Whose Muse lesse pregnant, present or acute,
Affording nought that with the age can sute,
    Like to the truant Bee, or lazie Drone,
    Robbe other Bee-hives of their hony-combe.

And which is worse; this worke they make their owne,
  Which they have pruned, purged, and refin'd,
  And aptly form'd it to the Author's mind;
When I'm assured, if the truth were knowne,
They reape the crop which was by others sowne:
    Yea, theese usurpers to that passe are brought,
    They'll foyst in that wee neither said nor thought.

(b)

(On 'The Miller's Tale', I, 3521-3.)

Thus shall mankind drenche, and lese her life,
This carpenter answered and said, alas my wife!
And shall she drenche?   Alas mine Alysoun &c.

There is nothing perplexeth him so much as the loss of
his dear *Alyson*. Pity it were, thinks he, that so prety
a Morsel of flesh should go the way of all Fish. So as
never till now begins he to provide for his own safety,
Wife, and Family.

Is there no remedy in this caas?

As if he sould say, Alas, my learned Guest *Nicholas,*
must we be all meat for Haddocks? No remedy? no means of
safety? 'Las, for my self I care not so much; for I have
the one foot i' th grave already; I am not a man long for
this world: But that my *Alyson*, who is in the very flower
and prime of her time, the very Daisie and Honey-suckle
of her time, that she should become Provender for a Sea-
horse, or lodge in the Guts of a Whale, it would make any
ones heart yern within him, that has any man's blood in
him. Besides, for her Age, she may have many pretty
Chips when I am gone. O then, good Guest *Nicholas,* provide for her safety, if not for mine. Who knows not, but
if you two can agree, she may be meat for you, when I am
Worms-meat. Thus might the poor Carpenter seem to have
expostulated with his learned Astronomer; as one desirous
to receive some small comfort from this profound Artist,
which might minister a remedy in cases of such urgent
necessity: and afford to his *Alyson* (whom he preferred
before all his Family) some promising hopes of safety.

(c)

('Wife of Bath's Prologue', III, 585-6, 587-8, 591-2.)

And now sir let me se, what shal I sain
A ha, by God I haue my tale again.

A excellent Rhetorical (1) Figure here used by our
Poet.
It seems the remembrance of the proper Personage of
her neat Clark, had like to have made her quite forget her
Tale. Yet, at last, she recals to mind the Story whereon

she is to treat, which Subject, sometimes, she was apt to
forget.

Whan that my fourth husband was on bere
I wept algate, and made sorie chere.

Or for want rather of natural Tears, she furnish'd her
self of other effectual means: She wrapt an Onion in the
one Nook of her Handkercher, or pump'd for Tears; or drew
her face into a Purse, purposely to feign a kind of sor-
rowing, when her Heart was full of Joy, in hope to enjoy
her *Jenkin*.

But for that I was purveied of a make
I wept but small, and that I undertake.

No doubt, but she had prov'd a better Mourner, had she
been a worser Purveior: Like to that Widow, whereof I have
heard this Story. That, having buried three Husbands, and
all those with a very small portion or quantity of Tears,
she came at last to the Grave with her Fourth, for whom
she wept bitterly; which her Neighbors much wondring at,
demanded of her the Cause why she should be so immoderate
in her Sorrow for that last Husband, who had been of so
harsh and rough a Disposition, and so patient at the
Deaths of all the other three, who were of loving and
affable Natures, and had deserved so well at her hands?
To whom she made this Answer; That she wept not so much
for that she was of her sweet Husband deprived, as that
she was now destitute and unprovided; whereas at the
Deaths of her other Husbands, she was ever of another
prepared before the other was buried.

Note

1   ʼΕπανοδος

56   HENRY PEACHAM, A DELICATE KERNELL OF CONCEIT AND
SWEET INVENTION

1622

Henry Peacham, educated at Trinity College, Cambridge, was

the son of a parson who himself published a book on rhetoric. He was a versatile, restless man who wrote many
books of which the best known is the treatise on general
education, 'The Compleat Gentleman', 1622. In this extract (p. 94) knowledge of Chaucer is put firmly among a
gentleman's literary accomplishments.

Of English Poets of our owne Nation, esteeme Sir *Geoffrey
Chaucer* the father; although the stile for the antiquitie,
may distast you, yet as vnder a bitter and rough rinde,
there lyeth a delicate kernell of conceit and sweete
inuention. What Examples, Similitudes, Times, Places, and
aboue all, Persons, with their speeches, and attributes,
doe as in his *Canterburie*-tales (like these threds of
gold, the rich *Arras*) beautifie his worke quite thorough?
And albeit diuers of his workes, are but meerely translations out of *Latine* and *French*, yet he hath handled them
so artificially, that thereby he hath made them his owne,
as his *Troilus* and *Cresseid*. The Romant of the Rose, was
the Inuention of *Iehan de Mehunes*, a French Poet, whereof
he translated but onely the one halfe: his *Canterburie*-
tales without question were his owne inuention, all circumstances being wholly English. Hee was a good Diuine,
and saw in those times, without his spectacles, as may
appeare by the Plough-man, and the Parsons tale: withall
an excellent Mathematician, as plainly appeareth by his
discourse of the Astrolabe to his little sonne *Lewes*. In
briefe, account him among the best of your English bookes
in your librarie.

---

57. JONATHAN SIDNAM (?), OBSOLETE

*c.*1630

'A Seventeenth-Century Modernisation of the First Three
Books of Chaucer's "Troilus and Criseyde"', ed. H.G.
Wright, 'The Cooper Monographs', Bern, 1960, from BM Add.
29494, dated about 1630, is attributed, on no very certain grounds, to a gentleman, Jonathan Sidnam, about whom
nothing is known. He sounds like an Oxford man, and may
have slipped from the records. There are two Sidenhams,
George and William (who may be the same person) recorded

in 'Brasenose College Register', Oxford, 1909, in 1598,
1601/2, but not recorded in J. Foster 'Alumni Oxonienses',
1891. Extracts (a) f.1 (ed.cit., p. 89), (b) ff. 69v-70
(cf. ed.cit., pp. 237-8).

(a)

A
Paraphrase
upon
The three first Bookes of
CHAUCERS
TROILUS and CRESIDA./
Translated into our Moderne English.
For the satisfaction of those.
Who either cannot, or will not, take ye paines to vnderstand.
The Excellent Authors.
Farr more Exquisite, and significant Expressions
Though now growen obsolete, and
out of vse./
By
J: S:

Semel insaniuimus omnes./

Quas habeat Meretrix, Merie-tricks, ediscere Nolj
Namque mere trux est, cum meretrice jocus.

(b)

260
Through you [Venus] I fullie haue describd at last
The sweete delight, and joye of Troilus
Though mixed now, and then wth some distast
As from mine Author it hath come to vs.
And though the Storie be not ended thus
    Yet I will heere leaue Troilus in rest
    wth Cresida the faire whom he loues best.

261
Tis true ye Storie saith shee wrongd his loue.
To her Eternall shame, and infamie.
For shee did after this vnconstant proue.
And fell from him, who lou'd her faithfullie.
Till shee prooud false, and vsd him treacherouslie,

And euen then, he pittied her sad case.
And greeu'd to see her branded wth disgrace.

262

But yet let him that list, goe on to tell
The wanton slipps of this deceitfull Dame.
And what misfortunes afterwardes befell
Poore Troilus, who vnderwent the shame.
Of her misdeedes, though he deseru'd noe blame.
    For I am loath to doe true loue that wrong.
    To make her fall, the subject of my song./

                    Finis./.

58. BRIAN WALKER, BELIEVED THE BIBLE TO BE AS TRUE AS
CHAUCER

1633

Brian Walker, of Bishop Auckland in the diocese of
Durham, a tradesman about whom nothing else is known, in
dispute with nephews and neighbours, was accused by them,
and found guilty, of denying, when drunk, the existence
of God and the devil. His further reported statement in
the testimony given by William Hutchinsonn is unusual
evidence of the general status of Chaucer at this date as
a classic of fiction amongst ordinary townspeople, not
courtiers nor gentry. (The Acts of the High Commission
Court within the diocese of Durham, 'Surtees Society',
1858, p. 116, for the year 1635.)

William Hutchinsonn of Bishopp Awckland, yeoman, aiged 30.
Aboute the beginninge of Lent, gone twelve monethes in
Lent last, happened to be in the house of Anthonie East-
gaite where other companie were present, as Thomas
Allansonn and Eastgait his wife. Walker happened to come
in and did fall into conference and discourse with exami-
nate [i.e. Hutchinsonn] and Thomas Allanson, and from such
discourse did fall to sweareinge and takeinge God's name
in vaine, uttering manie detestable oathes. Allanson
said, 'Fie, mann, doe yow not feare God?' Walker

answeared, 'I doe not beleive there is eyther God or
devill, neyther will I beleive anie thinge but what I
see.'   Aboute twoe yeares and a halfe now by gone, exami-
nate in the house of Anthonie Welfott of Bishopp Awckland
did heare Walker conferr and speake of the booke called
Chawcer, which booke he verie much commended, and said he
did beleive the same as well as he did the Bible, or
wordes to the same effect.   There was present Anthonie
Welfoote.

59.   EDWARD FOULIS, TIME CAN SILENCE CHAUCER'S TONGUE

1635

In 1635 Sir Francis Kynaston (1587-1642) educated at
Oriel College, Oxford and Trinity College, Cambridge, a
gentleman, courtier, and patron of learning, published a
Latin translation of the first two books of 'Troilus and
Criseyde, Amorum Troili et Creseidae libri duo priores
Anglico-Latini', at Oxford, with two prefatory addresses
and fifteen sets of prefatory flattering verses, in Latin
or English, addressed to Kynaston (all printed by Spurgeon) by Oxford men, mostly from New College and All
Souls.   Their constant refrain is the difficulty of understanding the ancient language, and the advantage of the
Latin translation.   The poem by Edward Foulis (b.1614?)
of All Souls, is representative, and adds a comment on
Chaucer's vivid realism which is soon to become a dominant
note.   Text from Sig. *4b.   Kynaston apparently completed
his Latin translation, with a Latin commentary on the
whole poem.   He also wrote a commentary in English, part
of which was edited and published by F.G. Waldron, 'The
Loves of Troilus and Creseid...with a Commentary', by
Sir Francis Kinaston, 1796.

True Poet! Who could words endue
With life, that makes the fiction true.
     All passages are seene as cleare
As if not pend, but acted here:
Each thing so well demonstrated,
It comes to passe, when 'tis but read.

Here is no fault, but ours: through vs
True Poetry growes barbarous:
While aged Language must be thought
(Because 'twas good long since) now naught.
    Thus time can silence *Chaucers* tongue
But not his witte, which now among
The Latines hath a lowder sound;
And what we lost, the World hath found.
    Thus the Translation will become
Th' Originall, while that growes dumbe:
And this will crowne these labours: None
Sees *Chaucer* but in *Kinaston*.
            Ed. Foulis, *Equitis & Baronetti filius*
                Coll. Om. An. Socius.

60. SAMUEL PEPYS, A VERY FINE POET

1663, 1664

Samuel Pepys (1633-1703), diarist and great administrator
of Charles II's navy, was educated at Magdalene College,
Cambridge. He worked in the Navy Office. In extract (a)
Penn, Batten and Mennes were all courtiers, his superiors
in rank, inferiors in ability and diligence, at the Navy
Office. Mennes (1599-1671) was possibly educated at
Corpus Christi College, Oxford, had a distinguished
career as a Royalist military and naval commander, and
had a reputation as a wit. In 1655 he published over his
initials, and in collaboration with Ja[mes] S[mith]
(1605-1667, a genial Royalist divine educated at Lincoln
College, Oxford) 'Musarum Deliciae', a small collection of
facetious, mainly scatological, verse, not without wit,
containing two Chaucerian burlesque and satirical 'characters' of a Cambridge clerk, i.e. don, William Nelson,
which incorporate a number of reminiscences of 'The
General Prologue'. It is clear that the comic, bawdy,
satirical elements in Chaucer mainly appealed to Mennes.
He probably represents quite well the sort of persons,
courtiers, wits, men of affairs, to whom Chaucer's work
continued to appeal. The third extract (c) shows that
Pepys himself, though responding to a particularly realistic detail (perhaps because of his anxiety about his own
eyesight) had read and absorbed the great poem of

'sentement', 'Troilus and Criseyde', referring to Book III,
1462. Pepys suggested to Dryden that he compose 'The
character of a good parson', translated and enlarged from
Chaucer's original in 'The General Prologue', and published
in the 'Fables', 1700. Dryden, whom Pepys had known at
Cambridge, showed Pepys the draft and invited his criticism ('Letters and the Second Diary of Samuel Pepys', ed.
R.G. Howarth, 1932, pp. 280-1). Exract (b) refers to
Pepys's own copy of Chaucer, Speght's edition of 1602,
which can still be seen in Pepys's Library, Magdalene College, Cambridge, No. 2365. Pepys also owned some MSS. of
Chaucer, and one of Caxton's editions of 'The Canterbury
Tales', Pepys's Library No. 2053. (These extracts taken
and information derived from the 'Diary', ed. R. Latham
and W. Matthews, IV, 1971, and Mr R. Latham, CBE, Pepys's
Librarian.)

(a)

14 June 1663...So to Sir W. Penn to visit him; and finding
him alone, sent for my wife, who is in her riding-suit, to
see him; which she hath not done these many months I think.
By and by in comes Sir J. Mennes and Sir W. Batten, and so
we sat talking; among other things, Sir J. Mennes brought
many fine expressions of Chaucer, which he dotes on might-
ily, and without doubt is a very fine poet (p. 184).

(b)

8 July 1664...So to Pauls churchyard about my books - and
to the binders and directed the doing of my Chaucer,
though they were not full neat enough for me, but pretty
well it is - and thence to the clasp-makers to have it
clasped and bossed (p. 199).

(c)

10 August 1664. Up; and being ready, abroad to do several
small businesses; among others, to find out one to engrave
my tables upon my new sliding-Rule with silver plates, it
being so small that Browne that made it cannot get one to
do it. So I found out Cocker, the famous writing-master,
and got him to do it; and I sat an hour by him to see him
design it all, and strange it is to see him with his

natural eyes to cut so small at his first designing it,
and read it all over without any missing, when for my life
I could not with my best skill read one word or letter of
it - but it is use; but he says that the best light, for
his life, to do a very small thing by (contrary to Chaucer's words to the sun: that he should lend his light to
them that small seals grave), it should be by an artifi-
ciall light of a candle, set to advantage as he could do
it (p. 237).

61.   THOMAS SPRAT, A CLOSE, NAKED, NATURAL WAY

1665

Thomas Sprat (1635-1713), bishop of Rochester, wit, man of
letters, Royalist sycophant, High-Church politician, popular preacher, *bon viveur*, was educated at Wadham College,
Oxford and is now most notable for 'The History of the
Royal Society', published in 1667, but of which he tells
us that the first parts (from which the quotations are
taken) were in print by 1665. He refers to Chaucer in
discussing the history of English, and in an allusion to
'The House of Fame' not previously noticed, but is also
important for representing the hostility to metaphor, to
fullness of language, and to eloquence which accompanied
the development of 'the mechanical philosophy'. Such an
attitude to language, though concerned with science,
inevitably tends to relegate all literature to triviality
or falsehood, and is particularly averse to literature
written, like Chaucer's, under a generally rhetorical
theory. At the same time it plainly promotes a relish for
the 'realistic', plain-spoken, 'lower-class', comic elements such as seem to appear in Chaucer's *fabliaux*, and
for which, in the eighteenth century, he was chiefly
marked. Text from the edition of 1667, pp. 41-2, 87, 90,
105, 111-12, 113.

The Truth is, it [the English language] has been hitherto
a little too carelessly handled; and I think, has had less
labor spent about its polishing, then it deserves. Till
the time of *King Henry* the *Eighth*, there was scarce any
man regarded it, but *Chaucer*; and nothing was written in

it, which one would be willing to read twice, but some of
his *Poetry*. But then it began to raise it self a little,
and to sound tolerably well....

   ...they [the members of the Royal Society] have indea-
vor'd, to separate the knowledge of *Nature*, from the colours of *Rhetorick*, the devices of *Fancy*, or the delightful
deceit of *Fables*....

   [London has advantages over all other European capit-
als.] It is, as the *Poets* describe their *House of Fame*, a
City, where all the noises and business in the World do
meet.....

   (p. 90) [An interest in rarity has up to now vitiated
Natural History and Philosophy.] It is like Romances, in
respect of *True History*; which by multiplying varieties of
extraordinary Events, and surprizing circumstances, makes
that seem dull and tasteless. And, to say no more, the
very delight which it raises, is nothing so solid: but, as
the satisfaction of *Fancy*, it affects us a little, in the
beginning, but soon wearies and surfets ....

   [(p. 105) The Royal Society] did not regard the credit
of *Names*, but *Things*...

   pp. 111-12 [Attacks 'superfluity of talking', and elo-
quence] this vicious abundance of *Phrase*, this trick of
Metaphors, this volubility of *Tongue*.

   (p. 113) [The Royal Society] have therefore been most
rigorous in putting in execution, the only Remedy, that
can be found for this *extravagance* [i.e. of language]: and
that has been, a constant Resolution, to reject all the
amplifications, digressions, and swellings of style: to
return back to the primitive purity, and shortness, when
men deliver'd so many *things*, almost in an equal number of
words. They have exacted from all their members, a close,
naked, natural way of speaking; positive expressions;
clear senses; a native easiness: bringing all things as
near the Mathematical plainness as they can: and preferring the language of Artizans, Countrymen and Merchants,
before that, of Wits, or Scholars.

62.   SIR JOHN DENHAM, MORNING STAR

1668

Denham (1615-69), gambler, wit, poet, Royalist, and Royalist cuckold, was educated at Trinity College, Oxford, at
least to the extent of failing to obtain his BA.   He exemplifies the court-poet's recognition of Chaucer, and seems
to be the first to call him 'morning Star'.   Text from the
poem 'On Mr Abraham Cowley, his Death', from 'Poems and
Translations', 1668, p. 89.

---

*On Mr Abraham Cowley, his Death and
Burial amongst the Ancient Poets.*

Old *Chaucer*, like the morning Star,
To us discovers day from far,
His light those Mists and Clouds dissolv'd,
Which our dark Nation long involv'd;
But he descending to the shades,
Darkness again the Age invades.
Next (like *Aurora*) *Spencer* rose,
Whose purple blush the day foreshows.

63.   EDWARD PHILLIPS, FACETIOUSNESS AND REAL WORTH

1675

Edward Phillips (1630-96?), Milton's nephew, was educated
by Milton.   In 1675 he published 'Theatrum Poetarum, or a
Compleat Collection of the Poets, especially the most eminent, of all Ages', and makes a clear distinction between
those who, like Mennes (see No. 60) enjoy Chaucer's 'facetiousness' and the quaintness of his antiquated language,
and those, doubtless few in any age, who appreciate
his real worth.   Extract (a) is from the Preface, Sig.
**2; (b) from pp. 50-1.

(a)

True it is that the style of Poetry till Henry the 8th's
time, and partly also within his Reign, may very well
appear uncouth, strange and unpleasant to those that are
affected only with what is familiar and accustom'd to
them, not but there were even before those times some that
had their Poetical excellencies if well examin'd, and
chiefly among the rest CHAUCER, who through all the neglect of former ag'd Poets still keeps a name, being by
some few admir'd for his real worth, to others not un-
pleasing for his facetious way, which joyn'd with his old
English intertains them with a kind of Drollery.

(b)

Sir Geoffry Chaucer, the *Prince* and *Coryphoeus*, generally
so reputed, till this Age, of our *English* Poets, and as
much as we triumph over his old fashion'd phrase, and
obsolete words, one of the first refiners of the *English*
Language, of how great Esteem he was in the Age wherein he
flourish'd, namely the Reigns of *Henry* the 4th, *Henry* the
5th, and part of *Henry* the 6th, appears, besides his being
Knight and Poet Laureat, by the Honour he had to be allyed
by marriage to the great Earl of *Lancaster, John* of *Gaunt.*
How great a part we have lost of his Works above what
Extant of him is manifest from an Author of good Credit,
who reckons up many Considerable Poems, which are not in
his publisht works; besides the Squires Tale, which is
said to be compleat in *Arundel-House* Library.

64. THOMAS RYMER, WILL NOT SPEAK OF CHAUCER

1674

Thomas Rymer (1614-1713) was educated at Sidney Sussex
College, Cambridge, and thereby offers an exception to a
good theory. He is notable for the great collection of
historical records, the 'Foedera' (1704-35) which include
some Chaucer life-records, and also for being an extreme
Neoclassical critic who condemned 'Othello' in his 'Short
View of Tragedy' (1692). Dryden (No. 66) is too kind to
him.

   With his critical principles he can find nothing to say
about Chaucer, whom he dismisses in his 'Preface of the
Translator' to the Neoclassical 'Reflections on Aristotle's Treatise of Poesie', by the French critic
R. Rapin, 1674, Sig. A 6b. He exaggerates Sidney's judgments. The concept of *design* is significant, as it denies
Gothic irregularity.

Nor shall I speak of *Chaucer*, in whose time our Language,
I presume, was not capable of any Heroick character. Nor
indeed was the most polite Wit of *Europe* in that Age sufficient to a great *design*....*Spencer* I think may be
reckon'd the first of our *Heroick Poets*.

65.   JOSEPH ADDISON, IN VAIN HE JESTS

1694

Addison (1672-1719), celebrated essayist and poet, was
educated at Magdalen College, Oxford, and wrote, according
to Pope (see No. 67), his account of the English poets
before he had read many of them, as a very young man; and
he would perhaps not have allowed this piece of crass
juvenilia to have been published; but it appeared after
his death in 'Miscellany Poems', 6 vols, ed. J. Dryden,
Vol. IV, p. 288.

      To Mr. H. S[acheverel] April 3, 1694

Since, dearest Harry, you will needs request
A short Account of all the Muse possest;
That, down from Chaucer's *days to* Dryden's *Times*
Have spent their noble Rage in British *Rhimes;*
Without more Preface, wrote in formal length,
To speak the Vndertaker's *want of Strength*
I'll try to make their sev'ral Beauties known,
And show their Verses worth, tho' not my own.
   Long had our dull Fore-Fathers slept Supine
Nor felt the Raptures of the tuneful Nine;
'Till Chaucer *first, a merry* Bard, *arose;*

And many a Story told in Rhime and Prose.
But Age has rusted what the Poet writ,
Worn out his Language, and obscur'd his Wit:
In vain he Jests in his unpolish'd Strain,
And tries to make his Readers laugh in vain.
    Old *Spencer* next...

66.   JOHN DRYDEN, GOD'S PLENTY

1700

Dryden (1631-1700), the great poet and critic, was educated at Trinity College, Cambridge, and translated a number
of Chaucer's poems. He shows the customary Cambridge
interest in the purity of English diction, and recognises
Chaucer's scientific learning, but particularly develops
what had only been lightly touched on earlier, his 'realism', his following 'Nature', and his sense of character.
This latter was particularly to be developed by Ogle (No.
76), Blake (No. 90), and many nineteenth- and twentieth-
century critics.
    Dryden rises above pedantic Neoclassical principles and
is the great master of informal, humane appreciation, but
emphasis on realism is in great part a Neoclassical characteristic. He is also a little worried by Chaucer's
Gothic mingling of trivial with greater things. He claims
to have consulted all the editions but seems to have used
Speght's 1598 edition to quote from, without worrying too
much about the spelling.

Spencer and *Fairfax* both flourish'd in the Reign of Queen
Elizabeth: Great Masters in our Language....*Milton* was the
Poetical Son of *Spencer*, and Mr. *Waller* of *Fairfax*; for we
have our Lineal Descents and Clans, as well as other Fami-
lies: *Spencer* more than once insinuates, that the Soul of
Chaucer was transfus'd into his Body; and that he was be-
gotten by him Two Hundred years after his Decease. *Milton*
has acknowledg'd to me that *Spencer* was his Original;...
    But to return: Having done with *Ovid* for this time, it
came into my mind, that our old *English* poet, *Chaucer*, in
many Things resembled him, and that with no disadvantage
on the Side of the Modern Author, as I shall endeavour to

prove when I compare them: And as I am, and always have
been studious to promote the Honour of my Native Country,
so I soon resolv'd to put their Merits to the Trial, by
turning some of the *Canterbury* Tales into our Language, as
it is now refin'd: For by this Means, both the Poets being
set in the same Light, and dress'd in the same *English*
habit, Story to be compar'd with Story, a certain Judgment
may be made betwixt them, by the Reader, without obtruding
my Opinion on him: Or if I seem partial to my Country-man,
and Predecessor in the Laurel, the Friends of Antiquity
are not few: And, besides many of the Learn'd, *Ovid* has
almost all the *Beaux*, and the whole Fair Sex his declar'd
Patrons. Perhaps I have assum'd somewhat more to my self
than they allow me; because I have adventur'd to sum up
the Evidence; but the Readers are the Jury; and their
Privilege remains entire to decide according to the Merits
of the Cause: Or, if they please, to bring it to another
Hearing, before some other Court. In the mean time, to
follow the Thrid of my Discourse (as Thoughts, according
to Mr. *Hobbs*, have always some Connexion) so from *Chaucer*
I was led to think on *Boccace*, who was not only his Contemporary, but also pursu'd the same Studies; wrote Novels in
Prose, and many Works in Verse; particularly is said to
have invented the Octave Rhyme, or *Stanza* of Eight Lines,
which ever since has been maintain'd by the Practice of
all *Italian* Writers, who are, or at least assume the title
of *Heroick Poets*: He and *Chaucer,* among other Things, had
this in common, that they refin'd their Mother-Tongues;
but with this difference, that *Dante* had begun to file
their Language, at least in Verse, before the time of
Boccace, who likewise receiv'd no little Help from his
Master *Petrarch*: But the Reformation of their Prose was
wholly owing to *Boccace* himself; who is yet the Standard
of Purity in the *Italian* Tongue; though many of his
Phrases are become obsolete, as in process of Time it must
needs happen. *Chaucer* (as you have formerly been told by
our learn'd Mr. *Rhymer*) first adorn'd and amplified our
barren Tongue from the *Provencall*, which was then the most
polish'd of all the Modern Languages: But this Subject has
been copiously treated by that great Critick, who deserves
no little Commendation from us his Countrymen. For these
Reasons of Time, and Resemblance of Genius, in *Chaucer* and
Boccace, I resolv'd to join them in my present Work; to
which I have added some Original Papers of my own; which
whether they are equal or inferiour to my other Poems, an
Author is the most improper Judge; and therefore I leave
them wholly to the Mercy of the Reader: I will hope the
best, that they will not be condemn'd; but if they should,
I have the Excuse of an old Gentleman, who, mounting on

Horseback before some Ladies, when I was present, got up
somewhat heavily, but desir'd of the Fair Spectators, that
they would count Fourscore and eight before they judg'd
him....

I proceed to *Ovid*, and *Chaucer*; considering the former
only in relation to the latter. With *Ovid* ended the Golden
Age of the *Roman* Tongue: From *Chaucer* the Purity of the
English Tongue began. The Manners of the Poets were not
unlike: Both of them were well-bred, well-natur'd, amorous, and Libertine, at least in their Writings, it may be
also in their Lives. Their Studies were the same, Philosophy, and Philology. Both of them were knowing in Astro-
nomy; of which *Ovid*'s Books of the *Roman* Feasts, and *Chaucer*'s Treatise of the *Astrolabe*, are sufficient Witnesses.
But *Chaucer* was likewise an Astrologer, as were *Virgil,
Horace, Persius,* and *Manilius*. Both writ with wonderful
Facility and Clearness; neither were great Inventors: For
Ovid only copied the *Grecian* Fables; and most of *Chaucer*'s
Stories were taken from his *Italian* Contemporaries, or
their Predecessors: *Boccace* his *Decameron* was first publish'd; and from thence our *Englishman* has borrow'd many
of his *Canterbury* Tales: Yet that of *Palamon* and *Arcite*
was written in all probability by some *Italian* Wit, in a
former Age; as I shall prove hereafter: The tale of *Gri-
zild* was the Invention of *Petrarch*; by him sent to *Boccace*; from whom it came to *Chaucer*: *Troilus* and *Cressida*
was also written by a *Lombard* Author; but much amplified
by our *English* Translatour, as well as beautified; the
Genius of our Countrymen, in general, being rather to improve an Invention than to invent themselves; as is evident not only in our Poetry, but in many of our Manufac-
tures. I find I have anticipated already, and taken up
from *Boccace* before I come to him: But there is so much
less behind; and I am of the Temper of most Kings, *who
love to be in Debt,* are all for present Money, no matter
how they pay it afterwards: Besides, the Nature of a Preface is rambling; never wholly out of the Way, nor in it.
This I have learn'd from the Practice of honest *Montaign*,
and return at my pleasure to *Ovid* and *Chaucer*, of whom I
have little more to say. Both of them built on the Inventions of other Men; yet since *Chaucer* had something of his
own, as *The Wife of Baths Tale, The Cock and the Fox*,
which I have translated, and some others, I may justly
give our Countryman the Precedence in that Part; since I
can remember nothing of *Ovid* which was wholly his. Both
of them understood the Manners; under which Name I com-
prehend the Passions, and, in a larger Sense, the Descriptions of Persons, and their very Habits: For an
Example, I see *Baucis* and *Philemon* as perfectly before me,

as if some ancient Painter had drawn them; and all the
Pilgrims in the *Canterbury* Tales, their Humours, their
Features, and the very Dress, as distinctly as if I had
supp'd with them at the *Tabard* in *Southwark*: Yet even
there, too, the Figures of *Chaucer* are much more lively,
and set in a better Light: Which though I have not time to
prove; yet I appeal to the Reader, and am sure he will
clear me from Partiality. The Thoughts and Words remain
to be consider'd, in the Comparison of the two Poets; and
I have sav'd my self one half of that Labour, by owning
that *Ovid* liv'd when the *Roman* Tongue was in its Meridian;
Chaucer, in the Dawning of our Language: Therefore that
Part of the Comparison stands not on an equal Foot, any
more than the Diction of *Ennius* and *Ovid*; or of *Chaucer*
and our present *English*. The Words are given up as a Post
not to be defended in our Poet, because he wanted the
Modern Art of Fortifying. The Thoughts remain to be consider'd: And they are to be measur'd only by their Propriety; that is, as they flow more or less naturally from
the Persons describ'd, on such and such Occasions. The
Vulgar Judges, which are Nine Parts in Ten of all Nations,
who call Conceits and Jingles Wit, who see *Ovid* full of
them, and *Chaucer* altogether without them, will think me
little less than mad for preferring the *Englishman* to the
Roman: Yet, with their leave, I must presume to say, that
the Things they admire are only glittering Trifles, and
so far from being Witty, that in a serious Poem they are
nauseous, because they are unnatural. Wou'd any Man, who
is ready to die for Love, describe his Passion like *Nar-*
cissus? Wou'd he think of *inopem me copia fecit*, and a
Dozen more of such Expressions, pour'd on the Neck of one
another, and signifying all the same Thing? If this were
Wit, was this a Time to be witty, when the poor Wretch,
was in the Agony of Death? This is just *John Littlewit*,
in *Bartholomew Fair*, who had a Conceit (as he tells you)
left him in his Misery; a miserable Conceit. On these
Occasions the Poet shou'd endeavour to raise Pity: But,
instead of this, *Ovid* is tickling you to laugh. *Virgil*
never made use of such Machines when he was moving you to
commiserate the Death of *Dido*: He would not destroy what
he was building. *Chaucer* makes *Arcite* violent in his
Love, and unjust in the Pursuit of it: Yet, when he came
to die, he made him think more reasonably: He repents not
of his Love, for that had alter'd his Character; but ack-
nowledges the Injustice of his Proceedings, and resigns
Emilia to *Palamon*. What would *Ovid* have done on this
Occasion? He would certainly have made *Arcite* witty on
his Death-bed. He had complain'd he was further off from
Possession, by being so near, and a thousand such Boyisms,

which *Chaucer* rejected as below the Dignity of the Subject.
They who think otherwise, would by the same Reason, prefer
Lucan and *Ovid* to *Homer* and *Virgil,* and *Martial* to all
Four of them. As for the Turn of Words, in which *Ovid*
particularly excels all Poets; they are sometimes a Fault,
and sometimes a Beauty, as they are us'd properly or im-
properly; but in strong Passions always to be shunn'd, because Passions are serious, and will admit no Playing.
The *French* have a high Value for them; and I confess, they
are often what they call Delicate, when they are intro-
duc'd with Judgment; but *Chaucer* writ with more Simplicity,
and follow'd Nature more closely, than to use them. I
have thus far, to the best of my Knowledge, been an upright Judge betwixt the Parties in Competition, not med-
ling with the Design nor the Disposition of it; because
the Design was not their own; and in the disposing of it
they were equal. It remains that I say somewhat of *Chaucer* in particular.

   In the first place, as he is the Father of *English*
Poetry, so I hold him in the same Degree of Veneration as
the *Grecians* held *Homer*, or the *Romans Virgil*: He is a
perpetual Fountain of good Sense; learn'd in all Sciences;
and, therefore speaks properly on all Subjects: As he knew
what to say, so he knows also when to leave off; a Conti-
nence which is practis'd by few Writers, and scarcely by
any of the Ancients, excepting *Virgil* and *Horace*. One of
our late great Poets is sunk in his Reputation, because he
cou'd never forgive any Conceit which came in his way; but
swept like a Drag-net, great and small. There was plenty
enough, but the Dishes were ill sorted; whole Pyramids of
Sweet-meats for Boys and Women; but little of solid Meat
for Men: All this proceeded not from any want of Knowledge, but of Judgment; neither did he want that in discerning the Beauties and Faults of other Poets; but only
indulg'd himself in the Luxury of Writing; and perhaps
knew it was a Fault, but hoped the Reader would not find
it. For this Reason, though he must always be thought a
great Poet, he is no longer esteemed a good Writer: And
for Ten Impressions, which his Works have had in so many
successive Years, yet at present a hundred Books are
scarcely purchased once a Twelvemonth: For, as my last
Lord *Rochester* said, though somewhat profanely, *Not being
of God, he could not stand.*

   Chaucer follow'd Nature every where, but was never so
bold to go beyond her: And there is a great Difference of
being *Poeta* and *nimis Poeta,* if we may believe *Catullus,*
as much as betwixt a modest Behaviour and Affectation.
The Verse of *Chaucer*, I confess, is not Harmonious to us;
but 'tis like the Eloquence of one whom *Tacitus* commends,

it was *auribus istius temporis accommodata*: They who liv'd
with him, and some time after him, thought it Musical; and
it continues so even in our Judgment, if compar'd with the
Numbers of *Lidgate* and *Gower*, his Contemporaries: There is
the rude Sweetness of a *Scotch* Tune in it, which is natural
and pleasing, though not perfect. 'Tis true, I cannot go
so far as he who publish'd the last Edition of him; for he
would make us believe the Fault is in our Ears, and that
there were really Ten Syllables in a Verse where we find
but Nine: But this Opinion is not worth confuting; 'tis
so gross and obvious an Errour, that common Sense (which
is a Rule in everything but Matters of Faith and Revelation) must convince the Reader, that Equality of Numbers,
in every Verse which we call *Heroick*, was either not known,
or not always practis'd, in *Chaucer*'s Age. It were an
easie Matter to produce some thousands of his Verses,
which are lame for want of half a Foot, and sometimes a
whole one, and which no Pronunciation can make otherwise.
We can only say, that he liv'd in the Infancy of our
Poetry, and that nothing is brought to Perfection at the
first. We must be Children before we grow Men. There was
an *Ennius*, and in process of Time a *Lucilius*, and a *Lucre-
tius*, before *Virgil* and *Horace*; even after *Chaucer* there
was a *Spencer*, a *Harrington*, a *Fairfax*, before *Waller* and
Denham were in being: And our Numbers were in their Nonage
till these last appear'd. I need say little of his Parentage, Life, and Fortunes: They are to be found at large
in all the Editions of his Works. He was employ'd abroad,
and favour'd by *Edward* the Third, *Richard* the Second, and
Henry the Fourth, and was Poet, as I suppose, to all Three
of them. In *Richard*'s Time, I doubt, he was a little dipt
in the Rebellion of the Commons; and being Brother-in-Law
to *John of Ghant*, it was no wonder if he follow'd the
Fortunes of that Family; and was well with *Henry* the
Fourth when he depos'd his Predecessor. Neither is it to
be admir'd, that *Henry*, who was a wise as well as a valiant Prince, who claim'd by Succession, and was sensible
that his Title was not sound, but was rightfully in *Morti-
mer*, who had married the Heir of *York*; it was not to be
admir'd, I say, if that great Politician should be pleas'd
to have the greatest Wit of those Times in his Interests,
and to be the Trumpet of his Praises. *Augustus* had given
him the Example, by the Advice of *Mecaenas*, who recommended *Virgil* and *Horace* to him; whose Praises helped to make

him Popular while he was alive, and after his Death have
made him Precious to Posterity. As for the Religion of
our Poet, he seems to have some little Byas towards the
Opinions of *Wickliff*, after *John of Ghant* his Patron;
somewhat of which appears in the Tale of *Piers Plowman*:
Yet I cannot blame him for inveighing so sharply against
the Vices of the Clergy in his Age: Their Pride, their
Ambition, their Pomp, their Avarice, their Worldly Interest, deserv'd the Lashes which he gave them, both in that,
and in most of his *Canterbury Tales*: Neither has his Contemporary *Boccace*, spar'd them. Yet both those Poets
liv'd in much esteem, with good and holy Men in Orders:
For the Scandal which is given by particular Priests reflects not on the Sacred Function. *Chaucer's Monk,* his
Chanon, and his *Fryar*, took not from the Character of his
Good Parson. A Satyrical Poet is the Check of the Laymen
on bad Priests....

I have followed *Chaucer*, in his Character of a Holy
Man, and have enlarg'd on that Subject with some Pleasure,
reserving to myself the Right, if I shall think fit hereafter, to describe another sort of Priests, such as are
more easily to be found than the Good Parson; such as
have given the last Blow to Christianity in this Age, by a
Practice so contrary to their Doctrine. But this will
keep cold till another time. In the mean while, I take up
Chaucer where I left him. He must have been a Man of a
most wonderful comprehensive Nature, because, as it has
been truly observ'd of him, he has taken into the Compass
of his *Canterbury Tales* the various Manners and Humours (as
we now call them) of the whole *English* Nation, in his Age.
Not a single Character has escap'd him. All his Pilgrims
are severally distinguish'd from each other; and not only
in their Inclinations, but in their very Phisiognomies and
Persons. *Baptista Porta* could not have describ'd their
Natures better, than by the Marks·which the Poet gives
them. The Matter and Manner of their Tales, and of their
Telling, are so suited to their different Educations,
Humours, and Callings, that each of them would be improper
in any other Mouth. Even the grave and serious Characters
are distinguish'd by their several sorts of Gravity: Their
Discourses are such as belong to their Age, their Calling,
and their Breeding; such as are becoming of them, and of
them only. Some of his Persons are Vicious, and some Vertuous; some are unlearn'd, or (as *Chaucer* calls them)
Lewd, and some are Learn'd. Even the Ribaldry of the Low
Characters is different: the *Reeve*, the *Miller*, and the
Cook, are several Men, and are distinguish'd from each
other, as much as the mincing Lady-Prioress, and the
broad-speaking, gap-tooth'd Wife of *Bathe*. But enough of

this: There is such a Variety of Game springing up before
me, that I am distracted in my Choice, and know not which
to follow.   'Tis sufficient to say according to the Proverb, that here is God's Plenty.   We have our Fore-fathers
and Great Grand-dames all before us, as they were in
Chaucer's Days; their general Characters are still remaining in Mankind, and even in *England*, though they are
call'd by other Names than those of *Moncks*, and *Fryars*,
and *Chanons*, and *Lady Abbesses*, and *Nuns*: For Mankind is
ever the same, and nothing lost out of Nature, though
every thing is alter'd.   May I have leave to do myself the
Justice, (since my Enemies will do me none, and are so far
from granting me to be a good Poet, that they will not
allow me so much as to be a Christian, or a Moral Man),
may I have leave, I say, to inform my Reader, that I have
confin'd my Choice to such Tales of *Chaucer* as savour
nothing of Immodesty.   If I had desir'd more to please
than to instruct, the *Reve*, the *Miller*, the *Shipman*, the
Merchant, the *Sumner*, and above all, the *Wife of Bathe*, in
the Prologue to her Tale, would have procur'd me as many
Friends and Readers, as there are *Beaux* and Ladies of
Pleasure in the Town.   But I will no more offend against
Good Manners: I am sensible as I ought to be of the Scandal I have given by my loose Writings; and make what Reparation I am able, by this Public Acknowledgment.   If anything of this Nature, or of Profaneness, be crept into
these Poems, I am so far from defending it, that I disown
it.   *Totum hoc indictum volo.*   *Chaucer* makes another
manner of Apologie for his broad-speaking, and Boccace
makes the like; but I will follow neither of them.   Our
Country-man, in the end of his Characters, before the
Canterbury Tales, thus excuses the Ribaldry, which is very
gross in many of his Novels.

> But firste, I pray you of your courtesy,
> That ye ne arrete it nought my villany,
> Though that I plainly speak in this mattere, [etc.].

[Quotes 'General Prologue' 725-42.   All sixteenth- and
seventeenth-century editions read *follie* for *villany*,
l.726, except Speght, 1598.]

Yet if a Man should have enquir'd of *Boccace* or of
Chaucer, what need they had of introducing such Characters, where obscene Words were proper in their Mouths,
but very undecent to he heard; I know not what Answer they
could have made: For that Reason, such Tales shall be left
untold by me.   You have here a *Specimen* of *Chaucer*'s Language, which is so obsolete, that his Sense is scarce to

be understood; and you have likewise more than one Example
of his unequal Numbers, which were mention'd before. Yet
many of his Verses consist of Ten Syllables, and the Words
not much behind our present *English*: as for Example, these
two Lines, in the Description of the Carpenter's Young
Wife:

>   *Wincing she was, as is a jolly Colt,*
>   *Long as a Mast, and upright as a Bolt.*

I have almost done with *Chaucer*, when I have answer'd some
Objections relating to my present Work. I find some
People are offended that I have turn'd these Tales into
modern *English*; because they think them unworthy of my
Pains, and look on *Chaucer* as a dry, old-fashion'd Wit,
not worth receiving. I have often heard the late Earl of
Leicester say, that Mr. *Cowley* himself was of that opinion; who, having read him over at my Lord's Request, declared he had no Taste of him. I dare not advance my
Opinion against the Judgment of so great an Author: But I
think it fair, however, to leave the Decision to the Publick: Mr. *Cowley*, was too modest to set up for a Dicta-
tour; and, being shock'd perhaps with his old Style, never
examin'd into the depth of his good Sense. *Chaucer*, I
confess, is a rough Diamond, and must first be polish'd,
e'er he shines. I deny not likewise, that, living in our
early Days of Poetry, he writes not always of a piece; but
sometimes mingles trivial Things with those of greater
Moment. Sometimes also, though not often, he runs riot,
like *Ovid*, and knows not when he has said enough. But
there are more great Wits beside *Chaucer*, whose Fault is
their Excess of Conceits, and those ill sorted. An
Author is not to write all he can, but only all he ought.
Having observ'd this Redundancy in *Chaucer*, (as it is an
easie Matter for a Man of ordinary Parts to find a Fault
in one of greater,) I have not ty'd my self to a Literal
Translation; but have often omitted what I judg'd unnecessary, or not of Dignity enough to appear in the Company of
better Thoughts. I have presum'd farther in some Places,
and added somewhat of my own where I thought my Author was
deficient, and had not given his Thoughts their true
Lustre, for want of Words in the Beginning of our Language. And to this I was the more embolden'd, because,
(if I may be permitted to say it of my self) I found I had
a Soul congenial to his, and that I had been conversant in
the same Studies. Another Poet, in another Age, may take
the same Liberty with my Writings; if at least they live
long enough to deserve Correction. It was also necessary
sometimes to restore the Sense of *Chaucer*, which was lost

or mangled in the Errors of the Press: Let this Example
suffice at present in the Story of *Palamon* and *Arcite*,
where the temple of *Diana* is describ'd, you find these
Verses in all the Editions of our Author:

> *There saw I* Dane *turned unto a Tree,*
> *I mean not the goddess* Diane,
> *But* Venus *Daughter, which that hight* Dane.

Which, after a little Consideration, I knew was to be
reform'd into this Sense, that *Daphne*, the daughter of
Peneus, was turn'd into a Tree. I durst not make thus
bold with *Ovid*, lest some future *Milbourn* should arise,
and say, I varied from my Author, because I understood him
not.

But there are other Judges, who think I ought not to
have translated *Chaucer* into *English*, out of a quite contrary Notion: They suppose there is a certain Veneration
due to his old Language; and that it is little less than
Profanation and Sacrilege to alter it. They are farther
of opinion, that somewhat of his good Sense will suffer in
this Transfusion, and much of the Beauty of his Thoughts
will infallibly be lost, which appear with more Grace in
their old Habit. Of this Opinion was that excellent
Person, whom I mention'd, the late Earl of *Leicester*, who
valued *Chaucer* as much as Mr. *Cowley* despis'd him. My
Lord dissuaded me from this Attempt, (for I was thinking
of it some Years before his Death,) and his Authority
prevail'd so far with me, as to defer my Undertaking
while he liv'd, in deference to him: Yet my Reason was
not convinc'd with what he urg'd against it. If the
first End of a Writer be to be understood, then, as his
Language grows obsolete, his Thoughts must grow obscure,
multa renascuntur, quae nunc cecidere; cadentque quae
nunc sunt in honore vocabula, si volet usus, quem penes
arbitrium est et jus et norma loquendi. When an ancient
Word for its Sound and Significancy, deserves to be
reviv'd, I have that reasonable Veneration for Antiquity,
to restore it. All beyond this is Superstition. Words
are not like Land-marks, so sacred as never to be remov'd:
Customs are chang'd, and even Statutes are silently
repeal'd, when the Reason ceases for which they were
enacted. As for the other Part of the Argument, that his
Thoughts will lose of their original Beauty by the innovation of Words; in the first place, not only their Beauty,
but their Being is lost, when they are no longer understood, which is the present Case. I grant, that something
must be lost in all Transfusion, that is, in all Translations; but the Sense will remain, which would otherwise

be lost, or at least be maim'd, when it is scarce intelligible; and that but to a few. How few are there who can
read *Chaucer*, so as to understand him perfectly? And if
imperfectly, then with less Profit, and no Pleasure. 'Tis
not for the Use of some old *Saxon* Friends, that I have
taken these Pains with him: Let them neglect my Version,
because they have no need of it. I made it for their
sakes who understand Sense and Poetry, as well as they;
when that Poetry and Sense is put into Words which they
understand. I will go farther, and dare to add, that what
Beauties I lose in some Places, I give to others which had
them not originally: But in this I may be partial to my
self; let the Reader judge, and I submit to his Decision.
Yet I think I have just Occasion to complain of them, who
because they understand *Chaucer*, would deprive the greater
part of their Countrymen of the same Advantage, and hoord
him up, as Misers do their Grandam Gold, only to look on
it themselves, and hinder others from making use of it.
In sum, I seriously protest, that no Man ever had, or can
have, a greater Veneration for *Chaucer* than my self. I
have translated some part of his Works, only that I might
perpetuate his Memory, or at least refresh it, amongst my
Countrymen. If I have alter'd him any where for the
better, I must at the same time acknowledge, that I could
have done nothing without him: *Facile est inventis
addere,* is no great Commendation; but I am not so vain to
think I have deserv'd a greater. I will conclude what I
have to say of him singly, with this one Remark: A Lady of
my Acquaintance, who keeps a kind of Correspondence with
some Authors of the Fair Sex in *France*, has been inform'd
by them, that *Mademoiselle de Scudery,* who is as old as
Sibyl, and inspir'd like her by the same God of Poetry, is
at this time translating *Chaucer* into modern *French*. From
which I gather, that he has been formerly translated into
the old *Provencall*; (for, how she should come to understand Old *English*, I know not). But the Matter of Fact
being true, it makes me think, that there is something in
it like Fatality; that after certain Periods of Time, the
Fame and Memory of Great Wits should be renew'd, as
Chaucer is both in *France* and *England*. If this be wholly
Chance, 'tis extraordinary; and I dare not call it more,
for fear of being tax'd with Superstition.

Boccace comes last to be consider'd, who, living in the
same Age with *Chaucer*, had the same Genius, and followed
the same Studies: Both writ Novels, and each of them
cultivated his Mother-Tongue: But the greatest Resemblance
of our two Modern Authors being in their familiar Style,
and pleasing way of relating Comical Adventures, I may
pass it over, because I have translated nothing from

Boccace of that Nature. In the serious part of Poetry,
the Advantage is wholly on *Chaucer*'s Side; for though the
Englishman has borrow'd many Tales from the *Italian*, yet
it appears, that those of *Boccace* were not generally of
his own making, but taken from Authors of former ages, and
by him only modell'd: So that what there was of Invention,
in either of them, may be judg'd equal. But *Chaucer* has
refin'd on *Boccace*, and has mended the Stories which he
has borrow'd, in his way of telling; though Prose allows
more Liberty of Thought, and the Expression is more easie,
when unconfin'd by Numbers. Our Countryman carries Weight,
and yet wins the Race at disadvantage. I desire not the
Reader should take my Word; and, therefore, I will set two
of their Discourses on the same Subject, in the same
Light, for every Man to judge betwixt them. I translated
Chaucer first, and amongst the rest, pitch'd on The Wife
of *Bath*'s Tale; not daring, as I have said, to adventure
on her Prologue, because 'tis too licentious: There
Chaucer introduces an old Woman of mean Parentage, whom a
youthful Knight of Noble Blood, was forc'd to marry, and
consequently loath'd her: The Crone being in bed with him
on the wedding Night, and finding his Aversion, endeavours
to win his Affection by Reason, and speaks a good Word for
herself, (as who could blame her?) in hope to mollifie the
sullen Bridegroom. She takes her Topiques from the Benefits of Poverty, the Advantages of old Age and Ugliness,
the Vanity of Youth, and the silly Pride of Ancestry and
Titles, without inherent Vertue, which is the true Nobility. When I had clos'd *Chaucer*; I return'd to *Ovid*, and
translated some more of his Fables; and, by this time, had
so far forgotten The Wife of *Bath*'s Tale, that when I took
up *Boccace*, unawares I fell on the same Argument of preferring Virtue to Nobility of Blood, and Titles, in the
Story of *Sigismonda*; which I had certainly avoided for the
Resemblance of the two Discourses, if my Memory had not
fail'd me. Let the Reader weigh both; and if he thinks me
partial to *Chaucer*, 'tis in him to right *Boccace*.
   I prefer in our Countryman, far above all his other
Stories, the Noble Poem of *Palamon* and *Arcite*, which is of
the *Epique* kind, and perhaps not much inferiour to the
Ilias or the *Aeneis*: the Story is more pleasing than either
of them, the Manners as perfect, the Diction as poetical,
the Learning as deep and various; and the Disposition full
as artful: only it includes a greater length of time; as
taking up seven years at least; but *Aristotle* has left un-
decided the Duration of the Action; which yet is easily
reduc'd into the Compass of a year, by a Narration of what
preceded the Return of *Palamon* to *Athens*. I had thought
for the Honour of our Nation, and more particularly for

his, whose Laurel, tho' unworthy, I have worn after him,
that this Story was of *English* Growth, and *Chaucer*'s own:
But I was undeceiv'd by *Boccace*; for casually looking on
the End of his seventh *Giornata*, I found *Dioneo*, (under
which name he shadows himself,) and *Fiametta*, (who represents his Mistress, the natural Daughter of *Robert*, King
of *Naples*) of whom these Words are spoken. *Dioneo e Fiametta gran pezza cantarono insieme d'Arcita, e di Pale-
mone:* by which it appears, that this Story was written
before the time of *Boccace*; but the Name of its Author
being wholly lost, *Chaucer* is now become an Original; and
I question not but the Poem has receiv'd many Beauties, by
passing through his Noble Hands. Besides this Tale, there
is another of his own Invention, after the manner of the
Provencalls, call'd *The Flower and the Leaf*; with which I
was so particularly pleas'd, both for the Invention and
the Moral; that I cannot hinder myself from recommending
it to the Reader.

67. ALEXANDER POPE, THE PLEASURE OF CHAUCER

1711, 1728-30

Pope (1688-1744), the great satirical poet, was privately
educated and had a generously catholic love of many different kinds of poetry: conscious of Chaucer's antiquity,
he 'modernised' 'The House of Fame'; he also produced an
amusing little 'imitation' more bawdy than anything Chaucer himself actually wrote, and he read Chaucer with pleasure all his life. Extract (a) comes from 'An Essay on
Criticism', 1711 (written 1709), p. 28; and (b) is from
his conversations 1728-30, in 'Anecdotes ... collected
from the Conversations of Mr. Pope ... by the Rev. Joseph
Spence', ed. S.W. Singer, 1820.

(a)

Short is the Date, alas, of *Modern Rhymes*;
And 'tis but just to let 'em live *betimes*.
No longer now that Golden Age appears,
When Patriarch-Wits surviv'd a *thousand* Years

Now Length of Fame (our *second* Life) is lost,
And bare Threescore is all ev'n That can boast:
Our Sons their Father's *failing Language* see,
And such as *Chaucer* is, shall *Dryden* be.

(b)

I read Chaucer still with as much pleasure as almost any
of our poets. He is a master of manners, of description,
and the first tale-teller in the true enlivened natural
way (p. 19).

   There is but little that is worth reading in Gower: he
wants the spirit of poetry, and the descriptiveness, that
are in Chaucer (p. 20).

[Of Addison's comment on Chaucer, No. 65, 1694.] He
wrote it when he was very young; and as such, gave the
characters of some of our best poets in it, only by hear-
say. Thus his character of Chaucer is diametrically opposite to the truth. He blames him for want of humour
(p. 50).

68. JOHN HUGHES, NATIVE STRENGTH

1715

John Hughes (1677-1720), miscellaneous writer, was educated at a dissenting academy, and edited the works of Spenser in 1715, with an Essay on Allegorical Poetry referring
to Chaucer's enduring value (pp. xxvi-vii), which sets
him, like Pope, apart from fashionable ignorance, when
discussing the poet Waller's view that since English is so
changeable poets should write in Latin or Greek if they
wish to be remembered.

Notwithstanding the Disadvantage he has mention'd, we have
two Antient *English* Poets, *Chaucer* and *Spenser*, who may
perhaps be reckon'd as Exceptions to this Remark. These
seem to have taken deep Root, like old *British* Oaks, and
to flourish in defiance of all the Injuries of Time and

Weather. The former is indeed much more obsolete in his
Stile than the latter; but it is owing to an extraordinary
native Strength in both, that they have been able thus far
to survive amidst the Changes of our Tongue, and seem
rather likely, among the Curious at least, to preserve the
Knowledg of our Antient Language, than to be in danger of
being destroy'd with it, and bury'd under its Ruins.

Tho Spenser's Affection to his Master *Chaucer* led him
in many things to copy after him, yet those who have read
both will easily observe that these two Genius's were of
a very different kind. *Chaucer* excell'd in his Characters;
Spenser in his Descriptions. The first study'd Humour,
was an excellent Satirist, and a lively but rough Painter
of the Manners of that rude Age in which he liv'd.

69. DANIEL DEFOE, NOT FIT FOR MODEST PERSONS TO READ

1718

Daniel Defoe (1661?-1731), prolific journalist and novelist, a Dissenter, regards Chaucer as both indecent and
forgotten, in a letter in 'Mist's Weekly Journal', 69,
5 April, in 'Daniel Defoe: His Life and Recently Discovered Writings', ed. W. Lee, 1869, II, 31, reprinted in
Alderson and Henderson, p. 205 (see Bibliographical note).

The inimitable brightness of [Rochester's] Wit has not
been able to preserve [his poems] from being thought
worthy, by wise Men, to be lost, rather than remember'd;
being blacken'd and eclips'd by the Lewdness of their
Stile, so as not to be made fit for Modesty to read or
hear. Jeffrey Chaucer is forgotten upon the same Account;
and tho' that Author is excused, by the unpoliteness of
the Age he lived in, yet his Works are diligently buried,
by most Readers, on that very Principle, that they are not
fit for modest Persons to read.

70.   AMBROSE PHILLIPS (?), BRIGHT IMAGES

1720

A slight, twice-weekly, brief-lived periodical, 'The Free-
Thinker', mostly written probably by Ambrose Phillips,
published a modernisation of 'The Cuckoo and the Nightingale' (now better known as 'The Boke of Cupide') which has
the following introduction, ccxxvii, 24 May 1720.   Phillips (1675-1749) (known as Namby-Pamby), was a pastoral
poet and fellow of St John's College, Cambridge.   The
influence of Dryden is apparent.

I was not willing to let the present Month, the fairest in
the whole Circle of the Year, pass over, without entertaining my youthful Readers of either Sex, with something
suitable to the Gayety of the Season.   And yet, I should
have been greatly at a Loss for a proper Entertainment,
had not a Gentleman, whose Knowledge of the Polite Writers in every Language is the least of his Commendations,
obliged me with a Piece of fine Invention out of *Chaucer*,
which is properly a very elegant *May-poem*....
     It is hard to say, whether the copiousness of *Chaucer*'s
Invention, or the Liveliness of his Imagination, is most
to be admired through all his Writings.   He flourished
above Three Hundred Years ago: And yet through the Cloud
of his antiquated Language, his Images still shine out
with greater Brightness, than those, which appear in any
of our succeeding Poets, if we except *Spencer*, and *Shakespear*, and *Milton*.   He was a great Master of Perspicuity
and Simplicity in all his Narrations; and his Expression
is always precise to the Justness of his Ideas.... *Chaucer*
is, likewise, a diligent observer of Nature, whether he
deals in Realities or in Fables.

71.   JOHN DART AND WILLIAM THOMAS, THUS CHAUCER PAINTED
      LIFE

1721, 1722

John Dart (d. 1730), attorney, clergyman, antiquary and
author, is of unknown education. He contributed the Life
of Chaucer to Urry's edition of 1721, sections of which
constitute extract (a), Sig. b2 et seq. He complained in
a later work ('Westmonasterium', 1723, I, p. 87), that he
was not allowed to revise his work, and that it was
altered without his knowledge or consent, before printing.
According to Timothy Thomas's annotations, in the British
Museum copy, the reviser was W. Thomas, who was concerned
especially in the account of the works. The Life perpetu-
ates the old errors, but also makes sensible remarks,
which may be Thomas's. Some inconsistency in the question
of metre may be due to his intervention. See Alderson and
Henderson. Extract (b) consists of sections from Dart's
'A Poem on Chaucer and his Writings', T. Paine, 1722,
pp. 1ff., discovered and printed by Alderson and Henderson, pp. 209-10, Copyright © 1970 by The Regents of the
University of California, reprinted by permission of the
University of California Press.

(a)

[(Sig. b2) After the usual (erroneous) account of Chaucer's education in both universities, and of foreign
travel, the writer continues that it is probable that
Chaucer acquired] knowledge of our Laws in his youth, in
order to qualify himself for publick Affairs, in which he
afterwards was concerned.

   But he had not long followed those studies, before his
singular accomplishments were discovered by some persons
at Court, whither he next made his approaches. A glorious
and successful Reign, as it affords subjects for the
praises of the Learned, so it gives them encouragement to
employ their abilities on such occasions; and *Edw*. III.
who was a discerning Prince to judge of, and generous to
reward Learning, invited Men of Letters to him, and by his
example induced his Court to encourage them: So that in
his Reign Valour was not more esteemed than Learning, and
Cowardice and Ignorance were equally despised. The Court
at that time consisted of all that was great and splendid,
and every thing that could be desired contributed to make

it the most glorious in *Europe*. A long and happy Reign,
successful in Victories abroad, filled it with Heroes, and
a just Administration at home supply'd it with Men of
Learning. These are so inseparably linked together for
the encouragement of each other, that where there are men
of Valour, there can be no Slavery and Oppression, and
where there is Slavery and Oppression, there can be no Men
of Learning. They equally flourished in this Reign, being
encouraged by a Prince who was Master of both, and applauded by a Court of Ladies remarkable for Beauty, Wit and
Gaiety. In short, there was nothing going forward in that
Court but perpetual Mirth, Tilts and Tournaments, and Rom-
antick Gallantry, which has been only parallel'd by the
late Reign of K. *Charles* the Second. And how well qualify'd our Poet was to be a Member of such an Assembly, we
may judge by his learning, wit, amorous disposition, gay
humour and gallantry: To which his Person gave no small
addition, being about the age of Thirty (as appears by a
Picture of him about that age) of a fair, beautiful complexion, his lips red and full, his size of a just *medium*,
and his port and air graceful and majestick. So that
every Ornament that could claim the approbation of the
Great and Fair, his Abilities to record the Valour of the
one, and celebrate the Beauty of the other, and his wit
and gentile behaviour to converse with both, conspired to
make him a compleat Courtier....

Our Poet being thus placed near the King, found respect and encouragement from all the chief persons of the
Court: Queen *Philippa*, a Princess of extraordinary merit,
esteemed him; *John* of *Gaunt* Duke of *Lancaster* had a
singular value for him, as had likewise his Dutchess
Blanch, at whose request he made the Poem called *La Priere
de notre Dame*. The Lady *Margaret*, the King's Daughter and
Countess of *Pembroke*, was the chief of his Patronesses,
and would frequently complement him upon his Poems. But
this is not to be meant of his *Canterbury Tales*, they
being written in the latter part of his Life, when the
Courtier and the fine Gentleman gave way to solid Sense
and plain Descriptions. In his Love pieces he was obliged
to have the strictest regard to Modesty and Decency; the
Ladies at that time insisting so much upon the nicest
punctilio's of honour, that it was highly criminal to depreciate their Sex, or do any thing that might offend
Virtue: The first of these *Chaucer* had been guilty of,
which he afterwards attoned by the *Legend of Good Women*;
a Task enjoined him by the Lady *Margaret*, whom he veils
under the name of the Daisy, as he does in several other
pieces....

Thus beloved, esteemed and honoured, he spent his

younger years in a constant attendance upon the Court, and
for the most part living near it, when residing at *Woodstock*, in a square stone house near the Park Gate, still
called *Chaucer's House*. That this was the chief place of
his abode, appears by his frequent descriptions of the
Park; as particularly a *Park walled with green stone*,
that being the first Park walled in *England*, and not many
years before his time. In most of his pieces, where he
designs an imaginary Scene, he certainly copies it from a
real Landskape: So in his *Cuckow* and *Nightingale*, the
Morning walk he takes was such as at this day may be
traced from his House through part of the Park, and down
by the Brook into the Vale under *Blenheim* Castle, as certainly as we may assert that Maples instead of *Phylireas*,
were the ornaments round the Bower; which place he likewise describes in his Dream, as a white Castle standing
upon a hill; the Scene in that Poem being laid in *Woodstock* Park.

   (Sig. cl) Most of those about the King countenanced
Wickliffe in a particular manner, as the Lord *Latimer*, Sir
Richard Sturry, Sir *Lewis Clifford*, &c. And *Capgrave*
asserts that the King himself was a Favourer of his
Opinions.

   And now the Parliament intermeddling with the Affairs
of the Church, Pope *Gregory* IX. thought it high time to
put a stop to those Proceedings, and therefore issued out
a Bull directed to the Archbishop of *Canterbury*, and the
Bishop of *London*, for apprehending *Wickliffe*; whereupon
the Bishop convened a Synod at St. *Paul*'s, where, upon
citation *Wickliffe* appeared, and with him his Patron the
Duke of *Lancaster*, and *Piercy* Lord Marshal. A Quarrel
happening between the Duke of *Lancaster* and the Bishop of
London about *Wickliffe*'s sitting down, the Duke told the
Bishop he would pull down his pride, and that of all the
Prelacy in *England*, with other opprobrious words; upon
which the *Londoners* rose, and plunder'd his Palace of the
Savoy, and reversed his Arms, the Duke himself hardly
escaping their fury.

   Our *Chaucer* had no small hand in furthering these Proceedings, both by his publick Interest, and his Writings;
tho' I cannot go so far as to suppose he scurrilously
reviled the Established Religion of those times, and
therefore cannot think that either the *Plowman's Tale* or
Jack Upland were written by him, as shall be further discussed in the Account of his Works: But that he was a
Favourer of the *Lollards* (as were likewise most of his
friends, and particularly *Occleve*) is evident from several
places in his Writings, where he bitterly inveighs against
the Priests and Fryers: Not that he disliked all of that

Order; for he mentions Fryer *John Some* and Fryer *Nicholas
Lenne*, or *Lynne*, with respect, calling them *Reverent
Clerkes*, and expresses his regard for the secular Clergy
who lived up to their Profession, in his Description of
the Parson.   Nor was he disesteemed by the Clergy of those
times; *Lidgate*, who was a Monk of St. *Edmondsbury*, and
several others entertaining a great reverence for him, and
speaking of him with the utmost respect: Nor was he less
esteemed by *Gower*, tho' a violent Bigot to the Church of
Rome, and a perpetual exclaimer against *Wickliffe* and his
Followers.

(Sig. c3) *Chaucer* how much soever he had espoused those
[Wycliffe's] Opinions, thought it prudence to conceal
them more than he had done, seeing the inconveniences and
danger they had occasioned; so that after the Prosecution
by *Rich.* II. and the Duke of *Lancaster*'s changing his mind,
he thought it proper to be more circumspect.   Nor doth it
appear that at any time time he ran all the lengths of
that Opinion.   His resentments were chiefly against the
personal Vices of the Clergy, not their Doctrines; for the
Pilgrimage to *Canterbury* is spoken of with reverence; and
he calls *Becket* the *holy blissful Martyr*: And the Parson,
tho' he would not *ren to St. Powles* to procure Livings,
makes one in the Expedition to *Canterbury*.   This I say,
not as if that Journey was real; but *Chaucer* would never
have been guilty of so great an impropriety as to make
Persons act contrary to their Opinions.   Nor did even the
Leaders of that Party scruple the Ceremonies then used:
They opposed them in opinion, but seldom differed from
them in practice.   Even *Wickliffe* himself always conformed,
and held his Living of *Lutterworth* without interruption,
and died in it of a Fit of the Palsy, which seized him
while he was saying Mass.   But *Chaucer* differed much from
them even in Opinion; for in his *Testament of Love*, he
confesses the Real Presence; which passage, because it
exposes the neglect of Religion in his time, and shews his
regard for Divine Worship, shall be here set down at large.

(Sig. c4) The Duke [of Lancaster] passing over Sea, his
Friends felt all the malice of the opposite Party, which
had long waited for revenge, and in order to it, sought
all possible means of oppressing them.   This put the
others upon calling in a number of the Populace to their
assistance, which is the general refuge of an oppressed
Party.   By these means several popular Commotions ensued,
and particularly that in the City of *London*.   As in this
affair our Poet was no unartful Prompter behind the Curtain, so he felt the consequences of it in his downfal
and ruin.   Strict search was made for *Chaucer*, but he made
his escape into *Hainault*, and afterwards into *France*, and

finding the King resolved to get him if possible into his
hands, (as the fittest person to discover the Abettors of
those Commotions) he fled thence into *Zealand*, with this
intent chiefly (as he says) *their privitie to conceale*.

   Several of the Accomplices in this affair were with
him, whom he supported in their Exile, while the chief
Ringleaders (except *Northampton*, who was condemned at
Reading, upon the evidence of his Clerk) had here at
London made their peace, by acknowledging their Crime, and
making Submission, and had now forgot the Honour and
Integrity of *Chaucer*, who suffered Exile to secure their
Secrets. Nay, to such a base height of Ingratitude were
they arrived, that they wished his death, and endeavoured
it, by keeping all supplies of Money from him: And while
he expended his Fortune in removing from place to place,
and in assisting his Fellow-exiles, he was so far from
receiving any assistance at home, that his Apartments were
let, and the Money received for Rent was never accounted
for to him; nor could he recover any from those who owed
it him, they being fully perswaded it was impossible for
him ever to return into *England*. The Government still
pursuing their Resentment against him and his friends,
they were constrained to leave *Zealand*; and *Chaucer* having
no possible means left of struggling longer with the difficulties of Exile and Poverty, and finding no security
wherever he fled, chusing to submit his Life to the Laws
of his Country, rather than lose it through hunger and
want in foreign parts, returned into *England*.

   He had not been long here before he was arrested by
order from the King, and imprisoned (as it is probable) in
the Tower of *London*. And now the Government thought they
had it in their power to make a full Discovery of the late
Rebellion, and sending for him, told him that in order to
obtain Mercy of the King, his only way was to confess the
secrets of his Treason, and discover the Confederates in
it; desiring him to propose in which manner those differences might be composed. But he a long while evaded all
the arts used to make him confess, and was very unwilling
to bring the malice of so powerful a Party upon him by
betraying their secrets, which he says he conceal'd longer
than he ought; but *the King and his Princes* (to use his
words) having obliged him upon Oath to declare what he
knew, and *with huge words and grete* urged him to confess,
and watching his words strictly and narrowly to catch him,
if they could, varying in his Confession, he very freely
disclosed all he knew, and impeached the Persons concerned
with him; and not only so, but (according to the custom of
Trials at that time) offered to prove the truth of his
Confession by Combat....

(Sig. d1) What the consequence of this Discovery was
with respect to his Accomplices doth not appear. It
brought upon him the ill will of most people, who (as he
says) called him *false*, *lyer*, *base*, *ingratefull*, &c. But
the King regarding him as a person beloved by his Grand-
father, and a faithful servant to himself, pardoned him.

This miserable condition, so different from his former
prosperity, as it is a proof of the uncertainty of human
Happiness, so it gave occasion to his writing that excellent Treatise called *The Testament of Love*....

Thus dispossessed of places, power and wealth, through
a misapplication of them and an unguarded conduct, he
retired to *Woodstock*; and weary of a long series of hurry,
noise, danger and confusion, he shifted it for quiet and
the calm pleasures of a studious safety, which produced
his excellent Treatise of the *Astrolabe*, which is calculated for the Latitude of *Woodstock*, being a small matter
different (as he says) from that of *Oxford*. It appears
from that piece, that the severe treatment which *Chaucer*
received from the Government did not make him a firm Male-
content; for he strictly enjoins his Son to pray for the
King.

(Sig. d3) But to return to our *Chaucer*: The King, about
the Twenty second year of his Reign, confirmed again to
him the Grant for the Pipe of Wine annually; and by means
of these Grants and the Influence he recovered by the Duke
of *Lancaster*'s Marriage, he again grew to a considerable
share of wealth. But being now near Seventy years of age,
and tired with a tedious view of hurried greatness, he
thought it high time to withdraw from the Court Stage,
where he had acted so considerable a part and with such
various success, to consider and at distant leisure reflect upon what he had been doing. In order to which, he
retired to *Dunnington* Castle near *Newbury*, where he spent
the two or three last years of his Life.

(Sig. d4) It stands in a pleasant Park, and is at present the Estate of *Robert Packer* Esq; in right of his Wife,
one of the Daughters and Coheirs of Sir *Humphrey Winch-
combe* of *Bucklebury*. In this Park stood an Oak called
Chaucer's Oak, under which he is said to have written
several of his Poems. Mr. *Evelin* gives a particular
account of this Tree, and says there were three of them
planted by *Chaucer*; the King's Oak, the Queen's Oak, and
Chaucer's Oak. In this pleasant Retirement *Chaucer* spent
the few last years of his Life, living in honour, and
esteemed by all, famous for his Learning, not only in
England, but in foreign Countries.

He was universally beloved, and even Party-Zeal could
not raise him Enemies. Of Friendships he selected the

best, being familiar with, and received by all the Men of
Learning at that time....

(Sig. e3) He was, as before observed, of a middle
stature, the latter part of his Life inclinable to be fat
and corpulent, as appears by the Host's bantering him in
the Journey to *Canterbury*, and comparing shapes with him.
His face was fleshy, his features just and regular, his
complexion fair, and somewhat pale, his hair of a dusky
yellow, short and thin; the hair of his beard in two
forked tufts, of a wheat colour; his forehead broad and
smooth; his eyes inclining usually to the ground, which is
intimated by the Host's words; his whole face full of
liveliness, a calm easy sweetness, and a studious venerable aspect. As in the Characters of his Pilgrims he so
naturally described them, that the nicest pencil could not
possibly give us so full an Idea of them as his words; so
likewise he has given us as just a Picture of himself....
The down-cast look, the strict attention, the labouring
thought, the hand waving for silence, the manner of address in speaking, the smooth familiar way of arguing, the
respectful way of starting his objections, and in short
every expression in that dispute figures a lively Image of
him in the mind of the Reader.

As to his Temper, he had a mixture of the gay, the
modest, and the grave. The spright lines of his humour
was more distinguished by his Writings, than by his Appearance; which gave occasion to *Margaret* Countess of *Pembroke* often to rally him upon his silent Modesty in company, telling him, that his absence was more agreeable to
her than his conversation, since the first was productive
of agreeable Pieces of Wit in his Writings, but the latter
was filled with a modest deference, and a too distant respect. We see nothing merry or jocose in his behaviour
with his Pilgrims, but a silent attention to their mirth,
rather than any mixture of his own; and when he is called
upon by *Harry Baily* the Host, and rouzed out of his
thoughtful Lethargy to tell a Tale, he endeavours to put
it off by singing an old Ballad; but that not satisfying
the Company; the Tale he tells is grave, moral and
instructive.

In his early years his Temper and Inclination were
somewhat too gay and loose; nor did even Marriage confine
his amorous humour, as appears by the Banter which passed
between him and his Man in some Verses written by them
with a Diamond in the glass Window where he lived; and he
himself speaks with a penitent concern of the many wanton
Songs he had writ in his younger years. Towards the
latter part of his Life, the gay Gentleman gave way to
the grave Philosopher and pious Divine.

When disengaged from publick Affairs, his time was
entirely spent in study and reading: So agreeable to him
was this exercise, that he says, he preferred it to all
other sports and diversions. He lived within himself,
neither desirous to hear nor busy to concern himself with
the affairs of his Neighbours. His course of living was
temperate and regular; he went to rest with the Sun, and
rose before it, and by that means enjoyed the pleasures of
the better part of the day, his morning walk and fresh
contemplations. This gave him the advantage of describing
the Morning in so lively a manner as he does everywhere in
his Works: The springing Sun glows warm in his lines, and
the fragrant Air blows cool in his descriptions; we smell
the sweets of the bloomy Haws, and hear the Musick of the
feathered Choir, when ever we take a Forrest walk with him.
The hour of the day is not easier to be discovered from the
Reflexion of the Sun in *Titian*'s Paintings, than in *Chaucer*'s Morning Landskapes. 'Tis true, those Descriptions
are sometimes too long, and (as it is before observed) when
he takes those early rambles, he almost tires his Reader
with following him, and seldom knows how to get out of a
Forrest, when once entered into it: But how advantageous
this beautiful extravagance is, most of his Successors well
know, who have very plentifully lopt off his exuberant
Beauties, and placed them as the chief Ornaments of their
own Writings.

His Reading was deep, and extensive, his Judgment sound,
and discerning; but yet (a thing rarely found in Men of
great Learning and poignant Wit) he was communicative of
his Knowledge, and ready to correct or pass over the Faults
of his Cotemporary Writers. He knew how to judge of, and
to excuse the slips of weaker Capacities, and pitied rather
than exposed the Ignorance of that Age.

In one word, he was a great Scholar, a pleasant Wit, a
candid Critick, a sociable Companion, a stedfast Friend, a
grave Philosopher, a temperate Oeconomist and a pious Christian. He was not unacquainted with the ancient Rules of
Poetry, nor did he disdain to follow them, tho' he thought
it the least part of a Poet's perfections. As he had a
discerning Eye, he discovered Nature in all her appearances, and stript off every disguise with which the *Gothick*
Writers had cloathed her: He knew that those Dresses would
change as Times altered; but that she her self would always
be the same, and that she could never fail to please in her
simple attire, nor that Writer who drew her so; and therefore despising the mean assistances of Art, he copied her
close. He knew what it was to be *nimis Poeta*, and avoided
it as the most dangerous extreme. His Strokes are bold,
and his Colours lively; but the first not too much

laboured, nor the other too showy or glaring. There is a
wild Beauty in his Works, which comes nearer the Descriptions of *Homer*, than any other that followed him: And
though his Pieces have not that regular disposition as
those of the *Grecians*, yet the several Parts separately
compared, bear an equal value with theirs; and Mr. *Dryden*,
than whom there was no better Judge of the Beauties of
Homer and *Virgil*, positively asserts that he exceeded the
latter, and stands in competition with the former. Whoever reads the *Knight's Tale*, which is the best of his
Performances, being a finished Epick Poem, and examines
the Characters, the Sentiments, the Diction, Disposition
and Time, will find that he was not unacquainted with the
Rules of that way of Writing; but this requires an abler
hand, and longer time to enlarge upon it.
  That he was a true Master of Satyr, none will deny. It
is true the Persons levelled against, and the Crimes
exposed, would not allow of the severe Scourge *Juvenal*
made use of, nor was there such a variety of Follies as
Horace facetiously exploded: Not but that *Chaucer* had a
Scene of Vice in the Court of that time, capable of supplying him with matter sufficient for the sharpest strokes of
Satyr; but he was wise enough not to exasperate a Court by
which he was supported, and in which he had interest little
enough to skreen himself from malice, without provoking it:
He knew he had a fair Province for the exercise of that
Talent without exposing himself to it's resentment; and
having a Court to back him, he has shewn by severely lash-
ing an ignorant and corrupt Clergy, that he could (had it
been safe) have applied as severe a lash to a vicious
irreligious Laity. Yet there are some strokes which shew
he was not uncapable of writing in the *Horatian* way; of
which the Physician whose *studie was but litil in the
Bible,* the Lawyer who *semed besier than he was,* the libidi-
nous Wife of *Bath*, and the testy cholerick Reve, and several other Characters are sufficient Instances.
  That in the Elegiack kind of Poetry he was a compleat
Master, appears plainly by his *Complaint of the Black
Knight,* the Poem called *La belle Dame sans mercy,* and
several of his Songs. He was an excellent Master of Love-
Poetry, having studied that Passion in all it's turns and
appearances; and Mr. *Dryden* prefers him upon that account
to *Ovid*. His *Troilus* and *Creseide* is one of the most
beautiful Poems of that kind; in which Love is curiously
and naturally described in it's early appearances, it's
hopes and fears, it's application, fruition, and despair
in disappointment.
  It is thought by some that his Verses every where consist of an equal number of feet, and that if read with a

right accent, are no where deficient; but those nice discerning Persons would find it difficult, with all their
straining and working, to spin out some of his Verses
into a measure of ten Syllables. He was not altogether
regardless of his Numbers; but his thoughts were more
intent upon solid sense than gingle, and he tells us
plainly that we must not expect regularity in all his
Verses.

His Language, how unintelligible soever it may seem, is
more modern than that of any of his Cotemporaries, or of
those that followed him at the distance of Fifty or Sixty
years, as *Harding*, *Skelton*, and others; and in some places
it is to this day so smooth, concise and beautiful, that
even Mr. *Dryden* would not attempt to alter it, but has
copied some of his Verses almost *literatim*: And *Chaucer*
was the first that adorned and amplified the *English*
Tongue from the *Provencal*, which was the most polished of
all the Languages used at that time. It would require a
just Dissertation to trace the old *French* Idiom through all
his Works; but some notice being occasionally taken of it
in the Glossary, the Reader must be referred thither.

(b)

   Whether he first prepares the Landskip clean
And e'er he mingles Life, describes the Scene:
'Strikes out the Sun that ruddy seems and broad,
'When early mounting through the misty Road;
Or when he spreads around a clearer Ray,
'And all th'Horizon laughs to see the Day;
Seiz'd with Delight, we see the Prospect spread
'O'er the dun Heath, or through the woodland Shade;

   If Life he draws, and earliest Love pursues,
How artless sighs the Elegiack Muse!

   But when he boldly strikes the'embattled Plain,
And daring Actions of the Warrior train;
Draws *Arcite*, like *Atrides*, fiercely Brave,
Slave to Desire, to head-strong Lust a Slave;

Such Strength, such Vigour, glows in ev'ry Line,
An *Iliad* rises through the great Design.
   If lowly Life he offers to the View,
And takes the Vizor off, or gives a new;
Thrown in its Shade, we see the Face appear;
The Look design'd, the artificial Leer,
The Features drawn so true, the Men explain:
The grave Physician, studious of his Gain;

The Glutton *Frankleyn*, with his pamper'd Case;
The Lawyer, seeming busier than he was.
The Prioress, fond of Rev'rence, courtly nice;
The Friar with Eyes expressive of his Vice.
The Monk with thoughtless Face and double Chin;
The waspish *Reeve* with Visage soure and thin.
The buxom Wife, industrious to explain
The Pride and Folly of the Female Train;

  Nor less exact, the Picture charms the Sight,
Where shines in Fairer View th'obliging Knight.
The Scholar humble, mild, and slow of Speech,
Submissive to be taught, and glad to teach.
The Peasant poor, with calm Contentment blest:
And, far the finest Draught, the Parish Priest.

Thus Chaucer painted Life in different Ways;
Earnest to blame, yet not displeas'd to praise.

  Great was his Task, who singly durst engage,
To draw at once the Humours of an Age;
Mankind the Actors, and the World his Stage:
Where ev'ry Character's so just design'd,
We see the Person, and we read his Mind;
View Nature as she seems in all Degrees,
All various, just, and ever of a-piece.
Tho' different, tending still to moral Use;
The chief Intent and Glory of the Muse.

72.   LEONARD WELSTED, OBSOLETE AND UNINTELLIGIBLE

1724

Leonard Welsted (1688-1747), gentleman, civil servant and
poet, enemy of Pope, who ridiculed him, for a short time
attended Trinity College, Cambridge, and published in 1724
'Epistles, Odes, &c', prefaced by a 'Dissertation concerning the Perfection of the *English* Language, the State of
Poetry, etc.'. In this he is probably the first to describe his own age as Classical, with its language hardly
to be improved, and is also perhaps original in introducing a Romantically organic image of the development of
the language. Chaucer is fashionably referred to merely as

an example of obscurity.   Extracts from pp. x, xii, xiii.

The vulgar Opinion therefore is a vulgar Error, *viz.* that
our Language will continue to go on from one Refinement to
another, and pass through perpetual Variations and Improvements, till in Time the *English*, we now speak, is become
as obsolete and unintelligible as that of *Chaucer*, and so
on, as long as we are a People; this is what one of our
Poets laid down some years ago as an undoubted Maxim.

And what now *Chaucer* is, shall *Dryden* be.

But whoever this Writer is [Pope, 'Essay on Criticism'
483] he certainly judg'd the Matter wrong; it is with
Languages, as it is with Animals, Vegetables, and all other
Things; they have their Rise, their Progress, their Maturity, and their Decay....
    The Notion I have... is, that the *English* Language does,
at this Day, possess all the Advantages and Excellencies,
which are very many, that its Nature will admit of.

73.   JOHN ENTICK - THOMAS MORELL, NO HYPERBOLE

1736

John Entick (1703?-73), writer of schoolbooks, classical
editions, etc., whose education is unknown, though he sub-
scribed himself 'MA', issued proposals in 1736 to publish
an edition of Chaucer that express with crude simplicity
a Neoclassical view of literature, including the need to
avoid hyperbole.   Extract (a) from 'Proposals for Printing
by Subscription in Two Volumes Folio, the Works of that
Most Learned, Facetious, and Ancient English Poet Sir
Geoffrey Chaucer, Knt. Poet Laureat', pp. 2, 3, 5.   The
'Proposals' were attacked (though *not* signed) by the
Rev. T. Morell (see No. 74) in 'The Daily Gazetteer', 340,
Thursday, 29 July 1736, from which extract (b) is taken
(cf. Alderson and Henderson, pp. 166-7).   Entick replied
in 'The London Daily Post and General Advertiser', 546,
Saturday 31 July 1736, from which extract (c) is taken

(Alderson and Henderson, pp. 168-9).

(a)

...I call it [the Art of Poetry] divine because it appears
from its Use among the most barbarous Nations, that GOD
has implanted That in them as a proper manner to adore him
in. Thus
   If we consider *Poesy* in her first Institution, e're she
became a common Prostitute to Lust, Flattery, Ignorance
and Ambition, we shall find her alone acknowledged as the
Sovereign Princess of the Civiliz'd World, and behold her
from her Throne giving Laws, not only to their *Religion*
and *Policy*, but also to their Manners. Her Court was
esteem'd the proper and only School of *Vertue*, to which the
greatest Princes form'd theirs, and under her Custody alone
was kept seal'd that Fountain, whence all the profitable
Instructions of Life were to be drawn. *Philosophy* itself
was a thing of no Use and destitute of Arms, 'till she
supply'd 'em; nor durst it appear in the World without the
easy Chain of *Verse*, in Token of Submission to her for its
Passport. The same may be said of all other *Arts*, That
from *Her* they've received their *Birth* and *Vigour*. And our
Author was so well convinced of this Truth, and was so
well qualify'd in the Art of *Poetry*, that he has adapted it
to all Parts of Literature: An Assertion not broach'd by
me, with bare-fac'd Impudence, to serve a *Turn*, but deriv'd
and confirm'd to us from the latest Antiquity and constant
Testimony....

[Quotes Denham and Lidgate.]

   But, as daily Example instructs us, that neither *Eloquence* nor *Language* are more able to propagate the deserved Character of an Author to Posterity, than *Vertue* and
Honesty to recommend a Politician; so our AUTHOR, thro'
the Grossness and Barbarity of the Age wherein he writ,
and for some Time after, when all good Learning was almost
asleep, was thrown aside in the Crowd, or; at least, so
wretchedly maim'd and deprav'd by the Ignorance of his
Transcribers, that he ran a manifest Risque either of
being lost to succeeding Ages, or to have his Sense so
basely confounded, that his Meaning could scarce be found
out....

[Quotes Spenser, Wm. Thynne, Beaumont, Peacham, Dryden, Savil.]

These Prologues are a Key to, and were design'd by the Author, to give the Reader a general Idea of those Characters, that are more lively represented in his 'Canterbury Tales'; as well as to prepare him for what might be expected under each State and Condition of Life, as that they might, I presume, serve for Arguments to each respective Tale. The Method herein observed, is, like his *Genius*, entirely new; his List of Persons are of his own Invention; nor did he borrow his Application from any other, but good and strong Natural Parts of his own Improvement, which not only enabled him to make just Reflections on the Age he lived in; but under the severest Satyr, to reprimand and condemn their Vices and Superstition.... This *Thomas of Canterbury* was of most note in *England*, for these kind of devotions (v. 15, etc.) and therefore our Author wisely considered, that a Company of such Pilgrims was the properest *Medium* by which he cou'd convey his Sentiments without incurring the Charge of *Hyperbole*, which is always to be avoided as much as may be.

(b)

Pity it is so excellent a Poet, the first of any Account, and, I had almost said, the best this Nation boasts, should be hawked about the Streets in Scraps, and made unintelligible by Explanations; but how should he expect better Treatment, when the *Sacred Scriptures* have not escaped the Hands of these little Pilferers! tho' this Artifice of imposing upon the Publick is now grown so stale, as to meet with but small Encouragement. - I cannot deny but that I am somewhat prejudiced in favour of a Friend of mine, who has, for some Time, been employed in preparing a new Edition of the same Works, and has now in his Possession, or has had within this Twelvemonth, most of the best MSS. in the Kingdom, and been honoured with the Assistance of several competent Judges in that Way of Writing: However, I intend to say nothing but what, I think, I can defend; and, in the first Place, do affirm, there are not in all *Chaucer* two such uncouth, inharmonious Lines, as this Retaler has made of the two first,

When that April *with his Shoures sotè,*
The Drought of March *had perc'd to the Rotè.*

The *E* feminine or obscure, is never used in any even Place,

except the 2d; I mean, it is never used in the 4th, 6th,
8th, and much less in the last Syllable of the Verse; in
the 2d indeed it is sometimes used, when the Accent is
strong upon the 4th; and therefore in the Critic's Style,
meo periculo, read them thus:

> Whannè *that* Apryl *with his Schouris sote,*
> *The Drought of* March *had percid to the Rote.*

His note upon these Lines, 'That the Poet intended, by
the Drought of *March*, to imitate that State of Avidity or
Dryness, from which the Pilgrims pretended to be roused by
the Impulse of the Holy Spirit,'- is past my Comprehension;
and therefore I shall pass on to the next.

> When Zephyrus, *eke with his sote Breath,*
> Espired *hath, in every Holt and Heath,*
> *The tender* Croppes. -

'*Espired,* says he, *Lat. Exspiro, to send forth, blow
from, or out of,* agreeable to the poetical Fiction, that
assigns a Den or Cavern to the Winds, from which they
blow.' I know not in which of these Senses the Retaler
takes it, but either of them is Nonsense; nor is there any
Allusion here to *Aeolus*'s Den. In Truth he has mistook
the Word; it is *enspired* (Lat. *inspiro*) *i.e.* inspired,
refreshed, enlivened; and there is the very same Expression in *Quintilian*, lib. 10. c. 3. *Inspirantes Ramis
Arborum Aurae.* For *Crop* (which, by the Way, I suppose he
takes in the common Acceptation of the Word, since he has
not explained it) signifies in old *English*, the Top of any
thing, and is here put for the Tops or Twigs of Trees; as
in another Place of *Chaucer:*

> And *for to kepe out well the Sunne,*
> *The* Croppis *were so thick yrunne,*
> *And every Braunch in other knitt.-*

R.R.

I shall take no Notice at present of the material Compliment he pays to *mine Host of the Talbot* (which, I fear,
he takes to be the same with the old Sign of the *Tabard,*
since this Word likewise is left unexplained, tho' he
thought it necessary to tell us, that *Array* signifies
Dress, and *Knight* a Soldier or Warriour) nor of the Non-
compliment to the Gentlemen of the Sword, when speaking of
Truth, Honour, Freedom, Courtesy, he is pleased to say,
these are Virtues very rarely to be found in the martial

Composition of a Soldier: But, with regard to the Text of
Chaucer, I must observe, that it has been Matter of Dispute, whether he wrote his Verses in exact Metre or not.
Some Writers have declared for one Side, some for the
other; but on which Side this Retaler is, I cannot guess.
By his foisting in some Words and Syllables of his own,
which indeed, as Mr. *Urry* once designed, he has honestly
distinguish'd by *Italicks*, he seems inclined to the former
Opinion; but then having curtailed some Verses of their due
Measure, and lengthened others out beyond their Complement;
as

> *'Specially fro every Shires End -*
> *Of Twenty Year of Age he was,* as *I* do *gesse.* -

He seems not at all concerned about the Matter; and
whatever Preamble the Notes may contain, as to the Text,
Chaucerum in Chaucero Quaeras.

(c)

To my Friend -   *July* 29, 1736

SIR,

At your Request alone I have taken pains to consider the
Paper signed R.R. in this Day's daily *Gazetteer;* and because
you intimate that in Honour I should defend my Work, I prefer your Pleasure to that deserved Obscurity in which such
a wretched Opponent ought to be suffer'd to wallow with his
own *dark* Sentiments: for such a one, it is plain, writes
for Information, and all I can expect from setting of
him *Right,* is, That like a Swine he'll rowl himself again
in the Mire. The whole Drift of his scurrilous Ribaldry
will prove my Assertion. He gilds his Inveteracy with the
noble Epithets of Justice and Liberty; *No one,* says he,
*can take Umbrage at just Censure - I shall therefore beg
Leave* FREELY *to animadvert.* One might from such a Preface
as this, reasonably expect, that the Letter-Writer was
acting upon *English* Principles, JUSTICE and LIBERTY; but
on the contrary, without any *Justice,* he takes the *Liberty*
to assert a Lie, That my Work is *hawk'd about the Streets
in Scraps,* and before he has proved the Premises, concludes
in Triumph, That the Works of CHAUCER are *made unintelligible by Explanations:* and why so? because says he, *I cannot deny but that I am somewhat prejudiced,* &c. Therefore his Pretence to *a just Censure,* and begging *Leave
freely to animadvert,* are Nonsense in the highest Degree.
But after all he adds, *I intend to say nothing but what,*

I think, I can defend. And my Pleasure is to find he can
say *nothing* to the Purpose: for in Relation to the two
first Lines of CHAUCER, which according to the best Copies,
I have publish'd in these Terms:

> When that *April* with his Shoures sotè,
> The Drought of *March* had perc'd to the Rotè,

He cavils at the è in *sotè* and *Rotè*, and affirms it is
never used but in the 2d Place: and therefore says he, in
the *Critick's* Style, *meo piriculo* [sic] (*i.e.* upon my
Reputation) read them thus,

> *Whannè that* Apryl *with his Schoures sote,*
> *The Drought of* March *had percid to the Rote.*

Judge now between him and me, Whether the Difference of
the final è deserves the harsh Epithets of *uncouth and inharmonious;* and if you please to consult *Urry* in the
Knight's Tale, you shall see the è in the 3d Place l.
2441. in the 4th l. 2430. in the 5th l. 2445. in the
Miller's Tale you read it in the 6th Place l. 718. the
7th l. 667. in the 9th 684. and in the last Place 591.
and yet this *ipse dixit* Critick ventures his Reputation,
That the è is only to be found in the 2d Place, because
he would begin his Verses with a *Whannè*; and this he calls
a just Censure! But what he adds relating to my Note is
most barbarous, and the most Revengeful Rascality would
scarce stoop so low to forfeit the Name of HONESTY in
quoting *Words* from PRINT that were never *printed*; yet the
Letter-Writer R.R. affirms, That I have given *this Note
upon the foregoing Lines*, 'That the Poet intended by the
Drought of *March* to *imitate* that State of *Avidity* or Dryness, from which the Pilgrims pretended to be roused by
the Impulse of the Holy Spirit.' This, says he, is past
my Comprehension; and indeed, it is not only so to me,
but adds to my Admiration, to think that a Man, who pretends to write as a Critick, should take such Liberty to
change SENSE into Words of *Nonsense*: I deny the Words
imitate and *Avidity*, they never were publish'd by me, but
are the impudent Product of a distemper'd Brain, which is
resolved to attempt any base Stratagem to depreciate, if
it were in his Power, a Work he sees likely to obstruct
the Birth of his own *Brat*

74. THOMAS MORELL, NOBLE FICTION

1737

The Rev. Thomas Morell (1703-84), classical scholar, miscellaneous writer, editor of schoolbooks, Handel's libret-
tist, good companion, projected a complete edition of 'The
Canterbury Tales' but published only 'The General Prologue'
and 'The Knight's Tale' in 1737. His textual method was
an improvement on those of his predecessors. The threat
to his project from Entick's proposals produced the caustic
criticism already noted (see No. 73). His Dedication (a),
pp. iv-v, reveals a strong sense both of the art of 'The
Knight's Tale' and its fictionality; in his Preface (b) he
comments as an editor very sensibly on Chaucer's metre,
and very typically on Chaucer's descriptions, pp. xx,
xxii-xxvii, xxxiv-xxxv.

(a)

This Tale, May it please your HIGHNESS, sets forth a
Princess, under the Name of *Emelia*, endowed with all the
Accomplishments that can adorn her Sex; and concludes, as
most Stories do, with giveing her in Marriage to a Prince
of the Blood Royal, in all respects worthy so great a
Blessing: There is no Art wanting in the Poet to embellish this noble Fiction, and to set off the lovely Characters of the Persons introduced: Truth, Honour, Beauty,
Virtue, are their lowest Qualifications; but after all,
'tis but a Fiction: Whereas the Joy, that is now diffused
thro' this our Nation, arises from the like Incident in
real Life: There is no need to mention your ROYAL HIGH-
NESS'S Marriage with a Princess of the most Illustrious
House of *Saxe-Gotha*: Amidst the many congratulatory Enco-
miums upon this happy Occasion, from every Press, from
every Mouth, permit me, Sir, to lay this my humble Tribute
at your Feet, and to subscribe myself,

May it please your Highness,
Your Highness's
Most Dutiful, and
Most Obedient Servant

THE EDITOR

(b)
Some account of the Poet's Life

For a more particular Description of his Person, and his
several Accomplishments, I must refer my Reader to the
aforesaid Writer of his Life [*i.e. in Urry's edition*]:
Only this in general, As to his Person, he was of a fair
and beautiful Complexion, his Lips red and full, his Size
of a just Medium, and his Port and Air graceful and majestic; and for his other Qualifications, he was an universal
Scholar, a pleasant Wit, a candid Critic, a sociable Companion, a stedfast Friend, a grave Philosopher, a temperate
Oeconomist, and, above all, a pious Christian....
    This ancient Poet *Jeoffery Chaucer*, has now stood the
Test of above 300 Years, still read, and still admired,
notwithstanding he hath been so wretchedly abused, *mis-
wrote* and *mismetred* by all his Editors, the last not
excepted. I speak not this to derogate from the Fame of
the late Mr. *Urry*, who died before he had completed his
Work, and left behind him a more amiable Character than
the nicest Skill in Criticism, or the whole Cycle of
Learning could procure; I mean, for his constant Integrity, and most extensive Charity: Nor would I be thought
to reflect upon his ingenious Editor, who carried on the
Work, by Command, it seems, rather than by Choice, in
Mr. *Urry's* Method; and I am persuaded would have done it
much better, had he never seen Mr. *Urry's* Design at all.
    This Gentleman tells us, that Mr. *Urry* 'intended, not
only to correct the Text, but to make some Observations on
the Author, and among other Things, to shew where he had
imitated or borrowed from the *Greek* and *Latin* Poets, but
had proceeded no farther herein than a single Reference to
Ausonius.' We shall endeavour, therefore to carry on this
Improvement, (such as it is) and to shew likewise, wherein
the Moderns have imitated or borrowed from him.
    But, what is more material, the said Editor tells us,
'That Mr. *Urry* found it was the Opinion of some learned
Men, that *Chaucer's* Verses originally consisted of an
equal Number of Feet, and he himself was persuaded that
Chaucer made them exact Metre; and therefore he proposed,
in this Edition, to *restore him to his Feet again.*' But
if *Chaucer* was a Cripple before Mr. *Urry* restored *him to
his Feet*, to keep to his own Expression, he was really
born such; 'twas a natural Lameness, and no more a Blemish
in *Chaucer's* Time, than Round-Shoulders were in the Days
of *Alexander* the Great: But he improved it with a manly
Air, and becoming Grace; whereas, since his fancied Cure,
he has minc'd it along like a Child telling his Steps, or,
not to run the Figure quite out of Breath, he must be read

as School-boys scan their Verses on the Tops of their
Fingers. I propose therefore to reduce him to his own
true Shape, and, not by servilely following any one
particular MS. but by collating several of the best
Authority, some of which Mr. *Urry* had never seen, to
select, if possible, the genuine Reading; and, if after
all, some Verses should want their full-Measure, to leave
them so, as I am confident, and shall immediately prove,
that *Chaucer* left many; without foisting in any wild
Conjecture of my own.

'But Mr. *Urry*, we are told, whenever he could by no
other Way help a Verse to a Foot which he fancied it had
lost, made no Scruple to supply it with some Word or
Syllable that served for an Expletive.' And this he did
indeed without any Authority, or the least Mark of Distinction, whereby we might know such Interpolations for
the Production of his own Fancy. But surely this is an
unwarrantable Liberty, and what lead Mr. *Urry* into several
Mistakes, as it put him upon using any Copy indiscrimi-
nately, so it served but his Scheme to complete the Verse.

'Tis true, Mr. *Speght* in his Edition 1602. affirms,
that *Chaucer* wrote in equal Measure; but of other learned
Men know I none of the same Opinion; I am sure, none that
I have had the Honour particularly to converse with on
this Occasion. Mr. *Dryden* thinks it not worth while to
confute so gross an Error; and the ingenious Editor of
Chaucer's Life, prefixed to Mr. *Urry*'s Edition, greatly
condemns it. But, if I am not mistaken, *Chaucer* himself
has put the Matter out of Dispute, in his Poem, called
'The House of Fame', 1. ₃.

> God of Science, and of Light,
> *Apollo*, thro thy greté Myght,
> This lytel last Book now thou gye,
> Now that I wol for Maisterie.
> Here Art *Poetical* be shew'd;
> But, for the Rhyme is lyght and lewde,
> Yet make it somewhat agreeable,
> *Tho som Verse fail of a Syllable.*

From this last Line, I conclude, that an exact Numerosi-
ty (as Bp. *Sprat* expresses it in his Life of *Cowley*, which,
by the way, runs parallel with our Author's in many Cases)
was not *Chaucer*'s main Care; but that he had sometimes a
greater Regard for the Sense, than the Metre: His Numbers,
however, are, by no Means so rough and inharmonious as
some People imagine; there is a charming Simplicity in
them, and they are always musical, whether they want or
exceed their Complement: The former Case, I have observed,

when it happens, is generally at the Beginning of a Verse, when a Pause is to be made, or rather two Times to be given to the first Syllable, as v. 368.

Not in Purgatory, but in Hell.

Mr. *Urry*, to make out his ten Syllables, reads it, *right* in Hell, which *right*, tho' I am no great Admirer of a Pun, is *wrong,* as it renders the Verse very harsh and dissonant: But this is only one Verse among hundreds that are false accented in Mr. *Urry*'s Edition, as may be seen by any one that thinks it worth while to consult the various Readings annexed to this.

Some Verses are charg'd with an additional Syllable that were full before, as v. 1050, 1537, &c. others are as unnecessarily curtailed, for want of knowing, that as *Chaucer* sometimes gives two Times to one long Syllable, so he often uses two short Syllables, I mean, such as do not require a strong Accent, instead of one, v. 734, 309, 1219, 2056. In others, the *Apostrophe* or *Elision* is not obser- ved, when it is necessarily required, v. 214, &c. But what I am more surpriz'd at is, that Mr. *Urry* very often disallows, the *double Rhime*, as v. 804, 325, &c. than which nothing can be more absurd.

As to the final *E*, it was anciently pronounc'd, no doubt, in feminine Adjectives, both from the *Saxon* and *French*, and in those Substantives, that from the old *Saxon* are made *English*, by changing *a* into *e*, as Gereva, *Nama*, *Revè*, *Namè*; as, we are told, it is still used in *Dorsetshire*, in the Words *Pipé*, *Buttoné*, *Finé*, &c.

However, our Author seems to have taken the Liberty to use it or not, as it best served his Metre: But give me leave to observe, that he has never used it in any even Place, except the 2d, where it is allowable, especially if the Accent be strong upon the 4th.

Whanné that Apryl, v. 1.
Thatté no Drop, v. 131.

I say, that the final *E*, (and I believe I might say the same of the plural *es* or *is*, especially of Monosyllables, v. 174. &c.) is never used in the 4th, 6th, 8th, or last Syllable of the Verse, which is a Fault that most injudi- ciously runs thro' Mr. *Urry*'s whole Edition.

In a Gounè, v. 393.
And in a Glass haddè he, 699.
Purse is the Archdekyns Hellé sayd he, 660.
He couth rosté, boilé, grillé, and frye, 385.

At my first reading *Chaucer*, I thought it a Trouble to
turn to the Glossary for every Word that required Explanation, and indeed it was what took off almost all the Pleasure of reading so excellent a Poet; to remedy this Incon-
venience, I have not only lessened the Bulk of the Book,
but have set before the Eye the Explanation of every obsolete Word and difficult Passage, and this in as concise a
Manner as possible, that I might not load the Text; and
therefore have given the Etymology of but few Words in
common Use, referring the Reader for a fuller Account to
an Appendix, wherein I have likewise given a short History
of the Persons, and ancient Customs alluded to in this
Work; and not intending to explain any Word twice, I shall
add an Index to each Volume of the Words and Passages
therein explained, for the Direction of the Reader; and
also to serve as a Glossary, not only to our Author, but
to all the Writers about his Time.
And lest some should still disrelish our Author in his
ancient Garb, by the Assistance of the most eminent Hands,
I have prepared him a modern one, which cannot but please
the nicest Taste; for as I have but little Hand in them
myself, I may venture to say, that some of these Poems, so
modernized, are the noblest and most finished Pieces we
have extant in our Language.
This then has been my Amusement for some Time, and I
hope with no great Detriment to the more severe and
decent Studies required by my Place and Character: I
believe many a leisure Hour might have been spent worse;
I am sure less pleasurably, than in this Sort of Conversation with our Forefathers; for so lively are *Chaucer*'s
Descriptions, that only to read them, is to carry Life
back again, as it were, 300 Years, and to join Conference
with his merry Crew in their Pilgrimage to *Canterbury*.
From whence we may observe, that Nature is still the same,
however alter'd in her outward Dress, and the Man that,
like *Chaucer* and *Shakespear*, can trace her in her most
secret Recesses, will be sure, in every Age, to please.
I doubt not, therefore, courteous Reader, but if you have
an idle Hour to spare, you will here find an agreeable
Entertainment.

75.   ELIZABETH COOPER, SOARING IN HIGH LIFE, PLEASANT
IN LOW

1737

Elizabeth Cooper (fl.1737), playwright and widow of an
auctioneer, about whom little is known, compiled an
unusually full, original and sensible anthology of earlier
English poetry, with the help of the antiquary William
Oldys, 'The Historical and Poetical Medley or Muses
Library', 1737. She discusses the importance of literature, its relation to the general language and culture,
the significance of a sense of the past, and has a fresh
appreciation of Chaucer's relationship with his contemporaries. Extracts from pp. xi-xiii, 1, 7-9, 19, 23-4, 30-1.

We need only look back to the Days of *Langland*, the first
English Poet we can meet with, who employ'd his Muse for
the Refinement of Manners, and, in the Rudeness of his
Lines, we plainly discover the Rudeness of the Age he
wrote in. —— *Chaucer*, not the next Writer, tho' the next
extraordinary Genius, encountered the Follies of Mankind,
as well as their Vices, and blended the acutest Raillery,
with the most insinuating Humour.—— By his Writings, it
plainly appears that Poetry, and Politeness grew up
together; and had like to have been bury'd in his Grave;
For War, and Faction, immediately after restor'd Ignorance, and Dulness almost to their antient Authority.
Writers there were; but Tast, Judgment, and Manner were
lost: Their Works were cloudy as the Times they liv'd in,
and, till *Barclay*, and *Skelton*, there was scarce a Hope
that Knowledge would ever favour us with a second Dawn.
—— But soon after these, Lord *Surrey*, having tasted of
the *Italian* Delicacy, naturaliz'd it here, gave us an
Idea of refin'd Gallantry, and taught Love to polish us
into Virtue.

[Comments on successive writers, concluding with the
'divine' Milton.]

So many and variously-accomplish'd Minds were necessary to remove the *Gothique* Rudeness that was handed down
to us by our unpolish'd Fore-Fathers; and, I think, 'tis
manifest all the Ornaments of Humanity, are owing to our

Poetical Writers, if not our most shining Virtues. 'Tis
not reasonable, therefore, that while the Work remains,
the Artist should be forgot; and yet, 'tis certain, very
Few of these great Men are generally known to the present
Age: And tho' *Chaucer*, and *Spencer* are ever nam'd with
much Respect, not many are intimately acquainted with
their Beauties. ----- The Monumental Statues of the Dead
have, in all Ages, and Nations, been esteem'd sacred; but
the Writings of the Learned, of all others, deserve the
highest Veneration; The Last bear the Resemblance of the
Soul, the First only of the Body. The First are dumb,
inanimate, and require the Historian to explain them;
while the Last live, converse, reason, instruct, and
afford to the Contemplative, one of their sincerest
Pleasures. They are likewise to Authors, what Actions are
to Heroes; In His Annals you must admire the one, in his
Studies the other; and an elegant Poem should be as lasting a Memorial of the Scholar's Wit, as a pompous Trophy
of the General's Conduct, or the Soldier's Valour. And
yet, for want of certain periodical Reviews of the Learning of former Ages, not only many inestimable Pieces have
been lost, but Science itself has been in the most immi-
nent Danger.
     I have often thought there is a Kind of Contagion in
Minds, as well as Bodies; what we admire, we fondly wish
to imitate; and, thus, while a Few excellent Authors
throw a Glory on the Studies they pursue, Disciples will
not be wanting to imitate them: But, when those Studies
fall into Disesteem, and Neglect, instead of being pro-
fess'd, or encourag'd, 'tis more than probable they will
not be understood. I have read 'twas thus in *Greece*, and
Rome, and all the considerable Nations of *Europe* beside:
In *England* 'tis notorious; and I wish our share of Re-
proach on this Head, may be confin'd to the Ignorance,
and Inhumanity of former Times.

                         The Muses Library

Philosophers, in a Series of Fossils, begin with Nature
in her crudest State, and trace her, Step by Step, to the
most refin'd. --- In this Progress of *English* Poetry we
must do the same; and they, who desire to see the Connexion, must bear with the rude Pebble, in order to be
better pleas'd with the Ruby, and the Diamond.
     To set aside the Metaphor, few People suppose there
were any Writers of Verse before *Chaucer*, but, as it
appears there were many, 'tis absolutely necessary to give
a Specimen from a few of them, both as Curiosities in

themselves, and to manifest from what a low and almost
contemptible Original, that happy Genius rais'd his Profession at once....

Robert de Langland

The Author of the Satire, intitled, *The Vision of Piers
the Plowman*, and who may be truly call'd the first of the
English Poets. *Selden*, in his Notes on *Draiton's Poly-
Olbion*, quotes him with Honour; but he is not so much as
mention'd either by *Philips* or *Winstanly*; though, in my
Judgment, no Writer, except *Chaucer*, and *Spencer*, for many
Ages, had more of real Inspiration. I must own I can't
read his Work, without lamenting the Unhappiness of a
fluctuating Language, that buries even Genius it self in
its Ruins: 'Tis raising Edifices of Sand, that every
Breath of Time defaces; and, if the Form remains, the
Beauty is lost. This is the Case of the Piece before us;
'Tis a Work of great Length, and Labour; of the Allegorick-
kind; animated with a rich Imagination, pointed with great
Variety of just Satire, and dignify'd with many excellent
Lessons of Morality and Virtue: And, to say all in a Word,
if I may presume to say so much, *Chaucer* seems to have
this Model in his Eye; and, in his *Pardoners Prologue*,
particularly, has a Feature or two nearly resembling the
Speech and Character of *Sloth* hereafter quoted.
   I am not ignorant that the Author of the Art of
English Poesy, mention'd in the Preface, ranks him, in
Point of Time, after *Chaucer*; but as he is not so much
acquainted with his Name, there is little Reason to
depend on his Authority. Besides, 'tis notorious *Langland* copies his Characters, and Manners from the Age he
lived in, and we find him, in one Passage, seating *Reason*
between the King and his Son: In another, *Conscience*
reproaches *Mede* with causing the Death of the King's
Father, which exactly tallies with the Fall of *Edward* II.
And, in a Third, *Mede* speaks of the Siege of *Calais*, as a
recent Fact, and upbraids *Conscience* as the only Impediment to the Conquest of *France*; which, says she, if I had
govern'd, could have been easily effected. From which
Historical References, I make no Scruple to place him in
the Reign of *Edward* III. or that of *Richard* II. his
Successor. To this may be added; That the worst Writer,
after *Chaucer*, had some regard to Measure, and never
neglected Rhymes: Whereas this is greatly defective in
both; seldom affording a perfect Verse, and using a Dialect hardly intelligible. But of this enough! This work
is divided into *Twenty* Parts; the Arguments of which are

wrote with uncommon Spirit; and several Passages in it
deserve to be immortal; But, as to the Conduct of the
whole, I must confess it does not appear to me of a Piece;
every Vision seeming a distinct Rhapsody, and not carrying
on either one single Action, or a Series of many. But we
ought rather to wonder at its Beauties, than cavil at its
Defects; and, if the Poetical Design is broken, the Moral
is entire; which is, uniformly, the Advancement of Piety,
and Reformation of the *Roman* Clergy.--- I hope the following
Quotations will not be thought too long; tho' the stile
is so obsolete; since they are not inserted for want of
other Materials; but because 'tis presum'd they are really
Curious and Entertaining. *Civil*, and *Symony* publish the
Marriage-Contract, between *False* and *Mede*, *Theologie* steps
in, forbids the Banns, and cites them to appear before
Conscience and the *King*....

Sir *John Gower*

Flourish'd in the Reign of *Richard* the Second, and
wrote his Poems by the King's Command. He was a Man of
Family, and Learning, but does not appear to have much
Genius; his whole Work being little better than a cool
Translation from other Authors: The Tale annex'd has,
however, something truly excellent both in the Incidents
and Moral. That he was a Man of Judgment, may be understood by *Chaucer*'s submitting his *Troilus*, and *Cressida*
to his Censure, as appears by the following Lines.

O Morall *Gower*, this Boke I directe
    To thee, and to the Philosophic *Strode*
To vouchsafe, where need is, to correcte
    Of your Benignitees, and Zeles good.

He was bred a Lawyer, tho' a Man of Fortune, survived
both *Chaucer* and *Lidgate*; being quite blind before he
dy'd, and was bury'd in St. *Mary's Southwark*....

Chaucer

The Morning-Star of the *English* Poetry! was, by his own
Record, in the 'Testament of Love', born in *London*; in the
Reign of *Edward* the Third. His Family is suppos'd to come
in with *William* the *Norman*, and, some day, his Father was
a Merchant. He had his Education partly at *Oxford*, partly
at *Cambridge*, and, by Circumstance, we find he was enter'd
a Student of the *Inner-Temple*. He travelled in his Youth,

thro' *France* and *Flanders*; and, in the Reign of *Richard*
the Second, was famous for his Learning. After this he
marry'd the Daughter of a Knight of *Hainault*, by which
Alliance he is said to become Brother-in-Law to *John* of
Gaunt Duke of *Lancaster*: He had several Children, a large,
and ample Revenue, resided chiefly at *Woodstock*, was
employ'd on several Embassies, received many great Rewards
from the Crown, and was in high Esteem with the most Noble
and Excellent Persons of his Time. --- In the latter Part
of his Life, he met with many Troubles, of which he complains, very pathetically, in some of his Pieces; yet
liv'd to the Age of Seventy Two Years, and was bury'd at
Westminster.

All agree he was the first Master of his Art among us,
and that the Language, in general, is much oblig'd to him
for Copiousness, Strength, and Ornament. It would be endless, almost, to enumerate the Compliments that have been
paid to his Merit, by the Gratitude of those Writers, who
have enrich'd themselves so much by his inestimable Legacies. --- But his own Works, are his best Monument. In
those appear a real Genius, as capable of inventing, as
improving; equally suited to the Gay, and the Sublime;
soaring in high Life, and pleasant in low: Tho' I don't
find the least Authority in History to prove it. Ever
both entertaining, and instructive! All which is so well
known, 'tis, in a Manner, needless to repeat: But the
Nature of this Work requires it, and I should not be
excus'd for saying less, or omitting a Quotation; tho it
is not a little difficult to chuse one that will do him
Justice: Most of his principal Tales have been already
exhausted by the Moderns, and, consequently, neither of
them would appear to Advantage in their antiquated, original Dress; tho' the same in Complexion and Harmony of
Parts....

[Quotes 'The Pardoner's Tale'.]

John Lidgate

Commonly call'd the Monk of *Bury*, because a Native of
that Place, was a Disciple of *Chaucer*'s. Many Authors
are so profuse in his Praise as to rank him very little
below his Master, and, often, quote them together; which
rais'd my Curiosity so high, that I gave a considerable
Price for his Works, and waded thro' a large Folio, hoping
still to have my Expectation gratified. --- But I must,
either, confess my own want of Penetration, or beg Leave
to dissent from his Admirers. --- Modesty, indeed, he has

to a very great Degree; ever disavowing all Pretence to
Merit, speaking of *Chaucer* with a religious Reverence, and
pleading the Command of Princes for following his Track.
--- But, as to the Compliments that are made him, of deep
Scholar, Logician, Philosoper, &c. let his own Words
answer, in the Close of his *Fall* of *Princes*; which will,
at once, illustrate my Idea both of the Poet, and the
Man....

Thomas Occleve, or Okeleafe

Another Disciple in the same School, and an officer in
the Houshold of the Immortal *Henry* the Fifth, to whom he
dedicated his Book 'De Regimine Principis'; a Work which
I have bever been able to attain a Sight of; consequently
can't presume to determine what is due to its Author.   By
some he is highly applauded, by others not so much as mention'd. --- To his Care and Affection is owing the Original of that Print, which is now so common of *Chaucer*, and
certain tender and pathetick Lines to his Memory, are the
only Instance in my Power to give of the Merit of his Muse.

76.   GEORGE OGLE, DRAMATIC CHARACTERISATION

1739

Ogle (1704-46), son of an Irish gentleman, published in
1739 'Gualtheris and Griselda: or the Clerk of Oxford's
Tale; From Boccace, Petrarch and Chaucer', with a prefatory 'Letter to a Friend' which continues Dryden's vein of
comparative literary discussion and develops Dryden's
dramatic concept of self-subsistent realistic character.
With this illusionist concept of literature goes the
emphasis on pretence.   At the same time there is an assimilation to Neoclassical models, or assumed models, no
longer Homer or Ennius, but even, among others, the
Augustan Horace.   Text, pp.vii-viii.

By What has been said, it is evident, that this Tale,
take it either as a Fact of History, or as a Fiction of

Fable, has already pass'd thro' the Hands of BOCCACE,
PETRARCH, and CHAUCER; that is, thro' the Hands of three
Men of as great Genius as ever appear'd in one Age.
BOCCACE may be suppos'd to have improv'd on Those He
follow'd; PETRARCH most certainly improv'd on Him; and
our Countryman undeniably improv'd on them Both. At the
same Time that I say This, I must ingenuously confess,
that tho' upon the Whole, I give the Preference to
CHAUCER's Manner of Treating this Story, yet, here and
there, I thought He had omitted some Beauties discernible
in PETRARCH; and still think, there are Others remaining
in BOCCACE, which PETRARCH has omitted. I have compared
them One with the Other; and have endeavoured to glean
after Them, and found Occasion rather to add than to dimi-
nish. So that should You pronounce Me guilty on the
Whole, I hope You will not condemn Me for Sins of Ommis-
sion. Tho' CHAUCER was my chief Guide, I could not forbear Consulting the other Two; And if by this Method the
Story has receiv'd any Improvement, I will fairly acknowledge (to apply with Justice what a great Writer on a like
Occasion said out of Modesty) That, I could have done
Nothing without their Assistance; That, *Facile est inventis addere*, is no great Commendation; and That, I am not
so vain as to think I deserve a greater.

I shall not trouble You here with any Account or Defence of this Kind of Translation; Mr. DRYDEN has sufficiently establish'd the Use and Advantage of it, as far
as it regards the modern ENGLISH Reader....

As to the Point of Characterizing, at which CHAUCER
was most singularly happy; You can name no Author even of
Antiquity, whether in the Comic or in the Satiric Way,
equal, at least superior, to Him. Give Me Leave, only to
throw together a few Touches taken from his Descriptions
of the Pilgrims. The *Knight*, or *old Soldier*; Who, *tho'*
that He was *worthy* (meaning a Man of excessive Bravery)
yet was *wise*! The *Squire*; with Locks curl'd, just fresh
from the *Press*! The *Squire's Yeoman*; so *smartly* equip'd
in his *Coat* and *Hood* of *Green*! The Lady *Prioress*; Who
wept if She saw a *Mouse* taken in a *Trap*! The *Monk*; a
bold Rider, Who had *many* an able *Horse* in his *Stable*! The
Frier; Who so *sweetly* heard *Confession*, and whose *Absolu-
tion* was so *pleasant*! The *Merchant*; Who *reason'd* so *sol-
emnly*, showing always the *Increase* of his *Winning*! The
Clerk of Oxford; Who was a *great Philosopher*, yet had but
little Gold in his *Coffer*! The *Frankelin*, or *Country
Gentleman*; of *sanguine* Complexion, whose *Table dormant*
stood always *ready cover'd* in his *Hall*! The *Haberdasher*,
with the rest of the *London Cits*; whose *Intellects* and
Shapes pronounced Them Each, an *Alderman*!....(etc.)

All these, I say, are the Strokes of no common Genius,
but of a Man perfectly conversant in the Turns and
Foibles of human Nature. Observe but his Manner of Throwing Them in, and You will not think I exaggerate, if I say,
these Turns of Satire, are not unworthy of PERSIUS,
JUVENAL or HORACE himself. Before I cool upon this Subject, I shall venture (as far as the Ludicrous may hold
Comparison with the Serious) to rank our CHAUCER with
whatever We have of greatest Perfection in this Character
of Painting; I shall venture to rank Him (making this
Allowance) either with SALUST or CLARENDON; Who in History
are allowed to have been the greatest Masters of the Picturesque; I mean the best Drawers of Characters. Even
here some Criticks will not allow that the Persons, so
described, are always consistent with themselves, at least
that their Actions are always conformable to the Characters given of Them by their Historians; they will never be
able to lay that Charge to CHAUCER. A Fault, however,
more applicable to CLARENDON than to SALLUST.
     For it was not to the Distinguishing of Character from
Character, that the Excellence of CHAUCER was confin'd; He
was equally Master of Introducing them properly on the
Stage; and after having introduced them, of Supporting
them agreeably to the Part They were formed to personate.
In This, He claims equal Honour with the best Comedians;
there is no Admirer of PLAUTUS, TERENCE, or ARISTOPHANES,
that will pretend to say, CHAUCER has not equally, thro'
his 'Canterbury Tales', supported his Characters. And All
must allow, that the Plan, by which He connects and unites
his Tales, one with another, is well designed, and well
executed. You will not think it Loss of Time, if I enter
into it, so far as may be requisite to our present Subject.
     The Scheme of the 'Canterbury Tales' is this. CHAUCER
pretends, that intending to pay his Devotions to the
Shrine of THOMAS A BECKET, He set up his Horse at the
Tabbard Inn in *Southwark*.

77. ASTROPHIL, MEER FICTIONS FOR REALITIES WE TAKE

1740

The pseudonymous Astrophil, whose identity is unknown,

author of the following poem In Praise of Chaucer, in 'The
Gentleman's Magazine', X, p.31 (January 1740), well sums
up the universality of Chaucer's genius, and continues to
develop the illusionist power of Chaucer's fictions, as
well as the vividness of his characterisation. He also
introduces a series of Classical comparisons, while
repeating the usual contrast between Chaucer and his
Gothick times.

Long veil'd in *Gothick* mists our *Britain* lay,
Ere dawning science beam'd a cheering ray,
Dark monkish systems, and dull senseless rhymes
Swell'd the vain volumes of those ruder times:
When *Chaucer* rose, the *Phoebus* of our isle,
And bid bright art on downward ages smile;
His genius pierc'd the gloom of error through,
And truth with nature rose at once to view.
    In regal courts by princely favours grac'd
His easy muse acquir'd her skilful taste:
A universal genius she displays
In his mixt subject tun'd to various lays.
If in heroic strain he tries his art,
All *Homer*'s fire and strength his strains impart.
Is love his theme? How soft the lays, how warm!
With *Ovid*'s sweetness all his numbers charm
His thoughts so delicate, so bright his flame,
Not juster priase we owe the *Roman* name.
What pious strains the heavenly piece adorn,
Where guilty *Magdalen* is taught to mourne.
Devotion's charms their strongest powers combine,
And with the poet equal the divine.
When he some scene of tragic woe recites,
Our pity feels the strong distress he writes;
Like *Sophocles* majestic he appears,
And claims alike our wonder and our tears.
Does he to comic wit direct his aim?
His humour crowns th'attempt with equal fame.
Meer fictions for realities we take,
So just a picture his descriptions make;
So true with life his characters agree,
What e'er is read we almost think we see.
    Such *Chaucer* was, bright mirror of his age
Tho' length of years has quite obscur'd his page:
His stile grown obsolete, his numbers rude,
Scarce read, and but with labour understood.
Yet by fam'd modern bards new minted o'er,
His standard wit has oft enrich'd their store;

Whose *Canterbury Tales* could task impart
For *Pope*'s and *Dryden*'s choice-refining art;
And in their graceful polish let us view
What wealth enrich'd the mind where first they grew.

                              Astrophil.

78.   THOMAS SEWARD, GROSS EXPRESSIONS

1750

Thomas Seward (1708-90), canon of Lichfield and Salisbury,
father of Anna, to the 'Works of Beaumont and Fletcher',
1750, contributed a preface in which he analyses Chaucer's
use of gross expressions in terms of dramatic propriety:
Preface, I, lvi (cf. Alderson and Henderson, p. 220).

Yet of this Play ['The Custom of the Country'] *Dryden*
asserts that it contains more Bawdry than all his Plays
together. What must we say of these different Accounts?
Why 'tis clear as Day, that the Stile of the Age was so
chang'd, that what was formerly not esteem'd in the least
Degree indecent, was now become very much so; just as in
Chaucer, the very filthiest Words are us'd without Disguise, and says Beaumont in excuse for him, he gave those
Expressions to low Characters, with whom they were then in
common Use, and whom he could not therefore draw naturally
without them. The same Plea is now necessary for *Beaumont*
himself and all his contemporary Dramatic Poets; but there
is this grand and essential Difference between the gross
Expressions of our old Poets, and the more *delicate Lewdness* of modern Plays. In the former, gross Expressions
are generally the Language of low Life, and are giv'n to
Characters which are set in despicable Lights: In the
latter, *Lewdness* is frequently the Characteristic of the
Hero of the Comedy, and so intended to inflame the Passions and corrupt the Heart.

79. SAMUEL JOHNSON, HIS DICTION WAS IN GENERAL LIKE THAT
OF HIS CONTEMPORARIES

1755, 1765

Johnson (1709-84), critic, poet, biographer and lexicographer, was educated at Pembroke College, Oxford, and
shows no enthusiasm for Chaucer, though he once projected
an edition with full introduction and apparatus. In
extract (a), from his 'History of the English Language'
prefixed to 'A Dictionary of the English Language', 1755,
I, pp. 9ff., with a rare inattentiveness that betrays his
lack of sympathy, he mistakenly attributes the words
actually spoken by Venus, to Gower in his own person
('Confessio Amantis', ed. G.C. Macaulay, 1901, Vol. 2,
Book VIII, 2941*), and so confuses Gower's relationship to
Chaucer. He has not noticed Lydgate's indebtedness to
Chaucer. In extract (b), from his Preface to 'The Plays
of Shakespeare', Sigs B 7ff. C 4, E 3 he expresses his
critical principles and makes clear his sense that
Shakespeare wrote before the (Neoclassical) rules were
known. He associates Chaucer with Shakespeare in characterisation, and much of what he says about Shakespeare
clarifies his response to Chaucer, except that his view of
Chaucer is darkened by his Oxfordian feeling that Chaucer
lived in a barbarous age and is difficult to understand.
In his 'Life of Dryden', treating of the 'Fables', Johnson remarks that the works of Chaucer 'require little
criticism'.

(a)

The first of our authours, who can be properly said to have
written *English*, was Sir *John Gower*, who in his 'Confession of a Lover', calls *Chaucer* his disciple, and may
therefore be considered as the father of our poetry....
     The history of our language is now brought to the point
at which the history of our poetry is generally supposed
to commence, the time of the illustrious *Geoffry Chaucer*,
who may perhaps, with great justice, be stiled the first
of our versifiers who wrote poetically. He does not however appear to have deserved all the praise which he has
received, or all the censure that he has suffered. Dryden,
who mistaking genius for learning, and in confidence of

his abilities, ventured to write of what he had not examined, ascribes to *Chaucer* the first refinement of our numbers, the first production of easy and natural rhymes, and
the improvement of our language, by words borrowed from
the more polished languages of the Continent. *Skinner* contrarily blames him in harsh terms for having vitiated his
native speech by *whole cartloads of foreign words*. But he
that reads the works of *Gower* will find smooth numbers and
easy rhymes, of which *Chaucer* is supposed to have been the
inventor, and the *French* words, whether good or bad, of
which *Chaucer* is charged as the importer. Some innovations he might probably make, like others, in the infancy
of our poetry, which the paucity of books does [not] allow
us to discover with particular exactness; but the works of
Gower and *Lydgate* sufficiently evince that his diction was
in general like that of his contemporaries: and some
improvements he undoubtedly made by the various dispositions of his rhymes; and by the mixture of different numbers, in which he seems to have been happy and judicious.
I have selected several specimens both of his prose and
verse; and among them, part of his translation of
Boetius.... It would be improper to quote very sparingly
an author of so much reputation, or to make very large
extracts from a book so generally known.

(b)

(Sig. B7) He that, without diminution of any other excellence, shall preserve all the unities unbroken, deserves
the like applause with the architect, who shall display
all the orders of architecture in a citadel, without any
deduction from its strength; but the principal beauty of
a citadel is to exclude the enemy; and the greatest
graces of a play, are to copy nature and instruct life.
  Perhaps, what I have here not dogmatically but deliberately written, may recal the principles of the drama to a
new examination. I am almost frighted at my own temerity;
and when I estimate the fame and the strength of those
that maintain the contrary opinion, am ready to sink down
in reverential silence; as *Aeneas* withdrew from the defence of *Troy*, when he saw *Neptune* shaking the wall, and
Juno heading the besiegers.
  Those whom my arguments cannot persuade to give their
approbation to the judgment of *Shakespeare*, will easily,
if they consider the condition of his life, make some
allowance for his ignorance.
  Every man's performances, to be rightly estimated, must
be compared with the state of the age in which he lived,

and with his own particular opportunities; and though to
the reader a book be not worse or better for the circumstances of the authour, yet as there is always a silent
reference of human works to human abilities, and as the
enquiry, how far man may extend his designs, or how high
he may rate his native force, is of far greater dignity
than in what rank we shall place any particular performance, curiosity is always busy to discover the instru-
ments, as well as to survey the workmanship, to know how
much is to be ascribed to original powers, and how much to
casual and adventitious help. The palaces of *Peru* or
Mexico were certainly mean and incommodious habitations,
if compared to the houses of *European* monarchs; yet who
could forbear to view them with astonishment, who remembered that they were built without the use of iron?

The *English* nation, in the time of *Shakespeare*, was
yet struggling to emerge from barbarity. The philology of
Italy had been transplanted hither in the reign of *Henry*
the Eighth; and the learned languages had been success-
fully cultivated by *Lilly, Linacer,* and *More; by Pole,
Cheke,* and *Gardiner;* and afterwards by *Smith, Clerk,
Haddon,* and *Ascham.* Greek was now taught to boys in the
principal schools; and those who united elegance with
learning, read, with great diligence, the *Italian* and
Spanish poets. But literature was yet confined to professed scholars, or to men and women of high rank. The
publick was gross and dark; and to be able to read and
write, was an accomplishment still valued for its
rarity.

Nations, like individuals, have their infancy. A
people newly awakened to literary curiosity, being yet
unacquainted with the true state of things, knows not
how to judge of that which is proposed as its resemblance. Whatever is remote from common appearances is
always welcome to vulgar, as to childish credulity; and
of a country unenlightened by learning, the whole people
is the vulgar. The study of those who then aspired to
plebeian learning was laid out upon adventures, giants,
dragons, and enchantments. *The Death of Arthur* was the
favourite volume.

The mind, which has feasted on the luxurious wonders of
fiction, has no taste of the insipidity of truth. A play
which imitated only the common occurrences of the world,
would, upon the admirers of *Palmerin* and *Guy* of *Warwick*,
have made little impression; he that wrote for such an
audience was under the necessity of looking round for
strange events and fabulous transactions, and that
incredibility, by which maturer knowledge is offended, was
the chief recommendation of writings, to unskilful curiosity.

Our authour's plots are generally borrowed from novels, and it is reasonable to suppose, that he chose the most popular, such as were read by many, and related by more; for his audience could not have followed him through the intricacies of the drama, had they not held the thread of the story in their hands.

The stories, which we now find only in remoter authours, were in his time accessible and familiar. The fable of *As you like it* which is supposed to be copied from *Chaucer*'s Gamelyn, was a little pamphlet of those times; and old Mr. *Cibber* remembered the tale of *Hamlet* in plain *English* prose, which the criticks have now to seek in *Saxo Grammaticus*.

His *English* histories he took from *English* chronicles and *English* ballads; and as the ancient writers were made known to his countrymen by versions, they supplied him with new subjects; he dilated some of *Plutarch*'s lives into plays, when they had been translated by *North*.

His plots, whether historical or fabulous, are always crouded with incidents, by which the attention of a rude people was more easily caught than by sentiment or argumentation; and such is the power of the marvellous even over those who despise it, that every man finds his mind more strongly seized by the tragedies of *Shakespeare* than of any other writer; others please us by particular speeches, but he always makes us anxious for the event, and has perhaps excelled all but *Homer* in securing the first purpose of a writer, by exciting restless and unquenchable curiosity and compelling him that reads his work to read it through.

The shows and bustle with which his plays abound have the same original. As knowledge advances, pleasure passes from the eye to the ear, but returns, as it declines, from the ear to the eye. Those to whom our authour's labours were exhibited had more skill in pomps or processions than in poetical language, and perhaps wanted some visible and discriminated events, as comments on the dialogue. He knew how he should most please; and whether his practice is more agreeable to nature, or whether his example has prejudiced the nation, we still find that on our stage something must be done as well as said, and inactive declamation is very coldly heard, however musical or elegant, passionate or sublime.

Voltaire expresses his wonder, that our authour's extravagances are endured by a nation, which has seen the tragedy of *Cato*. Let him be answered, that *Addison* speaks the language of poets, and *Shakespeare*, of men....

(Sig. C4) There is a vigilance of observation and accuracy of distinction which books and precepts cannot

confer; from this almost all original and native excellence proceeds. *Shakespeare* must have looked upon mankind
with perspicacity, in the highest degree curious and atten-
tive. Other writers borrow their characters from preceding writers, and diversify them only by the accidental
appendages of present manners; the dress is a little
varied, but the body is the same. Our authour had both
matter and form to provide; for except the characters of
Chaucer, to whom I think he is not much indebted, there
were no writers in *English*, and perhaps not many in other
modern languages, which shewed life in its native colours.

   (Sig. E3) The criticks on ancient authours have, in the
exercise of their sagacity, many assistances, which the
editor of *Shakespeare* is condemned to want. They are
employed upon grammatical and settled languages, whose
construction contributes so much to perspicuity, that
Homer has fewer passages unintelligible than *Chaucer*.

80. JOSEPH WARTON, VERY SUDDEN TRANSITIONS FROM THE
SUBLIME TO THE RIDICULOUS

1756, 1782

Joseph Warton (1722-1800), brother of Thomas, was educated
at Oriel College, Oxford. His most significant work is
his 'Essay on the Genius and Writings of Pope', Vol. I,
1756; Vol. II, 1782; quoted here from the edition of 1806;
extract (a) from I, pp. 393-5, discussing the 'Temple of
Fame', Pope's version of Chaucer's 'House of Fame'; and
extract (b) from II, pp. 6-9. Warton is perturbed by
Chaucer's Gothic mixture, which violates that Neoclassical
criterion of *decorum* to observe which in poetry, as Milton
observed, 'is the grand masterpiece'. Warton considers
that Pope improved the design of 'The House of Fame' (ed.
cit., I, p. 338).

(a)

On the revival of literature, the first writers seemed not
to have observed any SELECTION in their thoughts and
images. Dante, Petrarch, Boccace, Ariosto, make very

sudden transitions from the sublime to the ridiculous.
Chaucer, in his Temple of Mars, among many pathetic pictures, has brought in a strange line,

The coke is scalded for all his long ladell. (1)

No writer has more religiously observed the decorum here
recommended than Virgil.

This having heard and seen, some pow'r unknown,
Strait chang'd the scene, and snatch'd me from the
throne;
Before my view appear'd a structure fair,
Its site uncertain, if in earth or air.(l. 417).

The scene here changes from the TEMPLE of FAME to that
of Rumour. Such a change is not methinks judicious, as it
destroys the unity of the subject, and distracts the view
of the reader; not to mention, that the difference between
Rumour and Fame is not sufficiently distinct and percept-
ible. POPE has, however, the merit of compressing the
sense of a great number of Chaucer's lines into a small
compass. As Chaucer takes every opportunity of satyrizing
the follies of his age, he has in this part introduced
many circumstances, which it was prudent in POPE to omit,
as they would not have been either relished or understood
in the present times.

While thus I stood intent to see and hear,
One came, methought, and whisper'd in my ear,
What could thus high thy rash ambition raise?
Art thou, fond youth, a candidate for praise?
'Tis true, (said I,) not void of hopes I came,
For who so fond as youthful bards, of Fame?

This conclusion is not copied from Chaucer, and is
judicious. Chaucer has finished his story inartificially,
by saying he was surprised at the sight of a man of great
authority, and awoke in a fright. The succeeding lines
give a pleasing moral to the allegory; and the two last
shew the man of honour and virtue, as well as the poet:

Unblemish'd let me live, or die unknown:
Oh grant an honest fame, or grant me none!

In finishing this Section, we may observe, that POPE's
alterations of Chaucer are introduced with judgment and
art; that these alterations are more in number, and more
important in conduct, than any Dryden has made of the same

author. This piece was communicated to Steele, who entertained a high opinion of its beauties, and who conveyed it
to Addison. POPE had ornamented the poem with the machinery of guardian angels, which he afterwards omitted....

Note

1 Thus again; ——— 'As Aesop's dogs contending for a
        bone;' ———and many others.

                              (b)

The WIFE OF BATH is the other piece of Chaucer which POPE
selected to imitate. One cannot but wonder at his choice,
which, perhaps, nothing but his youth could excuse.
Dryden, who is known not to be nicely scrupulous, informs
us, that he would not versify it on account of its
indecency. POPE, however, has omitted or softened the
grosser and more offensive passages. Chaucer afforded him
many subjects of a more serious and sublime species; and
it were to be wished. POPE had exercised his pencil on
the pathetic story of the Patience of Grisilda, or Troilus
and Cressida, or the Complaint of the Black Knight; or,
above all, on Cambuscan and Canace. From the accidental
circumstance of Dryden and POPE's having copied the gay
and ludicrous parts of Chaucer, the common notion seems
to have arisen, that Chaucer's vein of poetry was chiefly
turned to the light and the ridiculous.(1) But they who
look into Chaucer, will soon be convinced of this prevailing prejudice; and will find his comic vein, like that
of Shakespeare, to be only like one of mercury, imperceptibly mingled with a mine of gold.
    CHAUCER is highly extolled by Dryden, in the spirited
and pleasing preface to his fables; for his prefaces,
after all, are very pleasing, notwithstanding the opposite
opinions they contain, because his prose is the most numerous and sweet, the most *mellow* and *generous*, of any our
language has yet produced.

Note

1 Cowley is said to have despised Chaucer. I am not surprised at this strange judgment. Cowley was indisputably a genius, but his taste was perverted and narrowed
   by a love of witticisms.

81 THOMAS GRAY, CIRCUMSTANCES ALTER

c. 1760

Gray (1716-71), poet and scholar, was educated at Peterhouse, Cambridge, where he lived until removing to Pembroke College in 1756 because of the rude behaviour of
the Peterhouse men. His comments on Chaucer occur in
the second volume of his Commonplace Books (now in Pembroke College), Vol. II, pp. 743ff., written partly for
a projected history of English poetry. His comments on
Lydgate frequently suggest his views on Chaucer, while
his comments on Chaucer's metre are also those of a poet
concerned with technique. His observations on 'circumstances' (which we should call 'realism') reflect the
progressive interest in literary realism of the eighteenth
century, as well as general truth.

Gray reveals a capacity, truly remarkable in his own
time, for historical scholarly imagination and penetration without loss of critical standards. In contrast
with Johnson he seems quite free from Neoclassical prejudice, while in his appreciation of a 'certain terrible
greatness' in Chaucer he shows a Romantic quality that is
also rare.

Gray's prose is informal and admirably taut. His comments were edited in 1814 by T.J. Mathias, who cast a
haze of early nineteenth-century pedantry over Gray's
sometimes elliptical clarity, as well as introducing a
number of inaccuracies. All later versions reproduce
Mathias, plus their own errors. The following transcript appears to be the first to be taken direct from
the Commonplace Book, without intentional change, by
courtesy of the Master and Fellows of Pembroke College.
According to Gosse ('Life of Gray') it was written about
1760.

However little [Lydgate] might be *acquainted* with Homer &
Virgil, it is certain he was very much so with Chaucer's
compositions, whom he calls his master, & who (I imagine)
was so in a literal sense: certain 'tis Lydgate was full
30 years when Chaucer died. but whatever his skill were
in either of the learned languages, it is sure he has not
taken his 'Fall of Princes' from the original Latin prose

of Boccace, but from a French Translation of it by one
Laurence, as he tells us himself in the beginning of his
work; it was indeed rather a Paraphrase than a translation, for he took the liberty of making several additions,
& of reciting more at large many histories, that Boccace
had slightly passed over.

> And *he* saieth eke, that his entencion   Laurence
> Is to amende, correcten & declare,
> Not to condemne of no presumpcion,
> But to support plainly & to spare
> Thing touched shortly of the storie bare
> Under a stile brief and compendious,
> Them to prolonge when they be vertuous:
>   For a storie which is not plainly tolde,
> But constrained under wordes few,
> For lack of truth wher they ben new or old
> Men by reporte cannot the matter shewe:
> These okes great be not downe yhewe
> First at a stroke, but by long process,
> Ner long stories a word may not expresse.

These *Long processes* indeed suited wonderfully with the
attention & simple curiosity of the age, in which Lydgate
lived. many *a stroke* have he & the best of his Contemporaries spent upon a sturdy old story, till they had blun-
ted their own edge, & that of their readers. at least a
modern reader will find it so; but it is a folly to judge
of the understanding & of the patience of those times by
our own. they loved, I will not say Tediousness, but
length & a train of circumstances in a narration. the
Vulgar do so still; it gives an air of reality to facts,
it fixes the attention, raises and keeps in suspense their
expectation, & supplies the defects of their little &
lifeless imagination; it keeps pace with the slow motion
of their own thoughts. tell them a story as you would
tell it a Man of wit, it will appear to them as an object
seen in the night by a flash of lightening; but when you
have placed it in various lights & various positions, they
will come at last to see & feel it, as well as others.
but we need not confine ourselves to the Vulgar & to
understandings beneath our own. Circumstance was ever &
ever will be the Life & essence both of Oratory & Poetry.
it has in some sort the same effect upon every mind, that
it has on that of the populace; & I fear, the quickness &
delicate impatience of these polish'd times we live in,
are but forerunners of the decline of all those beautiful
arts that depend upon the imagination. whether these
apprehensions are well or ill grounded, it is sufficient

for me, that Homer, the Father of Circumstance, has occasion for the same apology I am making for Lydgate & his Predecessors. not that I pretend to make any more comparison between his beauties & theirs, than I do between the different languages they wrote in: ours was indeed barbarous enough at that time, the Orthography unsettled, the Syntax very deficient & confused, the Metre & Number of syllables left to the ear alone, and yet with all its rudeness our Tongue had then aquired an Energy & a Plenty by the adoption of a variety of words borrow'd from the French, the Provençal, and the Italian about the middle of the 14th century, that at this day our best Writers seem to miss & to regret, for many of them have gradually drop'd into disuse, & are only now to be found in the remotest Counties of England. Another thing, which perhaps contributed something to the making our ancient Poets so voluminous, was the great facility of rhiming, which is now grown so difficult. words of two & three syllables being then newly taken from foreign languages did still retain their original accent, & that (as they were mostly derived from the French) fell according to the Genius of that tongue upon the Last Syllable, which, if it still had continued among us, had been a great advantage to our Poetry. among the Scotch this still continues in many words, for they say, Envỹ, Practĩse, Pensĩve, Positĩve, &c: but we in process of time, have accustom'd ourselves to throw back all our accents upon the Antepenultima, in words of three or more syllables, and of our Dissyllables comparatively but a few are left, as Disdaĩn, Despaĩr, Repēnt, Pretēnd, &c: where the stress is not laid upon the Penultima; By this means we are almost reduced to find our Rhimes among the Monosyllables, in which our tongue too much abounds, a defect that will forever hinder it from adapting itself well to Musick, & must be no small impediment consequently to the sweetness & harmony of Versification....

   To return to Lydgate, I do not pretend to set him on a level with his master Chaucer, but he certainly comes the nearest to him of any contemporary writer that I am aquainted with. his choice of expression, & the smoothness of his verse far surpass both Gower & Occleve. he wanted not art in raising the more tender emotions of mind, of which I might give several examples, the first is of that sympathy which we feel for humble piety & contrition....

   (p. 747) it is observable, that in images of horrour & a certain terrible Greatness, our author comes far behind Chaucer. whether they were not suited to the Genius or the temper of Lydgate I do not determine; but it is sure

that, tho' they seem'd naturally to present themselves, he
has almost in general chose to avoid them. yet is there
frequently a stiller kind of majesty both in his thought
& expression, which makes one of his principal beauties...

   (p. 749) Lydgate seems to have been by nature of a more
serious & melancholick turn of mind than Chaucer: yet one
here & there meets with a stroke of Satyr and Irony that
does not want humour, & it usually falls (as was the custom of those times) either upon the Women or on the Clergy.
as the Religious were the principal Scholars of these
ages, they probably gave the tone in writing & in wit to
the rest of the nation. the celibacy imposed on them by
the Church had sower'd their temper, and naturally disposed them (as it is observed of Old-Bachelors in our
days) to make the Weaknesses of the other Sex their theme;
& tho' every one had a profound respect for his own particular order, yet the feuds and bickerings between one
Order & another were perpetual & irreconcileable: these
possibly were the causes that directed the Satyr of our
old Writers principally to those two objects....

   (p. 750) This kind of satyr I know, will appear to
modern Men of Taste a little stale & unfashionable: but
our reflections should go deeper, & lead us to consider
the fading & transitory nature of Wit in general. I have
attempted to shew above the source from whence the two
prevailing subjects of our Ancestor's Severity were
derived: let us observe their different success & duration from those times to our own....

(p. 757)   Metrum

   Though I would not with Mr. Urry, the last Editor of
Chaucer, insert words & syllables, unauthorized by the
oldest Manuscripts, to help out what seems lame and defective in the measure of our ancient writers; yet as I see
those MSS, and the first printed Editions, so extremely
inconstant in their manner of spelling one & the same
word, as to vary continually, often in the compass of two
Lines, & seem to have no fix'd Orthography at all, I can
not help thinking it probable, that many great inequali-
ties in the metre are owing to the neglect of Transcribers, or that the manner of reading made up for the defects
that appear in the writing. thus the y which we often see
prefix'd to Participles passive, as ycleped, yhewe, &c: is
not a mere arbitrary insertion to fill up the verse, but
the old Anglo-Saxon augment, always prefix'd formerly to
such Participles, as gelufod (loved) from lufian (to
love), geraed, from raedan (to read), &c....   this

syllable, tho' (I suppose) then out of use in common
speech, our Poets inserted, where it suited them, in verse.
the same did they by the final syllable of verbs, as *bren-
nin, correctin, dronkin*...this termination begun to be
omitted, after the Danes were settled among us...the tran-
sition is very apparent from thence to the English, we now
speak. as then our writers inserted these initial and
final syllables, or omitted them; & where we see them written, we do not doubt, that they were meant to fill up the
measure, it follows that these Poets had an ear not insen-
sible to defects in metre; & where the verse seems to
halt, it very probably is occasion'd by the Transcriber's
neglect who seeing a word differently spelt from the
manner then customary, changed or omitted a few letters
without reflecting on the injury done to the measure. the
case is the same with the genitive case singular, & nomin-
ative plural of many nouns, which by the Saxon inflexion
had an additional syllable, as *word*, a word, *wordes*, of a
word: *smith*, a Smith, *smithes*, of a smith; *smithas*,
Smiths. which (as Hickes observes) is the origin of the
formation of those cases in our present tongue; but we
now have reduced them by our pronunciation to an equal
number of syllables with their Nominatives-singular. this
was commonly done (I imagine) too in Chaucer & Lydgate's
time; but in verse they took the Liberty either to follow
the old language in pronouncing the final syllable; or to
sink the vowel, and abridge it, as was usual; according to
the necessity of their versification. for example, they
would read either vĭolēttĕs with four syllables, or vio-
lets with three; *bānkis*, or banks, *triūmphys*, or triūmphs,
indifferently. I have already mention'd the *e* mute &
their use of it in words derived from the French and
imagine, that they did the same in many of true English
Origin, which the Danes had before rob'd of their final
consonant, writing *bute*, for the Saxon *butan* (without)...
here we may easily conceive, that tho' the *n* was taken
away, yet the *e* continued to be pronounced faintly, and
tho' in time it was quite drop'd in conversation, yet,
when the Poet thought fit to make a syllable of it, it no
more offended their ears, than it now does those of a
Frenchman to hear it so pronounced, in verse...
    These reflections may serve to shew us, that Puttenham,
tho' he lived within about 150 years of Chaucer's time,
must be mistaken with regard to what the old Writers
call'd their *riding* ryme, for the Canterbury Tales, which
he gives as an example of it, are as exact in their measure & their pause as the Troilus and Creseide where he
says *the meetre is very grave and stately;* and this not
only in the Knight's Tale, but in the comic introduction
and characters...,

I conclude, he was misled by the change words had
undergone in their accents since the days of Chaucer, & by
the seeming defects of measure that frequently occur in
the printed copies.

82.   RICHARD HURD, GOTHIC AND NEOCLASSICAL

1762

Hurd (1720-1808), was educated at Emmanuel College, Cambridge, where he appears to have been unremarked, and
eventually became Bishop of Worcester, creating a notable
Library. He included literary scholarship and criticism
among his numerous writings, and his 'Letters of Chivalry
and Romance (1762)', from which the following extracts are
taken, was influential in developing Romantic taste for
the literary Gothic. His distinction between Gothic or
'classical' (what is now better called Neoclassical) is an
important contribution to the understanding of literary
form, and of the literary concepts, conscious and unconscious, that so largely determine literary taste and
judgment. In order to give his argument fair scope for
comprehension the extracts extend beyond the specific
references to Chaucer. He deserves comparison with Gray.

From LETTER VI, pp. 54ff.

We are upon enchanted ground, my friend; and you are to
think yourself well used that I detain you no longer in
this fearful circle. The glympse, you have had of it,
will help your imagination to conceive the rest. And
without more words you will readily apprehend that the
fancies of our modern bards are not only more gallant, but,
on a change of the scene, more sublime, more terrible,
more alarming, than those of the classic fablers. In a
word, you will find that the *manners* they paint, and the
superstitions they adopt, are the more poetical for being
Gothic.

LETTER VII

But nothing shews the difference of the two systems under
consideration more plainly, than the effect they really
had on the two greatest of our Poets; at least the Two
which an English reader is most fond to compare with Homer,
I mean SPENSER and MILTON.

It is not to be doubted but that each of these bards
had kindled his poetic fire from classic fables. So that,
of course, their prejudices would lie that way. Yet they
both appear, when most inflamed, to have been more particularly rapt with the Gothic fables of chivalry.

Spenser, tho' he had been long nourished with the
spirit and substance of Homer and Virgil, chose the times
of chivalry for his theme, and fairy Land for the scene of
his fictions. He could have planned, no doubt, an heroic
design on the exact classic model: Or, he might have
trimmed between the Gothic and Classic, as his contemporary Tasso did. But the charms of *fairy* prevailed. And
if any think, he was seduced by Ariosto into this choice,
they should consider that it could be only for the sake
of his subject; for the genius and character of these
poets was widely different.

Under this idea then of a Gothic, not classical poem,
the 'Faery Queen' is to be read and criticized. And on
these principles, it would not be difficult to unfold it's
merit in another way than has been hitherto attempted.

Milton, it is true, preferred the classic model to the
Gothic. But it was after long hesitation; and his favourite subject was *Arthur and his Knights of the round table.*
On this he had fixed for the greater part of his life.
What led him to change his mind was, partly, as I suppose,
his growing fanaticism; partly, his ambition to take a
different rout from Spenser; but chiefly perhaps, the discredit into which the stories of chivalry had now fallen
by the immortal satire of Cervantes. Yet we see thro' all
his poetry, where his enthusiasm flames out most, a certain predilection for the legends of chivalry before the
fables of Greece.

This circumstance, you know, has given offence to the
austerer and more mechanical critics. They are ready to
censure his judgment, as juvenile and unformed, when they
see him so delighted, on all occasions, with the Gothic
romances. But do these censors imagine that Milton did
not perceive the defects of these works, as well as they?
No: it was not the *composition* of books of chivalry, but
the *manners* described in them, that took his fancy; as
appears from his 'Allegro'---

> Towred cities please us then
> And the busy hum of men,
> Where throngs of knights and barons bold
> In weeds of peace high triumphs hold,
> With store of ladies, whose bright eyes
> Rain influence, and judge the prize
> Of wit, or arms, while both contend
> To win her grace, whom all commend.

And when in the 'Penseroso' he draws, by a fine contrivance, the same kind of image to sooth melancholy which he had before given to excite mirth, he indeed extolls an *author* of one of these romances, as he had before, in general, extolled the *subject* of them; but it is an author worthy of his praise; not the writer of *Amadis*, or *Sir Launcelot of the Lake*, but Chaucer himself, who has left an unfinished story on the Gothic or feudal model.

> Or, call up him that left half-told
> The story of Cambuscan bold,
> Of Camball and of Algarsife,
> And who had Canace to wife
> That own'd the virtuous ring and glass,
> And of the wondrous horse of brass,
> On which the Tartar king did ride;
> And if ought else great bards beside
> In sage and solemn tunes have sung
> Of turneys and of trophies hung,
> Of forests and inchantments drear,
> Where more is meant than meets the ear.

The conduct then of these two poets may incline us to think with more respect, than is commonly done of the *Gothic manners*, I mean as adapted to the uses of the greater poetry.

I say nothing of Shakespear, because the sublimity (the divinity, let it be, if nothing else will serve) of his genius kept no certain rout, but rambled at hazard into all the regions of human life and manners. So that we can hardly say what he preferred, or what he rejected, on full deliberation. Yet one thing is clear, that even he is greater when he uses Gothic manners and machinery, than when he employs classical: which brings us again to the same point, that the former have, by their nature and genius, the advantage of the latter in producing the *sublime*.

LETTER VIII

I spoke 'of criticizing Spenser's poem, under the idea,
not of a classical but Gothic composition.'

It is certain much light might be thrown on that singular work, were an able critic to consider it in this view.
For instance, he might go some way towards explaining,
perhaps justifying, the general plan and *conduct* of the
Faery Queen, which, to classical readers has appeared
indefensible.

I have taken the fancy, with your leave, to try my
hand on this curious subject.

When an architect examines a Gothic structure by Grecian rules, he finds nothing but deformity. But the Gothic
architecture has it's own rules, by which when it comes to
be examined, it is seen to have it's merit, as well as the
Grecian. The question is not, which of the two is conducted in the simplest or truest taste: but, whether there be
not sense and design in both, when scrutinized by the laws
on which each is projected....

LETTER XI

But you are weary of hearing so much of these exploded
fancies; and are ready to ask, if there be any truth in
this representation, 'Whence it has come to pass, that
the classical manners are still admired and imitated by
the poets, when the Gothic have long since fallen into
disuse?'

The answer to this question will furnish all that is
now wanting to a proper discussion of the present subject.

One great reason of this difference certainly was, That
the ablest writers of Greece ennobled the system of heroic
manners, while it was fresh and flourishing; and their
works, being master-pieces of composition, so fixed the
credit of it in the opinion of the world, that no revolutions of time and taste could afterwards shake it.

Whereas the Gothic having been disgraced in their
infancy by bad writers, and a new set of manners springing
up before there were any better to do them justice, they
could never be brought into vogue by the attempts of later
poets; who in spite of prejudice, and for the genuine
charm of these highly poetical manners, did their utmost
to recommend them.

But, FURTHER, the Gothic system was not only forced to
wait long for real genius to do it honour; real genius was
even very early employed against it.

There were two causes of this mishap. The old roman-
cers had even outraged the truth in their extravagant
pictures of chivalry: And Chivalry itself, such as it once
had been, was greatly abated.

So that men of sense were doubly disgusted to find a
representation of things *unlike* to what they observed in
real life, and *beyond* what it was ever possible should
have existed. However, with these disadvantages there was
still so much of the old spirit left, and the fascination
of these wondrous tales was so prevalent, that a more than
common degree of sagacity and good sense was required to
penetrate the illusion.

It was one of this character, I suppose, that put the
famous question to Ariosto, which has been so often repeated that I shall spare you the disgust of hearing it.
Yet long before his time an immortal genius of our own
(so superior is the sense of some men to the age they live
in) saw as far into this matter, as Ariosto's examiner.
This sagacious person was Dan Chaucer; who in a reign,
that almost realized the wonders of romantic chivalry, not
only discerned the absurdity of the old romances, but has
even ridiculed them with incomparable spirit.

His RIME OF SIR TOPAZ, in the Canterbury tales, is a
manifest banter on these books, and may be considered as
a sort of prelude to the adventures of Don Quixot. I call
it *a manifest banter*: For we are to observe that this was
Chaucer's own tale, and that, when in the progress of it
the good sense of the Host is made to break in upon him,
and interrupt him, Chaucer approves his disgust and,
changing his note, tells the simple instructive tale of
Meliboeus, *a moral tale virtuous*, as he chuses to charac-
terize it; to shew, what sort of fictions were most expressive of real life, and most proper to be put into the
hands of the people.

One might further observe that the Rime of Sir Topaz
itself is so managed as with infinite humour to expose the
leading impertinences of books of chivalry, and their
impertinencies only; as may be seen by the different conduct of this tale, from that of Cambuscan, which Spenser
and Milton were so pleased with, and which with great propriety is put into the mouth of the SQUIRE.

But I must not anticipate the observations which you
will take a pleasure to make for yourself on these two
fine parts of the Canterbury tales. Enough is said to
illustrate the point, I am now upon, 'That these phantoms
of chivalry had the misfortune to be laughed out of countenance by men of sense, before the substance of it had
been fairly and truly represented by any capable writer.'

STILL, the principal reason of all, no doubt, was, That

the Gothic manners of Chivalry, as springing out of the
feudal system, were as singular, as that system itself:
So that, when that political constitution vanished out of
Europe, the manners, that belonged to it, were no longer
seen or understood. There was no example of any such
manners remaining on the face of the Earth: And as they
never did subsist but once, and are never likely to subsist again, people would be led of course to think and
speak of them, as romantic, and unnatural. The consequence of which was a total contempt and rejection of
them; while the classic manners, as arising out of the
customary and usual situations of humanity, would have
many archetypes, and appear natural even to those who saw
nothing similar to them actually subsisting before their
eyes.

Thus, tho' the manners of Homer are perhaps as different from our's, as those of Chivalry itself, yet as we
know that such manners always belong to rude and simple
ages, such as Homer paints; and actually subsist at this
day in countries that are under the like circumstances of
barbarity, we readily agree to call them *natural*, and even
take a fond pleasure in the survey of them.

Your question then is easily answered, without any
obligation upon me to give up the Gothic manners as
visionary and fantastic. And the reason appears, why the
'Faery Queen', one of the noblest productions of modern
poetry, is fallen into so general a neglect, that all the
zeal of it's commentators is esteemed officious and impertinent, and will never restore it to those honours which
it has, once for all, irrecoverably lost.

In effect, what way of persuading the generality of
readers that the romantic manners are to be accounted
natural, when not one in ten-thousand knows enough of the
barbarous ages, in which they arose, to believe they ever
really existed?

Poor Spenser then,

> in whose gentle spright
> The pure well-head of Poesie did dwell,

must, for ought I can see, be left to the admiration of a
few lettered and curious men: While the many are sworn
together to give no quarter to the *marvellous*, or, which
may seem still harder, to the *moral* of his song.

However this great revolution in modern taste was
brought about by degrees; and the steps, that led to it,
may be worth the tracing in a distinct Letter.

LETTER XII

The wonders of Chivalry were still in the memory of men,
were still existing, in some measure, in real life, when
Chaucer undertook to expose the barbarous relaters of them.
   This ridicule, we may suppose, hastened the fall both
of Chivalry and Romance. At least from that time the
spirit of both declined very fast, and at length fell into
such discredit, that when now Spenser arose, and with a
genius singularly fitted to immortalize the land of faery,
he met with every difficulty and disadvantage to obstruct
his design....

83.   THOMAS WARTON, THE LUSTRE AND DIGNITY OF A TRUE POET

1774

Warton (1728-90), educated at Trinity College, Oxford,
professor of poetry and of history at Oxford, poet laureate, editor, wrote a pioneer 'History of English Poetry'
(1774-81) containing many sensible references to and a
long narrative account of Chaucer's works (in Vol. I,
1774), of which the following are examples. Warton
appreciates Chaucer's humour, and sees that Chaucer's
'Gothic' structure is genuinely different from 'modern'
structure, but he is in some ways more Romantically
Gothic than Chaucer himself. Like Gray and Hurd, Warton
signalises a new development in sensibility and his remarks on e.g. 'The House of Fame' should be contrasted with
those of Samuel Johnson, to whom they were no doubt intended as an answer. Nevertheless he persists in the commendation of Chaucer's realism, characterisation and humour as against a barbarous age.

(a) From Vol. I, Section XII, p. 341.

Hitherto our poets had been persons of a private and cir-
cumscribed education, and the art of versifying, like
every other kind of composition, had been confined to
recluse scholars. But Chaucer was a man of the world:
and from this circumstance we are to account, in great

measure, for the many new embellishments which he conferred on our language and our poetry. The descriptions
of splendid processions and gallant carousals, with which
his works abound, are a proof that he was conversant with
the practices and diversions of polite life. Familiarity
with a variety of things and objects, opportunities of
acquiring the fashionable and courtly modes of speech,
connections with the great at home, and a personal
acquaintance with the vernacular poets of foreign countries, opened his mind and furnished him with new lights.
In Italy he was introduced to Petrarch, at the wedding of
Violante, daughter of Galleazzo duke of Milan, with the
duke of Clarence: and it is not improbable that Boccaccio
was of the party. Although Chaucer undoubtedly studied
the works of these celebrated writers, and particularly of
Dante before this fortunate interview; yet it seems likely,
that these excursions gave him a new relish for their compositions, and enlarged his knowledge of the Italian
fables. His travels likewise enabled him to cultivate the
Italian and Provencal languages with the greatest success:
and induced him to polish the asperity, and enrich the
sterility of his native versification, with softer caden-
ces, and a more copious and varigated phraseology. In
this attempt, which was authorised by the recent and popular examples of Petrarch in Italy, and Alain Chartier in
France, he was countenanced and assisted by his friend
John Gower, the early guide and encourager of his studies.
The revival of learning in most countries appears to have
first owed its rise to translation. At rude periods the
modes of original thinking are unknown, and the arts of
original composition have not yet been studied. The
writers therefore of such periods are chiefly and very
usefully employed in importing the ideas of other languages into their own. They do not venture to think for
themselves, nor aim at the merit of inventors, but they
are laying the foundations of literature; and while they
are naturalising the knowledge of more learned ages and
countries by translation, they are imperceptibly improving
the national language. This has been remarkably the case,
not only in England, but in France and Italy....
    (p.344) But Chaucer manifestly first taught his
countrymen to write English; and formed a style by
naturalising words from the Provencal, at that time the
most polished dialect of any in Europe, and the best
adapted to the purposes of poetical expression.
    It is certain that Chaucer abounds in classical allu-
sions: but his poetry is not formed on the ancient models.
He appears to have been an universal reader, and his
learning is sometimes mistaken for genius: but his chief

sources were the French and Italian poets....

(b) From Section XIV, p. 396.

Pope has imitated this piece [i.e. 'The House of Fame',
rendered by Pope as 'The Temple of Fame'] with his usual
elegance of diction and harmony of versification. But in
the meantime, he has not only misrepresented the story,
but marred the character of the poem. He has endeavoured
to correct it's extravagancies, by new refinements and
additions of another cast: but he did not consider, that
extravagancies are essential to a poem of such a structure,
and even constitute its beauties. An attempt to unite
order and exactness of imagery with a subject formed on
principles so professedly romantic and anomalous, is like
giving Corinthian pillars to a Gothic palace. When I read
Pope's elegant imitation of this piece, I think I am walking among the modern monuments unsuitably placed in
Westminster-abbey.

(c) From Section XV, p. 414.

Every reader of taste and imagination must regret, that
instead of our author's tedious detail of the quaint
effects of Canace's ring [i.e. in 'The Squire's Tale'], in
which a falcon relates her amours, and talks familiarly of
Troilus, Paris and Jason, the notable achievements we may
suppose to have been performed by the assistance of the
horse of brass, are either lost, or that this part of the
story, by far the most interesting, was never written.

(d) From Section XVI, p. 433: after discussing the
'Reeve's' and 'Summoner's' Tales, Warton continues:

Genuine humour, the concomitant of true taste, consists in
discerning improprieties in books as well as characters.
We therefore must remark under this class another tale of
Chaucer, which till lately has been looked upon as a grave
heroic narrative. I mean the RIME OF SIR THOPAS. Chaucer,
at a period which almost realised the manners of romantic
chivalry, discerned the leading absurdities of the old
romances: and in this poem, which may be justly called a
prelude to Don Quixote, has burlesqued them with exquisite
ridicule. That this was the poet's aim, appears from many
passages....
     (p. 434) But it is to be remembered, that Chaucer's

design was intended to ridicule the frivolous descriptions,
and other tedious impertinencies, so common in the volumes
of chivalry with which his age is overwhelmed, not to degrade in general or expose a mode of fabling, whose sublime extravagancies constitute the marvellous graces of
his own CAMBUSCAN; a composition which at the same time
abundantly demonstrates, that the manners of romance are
better calculated to answer the purposes of pure poetry,
to captivate the imagination, and to produce surprise,
than the fictions of classical antiquity.

(e) From Section XVII, p. 435.

But Chaucer's vein of humour, although conspicuous in the
CANTERBURY TALES, is chiefly displayed in the Characters
with which they are introduced. In these his knowledge
of the world availed him in a peculiar degree, and enabled
him to give such an accurate picture of ancient manners,
as no cotemporary nation has transmitted to posterity. It
is here that we view the pursuits and employments, the
customs and diversions, of our ancestors, copied from the
life, and represented with equal truth and spirit, by a
judge of mankind, whose penetration qualified him to dis-
cern their foibles or discriminating pecularities: and by
an artist, who understood that proper selection of circumstances, and those predominant characteristics, which form
a finished portrait. We are surprised to find, in so
gross and ignorant an age, such talents for satire, and
for observation on life; qualities which usually exert
themselves at more civilised periods, when the improved
state of society, by subtilising our speculations, and
establishing uniform modes of behaviour, disposes mankind
to study themselves, and renders deviations of conduct,
and singularities of character, more immediately and
necessarily the objects of censure and ridicule. These
curious and valuable remains are specimens of Chaucer's
native genius, unassisted and unalloyed. The figures are
all British, and bear no suspicious signatures of classical, Italian, or French imitation. The characters of
Theophrastus are not so lively, particular and appropriated. A few traites from this celebrated part of our
author, yet too little tasted and understood, may be sufficient to prove and illustrate what is here advanced.

(f) From Section XVIII, p. 457.

It is not my intention to dedicate a volume to Chaucer,

how much soever he may deserve it; nor can it be expected,
that, in a work of this general nature, I should enter
into a critical examination of all Chaucer's pieces.
Enough has been said to prove, that in elevation and elegance, in harmony and perspicuity of versification, he
surpasses his predecessors in an infinite proportion: that
his genius was universal, and adapted to themes of unboun-
ded variety: that his merit was not less in painting
familiar manners with humour and propriety, than in moving
the passions, and in representing the beautiful or the
grand objects of nature with grace and sublimity. In a
word, that he appeared with all the lustre and dignity of
a true poet, in an age which compelled him to struggle
with a barbarous language, and a national want of taste;
and when to write verses at all, was regarded as a singular qualification.

84. THOMAS TYRWHITT, INTELLIGENCE AND SATISFACTION

1775

Tyrwhitt (1730-86), educated at the Queen's College,
Oxford, was a classical philologist and clerk in the
House of Commons; he combined learning and scholarship
with personal generosity to an unusual degree. His
remarkable range of linguistic learning in many languages
included a grasp of fourteenth- and fifteenth-century
English probably unique in his day. His edition of 'The
Canterbury Tales' is the first truly scholarly edition of
any part of Chaucer; he was the first to examine manuscript variants analytically. The following extracts
illustrate his purpose and the cool Oxonian sceptical
empiricism of his method: (a) from the Preface, Vol. I;
(b) from the Essay on the Language and Versification of
Chaucer, Vol. IV.

(a)

(p. i) The first object of this publication was to give
the text of 'The Canterbury Tales' as correct as the MSS.

within the reach of the Editor would enable him to make it.

The account of former Editions, in the Appendix to this Preface, will shew, that this object had hitherto been either entirely neglected, or at least very imperfectly pursued. The Editor therefore has proceeded as if his Author had never been published before. He has formed the text throughout from the MSS and has paid little regard to the readings of any edition, except the two by Caxton, each of which may now be considered as a Manuscript. A list of the MSS. collated, or consulted, upon this occasion is subjoined.

In order to make the proper use of these MSS., to unravel the confusions of their orthography, and to judge between a great number of various readings, it was necessary to enquire into the state of our language and versification at the time when Chaucer wrote, and also, as much as was possible, into the peculiarities of his style and manner of composition. Nor was it less necessary to examine with some attention the work now intended to be republished; to draw a line between the imperfections, which may be supposed to have been left in it by the author, and those which have crept into it since; to distinguish the parts where the author appears as an inventor, from those where he is merely a translator or imitator; and throughout the whole to trace his allusions to a variety of forgotten books and obsolete customs. As a certain degree of information upon all these points will be found to be necessary even for the reading of the Canterbury tales with intelligence and satisfaction, the Editor hopes he shall be excused for supposing, that the majority of his readers will not be displeased with his attempt to shorten at least the labour of their enquiries, by laying before them such parts of the result of his own researches as he judges will be most conducive to that purpose....

(p. iv) With respect to a life of Chaucer, he found, after a reasonable waste of time and pains in searching for materials, that he could add few facts to those which have already appeared in several lives of that poet; and he was not disposed, either to repeat the comments and inventions, by which former biographers have endeavoured to supply the deficiency of facts, or to substitute any of his own for the same laudable purpose. Instead therefore of a formal life of his author, which, upon these principles, must have been a very meagre narration, he has added to this Preface a short ABSTRACT OF THE HISTORICAL PASSAGES OF THE LIFE OF CHAUCER, with remarks, which may serve to separate for the future those passages from others, which have nothing to recommend them to credit, but the single circumstance of having been often repeated.

(b)

(p. 89) Let us consider a moment, how a sensible critic in
the Augustan age would have proceeded, if called upon to
examine a work of Ennius. When he found that a great proportion of the verses were strictly conformable to the
ordinary rules of Metre, he would, probably, not scruple
to conclude that such a conformity must have been produced
by art and design, and not by mere chance. On the other
hand, when he found, that in some verses the number of
feet, to appearance, was either deficient or redundant;
that in others the feet were seemingly composed of too few
or too many syllables, of short syllables in the place of
long or of long in the place of short; he would not, I
think, immediately condemn the old Bard, as having all at
once forgotten the fundamental principles of his art, or
as having wilfully or negligently deviated from them.
He would first, I presume, enquire, whether all these
irregularities were in the genuine text of his author, or
only the mistakes of Copyists: he would enquire further,
by comparing the genuine text with other contemporary
writings and monuments, whether many things, which
appeared irregular, were not in truth sufficiently
regular, either justified by the constant practice, or
excused by the allowed licence of the age: where authority failed, he would have recourse (but soberly) to etymology and analogy; and if, after all, a few passages
remained, not reducible to the strict laws of Metre by
any of the methods above mentioned, if he were really (as
I have supposed him) a sensible critic, he would be apt
rather to expect patiently the solution of his difficulties from more correct manuscripts, or a more complete
theory of his author's versification, than to cut the
knot, by deciding peremptorily, that the work was composed
without any regard to metrical rules.

I beg leave to pursue the same course with respect to
Chaucer. The great number of verses, sounding complete
even to our ears, which is to be found in all the least
corrected copies of his works, authorises us to conclude,
that he was not ignorant of the laws of metre. Upon this
conclusion it is impossible not to ground a strong pre-
sumption, that he intended to observe the same laws in the
many other verses which seem to us irregular; and if this
was really his intention, what reason can be assigned sufficient to account for his having failed so grossly and
repeatedly, as is generally supposed, in an operation,
which every Balladmonger in our days, man, woman, or
child, is known to perform with the most unerring exactness, and without any extraordinary fatigue?

(p. 104) It may be proper however to observe, that we are not to expect from Chaucer that regularity in the disposition of his accents, which the practice of our greatest poets, in the last and the present century has taught us to consider as essential to harmonious versification. None of his masters, either French or Italian, had set him a pattern of exactness in this respect; and it is rather surprising, that, without rule or example to guide him, he has so seldom failed to place his accents in such a manner as to produce the cadence best suited to the nature of his verse.

85.   UNKNOWN, WROTE LIKE A GENTLEMAN

1778

'The Encyclopaedia Britannica' first mentions Chaucer in its second edition, vol. III, pp. 1799-800. It is the usual account except for the following remark at the end.

He had read a great deal; and was a man of the world, and of sound judgment. He was the first English poet who wrote *poetically*, as Dr. Johnson observes in the preface to his dictionary, and (he might have added) who wrote like a gentleman.

86.   JOHN PINKERTON, CHAUCER AND THE SCOTS

1786

John Pinkerton (1758-1826) antiquary and literary forger, educated at grammar school and privately, brought out two volumes of 'Ancient Scotish Poems never before in print', 1786, with an essay full of energy, eccentricity and local patriotism, attempting to establish significant comparisons between Chaucer and Scottish poets; extracts from the

234   Chaucer: The Critical Heritage vol. 1

Preface, pp. ix-x, xviii, Essay, lxx, lxxii-lxxiii, xciv.

[After discussing apologetically the work of Gavin
Douglas.]

But the next two pieces require no apology, being *Tales*
equal to any that Chaucer has written. The first ['The
Tua Mariit Women and the Wedo'], which is by Dunbar, is
in a singular kind of blank verse, used by the old roman-
cers, and after them by the author of Piers Plowman's
Visions. It is full of knowlege of life, and rich description; and is also much tinctured with immodesty, which
Fontaine indeed looks upon as essential to this kind of
writing. But Horace says

   Sanctum est vetus omne poema:

and the reader has it as it stands in the MS. He will
however find it quite free from the nastiness of Chaucer,
which, tho foolishly confounded with immodesty, is a very
different matter, and only serves to disgust....
   These tales place Dunbar in quite a new and more important light; for it is believed they will be as much preferred to his Goldin Terge, and Thistle and Rose, tho
these pieces have an elegance and opulence which Chaucer
nowhere attains, as Chaucer's Tales are to his allegorical poems. Dunbar, having a genius at least equal to
Chaucer, and perhaps more original; and having the advantage of living a whole century after him, when the language was more rich and expressive; it is no wonder that
he should excell that venerable poet in every point, but
in the length of his pieces, a most dispensable quality...
   The old Scotish poets ought to be regarded in the same
light as Chaucer and the old English ones; and who sus-
pects that the perusal of the latter can injure the purity
of English conversation, or writing? The contrary is so
far true, that I will venture to say that a man who writes
a language, without acquaintance with it's early state,
may compose well from chance, but never from intelligence.
For knowledge of the primitive and progressive powers of
words is the only solid foundation of that rich and terse
style which posterity pronounces classic. As long as
Chaucer is read therefore, and he will be read till the
English language perishes, so long may we hope for equal
attention to Barbour and Dunbar. The English reader of
Chaucer will in them, with the slightest help of a glossary, be delighted with equal pictures of manners; and

235 Chaucer: The Critical Heritage vol. 1

unpolished diamonds of genuine poetry: and, at the same
time, enjoy every pleasure of variety from a Doric dialect
of his own language, venerable from it's antiquity, nay
sacred from it's primitive dedication to poetry; the old
English bards being all of the *north countrie,* and their
metrical romances being almost Scotish, because the language spoken in the North of England and the South of
Scotland was anciently almost the same; as it is at this
day....

And perhaps, if the mixture of French words with
English was a fault, Lermont, and not Chaucer, ought to
bear the blame; tho there be no doubt but that Lermont and
Chaucer only used the language of the politest people of
the period: for to alter a language is the work of time;
and no single writer can ever effect so prodigious a work;
indeed, no one ever made the attempt. Lermont and Chaucer
wrote for men of birth and education; and doubtless in the
language used by them.

The first Scotish writers, thus finding the English a
sister dialect already written, naturally in writing accommodated themselves to it; as the English authors had to
the French. Hence, written language becoming colloquial
by degrees, first among the higher classes, and then
partly among the vulgar, the Scotish has more and more
yielded to the English language, as a politer language,
down to this very day. Thus has the vulgar error crept in,,
that the Scotish is derived from the Anglo-Saxon; or that
it is in fact merely a dialect of the English imported
into that country. Tho the reader may well believe that I
should, with pleasure, give the Scotish language so respectable an origin as the English, yet much inquiry into
the subject forbids my subscribing to this hypothesis.

[Claims that Scottish and English are equally descendants
from Gothic.]

Another cause why many later Anglicisms appear in the
old Scotish language, is, that it was usual for many
Scotishmen to go to England to follow their studies at the
universities there. St. Andrews, the oldest university in
Scotland, was only founded in 1413; before that time students repaired to Cambridge, Oxford, or Paris. In the
'Reves Tale', Chaucer tells us the two Cambridge students

Of o toun were they born that highte Strother,
Fer in the north I cannot tellen where.

There never was even a village of this name in the North
of England: the place was apparently Anstruther in Fife.

Mr. Tyrwhitt, in a note to his Life of Chaucer, says,
'Chaucer's reputation was as well established in Scotland,
as in England: and I will take upon me to say, that he was
as much the father of poetry in that country, as in this.'
This is quite a mistake, Chaucer was in the highest admiration in Scotland, as he justly deserved: but not one
Scotish poet has imitated him: or is in the least indebted
to him. I wish the Scotish writers had owned him as
father of their poetry with all my heart: but not a trace
of this can be found. They praise him; but never imitate
either his language, stanza, manner, or sentiments; how
then can he be their model? Thomas of Ercildon wrote the
century before Chaucer: and Barbour knew nothing of him,
tho he wrote in 1375. Chaucer's fame was not wide till
after his death in 1400: Gower, the stupidest of all
writers, had always been preferred to him; and Chaucer
himself calls him his master. If Mr. Tyrwhitt will point
out one imitation of the slightest passage of Chaucer in
any Scotish poet whatever, it will operate to his purpose;
but I know from certain knowledge that he cannot; so must
refuse my assent to his opinion. The French and Italians
may indeed say, with great justice, that Chaucer is more
than the imitator, is the mere translator of their poets,
save in one or two of his comic tales: and would that he
had never translated!...
    The Historian of English poetry [Thomas Warton] pass-
ing to the Scotish poets of this time, says, 'the Scotish
writers have adorned the present period with a degree of
sentiment, and spirit, a command of phraseology, and a
fertility of imagination not to be found in any English
poet since Chaucer and Lydgate.' He might safely have
added, 'nor even in Chaucer, or Lydgate.' The same
excellent judge of poetry observes that the natural complexion of 'Dunbar's genius is of a moral, or didactic
cast:' but this remark must not be taken too strictly.
The 'Goldin Terge' is moral; and so are many of his small
pieces: but humour, description, allegory, great poetical
genius, and a vast wealth of words, all unite to form the
'complexion' of Dunbar's poetry. He unites in himself
and generally surpasses, the qualities of the chief old
English poets; the morals and satire of Langland; Chaucer's humour, poetry, and knowlege of life; the allegory
of Gower; the description of Lydgate.

87.   WILLIAM GODWIN, INTEGRITY AND EXCELLENCE OF THE
AUTHOR'S DISPOSITION

1803

Godwin (1756-1836), educated at Hoxton Academy and at
first a dissenting minister, became an atheist, vegetarian,
philosophical anarchist and political philosopher, who
deeply influenced Shelley. He gives his admirable reasons
for writing about Chaucer in his Preface, part of which
(pp. v-xii) is extract (a). Although Godwin rightly confesses the superficiality of his own researches, there is
originality in them, in his recognition of the achievements of medieval culture, and of the relationship of a
writer to his age. In the examples of his criticism,
mostly of 'Troilus and Criseyde', he is sensible. He
touches on a characteristically Romantic notion of poetry
as expression of the poet's disposition, and perhaps both
the virtues and faults he finds in 'Troilus' are not unlike his own, both the goodness and the tediousness. His
'Life of Chaucer' was almost universally condemned for its
speculativeness.

(a)

I

The two names which perhaps do the greatest honour to the
annals of English literature, are those of Chaucer and of
Shakespear. Shakespear we have long and justly been
accustomed to regard as the first in the catalogue of
poetical and creative minds; and after the dramas of
Shakespear, there is no production of man that displays
more various and vigorous talent than the Canterbury
Tales. Splendour of narrative, richness of fancy, pathetic simplicity of incident and feeling, a powerful style
in delineating character and manners, and an animated vein
of comic humour, each takes its turn in this wonderful
performance, and each in turn appears to be that in which
the author was most qualified to excel.
      There is one respect at least in which the works of
Chaucer are better fitted to excite our astonishment than
those of Shakespear. Ordinary readers are inclined to
regard the times of Shakespear as barbarous, because they

are remote. But in reality the age of queen Elizabeth was
a period of uncommon refinement. We have since that time
enlarged our theatres; we have made some improvements in
the mechanism of dramatical exhibition; and we have studied, with advantage or otherwise, the laws of the Grecian
stage. But we have never produced any thing that will
enter into comparison with the plays of Shakespear, or
even of some of his contemporaries. What age can be less
barbarous than that which, beside the dramatic productions
of Shakespear, Fletcher, Massinger and Jonson, is illustrated with the names of Raleigh, of Hooker, of Bacon, and
of Spenser?

But the times of Chaucer were in a much more obvious
and unquestionable sense, so far as poetry is concerned,
times of barbarism. The history of the revival of
literature in the twelfth and thirteenth centuries will
be treated in these volumes. The sole efforts in the art
of verse which had been made in Western Europe previously
to Chaucer, were romances of prodigious and supernatural
adventure, prolix volumes of unvaried allegory, and the
rhapsodies of the vagrant minstrel. These productions,
though not unrelieved by admirable flights of imagination,
were for the most part rugged in versification, prosaic in
language, and diffusive and rambling in their story and
conduct. What had been achieved in English, was little
better than a jejune table of events with the addition of
rhyme. Chaucer fixed and naturalised the genuine art of
poetry in our island. But what is most memorable in his
eulogy, is that he is the father of our language, the
idiom of which was by the Norman conquest banished from
courts and civilised life, and which Chaucer was the first
to restore to literature, and the muses. No one man in
the history of human intellect ever did more, than was
effected by the single mind of Chaucer.

These are abundant reasons why Englishmen should
regard Chaucer with peculiar veneration, should cherish
his memory, and eagerly desire to be acquainted with
whatever may illustrate his character, or explain the
wonders he performed. The first and direct object of this
work, is to erect a monument to his name, and, as far as
the writer was capable of doing it, to produce an interesting and amusing book in modern English, enabling the
reader, who might shrink from the labour of mastering the
phraseology of Chaucer, to do justice to his illustrious
countryman. It seemed probable also that, if the author
were successful in making a popular work, many might by
its means be induced to study the language of our ancestors, and the elements and history of our vernacular
speech; a study at least as improving as that of the

language of Greece and Rome.

A further idea, which was continually present to the
mind of the author while writing, obviously contributed
to give animation to his labours, and importance to his
undertaking. The full and complete life of a poet would
include an extensive survey of the manners, the opinions,
the arts and the literature, of the age in which the poet
lived. This is the only way in which we can become truly
acquainted with the history of his mind, and the causes
which made him what he was. We must observe what Chaucer
felt and saw, how he was educated, what species of learning he pursued, and what were the objects, the events and
the persons, successively presented to his view, before we
can strictly and philosophically understand his biography.
To delineate the state of England, such as Chaucer saw it,
in every point of view in which it can be delineated, is
the subject of this book.

But, while engaged in this study, the reader may expect
to gain an additional advantage, beside that of understanding the poet. If the knowledge of contemporary
objects is the biography of Chaucer, the converse of the
proposition will also be true, and the biography of Chaucer will be the picture of a certain portion of the literary, political and domestic history of our country. The
person of Chaucer may in this view be considered as the
central figure in a miscellaneous painting, giving unity
and individual application to the otherwise disjointed
particulars with which the canvas is diversified. No man
of moral sentiment or of taste will affirm, that a more
becoming central figure to the delineation of England in
the fourteenth century can be found, than the Englishman
who gives name to these volumes.

II

I can pretend only to have written a superficial work.
My studies, if any thing of mine deserves so serious a
name, have chiefly been engaged upon other subjects; and
I came in a manner a novice to the present undertaking.
Had the circumstances under which I have written been
different, I should have been anxious to investigate to
the bottom the various topics of which I have treated.

Perhaps however I have not wholly failed in the execution of my design. I was desirous of convincing my
countrymen that there existed mines of instruction and
delight, with which they had hitherto little acquaintance.
I have led my readers, with however unconfirmed a speech
and inadequate powers, to the different sources of information; and, if I have been unable to present what should
satisfy a vigorous and earnest curiosity, I have wished to

say enough to awaken their enquiries, and communicate to
them some image of men and times which have long since
been no more.

It was my purpose to produce a work of a new species.
Antiquities have too generally been regarded as the province of men of cold tempers and sterile imaginations,
writers who, by their phlegmatic and desultory industry,
have brought discredit upon a science, which is perhaps
beyond all others fraught with wisdom, moral instruction
and intellectual improvement. Their books may indeed be
considerably useful to the patient enquirer who would
delineate the picture of past times for himself; but they
can scarcely incite enquiry; and their contents are put
together with such narrow views, so total an absence of
discrimination, and such an unsuspecting ignorance of the
materials of which man is made, that the perusal of them
tends for the most part to stupify the sense, and to
imbue the soul with moping and lifeless dejection.

It was my wish, had my power held equal pace with my
strong inclination, to carry the workings of fancy and the
spirit of philosophy into the investigation of ages past.
I was anxious to rescue for a moment the illustrious dead
from the jaws of the grave, to make them pass in review
before me, to question their spirits and record their
answers. I wished to make myself their master of the
ceremonies, to introduce my reader to their familiar
speech, and to enable him to feel for the instant as if he
had lived with Chaucer.

(b)

(pp. 177-8) Chaucer therefore had a right to consider himself as fallen upon no barbarous or inglorious age. Among
his immediate predecessors in the period of their existence were Giotto and Dante; and their successors, his co-
equals, perhaps his friends, were fast advancing in the
career which they had opened. The achievements of the
human mind never appear so stupendous as when they exhibit
themselves in their newest gloss. After the lapse of ages
we may possibly find that we have been continually improving, and that in most, though not in all, the arts and
exercises of our nature, we have gained something in scope
and something in address. But our ancestors were so considerable, and our own additions have been so miscellaneous or minute, as to afford to an impartial and dispas-
sionate observer small cause for any high degree of ela-
tion. Chaucer had only to look back for a single century
to find the whole of Europe in a state comparatively

barbarous. The sun of science had risen, and the dews
which welcome its beams were not yet dissipated: he
smelled the freshness of the morning, and his heart dilated at the sight of its soft and unsullied hues....

(pp. 298-307) The plan of the Aeneid...is precisely
what the plan of an epic poem should be. The Troilus and
Creseide can advance no pretensions to enter into this
class of composition. It is merely a love-tale. It is
not the labour of a man's life; but a poem which, with
some previous knowledge of human sentiments and character,
and a very slight preparation of science, the writer might
perhaps be expected to complete in about as many months,
as the work is divided into books. It is certainly much
greater in extent of stanzas and pages, than the substrat-
um and basis of the story can authorise.

It is also considerably barren of incident. There is
not enough in it of matter generating visible images in
the reader, and exciting his imagination with pictures of
nature and life. There is not enough in it of vicissi-
tudes of fortune, awakening curiosity and holding expectation in suspense.

Add to which, the catastrophe is unsatisfactory and
offensive. The poet who would interest us with a love-
tale, should soothe our minds with the fidelity and disinterestedness of the mutual attachment of the parties,
and, if he presents us with a tragical conclusion, it
should not be one which arises out of the total unworthi-
ness of either. Creseide (as Mr. Urry, in his introduction to Henryson's epilogue to the Troilus, has very truly
observed), however prepossessing may be the manner in
which she appears in the early part of the poem, is 'a
false unconstant whore,' and of a class which the mind of
the reader almost demands to have exhibited, if not as
'terminating in extream misery,' at least as filled with
penitence and remorse. Virgil indeed has drawn the catastrophe of his tale of Dido from the desertion of the
lover. But the habits of European society teach us to
apprehend less ugliness and loathsome deformity in the
falshood of the lover, than of his mistress; and we repose
with a tenderer and more powerful sympathy upon the abandoned and despairing state of the female. Besides, Virgil
did not write a poem expressly upon the tale of Dido, but
only employed it for an episode. The story of Romeo and
Juliet is the most perfect model of a love-tale in the
series of human invention. Dryden thoroughly felt this
defect in the poem of Chaucer, and has therefore changed
the catastrophe when he fitted the story for the stage,
and represented the two lovers as faithful, but unfortunate.

But, when all these deductions have been made from the claims of the Troilus and Creseide upon our approbation, it will still remain a work interspersed with many beautiful passages, passages of exquisite tenderness, of great delicacy, and of a nice and refined observation of the workings of human sensibility. Nothing can be more beautiful, genuine, and unspoiled by the corrupt suggestions of a selfish spirit, than the sentiments of Chaucer's lovers: While conversing with them, we seem transported into ages of primeval innocence. Even Creseide is so good, so ingenuous and affectionate, that we feel ourselves as incapable as Troilus, of believing her false. Nor are the scenes of Chaucer's narrative, like the insipid tales of a pretended pastoral life, drawn with that vagueness of manner, and ignorance of the actual emotions of the heart, which, while we read them, we nauseate and despise. On the contrary, his personages always feel, and we confess the truth of their feelings; what passes in their minds, or falls from their tongues, has the clear and decisive character which proclaims it human, together with the vividness, subtleness and delicacy, which few authors in the most enlightened ages have been equally fortunate in seizing. Pandarus himself comes elevated and refined from the pen of Chaucer: his occupation loses its grossness, in the disinterestedness of his motive, and the sincerity of his friendship. In a word, such is the Troilus and Creseide, that no competent judge can rise from its perusal, without a strong impression of the integrity and excellence of the author's disposition, and of the natural relish he entertained for whatever is honourable, beautiful and just.

There is a great difference between the merits of any work of human genius considered abstractedly, taken as it belongs to the general stock of literary production and tried severely on its intrinsic and unchangeable pretensions, and the merits of the same work considered in the place which it occupies in the scale and series of literary history, and compared with the productions of its author's predecessors and contemporaries. In the former case the question we have to ask is, Is it good? In the latter we have to enquire, Was it good? To both these questions, when applied to Chaucer's poem of Troilus and Creseide, the fair answer will be an affirmative.

But it is in the latter point of view that the work we are considering shows to infinitely the greatest advantage. The poem will appear to be little less than a miracle, when we combine our examination of it, with a recollection of the times and circumstances in which it was produced. When Chaucer wrote it, the English tongue had long

remained in a languid and almost perishing state, overlaid
and suffocated by the insolent disdain and remorseless
tyranny of the Norman ravagers and dividers of our soil.
Previously to the eleventh century it had no cultivation
and refinement from the cowardly and superstitious Saxons,
and during that century and the following one it appeared
in danger of being absolutely extinguished. With Chaucer
it seemed to spring like Minerva from the head of Jove, at
once accoutered and complete. Mandeville, Wicliffe and
Gower, whom we may style the other three evangelists of
our tongue, though all elder in birth than Chaucer, did
not begin so early to work upon the ore of their native
language. He surprised his countrymen with a poem, eminently idiomatic, clear and perspicuous in its style, as
well as rich and harmonious in its versification. His
Court of Love, an earlier production, is not less excellent in both these respects. But it was too slight and
short to awaken general attention. The Troilus and Creseide was of respectable magnitude, and forms an epoch in
our literature.

Chaucer presented to the judgment of his countrymen a
long poem, perfectly regular in its structure, and unin-
terrupted with episodes. It contained nothing but what
was natural. Its author disdained to have recourse to
what was bloated in sentiment, or romantic and miraculous
in incident, for the purpose of fixing or keeping alive
the attention. He presents real life and human sentiments, and suffers the reader to dwell upon and expand
the operations of feeling and passion. Accordingly the
love he describes is neither frantic, nor brutal, nor
artificial, nor absurd. His hero conducts himself in all
respects with the most perfect loyalty and honour; and
his heroine, however she deserts her character in the
sequel, is in the commencement modest, decorous, affectionate, and prepossessing. The loves of the Troilus and
Creseide scarcely retain any traces of the preposterous
and rude manners of the age in which they were delineated.

This poem therefore, as might have been expected, long
fixed upon itself the admiration of the English nation.
Chaucer, by his Court of Love, and the ditties and songs
which had preceded it, had gratified the partiality of his
friends, and given them no mean or equivocal promise of
what he should hereafter be able to perform. But these,
we may easily conceive, were of little general notoriety.
The Troilus and Creseide was probably, more than any of
his other works, the basis of his fame, and the foundation
of his fortune. He wrote nothing very eminently superior
to this, till his Canterbury Tales, which were the production of his declining age. Owing perhaps to the confusion

and sanguinary spirit of the wars of York and Lancaster,
English literature rather decayed than improved during the
following century; and we had consequently no poem of magnitude, and of a compressed and continued plan, qualified
to enter into competition with the Troilus and Creseide,
from the earliest periods of our poetry to the appearance
of the Fairy Queen. Accordingly, among many examples of
its praises which might be produced, sir Philip Sidney in
his Defense of Poesy has selected this performance, as the
memorial of the talents of our poet, and the work in which
he 'undoubtedly did excellently well.'

There are some particular defects belonging to this
production beside those already mentioned, which are the
more entitled to our notice, as they are adapted to characterise the stage of refinement to which our literature
was advanced in the fourteenth century. In the first
place, the poem is interspersed with many base and vulgar
lines, which are not only unworthy of the poet, but would
be a deformity in any prose composition, and would even
dishonour and debase the tone of familiar conversation.
The following specimens will afford a sufficient illustration of this fact. Cupid is provoked at the ease and
lightness of heart of the hero, and prepares to avenge
himself of the contempt.

-Sodainly he hitte him at the full,
And yet as proude a pecocke can be pul.

B. I, ver. 210.

Thus wol she saine, and al the toune at ones,
The wretch is dead, the divel have his bones.

ver. 806.

Withouten jelousie, and soche debate,
Shall no husbonde saine unto me checke mate.

B. II, ver. 754.

For him demeth men hote, that seeth him swete.

ver. 1533.

Now loketh than, if thei be nat to blame,
That hem avaunt of women, and by name,
That yet behight hem never this ne that,
Ne knowen hem more than mine oldé hat.

B. III, ver. 321.

I am, til God me better mindé sende,
At Dulcarnon, right at my wittés ende.

ver. 933.

> For peril is with dretching in ydrawe,
> Nay suche abodés ben nat worthe an hawe.
>
> ver. 856.

> Soche arguments ne be nat worthe a bene.
>
> ver. 1173.

> But soche an ese therwith thei in her wrought,
> Right as a man is esed for to fele
> For ache of hedde, to clawen him on his hele.
>
> B. IV, ver. 728.

> I have herd saie eke, timés twisé twelve.
>
> B. V, ver. 97.

There are also lines interspersed in the poem, which are not more degraded by the meanness of the expression, than by the rudeness, not to say the brutality, of the sentiment. We may well be surprised, after considering the delicacy and decorum with which Chaucer has drawn his heroine, to find him polluting the portrait of her virgin character in the beginning of the poem with so low and pitiful a joke as this,

> But whether that she children had or none,
> I rede it nat, therfore I let it gone.
>   .
> B. I, ver. 132.

The following sentiment must also be deeply disgustful to a just and well ordered mind. Calchas, the father of Creseide, languishes in the Grecian army for the restoration of his only child, and at length effects to his great joy the means of obtaining her in exchange for Antenor, a prisoner in the Grecian camp.

> The whiché tale anon right as Creseide
> Had herd, she (whiche that of her father rought,
> As in this case, right naught, ne whan he deide)
> Full busily, &c.
>
> B. IV, ver. 668.

Another defect in this poem of Chaucer, of the same nature, and that is not less conspicuous, is the tediousness into which he continually runs, seemingly without the least apprehension that any one will construe this feature of his composition as a fault. He appears to have had no idea that his readers could possibly deem it too much to peruse any number of verses which he should think proper to pour out on any branch of his subject. To judge from

the poem of Troilus and Creseide, we should be tempted to
say, that compression, the strengthening a sentiment by
brevity, and the adding to the weight and power of a work
by cutting away from it all useless and cumbersome excres-
cences, was a means of attaining to excellence which never
entered into our author's mind. A remarkable instance of
this occurs in the fourth book, where upward of one hundred verses upon predestination are put into the mouth of
Troilus, the materials of which are supposed to have been
extracted from a treatise 'De Causa Dei', written by
Thomas Bradwardine archbishop of Canterbury, a contemporary of our author. Other examples scarcely less offensive to true taste, might be cited.

It is particularly deserving of notice that scarcely
any one of the instances which might be produced under
either of these heads of impropriety, has a parallel in
the version made by Boccaccio of the same story, probably
from the same author, and nearly at the same time. Few
instances can be given in which the Italian writer has
degenerated into any thing mean and vulgar, and he never
suspends his narrative with idle and incoherent digressions. He seems to have been perfectly aware, that one
of the methods to render a literary production commendable
is to admit into it nothing which is altogether super-
fluous. The inference is, that, whatever may be the comparative degrees of imagination and originality between
England and Italy in the fourteenth century, what is commonly called taste had made a much greater progress in
the latter country than among us....

(pp. 372-4) The Palamon and Arcite is a fiction much
more to the taste of the present age, perhaps of every
age from the revival of learning under Leo X, than the
Troilus. Dryden has pronounced of it, that it 'is of
the Epique kind, and perhaps not much inferior to the
Ilias or the Aeneis; the story is more pleasing than
either of them, the manners as perfect, the diction as
poetical, the learning as deep and various, and the disposition full as artful; only it includes a greater
length of time, as taking up seven years at least.'

This eulogium must be acknowledged to be written in a
spirit of ridiculous and impertinent exaggeration. To
speak temperately however, the story of Palamon and
Arcite is full of novelty and surprise, is every where
alive, comprises the most interesting turns of fortune,
exhibits the most powerful portrait of chivalry that was
perhaps ever delineated, and possesses every thing in
splendour and in action that can most conspicuously paint
out the scenes of the narrative to the eye of the reader.
In all these respects it is strikingly contrasted with the

naked and desolate simplicity of the Troilus, at the same
time that it certainly does not fall short in delicacy of
sentiment, the principal beauty which the Troilus has to
boast.

Yet see the capriciousness and uncertainty of fame,
particularly at this period, when the power of truly
appreciating a poet's merit existed in so few individuals!
While the Troilus came down from age to age, the theme of
universal admiration, and, as a French critic has expressed himself in a similar case, surrounded with a triumphal
convoy of adulators and devotees, the Palamon and Arcite,
as Chaucer has informed us, near forty years after its
publication was 'knowen lite.' The poet, in sober confidence that his work, in its most essential particulars, was
worthy of public notice, recast it in the front of his
Canterbury Tales, and reduced it from about ten thousand
lines, which is the length of Boccaccio's poem, to little
more than two thousand. The consequence has been, that
Chaucer's original work is lost, and, unhonoured, con-
signed to oblivion; nor has one distinction been paid it
except in its compressed state, in which form it has furnished materials to the play of The Two Noble Kinsmen in
the works of Beaumont and Fletcher, where the play is,
though without probability, said to have been the joint
composition of Fletcher and shakespear; and in which form
it became the original of the first and longest piece in
the volume entitled Dryden's Fables, which is pronounced
by Warton to be 'the most animated and harmonious piece
of versification in the English language.'

The improvements which Chaucer has made upon Boccaccio,
or upon the author from whom Boccaccio translated his
Teseide, have been pointed out by Mr. Tyrwhit. They are
such as strongly mark the delicacy, perspicacity and power
of our poet's mind. He has been careful to contrast the
characters of his two principal personages, and to throw
the weight of interest and partiality in the reader's mind
into the scale of the successful lover.

88. WILLIAM WORDSWORTH, THE LUCID SHAFTS OF REASON

1805, 1822

Wordsworth (1770-1850), himself so great a poet, always

expressed his appreciation of Chaucer, with Spenser,
Shakespeare, and Milton, as the supreme English poets.
Remembering the various condemnations of Chaucer's bawdry,
it is interesting that Wordsworth's sister Dorothy notes
in her 'Journal' reading him 'The Miller's Tale' (26 Dec-
ember 1801) as well as numerous other poems of Chaucer's
at other times. Of a number of comments the two following
illustrate first his general youthful appreciation (reading as an undergraduate at Cambridge), (a) from 'The Prelude', ed. E. de Selincourt, 1932, Book III, 1805, 11.
276-9, by permission of the Oxford University Press. The
second (b) one of the 'Ecclesiastical Sonnets' (XXXI)
written 1822, published in 'Ecclesiastical Sketches', 1822,
Sonnet XXIII, p. 65, illustrates a sense of deeper significance, but is affected by the generally accepted tradition
that Chaucer wrote 'The Plowman's Tale'.

(a)

Beside the pleasant Mills of Trompington
I laugh'd with Chaucer; in the hawthorn shade
Heard him (while birds were warbling) tell his tales
Of amorous passion.

(b)
Edward VI

'Sweet is the holiness of Youth' - so felt
Time-honoured Chaucer when he framed the Lay
By which the Prioress beguiled the way,
And many a Pilgrim's rugged heart did melt.
Hadst thou, loved Bard! whose spirit often dwelt
In the clear land of vision, but foreseen
King, Child, and Seraph, blended in the mien
Of pious Edward kneeling as he knelt
In meek and simple Infancy, what joy
For universal Christendom had thrilled
Thy heart! what hopes inspired thy genius, skilled
(O great Precursor, genuine morning Star)
The lucid shafts of reason to employ,
Piercing the Papal darkness from afar!

89. LORD BYRON, OBSCENE AND CONTEMPTIBLE

1807

Byron (1788-1824), precocious poet and debauchee, in the
same year that he published his first book of poems, as a
nineteen-year-old boy, reprehended Chaucer in his Memoran-
dum book, 30 November 1807 (text from T. Moore, 'The Life,
Letters and Journals of Lord Byron', 1830, Chapter V, edition of 1860, p. 49.)

Chaucer. notwithstanding the praises bestowed on him, I
think obscene and contemptible:- he owes his celebrity
merely to his antiquity, which he does not deserve so well
as Pierce Plowman, or Thomas of Ercildoune. English living poets I have avoided mentioning:- we have none who
will survive their productions. Taste is over with us.

90. WILLIAM BLAKE, NAMES ALTER, THINGS NEVER

1809

Blake (1757-1827) engraver, poet and mystic, was not form-
ally educated and had a hard struggle all his life. In
his 'Descriptive Catalogue' (1809) he described some of
his engravings, among them that of the Canterbury Pilgrims.
Blake shows the penetration of his extraordinary genius in
his perception of Chaucer's 'superiority and generality'
(perhaps on a hint from Dart, No. 71), but he also reflects the times in his interest in individual character.
His rival was Stothard, who had produced a similar engraving. The present text is from 'Blake: Complete Writings',
edited by G. Keynes, 1966, pp. 566-75, reprinted by permission of the Oxford University Press.

NUMBER III.

Sir Jeffery Chaucer and the nine and twenty Pilgrims on their journey to Canterbury.

The time chosen is early morning, before sunrise, when the jolly company are just quitting the Tabarde Inn. The Knight and Squire with the Squire's Yeoman lead the Procession; next follow the youthful Abbess, her nun and three priests; her greyhounds attend her-

Of small hounds had she, that she fed
With roast flesh, milk and wastel bread.

Next follow the Friar and Monk; then the Tapiser, the Pardoner, and the Somner and Manciple. After these 'Our Host,' who occupies the center of the cavalcade, directs them to the Knight as the person who would be likely to commence their task of each telling a tale in their order. After the Host follows the Shipman, the Haberdasher, the Dyer, the Franklin, the Physician, the Plowman, the Lawyer, the poor Parson, the Merchant, the Wife of Bath, the Miller, the Cook, the Oxford Scholar, Chaucer himself, and the Reeve comes as Chaucer has described:

And ever he rode hinderest of the rout.

These last are issuing from the gateway of the Inn; the Cook and the Wife of Bath are both taking their morning's draught of comfort. Spectators stand at the gateway of the Inn, and are composed of an old Man, a Woman, and Children.

The Landscape is an eastward view of the country, from the Tabarde Inn, in Southwark, as it may be supposed to have appeared in Chaucer's time, interspersed with cottages and villages; the first beams of the Sun are seen above the horizon; some buildings and spires indicate the situation of the great City; the Inn is a gothic building, which Thynne in his Glossary says was the lodging of the Abbot of Hyde, by Winchester. On the Inn is inscribed its title, and a proper advantage is taken of this circumstance to describe the subject of the Picture. The words written over the gateway of the Inn are as follow: 'The Tabarde Inn, by Henry Baillie, the lodgynge-house for Pilgrims, who journey to Saint Thomas's Shrine at Canterbury.'

The characters of Chaucer's Pilgrims are the characters which compose all ages and nations: as one age falls, another rises, different to mortal sight, but to immortals only the same; for we see the same characters repeated

again and again, in animals, vegetables, minerals, and in
men; nothing new occurs in identical existence; Accident
ever varies, Substance can never suffer change nor decay.
Of Chaucer's characters, as described in his Canterbury
Tales, some of the names or titles are altered by time,
but the characters themselves for ever remain unaltered,
and consequently they are the physiognomies or lineaments
of universal human life, beyond which Nature never steps.
Names alter, things never alter. I have known multitudes
of those who could have been monks in the age of monkery,
who in this deistical age are deists. As Newton numbered
the stars, and as Linneus numbered the plants, so Chaucer
numbered the classes of men.

The Painter has consequently varied the heads and forms
of his personages into all Nature's varieties; the Horses
he has also varied to accord to their Riders; the costume
is correct according to authentic monuments.

The Knight and Squire with the Squire's Yeoman lead the
procession, as Chaucer has also placed them first in his
prologue. The Knight is a true Hero, a good, great, and
wise man; his whole length portrait on horseback, as written by Chaucer, cannot be surpassed. He has spent his
life in the field; has ever been a conqueror, and is that
species of character which in every age stands as the
guardian of man against the oppressor. His son is like
him with the germ of perhaps greater perfection still, as
he blends literature and the arts with his warlike studies. Their dress and their horses are of the first rate,
without ostentation, and with all the true grandeur that
unaffected simplicity when in high rank always displays.
The Squire's Yeoman is also a great character, a man perfectly knowing in his profession:

And in his hand he bare a mighty bow.

Chaucer describes here a mighty man; one who in war is the
worthy attendant on noble heroes.

The Prioress follows these with her female chaplain:

Another Nonne also with her had she,
That was her Chaplaine, and Priests three.

This Lady is described also as of the first rank, rich
and honoured. She has certain peculiarities and little
delicate affectations, not unbecoming in her, being
accompanied with what is truly grand and really polite;
her person and face Chaucer has described with minuteness;
it is very elegant, and was the beauty of our ancestors,
till after Elizabeth's time, when voluptuousness and folly

began to be accounted beautiful.

Her companion and her three priests were no doubt all
perfectly delineated in those parts of Chaucer's work
which are now lost; we ought to suppose them suitable
attendants on rank and fashion.

The Monk follows these with the Friar. The Painter has
also grouped with these the Pardoner and the Sompnour and
the Manciple, and has here also introduced one of the rich
citizens of London: Characters likely to ride in company,
all being above the common rank in life or attendants on
those who were so.

For the Monk is described by Chaucer, as a man of the
first rank in society, noble, rich, and expensively
attended; he is a leader of the age, with certain humorous
accompaniments in his character, that do not degrade, but
render him an object of dignified mirth, but also with
other accompaniments not so respectable.

The Friar is a character also of a mixed kind:

A friar there was, a wanton and a merry.

but in his office he is said to be a 'full solemn man':
eloquent, amorous, witty, and satyrical; young, handsome,
and rich; he is a complete rogue, with constitutional
gaiety enough to make him a master of all the pleasures
of the world.

His neck was white as the flour de lis,
Thereto strong he was as a champioun.

It is necessary here to speak of Chaucer's own character, that I may set certain mistaken critics right in
their conception of the humour and fun that occurs on the
journey. Chaucer is himself the great poetical observer
of men, who in every age is born to record and eternize
its acts. This he does as a master, as a father, and
superior, who looks down on their little follies from the
Emperor to the Miller; sometimes with severity, oftener
with joke and sport.

Accordingly Chaucer has made his Monk a great traged-
ian, one who studied poetical art. So much so, that the
generous Knight is, in the compassionate dictates of his
soul, compelled to cry out:

'Ho,' quoth the Knyght,-'good Sir, no more of this;
That ye have said is right ynough I wis;
And mokell more, for little heaviness
Is right enough for much folk, as I guesse.
I say, for me, it is a great disease,

Whereas men have been in wealth and ease,
To heare of their sudden fall, alas,
And the contrary is joy and solas.'

The Monk's definition of tragedy in the proem to his tale
is worth repeating:

Tragedie is to tell a certain story,
As old books us maken memory,
Of hem that stood in great prosperity,
And be fallen out of high degree,
Into miserie, and ended wretchedly.

Though a man of luxury, pride and pleasure, he is a master
of art and learning, though affecting to despise it.
Those who can think that the proud Huntsman and Noble
Housekeeper, Chaucer's Monk, is intended for a buffoon or
burlesque character, know little of Chaucer.

For the Host who follows this group, and holds the
center of the cavalcade, is a first rate character, and
his jokes are no trifles; they are always, though uttered
with audacity, and equally free with the Lord and the Peasant, they are always substantially and weightily expressive of knowledge and experience; Henry Baillie, the
keeper of the greatest Inn of the greatest City; for such
was the Tabarde Inn in Southwark, near London: our Host
was also a leader of the age.

By way of illustration, I instance Shakspeare's
Witches in Macbeth. Those who dress them for the stage,
consider them as wretched old women, and not as Shakspeare
intended, the Goddesses of Destiny; this shews how Chaucer
has been misunderstood in his sublime work. Shakspeare's
Fairies also are the rulers of the vegetable world, and so
are Chaucer's; let them be so considered, and then the
poet will be understood, and not else.

But I have omitted to speak of a very prominent character, the Pardoner, the Age's Knave, who always commands
and domineers over the high and low vulgar. This man is
sent in every age for a rod and scourge, and for a blight,
for a trial of men, to divide the classes of men; he is in
the most holy sanctuary, and he is suffered by Providence
for wise ends, and has also his great use, and his grand
leading destiny.

His companion, the Sompnour, is also a Devil of the
first magnitude, grand, terrific, rich and honoured in the
rank of which he holds the destiny. The uses to Society
are perhaps equal of the Devil and of the Angel, their
sublimity, who can dispute.

In daunger had he at his own gise,
The young girls of his diocese,
And he knew well their counsel, &c.

The principal figure in the next groupe is the Good
Parson; an Apostle, a real Messenger of Heaven, sent in
every age for its light and its warmth. This man is beloved and venerated by all, and neglected by all: He
serves all, and is served by none; he is, according to
Christ's definition, the greatest of his age. Yet he is
a Poor Parson of a town. Read Chaucer's description of
the Good Parson, and bow the head and the knee to him,
who, in every age, sends us such a burning and a shining
light. Search, O ye rich and powerful, for these men and
obey their counsel, then shall the golden age return: But
alas! you will not easily distinguish him from the Friar
or the Pardoner; they, also, are 'full solemn men,' and
their counsel you will continue to follow.
    I have placed by his side the Sergeant at Lawe, who
appears delighted to ride in his company, and between him
and his brother, the Plowman; as I wish men of Law would
always ride with them, and take their counsel, especially
in all difficult points. Chaucer's Lawyer is a character
of great venerableness, a Judge, and a real master of the
jurisprudence of his age.
    The Doctor of Physic is in this groupe, and the Frank-
lin, the voluptuous country gentleman, contrasted with the
Physician, and on his other hand, with two Citizens of
London. Chaucer's characters live age after age. Every
age is a Canterbury Pilgrimage; we all pass on, each sus-
taining one or other of these characters; nor can a child
be born, who is not one of these characters of Chaucer.
The Doctor of Physic is described as the first of his profession; perfect, learned, completely Master and Doctor in
his art. Thus the reader will observe, that Chaucer makes
every one of his characters perfect in his kind; every one
is an Antique Statue; the image of a class, and not of an
imperfect individual.
    This groupe also would furnish substantial matter, on
which volumes might be written. The Franklin is one who
keeps open table, who is the genius of eating and drinking, the Bacchus; as the Doctor of Physic is the Esculap-
ius, the Host is the Silenus, the Squire is the Apollo,
the Miller is the Hercules, &c. Chaucer's characters are
a description of the eternal Principles that exist in all
ages. The Franklin is voluptuousness itself, most nobly
pourtrayed:

It snewed in his house of meat and drink.

The Plowman is simplicity itself, with wisdom and strength for its stamina. Chaucer has divided the ancient character of Hercules between his Miller and his Plowman. Benevolence is the plowman's great characteristic; he is thin with excessive labour, and not with old age, as some have supposed:

> He would thresh, and thereto dike and delve
> For Christe's sake, for every poore wight,
> Withouten hire, if it lay in his might.

Visions of these eternal principles or characters of human life appear to poets, in all ages; the Grecian gods were the ancient Cherubim of Phoenicia; but the Greeks, and since them the Moderns, have neglected to subdue the gods of Priam. These gods are visions of the eternal attributes, or divine names, which, when erected into gods, become destructive to humanity. They ought to be the servants, and not the masters of man, or of society. They ought to be made to sacrifice to Man, and not man compelled to sacrifice to them; for when separated from man or humanity, who is Jesus the Saviour, the vine of eternity, they are thieves and rebels, they are destroyers.

The Plowman of Chaucer is Hercules in his supreme eternal state, divested of his spectrous shadow; which is the Miller, a terrible fellow, such as exists in all times and places for the trial of men, to astonish every neighbourhood with brutal strength and courage, to get rich and powerful to curb the pride of Man.

The Reeve and the Manciple are two characters of the most consummate worldly wisdom. The Shipman, or Sailor, is a similar genius of Ulyssean art; but with the highest courage superadded.

The Citizens and their Cook are each leaders of a class. Chaucer has been somehow made to number four citizens, which would make his whole company, himself included, thirty-one. But he says there was but nine and twenty in his company:

> Full nine and twenty in a company.

The Webbe, or Weaver, and the Tapiser, or Tapestry Weaver, appear to me to be the same person; but this is only an opinion, for full nine and twenty may signify one more or less. But I dare say that Chaucer wrote 'A Webbe Dyer,' that is, a Cloth Dyer:

> A Webbe Dyer, and a Tapiser.

The Merchant cannot be one of the Three Citizens, as
his dress is different, and his character is more marked,
whereas Chaucer says of his rich citizens:

All were yclothed in o liverie.

The characters of Women Chaucer has divided into two
classes, the Lady Prioress and the Wife of Bath. Are not
these leaders of the ages of men? The lady prioress, in
some ages, predominates; and in some the wife of Bath, in
whose character Chaucer has been equally minute and exact,
because she is also a scourge and a blight. I shall say
no more of her, nor expose what Chaucer has left hidden;
let the young reader study what he has said of her: it is
useful as a scarecrow. There are of such characters born
too many for the peace of the world.

I come at length to the Clerk of Oxenford. This
character varies from that of Chaucer, as the contemplative philosopher varies from the poetical genius. There
are always these two classes of learned sages, the poetical and the philosophical. The painter has put them side
by side, as if the youthful clerk had put himself under
the tuition of the mature poet. Let the Philosopher
always be the servant and scholar of inspiration and all
will be happy.

Such are the characters that compose this Picture,
which was painted in self-defence against the insolent and
envious imputation of unfitness for finished and scientific art; and this imputation, most artfully and industri-
ously endeavoured to be propagated among the public by
ignorant hirelings. The painter courts comparison with
his competitors, who, having received fourteen hundred
guineas and more, from the profits of his designs in that
well-known work, Designs for Blair's Grave, have left him
to shift for himself, while others, more obedient to an
employer's opinions and directions, are employed, at a
great expence, to produce works, in succession to his, by
which they acquired public patronage. This has hitherto
been his lot——to get patronage for others and then to be
left and neglected, and his work, which gained that patronage, cried down as eccentricity and madness; as unfinished and neglected by the artist's violent temper; he is
sure the works now exhibited will give the lie to such
aspersions.

Those who say that men are led by interest are knaves.
A knavish character will often say, 'of what interest is
it to me to do so and so?' I answer, of none at all, but
the contrary, as you well know. It is of malice and envy
that you have done this; hence I am aware of you, because

I know that you act, not from interest, but from malice,
even to your own destruction.' It is therefore become a
duty which Mr. B. owes to the Public, who have always
recognized him, and patronized him, however hidden by
artifices, that he should not suffer such things to be
done, or be hindered from the public Exhibition of his
finished productions by any calumnies in future.

The character and expression in this picture could
never have been produced with Rubens' light and shadow,
or with Rembrandt's, or anything Venetian or Flemish. The
Venetian and Flemish practice is broken lines, broken
masses, and unbroken colours. Their art is to lose form;
his art is to find form, and to keep it. His arts are
opposite to theirs in all things.

As there is a class of men whose whole delight is the
destruction of men, so there is a class of artists, whose
whole art and science is fabricated for the purpose of
destroying art. Who these are is soon known: 'by their
works ye shall know them.' All who endeavour to raise up
a style against Rafael, Mich. Angelo, and the Antique;
those who separate Painting from Drawing; who look if a
picture is well Drawn, and, if it is, immediately cry out,
that it cannot be well Coloured—those are the men.

But to shew the stupidity of this class of men nothing
need be done but to examine my rival's prospectus.

The two first characters in Chaucer, the Knight and the
Squire, he has put among his rabble; and indeed his prospectus calls the Squire the fop of Chaucer's age. Now
hear Chaucer:

Of his Stature, he was of even length,
And wonderly deliver, and of great strength;
And he had be sometime in Chivauchy,
In Flanders, in Artois, and in Picardy,
And borne him well, as of so litele space.

Was this a fop?

Well could he sit a horse, and faire ride,
He could songs make, and eke well indite
Just, and eke dance, pourtray, and well write.

Was this a fop?

Curteis he was, and meek, and serviceable;
And kerft before his fader at the table

Was this a fop?

It is the same with all his characters; he has done all
by chance, or perhaps his fortune,—money, money. According to his prospectus he has Three Monks; these he cannot
find in Chaucer, who has only One Monk, and that no vulgar
character, as he has endeavoured to make him. When men
cannot read they should not pretend to paint. To be sure
Chaucer is a little difficult to him who has only blund-
ered over novels, and catchpenny trifles of booksellers.
Yet a little pains ought to be taken even by the ignorant
and weak. He has put The Reeve, a vulgar fellow, between
his Knight and Squire, as if he was resolved to go contrary in everything to Chaucer, who says of the Reeve:

And ever he rode hinderest of the rout.

In this manner he has jumbled his dumb dollies together
and is praised by his equals for it; for both himself and
his friend are equally masters of Chaucer's language.
They both think that the Wife of Bath is a young, beautiful, blooming damsel, and H——says, that she is the Fair
Wife of Bath, and that the Spring appears in her Cheeks.
Now hear what Chaucer has made her say of herself, who is
no modest one:

But Lord when it remembereth me
Upon my youth and on my jollity
It tickleth me about the heart root,
Unto this day it doth my heart boot,
That I have had my world as in my time;
But age, alas, that all will envenime
Hath bireft my beauty and my pith
Let go; farewell: the Devil go therewith,
The flower is gone; there is no more to tell
The bran, as best I can, I now mote sell;
And yet to be right merry will I fond,—
Now forth to tell of my fourth husband.

She has had four husbands, a fit subject for this painter; yet the painter ought to be very much offended with
his friend H——, who has called his 'a common scene,' 'and
very ordinary forms,' which is the truest part of all, for
it is so, and very wretchedly so indeed. What merit can
there be in a picture of which such words are spoken with
truth?
But the prospectus says that the Painter has represented Chaucer himself as a knave, who thrusts himself among
honest people, to make game of and laugh at them; though
I must do justice to the painter, and say that he has made
him look more like a fool than a knave. But it appears in

all the writings of Chaucer, and particularly in his Canterbury Tales, that he was very devout, and paid respect
to true enthusiastic superstition. He has laughed at his
knaves and fools, as I do now. But he has respected his
True Pilgrims, who are a majority of his company, and are
not thrown together in the random manner that Mr. S——has
done. Chaucer has no where called the Plowman old, worn
out with age and labour, as the prospectus has represented
him, and says that the picture has done so too. He is
worn down with labour, but not with age. How spots of
brown and yellow, smeared about at random, can be either
young or old, I cannot see. It may be an old man; it may
be a young one; it may be any thing that a prospectus
pleases. But I know that where there are no lineaments
there can be no character. And what connoisseurs call
touch, I know by experience, must be the destruction of
all character and expression, as it is of every lineament.
     The scene of Mr. S——'s Picture is by Dulwich Hills,
which was not the way to Canterbury; but perhaps the painter thought he would give them a ride round about, because
they were a burlesque set of scare-crows, not worth any
man's respect or care.
     But the painter's thoughts being always upon gold, he
has introduced a character that Chaucer has not; namely, a
Goldsmith; for so the prospectus tells us. Why he has
introduced a Goldsmith, and what is the wit of it, the
prospectus does not explain. But it takes care to mention
the reserve and modesty of the Painter; this makes a good
epigram enough:

     The fox, the owl, the spider, and the mole,
     By sweet reserve and modesty get fat.

But the prospectus tells us, that the painter has
introduced a Sea Captain; Chaucer has a Ship-man a Sailor,
a Trading Master of a Vessel, called by courtesy Captain,
as every master of a boat is; but this does not make him a
Sea Captain. Chaucer has purposely omitted such a personage, as it only exists in certain periods: it is the soldier by sea. He who would be a Soldier in inland nations
is a sea captain in commercial nations.
     All is misconceived, and its mis-execution is equal to
its misconception. I have no objection to Rubens and Rembrandt being employed, or even to their living in a
palace; but it shall not be at the expence of Rafael and
Michael Angelo living in a cottage, and in contempt and
derision. I have been scorned long enough by these fellows, who owe to me all that they have; it shall be so no
longer.

I found them blind, I taught them how to see;
And, now, they know me not, nor yet themselves.

91. CHARLES LAMB, COMPREHENSIVENESS OF GENIUS

1811

The criticism of Lamb (1775-1834) is rich in penetrating
asides. He considered Blake's remarks (1809, No. 90) the
best criticism of Chaucer. The following comment occurs
in a criticism of Hogarth's works that first appeared in
the short-lived magazine 'The Reflector', edited by Leigh
Hunt: The Genius and Character of Hogarth, 'The Reflector'
II (part iii), 1811, p. 68.

In looking at Hogarth's principally comic works we do not
merely laugh at, we are led into long trains of reflection
by them. In this respect they resemble the characters of
Chaucer's 'Pilgrims', which have strokes of humour in them
enough to designate them for the most part as comic, but
our strongest feeling still is wonder at the comprehensiveness of genius which could crowd, as poet and painter
have done, into one small canvas so many diverse yet co-
operating materials.

92. GEORGE CRABBE, NAKED AND UNVEILED CHARACTER

1812

Crabbe (1754-1832), a fine but neglected poet, was
apprenticed to a doctor, and later took orders. The
Preface to the 'Tales', 1812, has a characteristically
suppressed fieriness, realism and sardonic humour. The
remarks on Chaucer's form, on 'realism', and on the nature
of poetry in general, are all so intertwined, so interesting, and relatively so neglected, that the whole Preface

is reprinted here.

That the appearance of the present Volume before the
Public is occasioned by a favourable reception of the
former two, I hesitate not to acknowledge; because, while
the confession may be regarded as some proof of gratitude,
or at least of attention from an Author to his Readers, it
ought not to be considered as an indication of vanity.
It is unquestionably very pleasant to be assured that our
labours are well received; but, nevertheless, this must
not be taken for a just and full criterion of their merit:
publications of great intrinsic value have been met with
so much coolness, that a writer who succeeds in obtaining
some degree of notice, should look upon himself rather as
one favoured than meritorious, as gaining a prize from
Fortune, and not a recompense for desert; and, on the contrary, as it is well known that books of very inferior
kind have been at once pushed into the strong current of
popularity, and are there kept buoyant by the force of the
stream, the writer who acquires not this adventitious help,
may be reckoned rather as unfortunate than undeserving;
and from these opposite considerations it follows, that a
man may speak of his success without incurring justly the
odium of conceit, and may likewise acknowledge a disappointment without an adequate cause for humiliation or
self-reproach.

But were it true that something of the complacency of
self-approbation would insinuate itself into an author's
mind with the idea of success, the sensation would not be
that of unalloyed pleasure: it would perhaps assist him
to bear, but it would not enable him to escape the mortification he must encounter from censures, which, though he
may be unwilling to admit, yet he finds himself unable to
confute; as well as from advice, which at the same time
that he cannot but approve, he is compelled to reject.

Reproof and advice, it is probable, every author will
receive, if we except those who merit so much of the
former, that the latter is contemptuously denied them;
now of these, reproof, though it may cause more temporary
uneasiness, will in many cases create less difficulty,
since errors may be corrected when opportunity occurs: but
advice, I repeat, may be of such nature, that it will be
painful to reject, and yet impossible to follow it; and in
this predicament I conceive myself to be placed. There
has been recommended to me, and from authority which neither inclination or prudence leads me to resist, in any
new work I might undertake, an unity of subject, and that

arrangement of my materials which connects the whole and
gives additional interest to every part; in fact, if not
an Epic Poem, strictly so denominated, yet such composition as would possess a regular succession of events, and
a catastrophe to which every incident should be subservient, and which every character, in a greater or less
degree, should conspire to accomplish.

In a Poem of this nature, the principal and inferior
characters in some degree resemble a General and his Army,
where no one pursues his peculiar objects and adventures,
or pursues them in unison with the movements and grand
purposes of the whole body; where there is a community of
interests and a subordination of actors: and it was upon
this view of the subject, and of the necessity for such
distribution of persons and events, that I found myself
obliged to relinquish an undertaking, for which the
characters I could command, and the adventures I could
describe, were altogether unfitted.

But if these characters which seemed to be at my disposal were not such as would coalesce into one body, nor
were of a nature to be commanded by one mind, so neither
on examination did they appear as an unconnected multi-
tide, accidentally collected, to be suddenly dispersed;
but rather beings of whom might be formed groups and
smaller societies, the relations of whose adventures and
pursuits might bear that kind of similitude to an Heroic
Poem, which these minor associations of men (as pilgrims
on the way to their saint, or parties in search of amusement, travellers excited by curiosity, or adventurers in
pursuit of gain) have in points of connection and importance with a regular and disciplined Army.

Allowing this comparison, it is manifest that while
much is lost for want of unity of subject and grandeur of
design, something is gained by greater variety of incident
and more minute display of character, by accuracy of description, and diversity of scene: in these narratives we
pass from gay to grave, from lively to severe, not only
without impropriety, but with manifest advantage. In one
continued and connected Poem, the Reader is, in general,
highly gratified or severely disappointed; by many independent narratives, he has the renovation of hope,
although he has been dissatisfied, and a prospect of reiterated pleasure should he find himself entertained.

I mean not, however, to compare these different modes
of writing as if I were balancing their advantages and
defects before I could give preference to either; with
me the way I take is not a matter of choice, but of necessity: I present not my Tales to the Reader as if I had
chosen the best method of ensuring his approbation, but as

using the only means I possessed of engaging his attention.

It may probably be remarked that Tales, however dissimilar, might have been connected by some associating
circumstance to which the whole number might bear equal
affinity, and that examples of such union are to be found
in *Chaucer*, in *Boccace*, and other collectors and inventors
of Tales, which considered in themselves are altogether
independent; and to this idea I gave so much consideration
as convinced me that I could not avail myself of the benefit of such artificial mode of affinity. To imitate the
English Poet, characters must be found adapted to their
several relations, and this is a point of great difficulty
and hazard: much allowance seems to be required even for
Chaucer himself, since it is difficult to conceive that on
any occasion the devout and delicate *Prioress*, the courtly
and valiant *Knight*, and 'the poure good Man the persone of
a Towne,' would be the voluntary companions of the drunken
Miller, the licentious *Sompnour*, and 'the *Wanton Wife of
Bath*,' and enter into that colloquial and travelling inti-
macy which, if a common pilgrimage to the shrine of *St.
Thomas* may be said to excuse, I know nothing beside (and
certainly nothing in these times) that would produce such
effect. *Boccace*, it is true, avoids all difficulty of
this kind, by not assigning to the ten relators of his
hundred Tales any marked or peculiar characters; nor,
though there are male and female in company, can the sex
of the narrator be distinguished in the narration. To
have followed the method of *Chaucer*, might have been of
use, but could scarcely be adopted, from its difficulty;
and to have taken that of the Italian writer, would have
been perfectly easy, but could be of no service: the
attempt at union therefore has been relinquished, and
these relations are submitted to the Public, connected by
no other circumstance than their being the productions of
the same Author, and devoted to the same purpose, the
entertainment of his Readers.

It has been already acknowledged, that these compositions have no pretensions to be estimated with the more
lofty and heroic kind of Poems, but I feel great reluct-
ance in admitting that they have not a fair and legitimate
claim to the poetic character: in vulgar estimation,
indeed, all that is not prose, passes for poetry; but I
have not ambition of so humble a kind as to be satisfied
with a concession which requires nothing in the Poet,
except his ability for counting syllables; and I trust
something more of the poetic character will be allowed to
the succeeding pages, than what the heroes of the *Dunciad*
might share with the Author: nor was I aware that by

describing, as faithfully as I could, men, manners, and
things, I was forfeiting a just title to a name which has
been freely granted to many whom to equal and even to
excel is but very stinted commendation.

In this case it appears that the usual comparison between Poetry and Painting entirely fails: the Artist who
takes an accurate likeness of individuals, or a faithful
representation of scenery, may not rank so high in the
public estimation, as one who paints an historical event,
or an heroic action; but he is nevertheless a painter, and
his accuracy is so far from diminishing his reputation,
that it procures for him in general both fame and emolu-
ment: nor is it perhaps with strict justice determined
that the credit and reputation of those verses which
strongly and faithfully delineate character and manners,
should be lessened in the opinion of the Public by the
very accuracy, which gives value and distinction to the
productions of the pencil.

Nevertheless, it must be granted that the pretensions
of any composition to be regarded as Poetry, will depend
upon that definition of the poetic character which he who
undertakes to determine the question has considered as
decisive; and it is confessed also that one of great
authority may be adopted, by which the verses now before
the Reader, and many others which have probably amused,
·and delighted him, must be excluded: a definition like
this will be found in the words which the greatest of
Poets, not divinely inspired, has given to the most noble
and valiant Duke of Athens——

> The Poet's eye, in a fine frenzy rolling,
> Doth glance from Heaven to Earth, from Earth to Heaven;
> And, as Imagination bodies forth
> The forms of things unknown, the Poet's pen
> Turns them to shapes, and gives to airy nothing
> A local habitation, and a name.
> (Midsummer Night's Dream, Act V, Scene 1.)

Hence we observe the Poet is one who, in the excursions of his fancy between heaven and earth, lights upon
a kind of fairy-land in which he places a creation of his
own, where he embodies shapes, and gives action and
adventure to his ideal offspring; taking captive the
imagination of his readers, he elevates them above the
grossness of actual being, into the soothing and pleasant
atmosphere of supra-mundane existence: there he obtains
for his visionary inhabitants the interest that engages
a reader's attention without ruffling his feelings, and
excites that moderate kind of sympathy which the realities

of nature oftentimes fail to produce, either because they
are so familiar and insignificant that they excite no
determinate emotion, or are so harsh and powerful that
the feelings excited are grating and distasteful.

Be it then granted that (as *Duke Theseus* observes)
'such tricks hath strong Imagination,' and that such Poets
'are of imagination all compact;' let it be further conceded, that theirs is a higher and more dignified kind of
composition, nay, the only kind that has pretensions to
inspiration; still, that these Poets should so entirely
engross the title as to exclude those who address their
productions to the plain sense and sober judgment of their
Readers, rather than to their fancy and imagination, I
must repeat that I am unwilling to admit,——because I conceive that, by granting such right of exclusion, a vast
deal of what has been hitherto received as genuine poetry
would no longer be entitled to that appellation.

All that kind of satire wherein character is skilfully
delineated, must (this criterion being allowed) no longer
be esteemed as genuine Poetry; and for the same reason
many affecting narratives which are founded on real
events, and borrow no aid whatever from the imagination of
the writer, must likewise be rejected: a considerable part
of the Poems, as they have hitherto been denominated, of
Chaucer, are of this naked and unveiled character; and
there are in his Tales many pages of coarse, accurate, and
minute, but very striking description. Many small Poems
in a subsequent age of most impressive kind are adapted
and addressed to the common sense of the Reader, and prevail by the strong language of truth and nature: they
amused our ancestors, and they continue to engage our
interest, and excite our feelings by the same powerful
appeals to the heart and affections. In times less remote,
Dryden has given us much of this Poetry, in which the
force of expression and accuracy of description have neither needed nor obtained assistance from the fancy of the
writer; the characters in his 'Absalom and Ahitophel' are
instances of this, and more especially those of *Doeg* and
Ogg in the second part: these, with all their grossness,
and almost offensive accuracy, are found to possess that
strength and spirit which has preserved from utter annihilation the dead bodies of *Tate* to whom they were inhumanly
bound, happily with a fate the reverse of that caused by
the cruelty of *Mezentius*; for there the living perished
in the putrefaction of the dead, and here the dead are
preserved by the vitality of the living. And, to bring
forward one other example, it will be found that *Pope*
himself has no small portion of this actuality of relation, this nudity of description, and poetry without an

atmosphere; the lines beginning *'In the worst inn's worst room,'* are an example, and many others may be seen in his Satires, Imitations, and above all in his Dunciad: the frequent absence of those *'Sports of Fancy,'* and *'Tricks of strong Imagination,'* have been so much observed, that some have ventured to question whether even this writer were a Poet; and though, as *Dr. Johnson* has remarked, it would be difficult to form a definition of one in which *Pope* should not be admitted, yet they who doubted his claim, had, it is likely, provided for his exclusion by forming that kind of character for their Poet, in which this elegant versifier, for so he must be then named, should not be comprehended.

These things considered, an Author will find comfort in his expulsion from the rank and society of Poets, by reflecting that men much his superiors were likewise shut out, and more especially when he finds also that men not much his superiors are entitled to admission.

But in whatever degree I may venture to differ from any others in my notions of the qualifications and character of the true Poet, I most cordially assent to their opinion who assert that his principal exertions must be made to engage the attention of his Readers; and further, I must allow that the effect of Poetry should be to lift the mind from the painful realities of actual existence, from its every-day concerns, and its perpetually-occurring vexations, and to give it repose by substituting objects in their place which it may contemplate with some degree of interest and satisfaction: but what is there in all this, which may not be effected by a fair representation of existing character? nay, by a faithful delineation of those painful realities, those every-day concerns, and those perpetually-occurring vexations themselves, provided they be not (which is hardly to be supposed) the very concerns and distresses of the Reader? for when it is admitted that they have no particular relation to him, but are the troubles and anxieties of other men, they excite and interest his feelings as the imaginary exploits, adventures, and perils of romance;—they soothe his mind, and keep his curiosity pleasantly awake; they appear to have enough of reality to engage his sympathy, but possess not interest sufficient to create painful sensations. Fiction itself, we know, and every work of fancy, must for a time have the effect of realities; nay, the very enchanters, spirits, and monsters of *Ariosto* and *Spenser* must be present in the mind of the Reader while he is engaged by their operations, or they would be as the objects and incidents of a Nursery Tale to a rational understanding, altogether despised and neglected: in truth, I can but

consider this pleasant effect upon the mind of a Reader,
as depending neither upon the events related (whether they
be actual or imaginary), nor upon the characters introduced (whether taken from life or fancy), but upon the
manner in which the Poem itself is conducted; let that be
judiciously managed, and the occurrences actually copied
from life will have the same happy effect as the inventions of a creative fancy;—while, on the other hand, the
imaginary persons and incidents to which the Poet has
given *'a local habitation, and a name,'* will make upon the
concurring feelings of the Reader, the same impressions
with those taken from truth and nature, because they will
appear to be derived from that source, and therefore of
necessity will have a similar effect.

Having thus far presumed to claim for the ensuing pages
the rank and title of Poetry, I attempt no more, nor venture to class or compare them with any other kinds of poetical composition; their place will doubtless be found
for them.

A principal view and wish of the Poet must be to engage
the mind of his Readers, as, failing in that point, he
will scarcely succeed in any other: I therefore willingly
confess that much of my time and assiduity has been devoted to this purpose; but, to the ambition of pleasing, no
other sacrifices have, I trust, been made, than of my own
labour and care. Nothing will be found that militates
against the rules of propriety and good manners, nothing
that offends against the more important precepts of morality and religion; and with this negative kind of merit,
I commit my Book to the judgment and taste of the Reader,
—not being willing to provoke his vigilance by professions of accuracy, nor to solicit his indulgence by apo-
logies for mistakes.

93.   JOHN GALT, ANYTHING BUT POETRY

1812

Galt (1779-1839), a copious novelist and miscellaneous
writer, acquaintance of Byron and Carlyle, takes a deriva-
tive 'Romantic' view, but is perhaps the first to attribute *naiveté* to Chaucer. On 'circumstances' cf. Gray,

c. 1760 (No. 81). Text from 'The Life and Administration
of Cardinal Wolsey', 1812, p. 191n.

I have never been able to bring myself to entertain any
feeling approximating to respect for the works of Chaucer,
Gower, Lydgate, and the other tribe of rhymers that preceded the reign of Henry VIII. They seem to me to have
acquired their fame before the nation knew anything of
poetry, and to have remained famous when their works are
no longer read. There is a little sprinkling, here and
there, of naiveté in Chaucer, but his lists and catalogues
of circumstances are anything but poetry. Lydgate is bare
naked prose.

94. GEORGE NOTT, VERSES OF CADENCE

1815

G.F. Nott (1767-1841), educated at Christ Church, Oxford,
scholar, dilettante and cleric, edited the works of the
sixteenth-century poets Surrey and Wyatt with a huge
introduction and an unreliable text, 'The Works of Henry
Howard, etc.', 1815. The comments on Chaucer occur in
Section IV. His concept of Chaucer's 'verses of cadence',
a notion not dissimilar to Puttenham's 'riding rhyme',
is sometimes revived. Nott is unscholarly (the
antithesis of Tyrwhitt; his remark about the manuscripts,
for example, is quite untrue), but his search for rhythm,
his emphasis on 'oral delivery', his observation of poetic
diction - in a word, his interest in rhetorical technique
- though usually mistaken or exaggerated, is unusual in
the nineteenth century, and of value.

(pp. clviii-clix)....The chief improvement introduced by
Chaucer into our versification was that of dropping altogether the use of the Alexandrine line, and substituting
the line of ten syllables in its stead. This alteration
was of importance; not only because it was adopted by all
subsequent writers, but because it led the way to that
further change which afterwards took place. It was the

first step towards bringing our versification to its present form.

But though Chaucer reduced our verse to ten syllables,
he suffered it to retain in other respects the properties
of the old Alexandrine verse. Like that it was divided by
the old caesura into hemistichs; had the pause at the end,
and was recited rhythmically. It was still what Lydgate
called 'the verse of Cadence.' It is true that many of
Chaucer's lines have the appearance of being pure Iambic
Decasyllables. This however was the effect of accident.
For accent and quantity, which are not of necessity the
same, would sometimes coincide, and when they did, a pure
Iambic Decasyllable was unavoidably the result. It was
the frequent occurrence of these fortuitous Iambic lines
that led Mr. Tyrwhitt, and before him Mr. Urry, and the
learned Mr. Morell, to believe that Chaucer's system of
versification was altogether metrical. But an impartial
consideration of the subject, and a reference to good MSS.
must I think lead us to conclude that Chaucer had not a
metrical system of numbers in contemplation; but that, on
the contrary, he designed his verses to be read, like
those of all his contemporaries, with a caesura and rhythmical cadence.

Should it be asked why so many Iambic lines are to be
found in Chaucer, the answer is obvious. Our language
had become more compressed. Most of the words in common
use had dropped their final syllables, and monosyllables
were multiplied. This could not but produce a corresponding effect on our versification, and lines of ten syllables would insensibly be written instead of lines of
twelve or fourteen....

(pp. clxii-clxiv) I will adduce some reasons why I
consider Chaucer's verses, though Decasyllabic, to have
been rhythmical, and not metrical.

First, because a large proportion of them cannot be
read as Iambic Decasyllables, without doing the utmost
violence to our language; all which verses are harmonious
as verses of cadence, if read with the caesura rhythmically. And further, because all those verses might easily
by a slight transposition have been made pure Iambic
Decasyllables, had Chaucer either known that mode of
versification, or intended to have adopted it: as in the
following instance.

In her is high beauty withouten pride.
                              'Cant. Tales.' 4522.

Unless this line be read rhythmically it has no principle of harmony at all; but when so read, it has all the

harmony that sort of versification aspires to.

In hèr ĭs hĭgh bĕautè ‖ wĭthòutĕn prĪde

Had the Iambic Decasyllabic measure been intended, the
line with the transposition of a single word, might have
been made a perfect Iambic Decasyllable. We cannot suppose that this would have escaped Chaucer's notice.

In her high beauty is, withouten pride.

The above observations apply to a large number of lines
of a similar construction, occurring in almost every page
of Chaucer's works.

Again; the incessant recurrence of defective and redundant verses seems to me wholly inconsistent with the
notion of a regular system of metrical versification, but
not so with rhythmical versification. On the contrary
those irregularities are, as I have said above, connected
with that system. That some licence in the use of defective or redundant lines, answering to the catalectic and
hypercatalectic lines of the Greek Poets, has ever been
claimed by our best writers in the regular metrical Decasyllabic system, will be readily admitted. Milton availed
himself of it. But that which is conceded as a licence,
must be used occasionally only: should it occur at almost
every other line, it is then no longer a licence; it forms
part of the system.

Another, and I conceive a conclusive reason for believing Chaucer's verses to have been rhythmical verses, or
verses of cadence, may be drawn from the Manuscripts themselves in which his poems are preserved. In these MSS.
either the caesura, or the pause at the end of the line,
and sometimes both the pause and the caesura are almost
always noted, and that in so careful a manner as makes it
questionable whether there be any MS. of good date and
authority in which one or both of them is not noted,
either by a point, or a virgule....

We must constantly bear in mind that Chaucer's verses
were not submitted to the eye like those of modern poets.
Few of the nobility, and still fewer of the common sort
could read. The generality of people therefore had no
other means of becoming acquainted with Chaucer's poems
than what the Minstrels supplied, who went about in troops
chanting them to the sound of the harp on days of public
festivity, or when the great feudal barons entertained
their vassals and dependents in their castle halls with
almost regal splendour. It was on these occasions, and by
those means alone that the English generally were made

acquainted with the animated compositions of their favourite national bard. Sometimes they heard chanted to them
his gayer tales of common life; and were told of the pains
and pleasures, the exultations and despondencies of love
as pourtrayed by him in his Troilus and Cressida. At
other times they were charmed with the lofty achievements
of Palamon and Arcite; or with the still wilder sublimity
of Cambuscan's eventful story. In every instance they
depended on their Minstrels, round whom they crowded, a
mixed unlettered multitude, greedily drinking in the
varied strains with wondering ears....

(p. clxxxviii) Chaucer did much towards refining our
poetic diction, but he left it indefinite: and therefore
open to subsequent innovation and experiment. Indeed he
was not consistent in the use of one uniform style. In
his Canterbury Tales what he seems to have particularly
aimed at was simplicity of construction and a not over-
curious selection of words. By these means he obtained a
sort of natural dignity, and simple elegance of style
which rose often into sublimity, and enabled him to present his thoughts in a manner singularly clear and distinct. In his Troilus and Cressida, which is evidently
his most laboured composition, he aimed at something more
like involution, and affected a greater nicety of terms.
But his diction was not sustained equally throughout. He
suffered mean expressions and prosaic forms of speech to
occur, mixed with phrases evidently of great study and
refinement.

That Chaucer's style of poetic diction was not considered unexceptionable is evident from the pains that were
taken after his death to improve upon it: something was
evidently wanting. But the absence of taste and genius
in the writers who succeeded him, led them, instead of
supplying what Chaucer had left defective, to frame a new
poetic diction altogether out of terms borrowed, or compounded from the Latin. By so doing they thought, no
doubt, to enrich our language; but the words they used
were not of a nature to incorporate themselves with it.
Therefore they never obtained any thing like common currency, and whenever they were employed they had the
appearance of pedantry and affectation. Such are the
following terms. *Aureate, amene, purpure, pulchritude,
celature, exornate, solatious, delectation, depured,
irous, facunde, termine, tenebrous, lacedation,* and a multitude of similar words. By means of which our poetry
was degraded to mere sound; all the real graces of diction
were neglected, and no attempt was made to obtain that
nice structure of period, that delicate arrangement of
words which produces a charm like the sweetness of a slow
protracted cadence in music.

95.   WILLIAM HAZLITT, CHAUCER ATTENDED CHIEFLY TO THE REAL
AND NATURAL

1817, 1818

The great critic Hazlitt (1778-1830) gives a fairly rou-
tine account of Chaucer, stuffed out with long quotations.
He emphasises character and realistic description and the
mixture of pathos and humour like everyone since Dryden,
but his perception of Chaucer's 'hardness and dryness' has
a touch of novelty, while Hazlitt's power of generalisation is always invigorating.   The first passage (a) comes
from 'Characters of Shakespeare's Plays', 1817 ('Troilus
and Cressida'); the second (b) from 'Lectures on the English Poets', 1818, Lecture I, On Poetry in General, and
(c) from Lecture II, On Chaucer and Spenser.

(a)

(p. 89) In Chaucer, Cressida is represented as a grave,
sober, considerate personage (a widow—he cannot tell her
age, nor whether she has children or no) who has an alter-
nate eye to her character, her interest, and her pleasure:
Shakespear's Cressida is a giddy girl, an unpractised
jilt, who falls in love with Troilus, as she afterwards
deserts him, from mere levity and thoughtlessness of
temper.   She may be wooed and won to any thing and from
any thing, at a moment's warning: the other knows very
well what she would be at, and sticks to it, and is more
governed by substantial reasons than by caprice or vanity.
Pandarus again, in Chaucer's story, is a friendly sort of
go-between, tolerably busy, officious, and forward in
bringing matters to bear: but in Shakespear he has 'a
stamp exclusive and professional:' he wears the badge of
his trade; he is a regular knight of the game.   The difference of the manner in which the subject is treated
arises perhaps less from intention, than from the different genius of the two poets.   There is no *double entendre*
in the characters of Chaucer: they are either quite serious or quite comic.   In Shakespear the ludicrous and iro-
nical are constantly blended with the stately and the
impassioned.   We see Chaucer's characters as they saw
themselves, not as they appeared to others or might have

appeared to the poet. He is as deeply implicated in the
affairs of his personages as they could be themselves.
He had to go a long journey with each of them, and became
a kind of necessary confidant. There is little relief, or
light and shade in his pictures. The conscious smile is
not seen lurking under the brow of grief or impatience.
Every thing with him is intense and continuous—a working
out of what went before.—Shakespear never committed himself to his characters. He trifled, laughed, or wept with
them as he chose. He has no prejudices for or against
them; and it seems a matter of perfect indifference
whether he shall be in jest or earnest. According to him
'the web of our lives is of a mingled yarn, good and ill
together.' His genius was dramatic, as Chaucer's was historical. He saw both sides of a question, the different
views taken of it according to the different interests of
the parties concerned, and he was at once an actor and
spectator in the scene. If any thing, he is too various
and flexible; too full of transitions, of glancing lights,
of salient points. If Chaucer followed up his subject too
doggedly, perhaps Shakespear was too volatile and heed-
less. The Muse's wing too often lifted him off his feet.
He made infinite excursions to the right and the left.

>   He hath done
> Mad and fantastic execution,
> Engaging and redeeming of himself
> With such a careless force and forceless care,
> As if that luck in very spite of cunning
> Bad him win all.

Chaucer attended chiefly to the real and natural, that
is, to the involuntary and inevitable impressions on the
mind in given circumstances: Shakespear exhibited also
the possible and the fantastical,—not only what things
are in themselves, but whatever they might seem to be,
their different reflections, their endless combinations.
He lent his fancy, wit, invention, to others, and borrowed
their feelings in return. Chaucer excelled in the force
of habitual sentiment; Shakespear added to it every variety of passion, every suggestion of thought or accident.
Chaucer described external objects with the eye of a painter, or he might be said to have embodied them with the
hand of a sculptor, every part is so thoroughly made out,
and tangible:—Shakespear's imagination threw over them a
lustre

> Prouder than when blue Iris bends.

We must conclude this criticism; and we will do it with
a quotation or two. One of the most beautiful passages in
Chaucer's tale is the description of Cresseide's first
avowal of her love.

> And as the new abashed nightingale,
> That stinteth first when she beginneth sing,
> When that she heareth any herde's tale,
> Or in the hedges any wight stirring,
> And, after, sicker doth her voice outring;
> Right so Cresseide, when that her dread stent,
> Opened her heart, and told him her intent.

See also the two next stanzas, and particularly that
divine one beginning

> Her armes small, her back both straight and soft, &c.

Compare this with the following speech of Troilus to
Cressida in the play.

> O, that I thought it could be in a woman;
> And if it can, I will presume in you,
> To feed for aye her lamp and flame of love,
> To keep her constancy in plight and youth,
> Out-living beauties out-ward, with a mind
> That doth renew swifter than blood decays.
> Or, that persuasion could but thus convince me,
> That my integrity and truth to you
> Might be affronted with the match and weight
> Of such a winnow'd purity in love;
> How were I then uplifted! But alas,
> I am as true as Truth's simplicity,
> And simpler than the infancy of Truth.

These passages may not seem very characteristic at
first sight, though we think they are so. We will give
two, that cannot be mistaken. Patroclus says to Achilles,

> Rouse yourself; and the weak wanton Cupid
> Shall from your neck unloose his amorous fold,
> And like a dew-drop from the lion's mane,
> Be shook to air.

Troilus, addressing the God of Day on the approach of
the morning that parts him from Cressida, says with much
scorn,

What! proffer'st thou thy light here for to sell?
Go, sell it them that smallé selés grave.

If nobody but Shakespear could have written the former,
nobody but Chaucer would have thought of the latter.
—Chaucer was the most literal of poets, as Richardson was
of prose-writers.

Every thing in Chaucer has a downright reality. A simile or a sentiment is as if it were given in upon evidence.
In Shakespear the commonest matter-of-fact has a romantic
grace about it; or seems to float with the breath of imagination in a freer element. No one could have more depth
of feeling or observation than Chaucer, but he wanted resources of invention to lay open the stores of nature or
the human heart with the same radiant light, that Shakespear has done. However fine or profound the thought, we
know what was coming, whereas the effect of reading
Shakespear is 'like the eye of vassalage encountering
majesty.' Chaucer's mind was consecutive, rather than
discursive. He arrived at truth through a certain process; Shakespear saw every thing by intuition. Chaucer
had great variety of power, but he could do only one thing
at once. He set himself to work on a particular subject.
His ideas were kept separate, labelled, ticketed and par-
celled out in a set form, in pews and compartments by
themselves. They did not play into one another's hands.
They did not re-act upon one another, as the blower's
breath moulds the yielding glass. There is something hard
and dry in them. What is the most wonderful thing in
Shakespear's faculties is their excessive sociability, and
how they gossipped and compared notes together.

(b)

ON POETRY IN GENERAL

(p. 1) The best general notion which I can give of poetry
is, that it is the natural impression of any object or
circumstance, bu its vividness exciting an involuntary
movement of imagination and passion, and producing, by
sympathy, a certain modulation of the voice, or sounds,
expressing it...

(p. 4) ...the vain, the ambitious, the proud, the cho-
leric man, the hero and the coward, the beggar and the
king, the rich and the poor, the young and the old, all
live in a world of their own making; and the poet does no
more than describe what all the others think and act. If
his art is folly and madness, it is folly and madness at
second hand. 'There is warrant for it.' Poets alone have

not 'such seething brains, such shaping fantasies, that
apprehend more than cooler reason' can.

> The lunatic, the lover, and the poet
> Are of imagination all compact.
> One sees more devils than vast hell can hold;
> The madman. While the lover, all as frantic,
> Sees Helen's beauty in a brow of Egypt.
> The poet's eye in a fine frenzy rolling,
> Doth glance from heav'n to earth, from earth to heav'n;
> And as imagination bodies forth
> The forms of things unknown, the poet's pen
> Turns them to shape, and gives to airy nothing
> A local habitation and a name.
> Such tricks hath strong imagination.

If poetry is a dream, the business of life is much the
same. If it is a fiction, made up of what we wish things
to be, and fancy that they are, because we wish them so,
there is no other nor better reality....
(p. 5) Poetry then is an imitation of nature, but the
imagination and the passions are a part of man's nature.
We shape things according to our wishes and fancies, without poetry; but poetry is the most perfect language that
can be found for those creations of the mind 'which
ecstacy is very cunning in.' Neither a mere description
of natural objects, nor a mere delineation of natural
feelings, however distinct or forcible, constitutes the
ultimate end and aim of poetry, without the heightenings
of the imagination.

(c)

(p. 39) Having, in the former Lecture, given some account
of the nature of poetry in general, I shall proceed, in
the next place, to a more particular consideration of the
genius and history of English poetry. I shall take, as
the subject of the present lecture, Chaucer and Spenser,
two out of four of the greatest names in poetry, which
this country has to boast. Both of them, however, were
much indebted as belonging, in a certain degree, to the
same school. The freedom and copiousness with which our
most original writers, in former periods, availed themselves of the productions of their predecessors, frequently transcribing whole passages, without scruple, or
acknowledgment, may seem contrary to the etiquette of
modern literature, when the whole stock of poetical
common-places has become public property, and no one is

compelled to trade upon any particular author. But it is
not so much to be wondered at, at a time when to read and
write was of itself an honorary distinction, when learning
was almost as great a rarity as genius, and when in fact
those who first transplanted the beauties of other languages into their own, might be considered as public bene-
factors, and the founders of a national literature.—There
are poets older than Chaucer, and in the interval between
him and Spenser; but their genius was not such as to place
them in any point of comparison with either of these celebrated men; and an inquiry into their particular merits
or defects might seem rather to belong to the province of
the antiquary, than be thought generally interesting to
the lovers of poetry in the present day.

Chaucer (who has been very properly considered as the
father of English poetry) preceded Spenser by two centuries. He is supposed to have been born in London, in the
year 1328, during the reign of Edward III. and to have
died in 1400, at the age of seventy-two. He received a
learned education at one, or at both of the universities,
and travelled early into Italy, where he became thoroughly
imbued with the spirit and excellences of the great Italian poets and prose-writers, Dante, Petrarch, and Boccace;
and is said to have had a personal interview with one of
these, Petrarch. He was connected, by marriage, with the
famous John of Gaunt, through whose interest he was introduced into several public employments. Chaucer was an
active partisan, a religious reformer, and from the share
he took in some disturbances, on one occasion, he was
obliged to fly the country. On his return, he was imprisoned, and made his peace with government, as it is said,
by a discovery of his associates. Fortitude does not
appear, at any time, to have been the distinguishing virtue of poets.—There is, however, an obvious similarity
between the practical turn of Chaucer's mind and the restless impatience of his character, and the tone of his
writings. Yet it would be too much to attribute the one
to the other as cause and effect: for Spenser, whose poetical temperament was as effeminate as Chaucer's was
stern and masculine, was equally engaged in public
affairs, and had mixed equally in the great world. So
much does native disposition predominate over accidental
circumstances, moulding them to its previous bent and
purposes! For while Chaucer's intercourse with the busy
world, and collision with the actual passions and conflicting interests of others, seemed to brace the sinews of
his understanding, and gave to his writings the air of a
man who describes persons and things that he had known and
been intimately concerned in; the same opportunities,

operating on a differently constituted frame, only served
to alienate Spenser's mind the more from the 'close-pent
up' scenes of ordinary life, and to make him 'rive their
concealing continents,' to give himself up to the unre-
strained indulgence of 'flowery tenderness.'

It is not possible for any two writers to be more opposite in this respect. Spenser delighted in luxurious
enjoyment; Chaucer, in severe activity of mind. As Spenser was the most romantic and visionary, Chaucer was the
most practical of all the great poets, the most a man of
business and the world. His poetry reads like history.
Every thing has a downright reality; at least in the rela-
tor's mind. A simile, or a sentiment, is as if it were
given in upon evidence. Thus he describes Cressid's first
avowal of her love.

> And as the new abashed nightingale,
> That stinteth first when she beginneth sing,
> When that she heareth any herde's tale,
> Or in the hedges any wight stirring,
> And after, sicker, doth her voice outring;
> Right so Cresseide, when that her dread stent,
> Open'd her heart, and told him her intent.

This is so true and natural, and beautifully simple, that
the two things seem identified with each other. Again, it
is said in the Knight's Tale—

> Thus passeth yere by yere, and day by day,
> Till it felle ones in a morwe of May,
> That Emelie that fayrer was to sene
> Than is the lilie upon his stalke grene;
> And fresher than the May with floures newe,
> For with the rose-colour strof hire hewe:
> I n'ot which was the finer of hem two.

This scrupulousness about the literal preference, as if
some question of matter of fact was at issue, is remarkable. I might mention that other, where he compares the
meeting between Palamon and Arcite to a hunter waiting for
a lion in a gap;—

> That stondeth at a gap with a spere,
> Whan hunted is the lion or the bere,
> And hereth him come rushing in the greves,
> And breking bothe the boughes and the leves:

or that still finer one of Constance, when she is condemned to death:—

Have ye not seen somtime a pale face
(Among a prees) of him that hath been lad
Toward his deth, wheras he geteth no grace,
And swiche a colour in his face hath had,
Men mighten know him that was so bestad,
Amonges all the faces in that route;
So stant Custance, and loketh hire aboute.

The beauty, the pathos here does not seem to be of the
poet's seeking, but a part of the necessary texture of the
fable. He speaks of what he wishes to describe with the
accuracy, the discrimination of one who relates what has
happened to himself, or has had the best information from
those who have been eye-witnesses of it. The strokes of
his pencil always tell. He dwells only on the essential,
on that which would be interesting to the persons really
concerned: yet as he never omits any material circumstance, he is prolix from the number of points on which he
touches, without being diffuse on any one; and is sometimes tedious from the fidelity with which he adheres to
his subject, as other writers are from the frequency of
their digressions from it. The chain of his story is composed of a number of fine links, closely connected together, and riveted by a single blow. There is an instance of the minuteness which he introduces into his most
serious descriptions in his account of Palamon when left
alone in his cell:

Swiche sorrow he maketh that the grete tour
Resouned of his yelling and clamour,
The pure fetters on his shinnes grete
Were of his bitter salte teres wete.

The mention of this last circumstance seemed a part of the
instructions he had to follow, which he had no discretion-
ary power to omit or introduce at pleasure. He is con-
tented to find grace and beauty in truth. He exhibits for
the most part the naked object, with little drapery thrown
over it. His metaphors, which are few, are not for ornament, but use, and as like as possible to the things themselves. He does not affect to shew his power over the
reader's mind, but the power which his subject has over
his own. The readers of Chaucer's poetry feel more nearly
what the persons he describes must have felt, than perhaps
those of any other poet. His sentiments are not voluntary
effusions of the poet's fancy, but founded on the natural
impulses and habitual prejudices of the characters he has
to represent. There is an inveteracy of purpose, a sincerity of feeling, which never relaxes or grows vapid, in

whatever they do or say. There is no artificial, pompous
display, but a strict parsimony of the poet's materials,
like the rude simplicity of the age in which he lived.
His poetry resembles the root just springing from the
ground, rather than the fullblown flower. His muse is no
'babbling gossip of the air,' fluent and redundant; but,
like a stammerer, or a dumb person, that has just found
the use of speech, crowds many things together with eager
haste, with anxious pauses, and fond repetitions to prevent mistake. His words point as an index to the objects,
like the eye or finger. There were none of the common-
places of poetic diction in our author's time, no reflected lights of fancy, no borrowed roseate tints; he was
obliged to inspect things for himself, to look narrowly,
and almost to handle the object, as in the obscurity of
morning we partly see and partly grope our way; so that
his descriptions have a sort of tangible character belonging to them, and produce the effect of sculpture on the
mind. Chaucer had an equal eye for truth of nature and
discrimination of character; and his interest in what he
saw gave new distinctness and force to his power of observation. The picturesque and the dramatic are in him
closely blended together, and hardly distinguishable; for
he principally describes external appearances as indicat-
ing character, as symbols of internal sentiment. There is
a meaning in what he sees; and it is this which catches
his eye by sympathy. Thus the costume and dress of the
Canterbury Pilgrims—of the Knight—the Squire—the Oxford
Scholar—the Gap-toothed Wife of Bath, and the rest, speak
for themselves.

[Quotes description of Prioress, 'Gen. Prol.', C.T, I,
118-50.]

   (p. 50) Chaucer, it has been said, numbered the
classes of men, as Linnaeus numbered the plants. Most of
them remain to this day: others that are obsolete, and may
well be dispensed with, still live in his descriptions of
them. Such is the Sompnoure....

[Quotes 'Gen. Prol.' C.T, I, 623-88, with some deliberate
omissions.]

   (p. 51) It would be a curious speculation (at least for
those who think that the characters of men never change,
though manners, opinions, and institutions may) to know
what has become of this character of the Sompnoure in the
present day; whether or not it has any technical representative in existing professions; into what channels and

conduits it has withdrawn itself, where it lurks unseen in
cunning obscurity, or else shews its face boldly, pampered
into all the insolence of office, in some other shape, as
it is deterred or encouraged by circumstances. *Chaucer's
characters modernised,* upon this principle of historic
derivation, would be an useful addition to our knowledge
of human nature. But who is there to undertake it?...

[Quotes 'Knight's Tale', C.T. I, 2128-86, with a few
deliberate omissions.]

(p. 53) What a deal of terrible beauty there is contained
in this description! The imagination of a poet brings
such objects before us, as when we look at wild beasts in
a menagerie; their claws are pared, their eyes glitter
like harmless lightning; but we look at them with a pleasing awe, clothed in beauty, formidable in the sense of
abstract power.
  Chaucer's descriptions of natural scenery possess the
same sort of characteristic excellence, or what might be
termed *gusto.* They have a local truth and freshness,
which gives the very feeling of the air, the coolness or
moisture of the ground. Inanimate objects are thus made
to have a fellow-feeling in the interest of the story;
and render back the sentiment of the speaker's mind. One
of the finest parts of Chaucer is of this mixed kind. It
is the beginning of the Flower and the Leaf, where he describes the delight of that young beauty, shrouded in her
bower, and listening, in the morning of the year, to the
singing of the nightingale; while her joy rises with the
rising song, and gushes out afresh at every pause, and is
borne along with the full tide of pleasure, and still
increases, and repeats, and prolongs itself, and knows no
ebb. The coolness of the arbour, its retirement, the
early time of the day, the sudden starting up of the birds
in the neighbouring bushes, the eager delight with which
they devour and rend the opening buds and flowers, are
expressed with a truth and feeling, which make the whole
appear like the recollection of an actual scene....

[Quotes 'The Flower and the Leaf', 34-133, with a few
omissions.]

(p. 56) There is no affected rapture, no flowery sentiment: the whole is an ebullition of natural delight 'wel-
ling out of the heart,' like water from a crystal spring.
Nature is the soul of art: there is a strength as well as
a simplicity in the imagination that reposes entirely on
nature, that nothing else can supply. It was the same

trust in nature, and reliance on his subject, which enabled Chaucer to describe the grief and patience of Griselda;
the faith of Constance; and the heroic perseverance of the
little child, who, going to school through the streets of
Jewry,

> Oh *Alma Redemptoris mater,* loudly sung,

and who, after his death, still triumphed in his song.
Chaucer has more of this deep, internal, sustained sentiment, than any other writer, except Boccaccio. In depth
of simple pathos, and intensity of conception, never
swerving from his subject, I think no other writer comes
near him, not even the Greek tragedians.

[Quotes 'Knight's Tale', C.T. I, 1355-71, 2771-9; and as
example of beauty and grandeur, 1967-80; and of 'terrific
images', 2041-8, with slight omissions.]

(p. 59) The story of Griselda is in Boccaccio; but the
Clerk of Oxford, who tells it, professes to have learned
it from Petrarch. This story has gone all over Europe,
and has passed into a proverb. In spite of the barbarity
of the circumstances, which are abominable, the sentiment
remains unimpaired and unalterable. It is of that kind,
'that heaves no sigh, that sheds ho tear;' but it hangs
upon the beatings of the heart; it is a part of the very
being; it is as inseparable from it as the breath we draw.
It is still and calm as the face of death. Nothing can
touch its ethereal purity: tender as the yielding flower,
it is fixed as the marble firmament. The only remons-
trance she makes, the only complaint against all the ill-
treatment she receives, is that single line where, when
turned back naked to her father's house, she says,

> Let me not like a worm go by the way.

The first outline given of the characters is inimitable

[Quotes 'Clerk's Tale', C.T. IV, 197-294, omitting 4
stanzas.]

(p. 63) The story of the little child slain in Jewry,
(which is told by the Prioress, and worthy to be told by
her who was 'all conscience and tender heart,') is not
less touching than that of Griselda. It is simple and
heroic to the last degree. The poetry of Chaucer has a
religious sanctity about it, connected with the manners
and superstitions of the age. It has all the spirit of

martyrdom.

It has also all the extravagance and the utmost
licentiousness of comic humour, equally arising out of
the manners of the time. In this too Chaucer resembled
Boccaccio that he excelled in both styles, and could pass
at will 'from grave to gay, from lively to severe;' but
he never confounded the two styles together (except from
that involuntary and unconscious mixture of the pathetic
and humorous, which is almost always to be found in
nature,) and was exclusively taken up with what he set
about, whether it was jest or earnest. The Wife of Bath's
Prologue (which Pope has very admirably modernised) is,
perhaps, unequalled as a comic story. The Cock and the
Fox is also excellent for lively strokes of character and
satire. January and May is not so good as some of the
others. Chaucer's versification, considering the time at
which he wrote, and that versification is a thing in a
great degree mechanical, is not one of his least merits.
It has considerable strength and harmony, and its apparent
deficiency in the latter respect arises chiefly from the
alterations which have since taken place in the pronunciation or mode of accenting the words of the language. The
best general rule for reading him is to pronounce the
final *e*, as in reading Italian.

It was observed in the last Lecture that painting describes what the object is in itself, poetry what it implies or suggests. Chaucer's poetry is not, in general,
the best confirmation of the truth of this distinction,
for his poetry is more picturesque and historical than
almost any other. But there is one instance in point
which I cannot help giving in this place. It is the
story of the three thieves who go in search of Death to
kill him, and who meeting with him, are entangled in their
fate by his words, without knowing him. In the printed
catalogue to Mr. West's (in some respects very admirable)
picture of Death on the Pale Horse, it is observed, that
'In poetry the same effect is produced by a few abrupt and
rapid gleams of description, touching, as it were with
fire, the features and edges of a general mass of awful
obscurity; but in painting, such indistinctness would be
a defect, and imply that the artist wanted the power to
pourtray the conceptions of his fancy. Mr. West was of
opinion that to delineate a physical form, which in its
moral impression would approximate to that of the visionary Death of Milton, it was necessary to endow it, if possible, with the appearance of super-human strength and
energy. He has therefore exerted the utmost force and
perspicuity of his pencil on the central figure.'—One
might suppose from this, that the way to represent a
shadow was to make it as substantial as possible. Oh,

no! Painting has its prerogatives (and high ones they
are), but they lie in representing the visible, not the
invisible. The moral attributes of Death are powers and
effects of an infinitely wide and general description,
which no individual or physical form can possibly represent, but by a courtesy of speech, or by a distant analogy. The moral impression of Death is essentially
visionary; its reality is in the mind's eye. Words are
here the only *things;* and things, physical forms, the mere
mockeries of the understanding. The less definite, the
less bodily the conception, the more vast, unformed, and
unsubstantial, the nearer does it approach to some resemblance of that omnipresent, lasting, universal, irresist-
ible principle, which everywhere, and at some time or
other, exerts its power over all things. Death is a
mighty abstraction, like Night, or Space, or Time. He is
an ugly customer, who will not be invited to supper, or to
sit for his picture. He is with us and about us, but we
do not see him. He stalks on before us, and we do not
mind him: he follows us close behind, and we do not turn
to look back at him. We do not see him making faces at us
in our life-time, nor perceive him afterwards sitting in
mock-majesty, a twin-skeleton, beside us, tickling our
bare ribs, and staring into our hollow eye-balls! Chaucer
knew this.

96. SAMUEL TAYLOR COLERIDGE, GOTHIC CHAUCER

1818, 1834

The teeming mind of Coleridge (1772-1834), educated at
Jesus College, Cambridge, always responded with enjoyment
to Chaucer, but his multifarious and fragmented writings
contain no regular discussion of Chaucer's poetry, despite
his intention to write a specific essay. The most suggestive remarks, never further developed, occur in the
course of lectures given in 1818, recovered from the notes
of various listeners, and published in 'Literary Remains
of S.T. Coleridge', ed. H.N. Coleridge, 4 vols, 1836-9,
Vol. I (a). Here Coleridge develops useful eighteenth-
century ideas of Gothic quality and form, of which Chaucer may be understood to be part, but where details are
missing. In his 'Table-Talk' (ed. H.N. Coleridge, 1835)

of 15 March 1834, four months before his death (extract
b), he repeats and elaborates the expression of enjoyment
of Chaucer found in 'Biographia Literaria', 1817, p. 32.
Elsewhere he claims how easy it is to understand Chaucer.

(a)

Lecture I

(p. 68) He then proceeded to describe the generic character of the Northern nations, and defined it as an indepen-
dence of the whole in the freedom of the individual,
noticing their respect for women, and their consequent
chivalrous spirit in war; and how evidently the participation in the general council laid the foundation of the
representative form of government, the only rational mode
of preserving individual liberty in opposition to the
licentious democracy of the ancient republics.

He called our attention to the peculiarity of their
art, and showed how it entirely depended on a symbolical
expression of the infinite,—which is not vastness, nor
immensity, nor perfection, but whatever cannot be circum-
scribed within the limits of actual sensuous being. In
the ancient art, on the contrary, every thing was finite
and material. Accordingly, sculpture was not attempted
by the Gothic races till the ancient specimens were discovered, whilst painting and architecture were of native
growth amongst them. In the earliest specimens of the
paintings of modern ages, as in those of Giotto and his
associates in the cemetery at Pisa, this complexion,
variety, and symbolical character are evident, and are
more fully developed in the mightier works of Michel
Angelo and Raffael. The contemplation of the works of
antique art excites a feeling of elevated beauty, and
exalted notions of the human self; but the Gothic
architecture impresses the beholder with a sense of self-
annihilation; he becomes, as it were, a part of the work
contemplated. An endless complexity and variety are
united into one whole, the plan of which is not distinct
from the execution. A Gothic cathedral is the petrefac-
tion of our religion. The only work of truly modern
sculpture is the Moses of Michel Angelo.

The Northern nations were prepared by their own previous religion for Christianity; they, for the most part,
received it gladly, and it took root as in a native soil.
The deference to woman, characteristic of the Gothic

races, combined itself with devotion in the idea of the
Virgin Mother, and gave rise to many beautiful associations.

Mr. C. remarked how Gothic an instrument in origin and
character the organ was.

He also enlarged on the influence of female character
on our education, the first impressions of our childhood
being derived from women. Amongst oriental nations, he
said, the only distinction was between lord and slave.
With the antique Greeks, the will of every one conflicting
with the will of all, produced licentiousness; with the
modern descendants from the northern stocks, both these
extremes were shut out, to reappear mixed and condensed
into this principle or temper;—submission, but with free
choice,—illustrated in chivalrous devotion to women as
such, in attachment to the sovereign, &c.

Lecture II

(p. 70) The Keltic and Teutonic nations occupied that part
of Europe, which is now France, Britain, Germany, Sweden,
Denmark, &c. They were in general a hardy race, possess-
ing great fortitude, and capable of great endurance. The
Romans slowly conquered the more southerly portion of
their tribes, and succeeded only by their superior arts,
their policy, and better discipline. After a time, when
the Goths,—to use the name of the noblest and most historical of the Teutonic tribes,—had acquired some knowledge of these arts from mixing with their conquerors,
they invaded the Roman territories. The hardy habits,
the steady perseverance, the better faith of the enduring
Goth rendered him too formidable an enemy for the corrupt
Roman, who was more inclined to purchase the subjection of
his enemy, than to go through the suffering necessary to
secure it. The conquest of the Romans gave to the Goths
the Christian religion as it was then existing in Italy;
and the light and graceful building of Grecian, or Roman-
Greek order, became singularly combined with the massy
architecture of the Goths, as wild and varied as the
forest vegetation which it resembled. The Greek art is
beautiful. When I enter a Greek church, my eye is
charmed, and my mind elated; I feel exalted, and proud
that I am a man. But the Gothic art is sublime. On
entering a cathedral, I am filled with devotion and with
awe; I am lost to the actualities that surround me, and
my whole being expands into the infinite; earth and air,
nature and art, all swell up into eternity, and the only
sensible impression left, is, 'that I am nothing!' This

religion, while it tended to soften the manners of the
Northern tribes, was at the same time highly congenial to
their nature. The Goths are free from the stain of hero
worship. Gazing on their rugged mountains, surrounded by
impassable forests, accustomed to gloomy seasons, they
lived in the bosom of nature, and worshipped an invisible
and unknown deity. Firm in his faith, domestic in his
habits, the life of the Goth was simple and dignified,
yet tender and affectionate.

Lecture III

(p. 79) In the present Lecture I must introduce you to a
species of poetry, which had its birth-place near the
centre of Roman glory, and in which, as might be anticipated, the influences of the Greek and Roman muse are far
more conspicuous,—as great, indeed, as the efforts of
intentional imitation on the part of the poets themselves
could render them. But happily for us and for their own
fame, the intention of the writers as men is often at
complete variance with the genius of the same men as
poets. To the force of their intention we owe their myth-
ological ornaments, and the greater definiteness of their
imagery; and their passion for the beautiful, the voluptuous, and the artificial, we must in part attribute to the
same intention, but in part likewise to their natural dispositions and tastes. For the same climate and many of
the same circumstances were acting on them, which had
acted on the great classics, whom they were endeavouring
to imitate. But the love of the marvellous, the deeper
sensibility, the higher reverence for womanhood, the
characteristic spirit of sentiment and courtesy,—these
were the heir-looms of nature, which still regained the
ascendant, whenever the use of the living mother-language
enabled the inspired poet to appear instead of the toil-
some scholar.
    From this same union, in which the soul (if I may dare
so express myself) was Gothic, while the outward forms and
a majority of the words themselves, were the reliques of
the Roman, arose the Romance, or romantic language, in
which the Romance, or romantic language, in which the
Troubadours or Love-singers of Provence sang and wrote,
and the different dialects of which have been modified
into the modern Italian, Spanish, and Portuguese; while
the language of the Trouveurs, Trouveres, or Norman-French
poets, forms the intermediate link between the Romance or
modified Roman, and the Teutonic, including the Dutch,
Danish, Swedish, and the upper and lower German, as being

the modified Gothic. And as the northernmost extreme of
the Norman-French, or that part of the link in which it
formed on the Teutonic, we must take the Norman-English
minstrels and metrical romances, from the greater predomi-
nance of the Anglo-Saxon Gothic in the derivation of the
words. I mean, that the language of the English metrical
romance is less romanized, and has fewer words, not originally of a northern origin, than the same romances in the
Norman-French; which is the more striking, because the
former were for the most part translated from the latter;
the authors of which seem to have eminently merited their
name of Trouveres, or inventors. Thus then we have a
chain with two rings or staples:—at the southern end
there is the Roman, or Latin; at the northern end the
Keltic, Teutonic, or Gothic; and the links beginning with
the southern end, are the Romance, including the Provençal, the Italian, Spanish, and Portuguese, with their different dialects, then the Norman-French, and lastly the
English....

(p. 88)   CHAUCER
              Born in London, 1328—Died 1400

Chaucer must be read with an eye to the Norman-French
Trouveres, of whom he is the best representative in English. He had great powers of invention. As in Shakspeare, his characters represent classes, but in a different manner; Shakspeare's characters are the representatives of the interior nature of humanity, in which some
element has become so predominant as to destroy the health
of the mind; whereas Chaucer's are rather representatives
of classes of manners. He is therefore more led to indi-
vidualize in a mere personal sense. Observe Chaucer's
love of nature; and how happily the subject of his main
work is chosen. When you reflect that the company in the
Decameron have retired to a place of safety from the
raging of a pestilence, their mirth provokes a sense of
their unfeelingness; whereas in Chaucer nothing of this
sort occurs, and the scheme of a party on a pilgrimage,
with different ends and occupations, aptly allows of the
greatest variety of expression in the tales.

                        Lecture XIV

(p. 231) In the northern or Gothic nations the aim and
purpose of the government were the preservation of the
rights and interests of the individual in conjunction
with those of the whole. The individual interest was

sacred. In the character and tendency of the Greek and
Gothic languages there is precisely the same relative difference. In Greek the sentences are long, and the structure architectural, so that each part or clause is insignificant when compared with the whole. The result is
every thing, the steps and processes nothing. But in the
Gothic and, generally, in what we call the modern, languages, the structure is short, simple, and complete in
each part, and the connexion of the parts with the sum
total of the discourse is maintained by the sequency of
the logic, or the community of feelings excited between
the writer and his readers. As an instance equally delightful and complete, of what may be called the Gothic
structure as contra-distinguished from that of the Greeks,
let me cite a part of our famous Chaucer's character of a
parish priest as he should be. Can it ever be quoted too
often?...
    (p. 238) It is, indeed, worthy of remark that all our
great poets have been good prose writers, as Chaucer,
Spenser, Milton; and this probably arose from their just
sense of metre. For a true poet will never confound
verse and prose; whereas it is almost characteristic of
indifferent prose writers that they should be constantly
slipping into scraps of metre.

(b)

(p. 297) I take unceasing delight in Chaucer. His manly
cheerfulness is especially delicious to me in my old age.
How exquisitely tender he is, and yet how perfectly free
from the least touch of sickly melancholy or morbid
drooping! The sympathy of the poet with the subjects of
his poetry is particularly remarkable in Shakspeare and
Chaucer; but what the first effects by a strong act of
imagination and mental metamorphosis, the last does without any effort, merely by the inborn kindly joyousness of
his nature. How well we seem to know Chaucer! How
absolutely nothing do we know of Shakspeare!
    I cannot in the least allow any necessity for Chaucer's
poetry, especially the Canterbury Tales, being considered
obsolete. Let a few plain rules be given for sounding the
final è of syllables, and for expressing the termination
of such words as ocëan, and natïon, &c. as dissyllables,
—or let the syllables to be sounded in such cases be
marked by a competent metrist. This simple expedient
would, with a very few trifling exceptions, where the
errors are inveterate, enable any reader to feel the perfect smoothness and harmony of Chaucer's verse. As to
understanding his language, if you read twenty pages with

a good glossary, you surely can find no further difficulty, even as it is; but I should have no objection to see this done:—Strike out those words which are now obsolete, and I will venture to say that I will replace everyone of them by words still in use out of Chaucer himself, or Gower his disciple. I don't want this myself: I rather like to see the significant terms which Chaucer unsuccessfully offered as candidates for admission into our language; but surely so very slight a change of the text may well be pardoned, even by black-letterati, for the purpose of restoring so great a poet to his ancient and most deserved popularity.

97.   THOMAS CAMPBELL, SO STRONG A GENIUS

1819

Campbell (1777-1844), educated at Glasgow University, once again demonstrates the nineteenth-century desire for 'reality' in fiction, by contrast with the later eighteenth-century's Romantic pleasure in fine fabling, but he also reveals some pleasure in fantasy. His comment is made in the introductory essay to his 'Specimens of the British Poets', 1819, p. 71. See also the next extract.

The simple old narrative romance had become too familiar in Chaucer's time, to invite him to its beaten track. The poverty of his native tongue obliged him to look round for subsidiary materials to his fancy, both in the Latin language, and in some modern foreign source that should not appear to be trite and exhausted. His age was, unfortunately, little conversant with the best Latin classics. Ovid, Claudian, and Statius, were the chief favourites in poetry, and Boethius in prose. The allegorical style of the last of those authors, seems to have given an early bias to the taste of Chaucer. In modern poetry, his first, and long continued predilection was attracted by the new and allegorical style of romance, which had sprung up in France in the thirteenth century, under William de Lorris. We find him, accordingly, during a great part of his poetical career, engaged among the dreams, emblems, flower-worshippings, and amatory parliaments, of that

visionary school.   This, we may say, was a gymnasium of
rather too light and playful exercise for so strong a
genius; and it must be owned, that his allegorical poetry
is often puerile and prolix.   Yet, even in this walk of
fiction, we never entirely lose sight of that peculiar
grace and gaiety which distinguish the Muse of Chaucer;
and no one who remembers his productions of the House of
Fame, and the Flower and the Leaf, will regret that he
sported for a season in the field of allegory.   Even his
pieces of this description, the most fantastic in design,
and tedious in execution, are generally interspersed with
fresh and joyous descriptions of external nature.

In this new species of romance, we perceive the youthful Muse of the language, in love with mystical meanings
and forms of fancy, more remote, if possible, from
reality, than those of the chivalrous fable itself; and
we could sometimes wish her back from her emblematic
castles, to the more solid ones of the elder fable; but
still she moves in pursuit of those shadows with an impulse of novelty, and an exuberance of spirit, that is
not wholly without its attraction and delight.

Chaucer was afterwards happily drawn to the more natural
style of Boccaccio, and from him he derived the hint of
a subject, in which, besides his own original portraits
of contemporary life, he could introduce stories of every
description, from the most heroic to the most familiar.

98.   UNKNOWN, AN IMAGE OF THOUGHTFUL INTELLECTUAL
CULTIVATION

1819

The extract from Campbell (No. 97) is quoted by a reviewer
in 'Blackwood's Edinburgh Magazine', IV (1819), pp. 703-4,
who then proceeds to remark, perhaps with some indebtedness to Godwin (see No. 87), that an age that can produce
a Chaucer has a high claim to culture.

Surely the reader misses something here.   He expects that
when the first mighty name of English Poetry is brought
before him, the author will dwell with some plenitude of
description on the great faculties and powers of a spirit,

which, if the age in which it lived among men had left of
itself no other memorial than the works that spirit produced, could still have avouched to us the existence, at
that day, in its young native vigour, of the whole character of the English mind. The existence of the works of
Chaucer changes, it may be said, to our apprehension, the
whole character of the age—raising up to our mind an
image of thoughtful intellectual cultivation, and of
natural and tender happiness in the simplicity of life,
which would otherwise be wanting in the dark stern picture
of warlike greatness and power. As a philosophical
critic, Mr Campbell ought, we think, to have said something more adequate to just expectation, respecting an
event which was a phenomenon in itself, and the cause of
subsequent phenomena.

99.   UNKNOWN, AN ESSENTIAL PORTION OF THE AUTHENTIC
HISTORY OF HIS COUNTRY

1823, 1825, 1826

'The Retrospective Review' was founded and edited, perhaps
largely written, by Henry Southern, and achieved fourteen
volumes from 1820 to 1826. It had a motto from Chaucer's
'Parliament of Fowls', 22-5, 'For out of olde feldes, as
men seyth,/Cometh al this newe corn... etc.' The intention was to review many topics and aspects of European
literary history, without being concerned with current
books. The history of literature 'is the history of the
mind of man' (I, viii). Southern (1799-1853), educated
at Trinity College, Cambridge, was a man of letters,
editor, magazine proprietor, who eventually became a
diplomat. Extract (a) is from a long essay in Vol. IX,
pp. 172-206, which reviews editions from Thynne to
Tyrwhitt; (b) is from XII, pp. 96-7; (c) from XII, pp. 299-
300; (d) from XIV, pp. 305-57, a long essay continued
from Vol. IX. He emphasises Chaucer's work as drama;
literature as an index of 'the national mind'; and Chaucer
as above all our gayest, most cheerful writer, not *protestant*.

(a)

(IX, p. 173) There are few circumstances connected with
the present taste for literature, more creditable than the
frequent recurrence that is made to the works of those
elder wits, with whom the frame and energies of our language may be said to have originated: who conduct us to
the well-head and fountains of our composite dialect, and
by shewing the sources and primal usages of our speech,
give us an accurate and distinctive perception of the significance of its terms and idioms. Researches of this kind
in every language, and particularly in languages which have
passed through such mutations as ours, appear to be indis-
pensible, not only to the attainment of that pregnant con-
ciseness, imaginative at once and definite, which is the
highest accomplishment of literary composition, but to the
preservation of that standard purity of phrase and idiom,
which the arbitrary affectations of fashion and the influence of foreign intercourse have a perpetual tendency to
disturb.
    It is true, that a taste for this kind of literature may
be carried to excess. Imitation may be substituted for
research; and instead of tracing derivatives, we may look
for models. The rust of antiquity may be mistaken for its
ore; and age may monopolise the veneration, which can only
belong to merit. By those who are infected by a mere rage
for the obsolete, neither the language nor the ideas of
succeeding generations are likely to be benefited. Instead of preserving from unmerited disuse what was nervous,
consonant, and expressive, they would intrude again what,
as crude and incongruous, has been deservedly dismissed
for more comprehensive terms, and more harmonious construc-
tions. Not satisfied with the correction of modern fop-
peries, they would strip us bare to the necessities of our
forefathers; without recollecting that what was simplicity
in them, might be quaintness and affectation in us. We
should know the past that we may make the best of the present, and avail ourselves of the wisdom, not assume the
ignorance, of former times. Even in the best wisdom of
our ancestors, every thing may not be fitting for their
posterity. We were born in the midst of modern associations, and therefore can never be ancients. In order to
write like our forefathers, we must learn to think and
feel as our forefathers felt and thought; and must re-
adopt their opinions, their prejudices, and their modes of
life, before we can resort again to the peculiarities of
their phraseology, or the modes and combinations of their
ideas.
    This is no reason, however, why the treasures of their

wit should not be among the objects of our study and research: why we should not preserve the memory of what is
estimable in their remains, and restore what has been un-
wisely neglected. Even their obscurities may occasionally
throw additional light upon what in present usage is but
loosely understood; and they have their points of brilliant light, which ought not to be lost from the intellectual horizon. They are the beacons and landmarks of
our language, to which our eyes should occasionally be
turned, to prevent us from floating too far on the sea of
innovation: and it should never be forgotten, that the
more fixed and permanent the standard of any language can
be rendered, the richer is the bank of accumulated knowledge: for the wisdom that is preserved in a language that
is obsolete, is a treasure buried in the earth, which we
know not where to delve for.

In treasures of this description, the neglected glebe
of Chaucer is particularly affluent—treasures both of
instruction and delight. As a fabulist and a poet, Dryden
gives him the decided preference over Ovid: though Dryden,
as we shall hereafter shew, was not capable of appreciating all his beauties. But there are other reasons for
recommending him to the attention of the English student.

To the philologist, he is a classic of the first order:
for he is pre-eminently the most conspicuous of the makers
and methodizers of the language: the first who taught it
to flow in expressive harmony, and gave to it consistency
and energy. Not that he invented and introduced a verb-
iage and idiom of his own, or compounded, as some have
supposed, a *melange* of imported phraseology; but because,
(as will be obvious to those who consult his contemporaries, Lydgate, Gower, Hocleve, Scogan, &c.) he selected
and methodised from the unsettled idioms then in use,
what was fittest and most congruous, and gave consist-
ence and solidity to that foundation, upon which the
polished structure of our present language has gradually
risen.

Even in point of rhythmical harmony, the obligations of
our language to Chaucer are not less decisive than in
phraseology and structure: and we shall endeavour to shew
hereafter, that in his versification are to be found, not
only the less rigid models of our present septasyllabic
and octosyllabic measures, but the exemplars also, which
Spenser has acknowledged, and of which Milton has availed
himself, of that heroic metre, to which the former gave so
much sweetness, and the latter such majestic sublimity;
and to which Pope has imparted all the elaborate terse-
ness of polished uniformity:—of that metre, in fact,
which has now become the established national *hexameter*

of our poesy, and the constant vehicle of our graver and
more stately modes of composition.

But it is not only to the philologist and the prosodist
that the memory of Chaucer should be dear. He has other
claims upon our admiration and gratitude, or he could
never have had these. The language and idiom of an author,
however erudite, can never become popular, nor his versification, however elaborate, a model of general imitation,
but from the merit or the fascination of his ideas. It is
the soul within that must give vital expression and influence to exterior form; and the most beautiful mechanism
of period or stanza, if only applied to the drawlings of
inanity, could but share in the oblivious slumber they
would facilitate. That Chaucer had the soul, as well as
the voice of poesy, is sufficiently evinced in the admiration he has excited in those who were neither familiar
with his language, nor in possession of the clue that
would unravel the harmony of his numbers: nay, who could
not, from the defective transcripts they consulted, or by
their mode of pronunciation, make out even the numerical
proportion of his feet, or his syllables. *'His style,'*
at any rate, notwithstanding the charm which undoubtedly
it had in his own day for ears familiar with the accents
and quantities he made use of, cannot now be considered
(as a paradoxical critic has considered that of Virgil)
'as the pickle that preserves his mummy from corruption.'
The imperishability of his works must be evidently ascribed to some thing more inherent, to that superiority of
poetical and intellectual merit—that pregnancy of thought
and brilliant versatility of genius which, commanding the
admiration of his contemporaries, gave currency to his
idioms, and rendered his rhythmical arrangements the
models of succeeding generations.

The history of the progress of English versification
(if this were a proper place to enter upon such a subject)
would place this suggestion beyond the pale of controversy. It would be seen how the successive experiments of
inferior, though far from despicable writers had their day
and perished; while the heroic and octo-syllabic measures
of Chaucer still continue to be the models of our serious
and our familiar versification.

But it is not merely in a literary point of view, as
works of amusement and effusions of a poetical imagination, that the writings of Chaucer are entitled to particular attention. They are pregnant with instruction of a
higher order. They are an essential portion of the authentic history of his country; not of its sieges, its
battles, and its revolutions—like *The Pharsalia* of Lucan,
or *The Civil Wars* of Daniel; or of the successions of

names and dates, the installations, and the demises of
kings and bishops, like our old monkish chronicles!—but
of the history of the national mind. It is something to
know even the tastes of former ages,—for taste has an
inseparable connection with the state of morals and of
intellect, and the general condition of society; and, in
this point of view, even the wildest and most extravagant
romance of antiquity may be read with some degree of profit, if we have any means of ascertaining its degree of
popularity in the age to which it is ascribed. But certainly the works of Chaucer, his 'Canterbury Tales' in
particular, minister to our information, in a more unequi-
vocal way, and on a much more extensive scale. They bring
the genuine picture of society alive and breathing before
us. We mingle with our long-buried ancestors, as though
they were cotemporary with us—converse with them, listen
to them, enter into their humours and their habits; and
become as familiar with the moral, the intellectual, and
the social state of the community of those times, as
though the living drama, with all its actual incidents,
had passed in review before us. This is an essential and
an edifying part of history, that of the progress and
revolutions of the social mind: a portion of history in
which the generality of us have, in reality, a more vital
interest, than in the changes of dynasties and the revolutions of empires.

In this point of view, indeed, works of imagination,
when its higher attributes are employed upon local scenes
and cotemporary subjects, are frequently more instructive
than the most elaborate pages of history. The latter
affect to perpetuate the actions of potentates and the
exploits of heroes; though the authors of those *panegyrics*
cannot but know how perpetually the record must be falsi-
fied; since those who are most interested in disguising
the truth, have also most the means, and have the passions, the prejudices, and the vanity of the cotemporaries generally on their side, to assist them in the imposi
tion: and he must have passed through the world with unob-
servant eyes, or had few opportunities of reading the
narrative of any transaction 'all of which he saw, and
part of which he was,' who has not been induced to reflect
how wide the difference is apt to be, between the doings
that have actually been done, and the deeds that are to
be recorded to posterity. But the imaginative historian,
who adorns his record with names of his own creation, and
selects the character he assigns to his imaginary agents
from the great book of nature, as it lies spread before
him, may use with freedom the genuine colours of truth,
and delineate man as he really is, with all the modifica-

tions of morals, manners, and characteristics, which the
institutions, the necessities, and the habitudes of the
age have imposed upon him. Whoever does this is, in fact,
an historian of the highest order: an historian, instructive, not to the statesman and the politician only, but to
all who may peruse his record. And such an historian is
the great father of our English poetry—the venerable
Geffrey Chaucer.

In these respects we trust that we have said enough to
justify the degree of importance we attach to this subject,
and the space to which we may probably find it necessary
to extend the present article: since every reader who has
a taste for the varied productions of original genius, or
is desirous of being acquainted with the habits, the manners, customs, and characters of our ancestors, and all
that belonged to the social frame of the community, at an
interesting and splendid period of our annals, when the
terror of our island-arms had begun to shake the continent, and captive kings bowed before the footstool of our
warlike Edwards, will be thankful, we should suppose, for
every effort to extend his familiarity with such a writer,
and facilitate his enjoyment of the intellectual treasures which these varied works contain.

In the way of this familiarity and enjoyment, there are
still (notwithstanding the praise-worthy and successful
labours of Mr. Tyrwhitt, with reference to one essential
portion of these works) considerable difficulties; more
especially with respect to those ample portions which that
diligent and ingenious editor has not collated and revised. The barbarous corruptions of the text, printed
originally, and of necessity, from imperfect transcrip-
tions, and (restricting the observation to all that followed the more careful edition of Mr. Thynne) still more
and more corrupted in each successive impression, are not
to be regarded as among the smallest of these difficulties; and we have already shewn that even the harsh judgment pronounced by his great admirer, Mr. Dryden, on the
versification of our poet, is in part at least attribut-
able to the blunders and injudicious innovations of these
successive editors. Independently however of those corruptions which have resulted from the errors of trans-
cription and of the press, there are still great and dis-
couraging difficulties to be encountered in Mr. Tyrwhitt's
revised edition of the 'Canterbury Tales': difficulties
resulting from the obscurity of obsolete language, and
still more obsolete spelling; from the obvious changes
that have taken place in our modes of pronunciation—particularly with respect to syllabication, and the seat of
the thesis, or percussive accent, and that indolent

elision of the vowel, which our Midas' ears have suffered
to be carried to such an extent, and by which so many of
our dissyllables have been melted, or rather crushed, into
monosyllabic words, &c. But if ever we should have such
an edition of the works of Chaucer as is still to be regarded among the *desiderata* of our restored literature—an
edition which would obviate the obscurity without impairing the venerable features of antiquity—which would remove some portion of the rust of time, without superadding
the varnish-like glare of the modern mint, or impairing
the lines and characteristics of the original impression,
—which would soften down some of those grossnesses of
diction, in the looser tales, which the *fashion* of Chaucer's days somewhat too freely admitted, without precisely
substituting that fastidious phraseology with which modern
prudery disguises its looser thoughts,—the difficulties
in the way of the complete enjoyment of these literary
treasures of the fourteenth century would disappear....
    (p. 182) But, obscure as are all the circumstances
relative to the birth and actual family of our poet, the
station to which he attained in the court of Edward, and
the functions and negociations in which we find him
employed, sufficiently prove that he must have been of
what is called *gentle blood;* for although Mr. Tyrwhitt
has sufficiently exposed the mistakes which have occasioned Speght to dignify his first entrance into the
royal household with the rank of *Page,* and afterwards to
grace him with that of *royal shield-bearer,* the first
authentic memorial in which we have any mention of Chaucer calling him only *Valetus noster* (our yeoman) and that
of 46 Edward III. in which the king appoints him one of
his envoys to Genoa, entitles him only *Scutifer noster*
(our *esquire*),—yet, as the former of these titles was
given in those days even to young men of the highest
quality before they were knighted, it is not likely it
should have been conferred, in the royal household, upon
any individual of mere plebeian family. The feudal, or
high aristocratic feeling was then in its full vigour;
even commercial wealth, however disproportionate, had not
yet been able to break into the ranks of the proud nobility; and rarely could any degree of plebeian merit enter
into official association with those who 'disdeigned to
consider the peasant or burgher as of the same species
with themselves.' The profession of the church furnished,
as yet, the only exceptions. The sacerdotal robe indeed
conferred a nobility of its own, and efficiently of the
first order; and, in episcopal mantle, or beneath a cardinal's hat, a vintner's son, or a butcher's, might jostle
or might trample the proudest peerage, and even maintain

equality with royalty itself: but by no other path could
the offspring of 'peasant or burgher' enter so far into
the ranks of gentlemanship, as to mingle with the high-
born pages of the court, or be *esquired* in royal patent:
and we may safely pronounce that, notwithstanding the
familiar patronage of John of Gaunt, Duke of Lancaster,
Chaucer would never have held the stations in which we
find him placed, if he had not been of what courts and
courtiers would have called *respectable family*: if
indeed we could readily believe that, under any circumstances, such familiar patronage would have been accorded
by that lofty aspiring prince to the son of a vinter or
city tradesman....

(p. 200) The 'Canterbury Tales' seem always to have
been the most popular of all our author's works. It was
the first, as we have shewn, that had the distinction
of being rescued from the danger of unmerited oblivion by
the intervention of the press; and it has invariably maintained its pre-eminence in favour. Nor is this pre-
eminence of popularity at all to be wondered at. It owes
that distinction not only to the excellence and variety
of its materials (though these alone might have justified
all its celebrity) but to the attractive form into which
those materials are wrought, and the ingenuity with which
what would otherwise have constituted a mere collection
of unconnected narratives, are coherently united into one
great and interesting drama, which, whoever takes up,
feels irresistibly impelled to pursue to its conclusion;
for the dramatic is the most interesting, and perhaps the
most instructive of all the forms of literary composition.

It was a favourite axiom of the celebrated philologist,
John Horne Tooke, that the cream of the literature of
every language was to be found in its dramatic poetry.
And it must be admitted that the popular diffusion of
intellectual civilization seems in almost every country to
have originated in the amusements of the stage. It must,
however, have happened in every language that some portion
of attention must have been devoted to literary composition long before the drama could become a source of intellectual excitement. Nor can it be forgotten that Homer
was anterior to Eschylus, Sophocles, and Euripides. He
wrote, however, dramatically; and has been regarded as
the greatest exemplar both of the tragic and comic drama.
If referring, however, to our language and country, we
look towards that splendid morning of our intellectual
day—the reign of Elizabeth (though we must not forget the
invaluable lucubrations of Bacon, or the mighty mass of
wisdom and of science which his philosophic spirit
bequeathed and generated), in what is generally understood

by literary genius, the contributions of dramatic talent
sustained an unrivalled pre-eminence. No other species of
literature can produce a name comparable to that of Shakspeare; and Beaumont, Fletcher, Massinger, Ben Jonson, and
a considerable catalogue of dramatists, who either flourished or were fostered in that intellectual reign, demon-
strate the superiority of the dramatic over every other
species of contemporary composition.

But our literature had also its Homer, if we may so express ourselves, before its Eschylus or its Menander....

(p. 202) ....it is sufficiently notorious, that our
dramatic literature, if it deserved that name, was in a
state of the most sordid abasement, till the time of
Elizabeth; while the poetic literature of the age of
Edward III. was adorned by the names of Chaucer, Gower,
Lydgate, and Occleve, the meanest of whom would at least
eclipse the very best of those mystery mongers, who mono-
polised during ten intervening reigns the dramatic function.

But the foundations of the drama had been already laid:
we find them in the work before us: the propension to the
dramatic form of composition, being indeed, as it should
seem, one of the universal instincts of the poetic mind.
The oldest poem, perhaps, extant in the world (the book of
Job) is cast in that mould; as are many of the choicest
specimens of oriental antiquity. The Eclogues of Theo-
critus, a large portion of the Iliad, and the finest episodes of the Odyssey, are essentially dramatic; and if
Homer be justly considered as the father of the ancient
tragedy, the venerable patriarch of English poesy is no
less entitled to be considered as the father of the modern
comedy. Both seem to have drawn their principal resources
from the pages of the great book of Nature spread before
them—to have collected their materials by observation of
the living realities of human character; and though the
machine, or fable of both, in detail at least, may be
equally fictitious, and the minds of both were probably
enriched with all the learning of their respective times,
both have contrived to embody the realities they had witnessed in the persons and transactions they have feigned,
and to render the knowledge, derived from the secondary
sources of written and traditionary science, subservient
to the more efficient and authentic intelligence derived
from actual intercourse with their species. One delighted,
indeed, in the contentions of camps and councils, the din
of arms and strife of the dusty field; the other was most
at home in the mingled intercourses of familiar life - its
occupations and its pastimes, its humours, passions,
absurdities; its squabbling garrulities, and ludicrous

intrigues. One shews us human nature, such as power and
public station, and ambition, and all the gigantic passions of the aspiring mind, have a tendency to make it;
the other, such as its instincts and propensities render
it, under the restriction of more humble or more sordid
circumstances; where ambition becomes dwarfed into petty
rivalry, and the same emulous and hostile feelings which
might have desolated realms and trampled nations in the
dust, vent themselves in breaking a head at cudgel-play,
or a scurrilous jest in the conflicts of conversational
recrimination. One pictures the splendid atrocities of
illustrious homicides, and thrills us with sublime and
pathetic descriptions of the miseries entailed on warring
nations by a lascivious queen; the other is content to
excite our laughter over the ludicrous consequences of a
clerk of Oxenford's intrigue with the light-heeled spouse
of a *sely* old carpenter; or the pleasant vengeance of a
brace of poor scholars on the crafty miller, who had
robbed them of a part of their grain. But the characters
of Homer in the highly imaginative adventures of the Odyssey, and the equally imaginative conflicts of the Iliad,
and those of Chaucer, whether in the suppositious adventures of the Pilgrims, or the comic stories they relate,
bear alike the authentic stamp of nature in every word and
circumstance ascribed to them. They are alike, indeed, in
every instance, distinct creations of the genius of the
respective authors; but endued with appropriate passions,
habitudes, and characteristics, evidently derived from the
co-existing realities of human life and incident. They
were fitted, therefore, alike to be the great exemplars,
one of the tragic, the other of the comic drama, in their
respective regions.

It has not, indeed, happened to Chaucer as to Homer, to
have his individual characters and incidents consecrated
by name and circumstance to the purposes of the stage.
But it was he, nevertheless, who first shewed the way how
comedy should be constructed, and its characters grouped
and diversified; and his is the storehouse into which
some of our best dramatic poets (Shakspeare among the
rest) were in the habit of looking, not only for examples,
but for specific materials, and from which the genuine
spirit of English comedy has been drawn.

This dramatic form of writing has indeed sufficient
advantages to recommend its adoption to all who have the
requisite endowments. It leaves the author at liberty to
escape out of his own individualities—to emerge from the
egotistical monotony of detailing merely his own sentiments and opinions, and to indulge his imagination without
responsibility for every sentiment he may amplify, or

every passion he may call into play. It duplicates and
multiplies him into a thousand shapes and distinct iden-
tities; and gives him the opportunity of adopting the
idiom of every vice, as well as every virtue; of every
humour, impulse, and caprice; of the lowest degradations,
as well as the most towering sublimities of human passion;
and even of the grossest ignorance and fatuity, without
taint or humiliation: provided only that in the selection
of persons and incidents there be so much discretion, as
not to shock the ear of modesty, or trespass beyond the
limits of moral decorum.

Chaucer, in his general prologue, has thought fit to
claim the full benefit of this dramatic privilege; and as
it may perhaps be thought, that he occasionally stands in
need of all the indulgence that can be granted to him, we
will let him speak for himself.

Having enumerated and described the several pilgrims
or persons of his drama, the poet thus proceeds.

[Quotes 'General Prologue' C.T. I, 720-42]

Chaucer, it will be seen, has thus, in the very outset,
put in his plea of indulgence pretty broad; and whether he
has, in all respects, or as far as morality is concerned,
complied with our premised condition of decorous selection, in the Tales especially which he has put into the
mouths of some of his characters, or how far, if now
brought to the bar of decorous criticism, he might avail
himself of excuse from those changes which have taken
place since his time in the *fashions of phraseology*, which
are sometimes mistaken for moral distinctions, it is not
necessary at present to discuss. Though perhaps it may
not be amiss to observe, by the way, that (however we may
admire the delicacy and refinement of the present age in
these respects, as far as manners are concerned) it is
not always the coarsest language, or even the coarsest
incident, that is most injurious. If we look, through
surfaces, to latent consequences, we perhaps may find,
that 'vice' is so far from 'losing half its evil by losing
all its grossness,' that the grossness is frequently, in
some degree, an antidote to the vice; and that morality is
never so much endangered as by the delicacy of

> that soft persuasive art,
> That can without the least offence impart
> The loosest wishes to the chastest heart.

It appears, however, by his own confession, that Chaucer was sufficiently aware that his *Miller and his Reve,*

&c. did not very strictly confine themselves even within
the *fashion* of the decorums of his own time; and he has
accordingly, in the prologue to the 'Miller's Tale',
thought it necessary not only to renew his plea of dramatic licence, but to accompany it with a warning, of which
the more modest of his readers may, if they please, avail
themselves.

(b)

(XII, pp. 96-7) The Jews are the most extraordinary
people, and their history is the most interesting history,
in the world. For ages out of number, they have not possessed one square mile of territory, and they still look
forward to universal dominion;—for generation after
generation they have run a troubled stream in the greater
stream of the population of all nations, without once
assimilating with any:—every where they live separate and
alone, sojourners rather than home-dwellers. They have at
all times possessed great wealth, and, at times, great
power; once, they had among them the greatest general information, in comparison with their numbers, and the most
learned men, without comparison, that Europe could then
boast of; they have been also the most ignorant as a body,
and had fewer men of eminence among them; they were at one
time, in Spain particularly, indirectly possessed of great
civil power; and at other times, and for long intervals
together, they have been the most abject and miserable
race throughout all Europe; their persecutions have been
fearful even to remember, and dreadful beyond all preced-
ent; and yet they are one, and still a people.
    Of late years indeed, at least in this country, the
current has set the opposite way to persecution. Cumber-
land's Jew is quite another man from Shakspeare's Jew, or
the Jew of Malta; and who can believe that Rebecca is a
lineal descendant of the 'Ebraike peple,' that slew young
'Hew of Lincoln!' But so it is! and, thanks to the genius
of our countrymen, the feeling of the ages in which they
severally lived has had permanency given to it in their
immortal works: for, when the Lady Prioress talked of

the serpent, Sathanas,
That hath in Jewe's herte his waspe's nest,

we may be quite sure that Chaucer had the authority of
many such ladies for such sentiments; and for the purity
of conduct and beautiful humanity of Rebecca, the modern
poet had the voucher for its possible truth in the agree-

ment of all men of sense; and both facts, as far as the
philosophy of mind is concerned, prove only that poets as
well as Jews, and Jews as well as poets (a much more
important point to establish) are very much the children
of circumstances. When lady prioresses talked after this
fashion, and other ladies and gentlemen too agreed with
her in opinion; when the Jews were every where persecuted,
despised, or hated—spit on, trampled on, and bearded;—
their sufferings made a jest, and the law made an instrument of infliction; was it not in human nature that 'the
serpent, Sathanas' should dwell in their hearts? But the
progress of knowledge has been accompanied with progressive liberality,and this feeling is much more distinctly
to be traced in our poets than our historians. In the
lady prioress's tale, there is not one redeeming circumstance for the poor Jews; they are isolated beings, cut
off from human society; in the want of all human sympathy,
they stand out naked and bare for universal hate and det-
estation.

But in Shakspeare and in Marlowe, the Jews have not
much the worst of it.

(c)

(XII, p. 299) Merry Old England! Why merry? Why old? In
antiquity, as well as in merriment, we seem far inferior
to our neighbours. Certainly, we possess not these acci-
dents in any such degree as entitles us to the epithets as
a distinction over other sadder and younger nations.
Gaiety, lightheartness, high animal spirits, are not the
characteristics of Englishmen now; and, as well as we can
judge, never have been. The character of seriousness is
engraven upon the chiefest part of our literature; and,
in cases of great excellence, the rising of the spirit has
not been especially shewn in compositions of wit and drollery, but in passages of wisdom, sublimity, and grandeur.
The period in the annals of our literature most distinguished for wit and gaiety was a period of imitation; the
style, the air, almost the matter, was imported; the
exotic never took deep root. The grave and earnest fanaticism of the Puritanic age, which preceded the times of
the witty courtiers of the Merry Monarch, took a far
stronger hold of the intellectual soil of this country.
Perhaps the tone of composition and the tenor of thought
most characteristic of England, is that which may be best
described by the epithet *biblical*. Throughout our national sentiment there breathes the zeal, the earnestness, the
sublimity, the sternness, of the Jewish Scripture—the

library of the peasant, the storehouse of the poet, the
model of the man of taste, the authority of the divine,
the guide of age, the terror of youth, the text-book of
all. Gaiety and lightness of heart are not *protestant*.
The gayest and most cheerful writer of our language is
Chaucer. Popery, by divesting religion of the spiritual,
and by converting its observances into mere ceremonies,
relieves the mind from the contemplation of the future and
the supernatural, and confines its circle of consideration
to the mere things of this world. What is lost in greatness is gained in lightness. Let our remarks be understood as simply literary. We take not here into account
the greater and vastly more important points of the comparison.

(d)

(XIV, p. 314) In our former article we particularly alluded to the circumstance of Chaucer having given the first
exemplifications of genuine dramatic character and invention exhibited in our language; or, in other words, of his
having been the first who 'shewed the way how Comedy
should be constructed, and its characters grouped and
diversified.' We proceed to shew, that although the state
of society, during the age which he illustrated, occasioned him to have taken his station among those who have
dramatised for the closet, nor for the scene, that he is
not therefore the less to be regarded as the Father of
English Comedy as well as of English Poetry in general; a
statement that may be fully substantiated, both from the
structure and execution of what has descended to us of
that comprehensive and yet unrivalled production, the Canterbury Tales; which, when duly analyzed, will be found to
have embraced and exemplified every essential requisite
of the Comic Drama.
     In that most indispensable of all the attributes of
dramatic genius, in particular, the delineation, grouping,
and sustainment of diversified character, he may be
proudly placed by the side of Shakspeare himself; nor has
any equal to them yet appeared to fill out a triumvirate.
     How finely, for example, does that admixture of the
observant and the *creative* faculty—that harmony of *faithful transcript* and *imaginative conception,* which constitutes the very essence of poetic nature and dramatic veri-
similitude, manifest itself in the inimitable character of
the Host! who, though he sustains, as has been justly
observed throughout, a function similar to that of the
Chorus in the ancient drama, has yet an attribute of

higher and more connective merit, inasmuch as he is at
once the contriver and conductor of the plot or main
action of the fable, and an essential part of the action
itself; and is endowed with a peculiarity of appropriate
humour, which gives him not only the truth and consonance
of personal identity, but also a *necessary* connexion with
the whole, which the ancient Choruses could seldom boast.
He does not seem to be placed among the other actors
merely to predicate and moralize upon characters and
incidents as they pass before him: he is the master
spirit—the motive principle that puts every thing in
action—the life and soul of all. His character is so
admirably kept up throughout the whole journey, with such
unabated wit and spirit, that he retains, to the very
last, all that freshness of originality which at the
outset seizes upon the imagination; and of which familiarity rather increases than abates the interest.

From this character that of 'mine host of the garter'
in 'The Merry Wives of Windsor,' is obviously derived:
and that even our immortal dramatist should, in his copy,
have been far from surpassing the original, is surely the
highest of imaginable tributes to the triumphant genius
of Chaucer....

(p. 322) The pilgrims proceed accordingly to the
ballot; and it is insinuated, that it is not without contrivance on the part of our politic host, that the lot of
precedency falls to the knight; who accordingly tells the
first tale: and certainly a subject more adapted for
knightly theme, or more appropriate to the character that
had been delineated—more sounding with chivalrous feats
of arms, and no less chivalrous devotion to the fair, at a
time when *tout a l'amour, tout a l'honor,* was the universal motto of the knighthood of Europe, could not well have
been put into knightly mouth. An observation, the spirit
of which will equally apply to all the rest: the adapta-
tion of the stories, as well as the dialogue, to the
characters from whom they proceed, being a circumstance
in which our author never loses sight of the dramatic
model of his machine.

This tale of Palemon and Arcite (epic in its subject,
and almost so in its construction, and extending almost
to epic length—nearly 2300 verses) is so well known, that
it is unnecessary to enter into any detail of the fable
and action, or to animadvert upon that curious admixture
of Gothic manners and classical mythology—the exploits
and jousts of chivalry, with the names and incidents of
the heroic age of Greece, (a usual characteristic in the
romantic compositions of the times) with which it abounds.

It has been popularised by the paraphrastic version of

Dryden, already alluded to, and dramatised by Fletcher:
assisted (as is pretended) by the master hand of Shakspeare.

With respect to Dryden's paraphrastic version, however,
of this, the *noblest* of the Canterbury Tales, we must have
the temerity (notwithstanding his high reputation) to con-
tend, that it does not do all the justice that might have
been expected to the venerable original. The incidents
indeed remain unaltered; and the language and versification of Dryden cannot fail of being more acceptable to the
modern ear than that of the great master harmonist of the
fourteenth century. Nor will it be doubted by those who
are acquainted with the voluptuous cast and character of
Dryden's style, that beauty would become more decorate,
and description more florid, under the colourings of his
hand. But these adornments seem to have been purchased
by a more than necessary sacrifice of the venerable simplicity of the original. The ornament is not always in
harmony with the subject—the style not always adapted to
the theme. It is Corinthian frieze on a Gothic edifice.
What is gained also in smoothness, is often lost in
strength; and amplification is not always atoned by the
value of what is added. In straining to be more poetical,
Dryden is apt to become occasionally *outré:* and when he
would be imaginative, his fancy sometimes evaporates
conceit, a fault from which even his translations from
the classics are not always exempt. Neither does he
always forbear, in his fondness for a not over delicate
vein of satire, to pervert the sentiment and enfeeble
the pathos of his author. There are, at any rate, many
passages in the Knight's Tale which, to those who have
sufficiently mastered the language to enter into the
spirit of the original, will appear more touching in the
comparative rudeness of their primitive simplicity, than
in the gloss and equanimity of their modern array.

(p. 337) The commendation of the Franklin, whose allusions to his own wayward son, that

> to virtue listeth not to intend,
> But for play at dice, and to dispend,

and some parade about 'learning gentilless,' the host
very unceremoniously cuts short, occasions his tale to
be called for;

> Straw for your gentilless,'——
> Tell on thy tale withouten wordes mo:'

and a legend of sentimental romance, deeply tinged with

that affectation of factitious ethics and preternatural
platonism (whose origin we are apt to ascribe to a somewhat later period of our literature) admirably illustrates
the tastes and intellectural habitudes of this well-drawn
character: whose rustic gentlemanship, not untinctured
with the accessible, or ex-collegiate literature of the
times, strongly reminded us of what, (though under modifi-
cations from the very altered state of knowledge and
society) we have occasionally met with, in our own day,
among persons in the same class of life.

It is introduced by some sensible observations, though
characteristically given in a somewhat sermonising strain,
(making the most it may be said of a small morality, as
country gentlemen, when they are sentimental, are still
apt to do!) about not treating wives as 'thralls;' for
that

Love will not be constrain'd by masterie;

and it relates the history of one Arviragus, (a husband
who carries this principle and that of the punctilious
obligation of a promise to a somewhat extraordinary
extent,) and of Dorigene, his wife, from whom, after
having lived with her 'a year and more in bliss and in
solas,' he is obliged by certain affairs to be absent for
two years; and who, in the mean while, though pining like
a widowed dove, gets entangled in a sort of amour, on her
side purely platonic, with a

lusty squire, servant of Venus,
Which that yclepped was Aurelius,

and which seems, at one time, even after the return of the
husband, very likely to terminate(though not without the
aid of a most extraordinary feat of magic on the part of
the gallant) as platonic amours every where, we believe,
but in the pages of novels and romances, pretty generally
do terminate; but which, *by means* of a sort of Cato-like
liberality on the husband's part, and his insisting upon
the religious fulfilment of the promise into which the
reluctant and grief-stricken Dorigene had been most
unwittingly, and upon a seemingly impossible condition
betrayed, is most sentimentally brought to a happy and
honourable conclusion: the gallant himself, (when the lady
meets him reluctantly obedient to her engagement and her
lord's most scrupulous command,) overcome by the example
of such punctilious honour and generosity, relinquishing
the long-sigh'd-for prize, and restoring her pure and
untainted to 'the bliss and the solas' of her nuptial

obligations.

The tale, strange and sentimentally extravagant as it is, is beautifully told, and in a style that marks the gradation of mind and culture between the rustic and mechanical characters, and those who, from profession and station, may be naturally supposed to have had all the advantages of the learned education of their times.

It is, indeed, worthy of particular note, how judiciously the poet has adapted throughout, not only the subjects of the respective narratives to the characters, conditions, and consequent associations of the respective narrators; but with what wonderful tact (or intuition rather) he has accommodated the style and language of each to the intellectual, educational, and moral habits, which should, in the course of things, pertain to them. The very *dialects* of the respective speakers are obviously, and, in many instances, strikingly different: marking their provincial, as well as their professional distinctions: in their tales, quite as much as in their dialogue. This of course must have been still more conspicuous to Chaucer's contemporaries than it can be to us: though still *we* may distinguish many essential varieties, in all their shades and gradations, from the patois of the provincial and mechanical vulgar, to the polished diction of the courtly and the classic book-style of the professionally learned.

It would be an exercise both amusing and instructive to trace the upward progress of these characteristic dialects, accordant with the educational privations or advantages of the respective speakers, and the degrees of approximation in their language towards the current English of the present day. Nor would the effect be unobvious, even upon the rhythmical emphasis, the differences in the syllabic disposition of which constitutes so much of the *apparent* difference between the harmony of the olden and of our present polished versification.

(p. 352) So far, however, as the work has proceeded, and the materials have been preserved and arranged, we trust that we have sufficiently substantiated the claim of Chaucer to the merit of dramatic invention and interest, in the two grand requisites, the structure of his fable or action, and the delineation, sustainment, and felicitous grouping of comic character.

Of the peculiar advantages of this form of composition, in connecting together a series of miscellaneous tales, Chaucer may be truly said to have given the first efficient, and yet unrivalled example. Boccaccio, indeed, in his 'Decameron,' had introduced the colloquial *form* of dramatic dialogue to string his stories together; but it

was the form only. The persons whom he has brought together as his narrators maintain a sort of connected conversation; but they have neither the diversity nor the
identifying peculiarities which comedy requires; nor is
there any definite action in the 'Decameron,' to constitute a comedy. His machine has neither plot nor fable—no
beginning, middle, or end—nothing in it to give it any
semblance of a dramatic whole, any more than there are, in
the narrators themselves, any of those discriminating
shades of contrast and variety, requisite to give to the
dialogue any portion of dramatic effect.

Mr. Tyrwhitt, in his 'Discourse on the Canterbury
Tales,' gives therefore, perhaps, somewhat more than
deserved praise to the 'Decameron,' when, in comparing it
with other collections of tales, &c. he ascribes to it
'the same advantage, that a regular comedy will necessarily have over an equal number of single unconnected
scenes.' For the analogy fails in its most essential
parts, namely the coherent dependence of the respective
scenes, by progressive incidents, naturally conducting
to some expected catastrophe; without which, the composition is still but a series of scenes, and not a drama.
And though Mr. Tyrwhitt adds—that 'Perhaps there would be
no great harm, if the critics would permit us to consider
the "Decameron" in the light of a comedy, not intended for
the stage,' 'the fundamental defects,' which he afterwards
mentions, in a note on the ensuing passage, effectually
destroy the pretensions of Boccaccio's work to this dramatic character.

(p. 354) What Mr. Tyrwhitt calls the *action* of the
'Decameron,' is therefore, in any dramatic sense of the
word, no action at all. It is merely an expedient, for
giving an arbitrary connexion to a variety of miscellaneous narratives. And, even in this point of view, the
merit of the invention is not due to Boccaccio. The
'Arabian Nights' Entertainments,' (which, may confidently
be inferred from sufficient evidence, were not unknown to
the novelists of the age of Boccaccio) had already given
an example of a better machine; for though the narrator in
that case be but one, and the other characters have a very
subordinate part to play, there is an action and object
running through the whole, (and that of deep interest)
which gives connexion to the successive stories, and for
the furtherance of which they are told. Here, then, we
have that unity of design, which the 'Decameron' wants,
and the only defect of the action is, that it has obviously no necessary limit.

Mr. Tyrwhitt is, however, much more happy in the succeeding observation:

That the closer any such composition shall copy the
most essential forms of comedy, the more natural and
defined the plan shall be, the more the characters
shall be diversified, the more the tales shall be
suited to the characters, so much the more conspicuous
will be the skill of the writer, and his works approach
the nearer to perfection.

And in this respect it is that the Canterbury Tales
have an advantage so conspicuous, as almost to entitle our
Chaucer to the whole merit of the original invention:—
that the work is, in reality, 'a Comedy not intended for
the stage.' It has a main action running through and
connecting the whole; with its obvious and necessary duration, and equally necessary catastrophe; its critical
unity of object; its natural beginning, middle, and end.
It is rich in all the requisite contrast and diversity of
character which can give amusing variety to the dialogue.
The respective Tales themselves become consistent and
necessary parts of that dialogue; and at once fill out and
sustain the respective characters, and constitute the
essential means of accomplishing the catastrophe which the
author has designed. The Tales of the Reve and the Miller,
the Frere and the Sompnour, for example, as naturally and
as forcibly elucidate the personal and professional ani-
mosities, and display the humourous and moral (or immoral)
habitudes of those personages, and of their class, as
their colloquial scurrilities and sarcasms: and the epic
narrative of the Knight, the Monastic Legend of the Prioress, the Witch Tale of the Wife of Bath, the Sermon of
the Good Parson, and so of the other Tales, as correctly
sustain the characters of the respective narrators, as the
dialogue, little or much, that is put into their respective mouths.

The main object in view is not in itself very important; but it is sufficiently comic for interest and effect;
and promises a termination in a scene of jollity and high
convivial enjoyment: and it is curious to observe, that
two compositions of such sterling merit, as the first
closet and the first stage Comedy in our language, should
have had, for the object of their respective actions, the
former the attainment of a jolly supper, cost-free, at the
Tabbard Inn in Southwark; and the latter, the finding of
Gammer Gurton's needle in the seam of her man Hodge's old
small-clothes, which she had been mending. But what possible subject is there, which, touched by the hand of
genius, may not become interesting and amusing?

100.   WILIAM ROSCOE, ILLUSTRATING THE PHENOMENA OF THE
MORAL AND PHYSICAL WORLD

1824

Roscoe (1753-81), biographer and poet, in his edition of
Pope's 'Works', 10 vols (1824), Vol. I, pp. x-xi, makes an
unusual and suggestive comparison and estimate.

Of English authors those to whom Pope stands the nearest
related in genius and poetical character, are Chaucer and
Dryden, both of them not only the objects of his warm
admiration, but of his avowed and frequent imitation.
Chaucer may be said to be, like Pope, a general poet. His
excellence was not confined to any particular department.
He was qualified

> happily to steer
> From grave to gay, from lively to severe.

In this respect Chaucer is unrivalled by any of his successors, except Shakspear and Pope, both of whom resemble
him also in that moral and contemplative character which
delights in comparing, and illustrating the phenomena of
the moral and physical world, and demonstrating that not
an incident or a sensation can take place in the one without exciting in the mind a decided sympathy with the
other.
   It was probably this similarity of taste that induced
Pope when young to imitate several of the pieces of Chaucer, and in particular to write his Temple of Fame, one
of the noblest, although one of the earliest of his productions. That the hint of this piece is taken from
Chaucer's House of Fame, is sufficiently obvious, yet the
design is greatly altered, and the descriptions, and many
of the particular thoughts, are his own; notwithstanding
which, such is the coincidence and happy union of the work
with its prototype, that it is almost impossible to distinguish those portions which are originally Pope's, from
those for which he has been indebted to Chaucer.
   In the establishment of the English language, Chaucer
may be said to have laid the foundation of a building
which it was the good fortune of Pope to complete.

101. ROBERT SOUTHEY, ORIGINAL GENIUS OF THE HIGHEST ORDER

1831

The poet and man of letters Southey (1774-1843) many times
refers to Chaucer with enjoyment, but here reflects the
Romantic dislike of ornate diction; an interesting contrast with earlier ages. The comment precedes his selection from Chaucer in 'Select Works of the British Poets',
1831, p. 1.   .

Chaucer is not merely the acknowledged father of English
poetry, he is also one of our greatest poets. His proper
station is in the first class, with Spenser, and Shakspeare, and Milton; and Shakspeare alone has equalled him
in variety and versatility of genius. In no other country
has any writer effected so much with a half-formed language: retaining what was popular, and rejecting what was
barbarous, he at once refined and enriched it; and though
it is certain that his poetry is written rhythmically
rather than metrically, his ear led him to that cadence
and those forms of verse, which, after all subsequent
experiments, have been found most agreeable to the general
taste, and may, therefore, be deemed best adapted to the
character of our speech. In some of his smaller pieces,
he has condescended to use the ornate style which began to
be affected in his age; but he has only used it as if to
show that he had deliberately rejected it in all his
greater and better works. He drew largely from French
and Italian authors; but in all his translations there is
the stamp of his own power; and his original works are
distinguished by a life, and strength, and vivacity, which
nothing but original genius, and that of the highest order,
can impart. Whoever aspires to a lasting name among the
English poets must go to the writings of Chaucer, and
drink at the well-head.

102.   UNKNOWN, CHAUCER BECAME AT ONCE THE POET OF A PEOPLE

1837

The increasing nineteenth-century emphasis on Englishry,
on the importance of the common people, and on the nature
of the English language, finds explicit and quite subtle
expression in this extract from an unknown reviewer's
remarks about Chateaubriand on the Literature of England,
'Edinburgh Review', LXIV (1837), pp. 520-3.

The Normans are, next to the Hellenes, the most splendid
people in history....The first influences of the Normans
in England were not favourable to our national poetry.
Their own songs and lyrics had not the freshness and simplicity which usually characterise an early literature:
they were for the most part at once rude and affected.
The Conquest necessarily imposed a sudden check upon the
growth of the native literature—the spirit of the people,
which is the true germ of a national poetry, was crushed
—their very language was ridiculed as barbarous—popular
Saxon writings became translations or imitations from the
French; and the Normans suggested not only the subject-
matter for legendary lore, but, by the fashion of rhyme,
the very mode in which the themes were to be shaped. But
although our romance-poetry, if it did not absolutely
spring out of that of France, must at least regard the
Trouvere as its foster-father; yet, until something of
the national and popular spirit began to revive under the
new shapes which our infant literature had been violently
constrained to assume, nothing could be more feeble and
wretched than its languid and unhealthful aspect. It was
not until a national spirit was once more formed that a
national bard arose. Then, all the foreign and French
adulterations began no longer to smother, but seemed to
embellish and enrich, an original and characteristic
muse; and Chaucer, though Norman by descent, a courtier
and a scholar, the favourite of clerks and nobles, became
at once the poet of a people; and united into one unique
and decided whole the attributes and characteristics not
more of the conquerors than the conquered....because in
writing English our first rude minstrels addressed themselves, perforce, to the large masses of men,—to burg-
hers, franklins, and boors,—that, despite the contagion
of a foreign and artificial muse, there sprung up, in the

ways and thoroughfares, a poetry especially robust, catholic, and manly. The very circumstance of there being two
languages in England,—one for the nobles, one for the
people,—though for a time it humbled and debased intellectual effort in the native language, imposed a certain
limit, defined and insurmountable, to the influence of an
alien and exotic tongue. And, while knights and nobles
were listening to Norman madrigals, amongst more popular
audiences the national genius was allowed to form itself;
often borrowing from the more courtly lyres, but amalgam-
ating every addition, and referring all to the best test
—that of the greatest number. Thus the literary feelings
kept pace, upon the whole, with the social advancement of
the people,—grew with their growth and strengthened with
their strength; and thus when Chaucer wrote, though borrowing largely from the early Italian poetry—though not
untinctured by the Norman—it was at once a national poet
formed by national circumstances, and appealing to a
nation! Though, as we before said, a scholar and a courtier, it was in Chaucer that the literary spirit of the
English people, vigorous, simple, and truthful, found its
voice. It was an immense encouragement to the English
language that a man so clerkly and so well with the great,
should have given it the preference to the French.
Unquestionably the extraordinary popularity of the 'Canterbury Tales,' and the 'Troilus and Cresseide' had a
prodigious effect in rendering the language of a conquered
people not only familiar but musical to the conquerors.
Chaucer wrote for the people, but it was in the style of
a gentleman. And he at once familiarized the Anglo-Norman
and refined the Anglo-Saxon genius. The sympathies of
Chaucer are not those of coteries and courts, they are
with common and universal feelings. He has a passionate
love of nature, and his minute and close descriptions are
very different indeed from the pastoral affectations of
the *Trouveres* and *Troubadours*. He has also that clear and
racy power of discriminating and individualizing character, which springs from an observant eye and a social
temper. Chaucer is the earliest writer in modern literature whose characters are strongly marked and distinct.
His personages are to those of Boccaccio what Homer's are
to those of Virgil; and the study of Chaucer would, like
that of Homer, conduce insensibly to the Drama. It was,
perhaps, his constitutional sympathy with broad interests
and universal feelings, no less than the concession of his
reason to the tenets of Wickliff, that made Chaucer a satirist of monks and priests. He seems to have had a practical and shrewd philosophy in his easy sarcasms on those
holy men, which is more subtle and thoughtful than the

careless gibes of the Troubadours. The active career of
Chaucer, his keen observation of the natural, whether in
men or scenery, tended, perhaps, to make him the great
founder of a very remarkable distinction of English literature,—namely, the mixture of the humorous and pathetic
—the solemn and the comic. Faithful to human life, from
which he insensibly drew his rules, he painted its changes
as he saw them; and it is difficult to say in which style
he excels the most, the grave or the gay. In his easy and
muscular play, as it were, with his subjects, he may have
found an example in Boccaccio. But it was Chaucer's
excellence, that he took no models of which Nature was not
the Original. Perhaps if we were to name that author who
had the greatest influence upon the English Drama, we
should select Chaucer. His spirit is more visible in that
department of our poetry, than any other. In fact the
poetry of tales, as literature became a more active agent
of society, passed into the poetry of plays. The same
individuality of character, correctness of purpose, and
admixture of the grave and humorous, which gave life to
narrative, took root in the drama, and became dialogue and
action.

103. JOHN HIPPISLEY, THE MATURE YOUTH OF POETRY

1837

J.H. Hippisley is presumably he who was educated at Oriel
College, Oxford, and became JP, DL, FRS, FRAS, but nothing has been discovered about his life. In 1837 Moxon
published his 'Chapters on Early English Literature', from
which the following extracts are taken. Though somewhat
rambling and diffuse (or even because it is so) his writing is a very representative account of the nineteenth-
century view of Chaucer by an intelligent, sensible,
thoughtful, well-read man. He has a genuine historical
sense of the development of English literature, clearly
differentiates the 'minor poems', registers both humour
and pathos, perceives the picturesque. His sense of Chaucer's description of professional characters, their relation to real persons, his treatment of 'The Canterbury
Tales' as dramatic expression of character, his rejection
of rhetoric, are exactly the concepts and interests that

impelled the research of Professor G.L. Kittredge and of
Professor J.M. Manly and other scholars nearly a century
later. Hippisley's survey of the criticism of Chaucer
seems to be quite original (though based on 'testimonies'
collected by editors from Speght in 1598 onwards) and, as
the present book demonstrates, here too he introduced an
interest still followed in Chaucer studies. The extracts
are from pp. 32-5, 39-55, 69-71, 111-12, 124-7, 140-1,
154-5, 174, 178-83, 317-19.

(p.32) By the choice of such subjects [i.e. in his minor
poems] various in most of their details, but uniting on
the topic of love, a revolution was effected in English
literature. The favourite themes of the middle classes of
society, the religious poems and legends, and the satires
on the clergy, in which ploughmen play a distinguished
part in exposing the fraud and hypocrisy of friars, were
exchanged for the favourite topics of knights and courtiers. In this change of theme, as well as in the excellence and lasting popularity of their respective productions, the age of Chaucer may be compared to that of the
Homeric poems. In both ages, the priest ceased to be the
only poet, and consequently literature ceased to be confined to religious subjects.

There is also another point in which these two epochs
in literary history may be compared, namely, as regards
the depression, or rather decline, of poetry which followed them. Nor are the causes apparently very different,
of a decline, which in both instances, seems to have been
owing to a distracted and unsettled state of political
affairs. But something, perhaps, may be attributed to
the want of a drama. In ages when books either do not
exist at all, or are very rare and dear, minstrelsy, reci-
tation, lectures, or the drama, one or the other, according to the existing state of society, are necessary to
connect literature with the great mass of the people.
Without means of this nature there can be no public, and
consequently there can be no poets. In both the literary
epochs, which we are comparing with each other, the drama
was not yet in existence. Besides this, the most interesting topics of the respective ages had been exhausted by
the genius of great poets. The feeble successors of Chaucer, at least on this side of the Tweed, are not more to
be compared with our poet than are the Cyclic poems, as
far as we can judge of their nature, with the Homeric.

(p. 39) The hostility to elegant literature, entertained

by the schoolmen and the clergy of Chaucer's day, was much
like that professed by the sophists and philosophers of
Athens towards the poets and dramatists. In all ages,
indeed, there have been two parties in literature, one of
which has been strongly opposed to all learning which did
not immediately bear, either upon religion, or practical
utility. In the age of St. Jerome, and in that of Gregory
the Great, the anti-classical spirit became conspicuous
amongst the Christian clergy. In the eleventh and twelfth
centuries, the style of their Latin writings evince some
degree of attention to the best authors; but the thirteenth and fourteenth centuries are marked, in Europe, by
a decline of learning among the clerical orders, caused
principally by the relaxed and indolent habits of the
seculars, as well as regulars, and by the introduction
into the universities, chiefly through the mendicant
friars, of the scholastic philosophy.
    Meanwhile the vernacular literatures received a polish
from the genius of distinguished laymen, which they had
scarcely hitherto possessed. Of these, Dante, Petrarch
and Bocaccio in Italy, and Chaucer in England, are the
most conspicuous in the fourteenth century.

CHAPTER II
REPUTATION OF CHAUCER IN VARIOUS AGES

The Canterbury Pilgrimage, upon which the poetical
reputation of Chaucer now chiefly rests, and which opens
to us the true character of his genius, does not appear
to have obtained avowed and universal admiration till a
comparatively late period. This circumstance is doubtless, in a great measure, to be attributed to the satire,
which the great work of our poet contains, on the Catholic
clergy. Hence perhaps it is, that we find the Canterbury
Tales distinctly mentioned, by the poets immediately
succeeding him, only on one occasion; and hence the earliest imitators of his satirical writings, such as the authors of the Plowman's Tale, the Merchant's Second Tale, and
Jack Upland, wrote only anonymously:
    But the neglect which this great work experienced at
the hands of critics, extends beyond the period of the
Reformation. Fox, the martyrologist, eulogises Chaucer,
not for his comic and satiric powers, but for 'his true
Wicklevian spirit;' and, with the exception of Beaumont's
apology for the ribaldry of the comic tales, and a passage
in Puttenham's Arte of Englishe Poetrie, there is scarcely
any distinct recognition of the poetical merits of the
Canterbury Pilgrimage anterior to Dryden.

Considering that, in all probability, this great work
was not begun at a very early period of our author's life,
and that it was never finished; considering also the
enmity which it must have excited against him from one
party in the State, it will not appear very surprising
that we find few allusions to it in his own works. Chaucer, indeed, always regards himself as the poet of Love.
On two occasions only he alludes to the Canterbury Tales;
once towards the conclusion of the Troilus and Cresseide,
where he seems to hint that the work is projected and perhaps begun: and again in a passage of doubtful genuine-
ness, called the Retraction, affixed to the Persoune's
Tale. This passage, which has sometimes been cited merely
as a proof of Chaucer's repentance for the ribaldry of
some of his comic tales, contains also a condemnation of
all his works not strictly of a religious character; a
spirit of criticism so exactly corresponding with that
shown by Richard of Bury in his Philobiblon, and so
thoroughly scholastic and monkish, that it is at once
evident, either that Chaucer towards the conclusion of his
life abjured all his former opinions on religion and literature, (a circumstance for which there is no ground, and
which is highly improbable) or that the words in question,
which are evidently out of place, were interpolated by the
hand of some pious catholic or schoolman.
     But be this as it may, on all other occasions at least,
Chaucer alludes to his own works as undertaken in the
service of the God of Love: and in this view they are
regarded also by his friend and contemporary, Gower. In
a well-known passage at the conclusion of the 'Confessio
Amantis,' Venus addresses Chaucer as her 'disciple and her
poete,' and enjoins him (in a message sent to him through
the author of the Confessio) 'to sette an ende of al his
worke by making his Testament of Love.' If the great
English work of Gower is not sufficient to afford us an
insight into the exalted nature, entertained in that age,
of the character of a true Lover, the Testament of Love
carries these extravagancies yet further. In that work,
Love (personified as Philosophy is by Boethius), under the
character of a beautiful woman, bequeaths to all those who
follow her instructions, the knowledge of truth from error
—the knowledge of one very God our Creator,—as also the
state of grace and of glory: all which things are typified
under the image of a 'margerite,' or pearl.
     After such sentiments as these, and considering the
nature of Chaucer's earlier works, all of which in one way
or another turn upon the subject of love; we shall not be
surprised at the view taken of his poetical character by
his contemporaries. No poet, perhaps, affords such a

contrast to himself as does the poet of the Miller's, or
of the Nonne's Priest's Tale, to the poet of the Court of
Love, of The Floure and the Leaf, and of the prologue to
the Legende.—The critics of the present day are accustomed to weigh the pathetic with the comic powers of our
author; and to admire the union of both in the same poet.
But a very slight review of the earlier criticisms on
Chaucer, will convince us, that in neither department was
his poetical character either valued or understood, previous to the days of Puttenham and of Spenser.

The earliest successors of Chaucer, John the Chaplain,
Occleve, and Lydgate, in celebrating the praises, or lamenting the death, of their 'greate maister,' all harp upon
one theme: the eloquence, or 'rhetoricke,' as they usually
style it, of the departed poet. And this, indeed, is the
term which Chaucer himself fixes upon, in praising Petrarch. But if any two poets afford a contrast to each
other, and exhibit qualities directly opposite, these two
are Chaucer and Petrarch. The latter is the poet of language and of style—the former the poet of vigorous
thought, and of matter: amongst other proofs, therefore,
of the very slight degree in which the poetical character
of Chaucer was felt and understood in a later, and a more
learned, age, I would refer the reader to a passage of
Ascham, from which it appears that Chaucer and Petrarch
were the rivals in his days for poetical reputation.

The term 'rhetoryke,' then, although not unaptly
applied to Petrarch, will not in the slightest degree
portray the characteristic excellencies of our eldest
English poet. Perhaps, indeed, the most striking quality
of Chaucer's works, at least on our first acquaintance
with them, will be the beauty and vigour which many of his
descriptive passages have attained, notwithstanding not
only the rudeness and imperfection of his metre and language, but even the homeliness of his style and diction.
Yet rude as this language, and unornamented as this style,
now appears to us, so manifest an improvement was it upon
that of his predecessors, that from his own day to that of
Leland and William Thynne—the one, his earliest biographer; the other, the first editor of his entire works—
this peculiar excellence of Chaucer, trifling as it is in
comparison with his real merits as a poet, seems to have
occupied the attention of his admirers, to the exclusion
of every other. Skelton, in his 'Crowne of Laurell,'
written in 1489, continues in the same strain with John
the Chaplain, Occleve, and Lydgate; and extols both Gower
and Chaucer as the garnishers and refiners of the rude
English tongue: and Hawes, in his 'Pastime of Pleasure,'
speaks of Chaucer much in the same strain. The Latin

verses of Leland inserted in his Life of Chaucer, and prefixed to William Thynne's edition, touch on this subject
alone. But Leland, in all that he has said of our poet,
seems to have been more careful of his own reputation for
eloquence, than for that of his author: he sacrifices fact
to style; and in the vagueness of his criticisms, shows as
much negligence of the poetry of Chaucer, as ignorance of
the authentic facts of his life, by unfounded detail.

In the dedication of Thynne to Henry the Eighth the
poet is praised, according to the affected pedantry of the
day, for his 'excellent learning in all kindes of doctrines and sciences,' and for 'his sharpnesse and quick-
nesse in conclusion, in a time, when either by the disposition and influence of the heavenly bodies, or, by the
ordinaunce of God, al good letters were laid asleepe
through the world.' Thus, in a contemporary dedication of
the 'Confessio Amantis' to the same monarch, that work is
praised as 'plentifully stuffed and fournished with mani-
folde eloquent reasons, sharpe and quicke argumentes, and
examples of great auctoritie, perswadynge unto vertue, not
onely taken out of the poetes, oratours, historie writers,
and philosophers, but also, our of the Holy Scriptures.'

This practical and philosophical view of the merits of
Chaucer continued in force till the latter years of the
sixteenth century. Webbe, in his 'Discourse of English
Poetry,' praises the poet in the spirit of Fox, Bale, or
the most zealous Protestants.

Puttenham, a contemporary of Webbe, is the first critic
who seems in any degree to understand either the history
of our author's works, or their poetical merits. 'Though
many of his bookes be but bare translations out of the
Latin and French, yet they are wel handled, as his bookes
of Troilus and Cresseide, and the Romaunt of the Rose,
whereof he translated but one halfe; the device was John
of Mehune's, a French poet: the Canterbury Tales were
Chaucer's own invention, as I suppose, and where he show-
eth more the natural of his pleasaunt wit than in any other
of his workes; his similitudes, comparisons, and all other
descriptions, are such as cannot be amended. His metre
heroical, of Troilus and Cresseide, is very grave and
stately, keeping the staffe of seven, and the verse of
ten: his other verses of the Canterbury Tales be but riding ryme, neverthelesse very well becoming the matter of
that pleasaunt pilgrimage, in which every man's part is
played with much decency.' This passage, though it does
not display any very deep knowledge in literary history,
may, considering the age in which it was written, be regarded as a masterly outline of the poetical character of
our author, and forms a striking contrast to the vagueness

with which Sidney, in his 'Defence of Poesie,' character-
ized the poet, 'as seeing clearly in a mystic time,' and
as 'beautifying our mother tongue.'

To enter into a history of the conflicting opinions
with regard to the merits of Chaucer's language, which
began about this time, and which even a late distinguished
critic has condenscended to notice, would be to imitate
the puerile spirit of the controversy itself. It may,
however, be amusing to observe, not only the opposite
statements which have been made by different critics on
this subject, but even the opposite inferences which have
been drawn from the same statement. Up to the days of
Leland and William Thynne, there was, as we have seen, but
one opinion on this subject. Chaucer was the 'floure of
rhetoricke,' the 'garnisher of Englishe rude.' Webbe
first ventures to hint that 'the manner of his style may
seeme blunt and course to many fine English eares at these
days.' In the days of which Webbe speaks, the English
tongue, besides the natural polish which it had acquired
from the labours of successive writers, was also affected-
ly interlarded with artificial ornaments, borrowed chiefly
from the Spanish and Italian languages. These 'ink-horn
terms,' as they were called, form a frequent theme of
ridicule in the comedies of Ben Jonson and Shakspeare.
Similar affectations and innovations were encouraged and
extended by the 'Euphues' of John Lilye; and Spenser,
finding the ornate style, which was then becoming popular,
abhorrent from the nature and subject of his romantic
poem, adopted at once the language of Chaucer, as a 'well
of English undefiled.' The genuine English style of this
age lay between the obsolete diction of Chaucer, and the
affectations above-mentioned. This is accurately felt,
and sensibly pointed out, by an old writer somewhat senior
to Spenser. Peter Asheton, in dedicating his translation
of a treatise by Paulus Jovius to Sir Ralph Sadler, desires him 'not so much to regarde and loke for picked
termes, and strange Englishe wordes, (whiche, indeed, be
not here,) as for the playne setting forthe of the sentence, and right declaration of the history. For truly
throughout al this simple and rude translation, I studyied
rather to use the most playn and famylier English speach,
then ether Chaucer's wordes, (whiche, by reason of antiquitie, be almost out of use,) or els ink-horne termes (as
they call them) whiche the common people, for lacke of
Latin, do not understand.'

Verstegan, in his Restitution of Decayed Intelligence,
and Skinner, in the preface to his Etymologicon Anglican-
um, have censured Chaucer for what formed the constant
argument in his praise, up to the Elizabethan period of

our literature: namely, for the introduction of French
terms into English. Rymer, in a passage which shows that
he has reaped the full advantage of the philological labours of our poet, first introduces him to us as a recruit-
ing officer of our language; and afterwards, proceeding
more scientifically to explain the chemical process, by
which that tongue was formed, he represents Chaucer as a
skilful brewer of English.

This tedious and puerile controversy may, perhaps, be
best disposed of by referring to a simple principle in the
history of language. In proportion as a nation becomes
literary, the study of foreign languages (whether modern
or those of antiquity) and the translations made from those
languages into the native tongue, bring with them a variety
of new expressions, by which the original poverty of that
tongue is enriched. Thus languages, like nations, or even
like the physical substances of nature, are formed by a
union of various elements, useless in themselves, but rendered valuable by combination. Amongst those who first
'employed themselves to the beautifying and bettering of
the English tongue,' (to use the words of his oldest editor,
William Thynne,) was 'that noble and famous clerke, Geffray
Chaucer.' But in the interval which had elapsed between the
days of

Old Dan Geffrey, in whose gentle spright
The pure well-head of poetry did swell

and those of his illustrious successor, who thus charac-
terises him, the innovations which Verstegan and Skinner
charge solely upon Chaucer, had been so far increased,
that his language had become obsolete; and the adoption
of it by Spenser is only to be justified, on the ground
of its being in harmony with his theme.

With the mention of the name of Spenser, we have arrived at a period in the history of Chaucer's reputation
more interesting and important. From this aera to the
present day, the morning star of English poetry has been
constantly either imitated or extolled by his successors.
To this general rule there seems, indeed, to be one solitary exception: Cowley is said to have despised Chaucer.
I must leave it to the judgment of the critical reader to
determine which of the two poets suffers the most by this
decision.

[Remarks that during the lifetime of Spenser 'the poetical
character of Chaucer was rather viewed in reference to his
pathetic, than to his comic powers' (p. 59). 'The
Knight's Tale' and 'the "Troilus and Cresseide" maintained
a precedency' (p. 60). Discusses the use of fairies in

literature; Chaucer's quite different from Shakespeare's
(p. 66).]

(p. 69) Shakspeare is the earliest of our great and distinguished poets, who gives evidence of a fine taste and
relish for the comic powers of Chaucer. There is indeed
much in the comic genius of our eldest poet which closely
resembles that of his admirer and imitator. In the use
of Satirical Parodies the two poets appear to have been
animated by the same spirit. Chaucer, in his 'Rhyme of
Sir Thopas,' openly ridicules the metrical romances of his
day. In the minute discriminations of trees and of birds
in the 'Parliament of Fowls,' and in the allusions to the
pomp of Cambuscan's feast, and in Custance's wedding, in
the Knight's, and in the Man of Law's Tale, the tedious
descriptions which frequently occur in contemporary
poetry seem to be tacitly satirized....From the days of
Shakspeare, the comic powers of Chaucer have been the
constant theme of admiration both with critics and poets.
In allegorical description he may have been excelled by
Spenser, in pathos by Shakspeare, in sublimity by Milton;
but in true comic humour, and more especially in the delineation of professional characters, he has few equals,
no superiors....His pathetic powers, which engaged the
admiration of the poets and critics of the age of Elizabeth, continue even now to rival his genuine comic humour.
Without, therefore, attempting to defend the ribaldry of
some of his ludicrous tales, the homeliness of his diction, or the occasional lameness of his versification (on
all of which failings he himself, with his usual candour
and modesty, I had almost said naivete, observes), in all
the sterling and substantial qualities of a true poet, he
may well bear a comparison with the master-spirit of all
ages.

(p. 111)   CHAPTER IV
   OBSERVATIONS ON SOME OF THE PRINCIPAL OF CHAUCER'S
                  EARLIER POEMS

Chaucer, like Ariosto and Spenser, is essentially a descriptive, rather than a dramatic poet. The action, at
least of his original poems, is limited and trifling; the
poet almost always speaks in his own person, and his
characters rarely come forward upon the stage, like those
of Homer or Milton, to illustrate their own qualities by
their sentiments. But his descriptive powers are of every
kind; satirical, pathetic, picturesque; which latter term
is not to be confined strictly to rural imagery, but may

extend to all description, in which the object of the poet
is merely to present a material image, and not to touch
upon the human character, either satirically or pathetically.
    (p. 124) Chaucer is a picturesque poet in the narrowest
and strictest sense of the term. In the 'Dutchesse,' the
woodland scene in which the mourning knight is discovered,
and in the 'Parliament of Fowles,' the description of the
garden, are genuine instances of landscape poetry. The
'Complaint of the Black Knight,' a poem remarkable for the
easy flow of the versification, is distinguished also by
the beauty of its rural imagery. In the prologue to the
Canterbury Tales, the description of the Reve's rural
dwelling, and that of the poor widow's cottage in the
Nonne's Priest's Tale, but more particularly, perhaps, the
picturesque description of fairies in the opening of the
Wife of Bathe's Tale, show a true and simple taste in
landscape scenery. Rural imagery, however, with Chaucer,
as indeed generally with the poets of the middle ages and
of antiquity, forms but a background to the picture.
Landscape painting and landscape poetry, that is, poetry
of which the prominent subject is landscape, is of modern
growth; there is no Thomson, Cowper, or Delille, previous
to the seventeenth and eighteenth centuries.
    The term picturesque may, however, in poetry, be exten-
ded generally to the description of external nature, as
opposed to that of moral qualities. The poet may be said
to be picturesque, when his object is, not to unfold the
heart of man, but merely to present an image or picture;
and this, not merely when the imitation is of objects
natural and real, but even when the poet is at once the
creator of the original, and the portrayer of the resemblance. Dante is not less a picturesque poet, because the
scene of his Commedia is removed from the visible world to
one of his own creation. Amongst the more modern names,
Ariosto and Spenser, who both wander into all the extravagances of romantic fiction, are for ever picturesque
poets.
    Perhaps, however, fewer of these extravagant images,
than may be commonly supposed, are to be attributed to the
invention of poets. It has been observed of Spenser, that
the originals of many of his allegorical monsters may be
found in the pageants of his day: the poet described what
he actually saw. This, it should seem, is the true source
of minuteness and detail in picturesque allegory; and
hence the reason why the ancient poets, as Homer, in his
description of Strife, Terror, &c.; Virgil, in his celebrated image of Fame; Statius, in the description of the
temples of Mars and Venus, are so vague and general in

their allegorical figures, when compared with the poets of
the middle ages. This may be strikingly exemplified by a
comparison of the passages in Statius, with the manifest
improvement upon them in the 'Knight's Tale' of Chaucer.
The English poet was assisted to details, by painted
representations which he had observed, or had seen described, and which in his day frequently formed the interior decoration of public edifices.

The 'Troilus and Cresseide,' a poem in five books, has
been in all ages, notwithstanding its prolixity, a general
favourite: indeed, with all its want of incident and of
characters, it contains descriptive passages of great
beauty, particularly of the pathetic kind. It is assigned
by Lydgate to Chaucer's youth: and it is dedicated, with
all the diffidence of a young pupil, to the moral Gower
and the philosophical Strode.

(p. 140)   CHAPTER V
HOW FAR, AND IN WHAT SENSE, THE CANTERBURY PILGRIMAGE MAY
   BE REGARDED AS DRAMATIC—CHARACTERS OF THE PILGRIMS
          —GENERAL REMARKS ON THE TALES

Tyrwhitt, in his introductory discourse to the Canterbury
Tales, seems to be of opinion that 'The Canterbury Pilgrimage,' as well as its prototype, the 'Decameron' of Bocaccio, might be classed as comedies not intended for the
stage. As illustrating the vices and follies of the day,
these works are, indeed, a substitute for (what did not
in their age exist) the comic drama: but this chiefly
when least dramatic, and when most purely descriptive.

As an historical illustration of contemporary vices or
absurdities, neither the Decameron, nor any similar work,
will bear a comparison with the Canterbury Tales. In the
prologue to the Decameron there is very little discrimination, even of character, and none of profession or class
of life. If we are to look for touches of contemporary
manners, these must be found chiefly in the tales themselves. The tales, also, of Chaucer abound with this kind
of historical interest; but in the general prologue we
find an accurate and varied portraiture of all the stations of middle life in the poet's day. All this, however, is not the drama, but descriptive satire substituted
for it. Something, perhaps, of dramatic effect may be
discovered in the support and illustration, which the
several characters receive from the aptness of the tales
put into their mouths; the moment the pilgrim begins to
speak he is brought upon the stage, and becomes an actor;
yet even here he is not essentially dramatic, but is

rather engaged in illustrating the characters and adventures of others, than in opening to view his own life and
actions.
(p. 154) It would be an amusing speculation to search
among the few friends or acquaintance of Chaucer, whose
names have come down to us, for the possible originals of
some of the Canterbury Pilgrims. Was the Parish Priest,
Wickliffe? or the Clerke of Oxenforde, the philosophical
Strode? Was Harry Bailey, the Host, a real character? A
name seems to stamp him with individuality. But if there
is any thing in a name, did Osewold the Reve ever enjoy
his picturesque rural dwelling, and

> Ride his right good stot,
> That was a pomelee grey, and highte Scot.

And did the poet, in this instance, as well as in that of
Huberd the Friar, indulge in the personal satire of the
older Greek comedy? All that can be offered in answer to
such questions is, that there is in many of the characters, as well those of the prologue as those described in
the tales, an individuality, which renders it highly probable that they were drawn from the life.
In remarking upon the Persoune's character, it may be
as well to observe upon the inconsistency of uniting a
Lollard, an avowed despiser of pilgrimages, with a gay
train of Catholic devotees. In his prologue, the Priest
speaks in the spirit of the Puritans of a later day.

> I wol you tell a litel tale in prose
> To knitte up all this feste, and make an ende,
> And Jesu for his grace wit me sende.

(p. 174) [The subject matter of medieval romances] as
well as the spirit in which they were written, continued
long to exercise a powerful influence on the literature
of Europe. The romance of the Cid, in Spain—the poetry
of Luigi Pulci, Boiardo, and Ariosto, in Italy—and that
of Spenser, in England, is grounded, in great measure, on
a chivalric basis; and the numerous prose romances which
amused the leisure hours of the unlettered baron, or even
occasionally of the scarcely more learned clerk, gave way
only to a taste for religious controversy, introduced by
the Reformation, and to the powerful ridicule of Rabelais
and Cervantes. Generally speaking, tales, such as we
find in the 'Confessio Amantis,' in the 'Canterbury Pilgrimage,' and in the 'Decameron,' may be said to form an
intermediate step between the romances of chivalry, and
the more modern schools (various as they are) of novelists....

(p. 178) In the incidents of his satirical tales Bocaccio,
though he may be less offensively gross, is more danger-
ously licentious, than our English poet; and for this he
offers us no apology: indeed he quietly informs us that
he writes 'per cacciar la malinconia delle femmine.' In
the poetical defence which Chaucer offers for his sins on
the score of decency, although he establishes no case for
himself, yet he proves that there was a class of his
readers, amongst whom we will hope were included the fair
sex, who would be scandalised at the immoral and indecent
incidents he relates; thus indirectly showing that the
moral tone of society in England, whether owing to the
reformers and puritans, or to whatever other cause, was
higher in his day, as it has been ever since, than that of
Italy. It should be observed, however, in defence of
Italy in a subsequent age, that Ariosto apprehended similar objections to his ribaldry, as will appear from the
following line of Sir John Harrington's translation, which
I give in preference to the original, because it approaches very nearly to the words of Chaucer—

Turn o'er the leaf, and let this tale alone.

With regard to the literary merits of the respective fictions of Chaucer and Bocaccio, the distinctions lie on the
very surface of the subject. In the choice of the occasion; in the variety and delicate discrimination of the
characters, and in the vivacity and dramatic effect with
which the whole plot is conducted; in all these respects,
Bocaccio, when compared with Chaucer, is but a mere shadow. As a lively and agreeable fabulist, the Italian,
especially in his serious tales, has the advantage. Prolixity, a fault common to all our old poets, is one of the
principal blemishes of Chaucer's serious productions.
With Bocaccio, the subject of the 'Knight's Tale' forms,
as it should do, a separate and a considerable poem: and
such, indeed, was its original destination in the hands
of the English poet. As it now appears, and as one of a
long series of tales, we cannot help feeling, with the
Knight who relates it,

I have got wot a largé felde to ere.

The field, indeed, large as it is, has been cultivated, in
parts at least, with triumphant success by Chaucer, though,
with his usual modesty, he complains, in the person of his
Knight, that 'weke ben the oxen in my plow;' yet we cannot
help suspecting, that, when once the verdant spots have
been discovered, the reader will scarcely be persuaded to

revisit any others. In one respect, however, the
'Knight's Tale' is admirably qualified for the situation
which it occupies amongst the tales of the Pilgrims;
though removed in time and scene to the heroic ages of
Greece, it is throughout, in the hands of Chaucer, a
feudal and chivalric story. But this aptness of the tale
to its relater is common to the whole series, with the
exception of those related by the poet himself. It is,
perhaps, the intention of Chaucer, by the expressions in
the Miller's Prologue, already alluded to, to excuse himself from the charge of ribaldry, on the ground that the
Miller's, and similar tales, are suited to the characters
who relate them. This, indeed, is the ground of defence
which Francis Beaumont, in his letter to Speght, endeavours to establish for the poet; and certainly the characters of the 'cherls' would have been less fully illustrated, had they been exhibited as drawling out the doleful
'tragedies' of the Monk, or the monastic legends of the
Nonne or the Prioresse.
      Some of the most pleasing instances of this attention
to dramatic effect, are to be found in the tales which
turn upon popular superstitions, and supernatural agency:
in the fairy tale of the Wife of Bathe, with its picturesque and appropriate introduction; and in the tales of
magic related by the Squier and the Frankelein, all of
which are admirably adapted to the notions and characters
of the respective narrators.
      (p. 317) These qualities [i.e. delicacy of sentiment,
freedom from ribaldry, polish, harmony of versification,
description of landscape] in which the modern school of
poetry has indisputably surpassed the more ancient, are,
it will be said, but the minor graces and embellishments
of the art; the dress rather than the graceful figure
itself; the Dutch school of painting compared to the
Roman. This degeneracy, if it must be so called, has been
the constant attendant of art in refined ages, but more
especially, perhaps, of poetry. Poetry is the natural
growth of a rude and uncultivated soil; and in that soil,
unfettered by the mechanical difficulties of sculpture of
painting, it soon springs to maturity. In an age entirely
destitute of letters, poetry is of necessity the only
literature. Metre is required to aid the memory; and even
metaphors, which, in after ages, are the work of art and
design, are at first adopted from poverty of language.
There is a youth also, and youthful feelings, in nations,
as well as in individuals. In rude ages, the mind is un-
occupied by more serious pursuits; the heart is not yet
rendered callous by the vices, the follies, and intrigues
of over-grown cities; and the pastoral, roving, or

adventurous life of enterprise in which infant nations
are engaged, at once supplies themes for the bard, and
disposes the minds of his audience to a rapturous admiration of his song. Hence that truth and simplicity, natural only to a rude period, but affected, and therefore
displeasing, in an age of comparative refinement. Hence
the impracticability, either of imitating or translating
the sublimity of Homer, or of modernising the simple diction of Chaucer. Poetry, in short, in order to progress,
must be born again.

What, then, are the characteristics by which the
literature of the present age is most advantageously distinguished from that. of almost all preceding periods?
Next to a purer tone of morals, the foremost of all
advantages, must be reckoned that critical and antiquarian
spirit in historical research, which we recognise but
indistinctly, and only in some rare instances, amongst
ancient classic authors; and which, in our country,
does not appear before the days of Leland, scarcely
before those of Camden, Selden, and Dugdale. This laborious exactness, fostered as it has been, as well by religious controversy as by the study of physical science, can
only be rendered available, through the facilities afforded to us, towards the preservation and inspection of
ancient documents, by the art of printing.

Wherever we cast our thoughts abroad, and into whatever
train of ideas we may fall, in comparing the present with
the past intellectual condition of the world, to this
powerfully effective art, and to its consequences, by one
channel or another, we must inevitably revert; and,
indeed, if there is one circumstance more than any other,
in which the literature of the present age displays an
undoubted pre-eminence over that of every preceding
period, it is not, generally speaking, so much in the
advancement, as in the diffusion, of knowledge.

Index

The index has been divided into two parts. The first index contains material on Chaucer: biographical details, literary qualities and themes and his works. The second index contains general topics, people, books and periodicals.

1. GEOFFREY CHAUCER

337 Index

2. GENERAL INDEX

338   Index

St. Paul's Gospel

ST. PAUL'S GOSPEL

by

RONALD KNOX

NEW YORK

SHEED & WARD

1950

NIHIL OBSTAT

Hugh F. Blunt, LL.D.
Censor Deputatus

IMPRIMATUR

✠Richard J. Cushing
Archbishop of Boston

Boston, November 8, 1950

This series of Lenten Conferences was preached by Msgr. Ronald Knox in Westminster Cathedral on the Sunday evenings in Lent, 1950.

CONTENTS

THE PAULINE APPROACH

Our brother Paul, with the wisdom God has granted him, has written you a letter (II Peter iii. 15).

WHEN YOU have been looking at a child's picture-book, it may have occurred to you to wonder, before now, how the printer ever managed to transfer those brightly-coloured illustrations from the block to the paper. The process, of course, is not a simple one; in reality, there are three processes, and the page you are looking at has been three times through the press, receiving successively its tints of red, yellow and blue. So it is, if you come to think of it, about the knowledge you and I have of the basic facts of our religion; three different layers of evidence have been superimposed, one on the next. First, there is tradition. The earliest Christians learnt their faith by word of mouth; you and I, if God had so ordered our destiny, might still, after all these centuries, be learning our faith by word of mouth. Next, there are the holy gospels; an account of our Lord's life deliberately composed, for your information and mine, by men who had witnessed the events of it, or had lived so close to first-hand witnesses that the question of tradition hardly comes in. And finally, in the remaining books of the New Testament, you have a set of documents, mostly in the form of letters, written during the life-time of men who had seen our Lord. They don't set out to give us a course of religious instruction, but they are all the better as evidence for that. We learn from such writers in the course of conversation (as it were) how Christian people lived and thought in that first age, an age lit up by the afterglow of our Lord's own life on earth.

Leave out the four gospels, and most of the New Testament comes to us from the mind of one man, St Paul. I say 'from the mind' not 'from the hand,' because St Paul didn't usually write, he dictated. And you can trace his influence, no doubt, in the writings of other men who derived their inspiration from him. The Acts of the Apostles was written, not by St Paul, but by his friend St Luke; yet I think it is clear that St Paul must have encouraged him to write it, and supplied him with a good deal of his material. What shall we say of the Epistle to the Hebrews? The Church holds by the tradition that it was, in some sense, the work of St Paul, but the style of it differs noticeably from that of his acknowledged epistles. Must we suppose that, this time, he wrote with his own hand, wrote carefully, as a man writes when he is working out a thesis, instead of blurting out the thoughts of his pregnant mind, as he did to the stenographer? Or is it possible that he drew up a skeleton of the things he wanted said, and left some trusted disciple, Silvanus or another, to clothe it in his own words? Be that as it may, for our present purposes we will not use either the Acts of the Apostles or the Epistle to the Hebrews except here and there, by way of illustration. We will build up our picture of St Paul's gospel from those vivid, personal letters of his, thrown off in the heat of the moment to the Christians in Rome, Corinth, Galatia, Ephesus, Philippi, Colossae, Thessalonica, and to one or two of his immediate friends.

I want to study St Paul's letters in isolation, forgetting for the moment that we have any Christian tradition, any Gospel narrative, to supplement them. So, I imagine, you might get the printer to give you a pull-off of that childish picture all in blue, with the yellows and the reds left out. I want you to see what an admirable blue-print you can get, even so, of the Christian world-picture, simply from listening to what St Paul has to tell us. It is rather like listening to one side of a telephone conversation; we can only guess, as we go along, what the people at the other end of the wire have been saying. Our pattern will be all built up out of bits and pieces, just fragments of talk overheard, sparks struck from the anvil of forgotten controversies, and problems that have no meaning for us now. But we shall see, already, the outlines of our Christian world-picture etched in for us, and with a firm hand, by a man who is not thinking about us or our difficulties; he is just talking to his friends.

It is an extraordinary thing, if you come to think of it, how the account of our Lord which you get in the Gospels dovetails in with the account of him you get in the epistles. Not in the sense that the two accounts agree;

that would be natural, that would be commonplace; rather in the sense that they disagree. I don't mean that they contradict one another; I mean that the things on which St Paul concentrates his attention are things upon which, apparently, the Evangelists do not concentrate attention, and vice versa. After all, ask anybody in the world who has heard of Jesus Christ to tell you what kind of Man he was. You will be told, at once, that Jesus Christ went about the world doing good, healing the sick, giving sight to the blind, and so on. There is no word of that in St Paul; with him, the whole of our Lord's earthly biography passes unnoticed. Watch him, for example, when he is recommending to the Philippians the virtue of humility (Phil. ii. 5 *sqq.*). You would expect him to remind them how our Lord was born in a stable, his Mother a peasant; how he lived as a poor man, how he died as a common criminal. But it isn't, you find, our Lord's behaviour as Man that he appeals to for his illustration; it is the condescension of our Lord in becoming Man at all. Always he misses the opportunity of telling us a story, the story of the greatest Man who ever lived.

Again, think how much space is occupied in all the Gospels by long extracts from what our Lord said. Very probably, even before the Gospels were written, there were collections of such sayings handed on to the faithful by word of mouth. How often does St Paul quote the words of his Master? In the epistles, never*; only once in

* Except incidentally, when he describes the institution of the Holy Eucharist in I Cor. XI. 24, 25.

a speech recorded in the Acts, and then it is a saying which the Gospels haven't preserved for us at all (Acts xx. 35). Think of it, here was the whole Sermon on the Mount at his disposal; here was St Luke at his elbow, writing our Lord's biography, and never once does St Paul reinforce his own authority by pointing to the things Christ said! What a lot of our Lord's teaching was devoted to shewing the Jews they could no longer claim a monopoly of the Divine mercies; they had got to make room for the Gentiles in the new kingdom! Parables which evidently pointed to that and nothing else, like the Labourers in the Vineyard and the Prodigal Son. All that was a subject on which St Paul felt and wrote furiously; all through the Galatians and the Romans he is talking about nothing else. But he never quotes our Lord as having said anything on the subject; never borrows an illustration, even, from our Lord's teaching. He must have known; and yet, somehow, the two streams of Christian tradition don't overflow into one another. Merely as a matter of literary curiosity, and quite apart from any bearing it has on religion, I should say that this lack of interdependence between the gospels and the epistles is a fascinating circumstance, a baffling circumstance.

If we want to understand what St Paul's approach to the matter was, I think we have to concentrate our attention on a passage in the second epistle to the Corinthians (II Cor. v. 15–17). 'Christ died for us all,' he writes, 'so that being alive should no longer mean living with our own life, but with his life, who died for us and has risen again. And therefore, henceforward, we do not think of anybody in a merely human fashion; even if we used to think of Christ in a human fashion, we do so no longer. It follows, in fact, that when a man has become a new creature in Christ, his old life has disappeared, everything has become new about him.' The interpretation of that passage is neither easy nor certain, but I think the kind of meaning St Paul means is this. It is for the beginner, for the man who is still finding his way into the Church, to study the proofs of our Lord's Divine mission, the miracles, the fulfilments of prophecy; it is for the beginner to learn by heart, if he will, our Lord's recorded sayings. But all that is to know Christ after a human fashion, to treat him as a Man who once lived but now is dead, the subject of a biography. Once you have learned to accept Christ, and to be united with him by baptism, everything becomes different; he who was once a dead Hero is now a living Friend. Difficult for us, after all these centuries, to think in those terms; we have to treasure up the least crumbs of information we can get about Jesus of Nazareth—it all happened so long ago. But in St Paul's time it was different; the Ascension had only happened the other day; the airs of grace were all about you; why should you go back over the past?

Some instinct of that kind it must have been, I think, which made St Paul and the other New Testament writers strike out a line for themselves, instead of constantly quoting our Lord, constantly appealing to his example, as we should have expected them to do. The Evangelists, you see, were so very much on their good behaviour; they were determined to tell a plain story, not dotting the I's or crossing the T's, leaving it to the reader to form his own conclusions. Every scene must be described just as it appeared to the people who saw it happen; there was to be no improving the occasion, no morals drawn, no theological footnotes. Their readers were to see the Hero of the gospels as a Man among other men, who lived and died at a given moment in history. All that he was, but for St Paul that was not the point. The point was that our Lord was alive; that he lived on in his mystical Body, the Church. When they met on the road to Damascus, our Lord said, 'Why dost thou persecute me?' and that ME remained in St Paul's thought as the keynote of all his theology.

No, they were not to think of Christ after a human fashion. His nature was Divine; if all things came from the eternal Father, they came from him through Christ; and that 'through' denoted, not a less ultimate responsibility, but somehow a more intimate relation. He was the Elder Brother of all created things, and it was suitable that when God determined to reconcile his rebel world to himself, Christ should be the focus in which all creation should be at once resumed and renewed. His nature was Divine, but the incommunicable privileges of Godhead were not allowed to detain him (Phil. ii. 6) ; somehow, he took upon himself the nature of Man, accepted all its inadequacies, shouldered all its responsibilities. He, our Elder Brother, our Representative, became our Victim, the Representative of our sin; hung upon the Cross, and, as if by the shock of that unparalleled encounter, shattered all the barriers that had existed till then (Eph. ii. 15) —the barrier between God and Man, the barrier between life and death, the barrier between Jew and Gentile. He died, and in his death mankind, as mystically associated with him, died too, so that the old debt incurred by Adam's sin was cancelled (Rom. vi. 6). He rose again, and thereby acquired a second title to the headship of the human race; he was the Elder Brother of all risen men (Col. i. 18). The life into which he rose was not a force that quickened his natural body merely; it quickened to birth a new, mystical body of his, the Church. In the power of that life the individual Christian becomes supernaturally alive; dead to sin, dead to the fetters of the old legal observance, he lives now in Christ, lives to God (Rom. vi. 10). Baptism, his initiation into his Master's death and Resurrection, leaves him, as it were, tongue-tied and gasping for breath, while the Holy Spirit within him cries out, 'Father, Father,' to claim the promise of adoption (Gal. iv. 6). Meanwhile, the Church as a whole is Christ's building, in which we all inhere, is Christ's Bride, inspiring and prescribing sanctity, is Christ's Body, of which we are cells. Our whole life now is Christ-conditioned, he is the medium in which we exist, the air we breathe; all our nature is summed up, all our activities are given supernatural play, in him.

That is St Paul's programme; and perhaps it is not to be wondered at if he passes over in silence the details of a biography, whose total effect so reverberates with theological significance. The Incarnation, for St Paul, did not mean primarily that God had become *a* Man; it meant primarily that God had become *Man,* had infected the human race, as it were, with his Divinity. 'The Life of Christ' is a phrase which suggests to you and me a book on a shelf, a book by Père Didon or Archbishop Goodier. For St Paul, the phrase had no such meaning; or anyhow, that was not the meaning which leaped to the mind. The Life of Christ was to him an energy that radiated all about him, was the very breath he drew in with his lungs.

Do you know what it is to meet some great man, or even some interesting personality that arrests you, and to go away quite forgetting how he was dressed or even what he looked like, because the inspiration of what he was saying riveted you at the time, so that you were unconscious of anything else? And afterwards, even what he said hardly remains in the memory; what exactly *did* he say? All you know is that a kind of glow pervades you, a kind of clarity that reveals your own thoughts to you, as the result of what passed. It is the man's personality that haunts you, something too subtle and too elusive to admit of analysis, something beyond the play of features or the sound of speech; the man himself has cast a kind of spell on you. Something like that happened to St Paul, I suppose, but in an infinitely higher degree, after his experience on the road to Damascus. The shock passed off, the blindness was cured; but always the interior sight of the apostle was dazzled by the memory of that interview. Stories about Christ, things Christ said, repeat them by all means, but St Paul wanted something more than that; he wanted Christ.

St Ignatius put it on record, that even if no documents of the Christian religion remained, he would have been prepared to die for the faith, in the light of what our Lord had made known to him at Manresa. And St Paul was in the same category.

There is, I think, something Providential about this attitude of the New Testament writers. Because St Paul contrives to fill in for us, like the blue plate which the printer superimposes on the red, our picture of what our Lord was like. I think there is, about the Synoptic gospels, a kind of deliberate objectiveness which sometimes makes it hard to understand the way in which their story develops. Why did the Apostles leave their nets and start out without a word, when our Lord said 'Follow me'? What was the magic of voice or look that drew them away, in those early days when no miracles had yet been done, when the campaign of preaching had not yet been opened? Something escapes us in their narrative; what we call, in the loose sense, 'personality'. The tremendous impact which his force of character made on people—do you remember how, according to St John, his captors in the garden went back and fell to the ground when he said, 'I am Jesus of Nazareth'? All that is difficult to realize in the Synoptist account. It becomes easier to realize when you watch the effect it had on St Paul; how, after that interview on the Damascus road, he saw Christ in everyone, Christ in everything; nothing but Christ.

Meanwhile, let us not be betrayed, even for one unguarded moment, into suggesting that St Paul's gospel was different from anybody else's gospel. There was no imputation which he would have met with a more vigorous protest; that we know, because the imputation was in fact made by rival teachers in his own day, anxious to undermine his influence. Always he describes his teaching as a tradition, something which he is handing on; beset with missionary problems, he will yet find time, not once or twice, to go back to Jerusalem and confer with those who were Apostles before him; 'Was it possible,' he asks, 'that the course I had taken was useless?' (Gal. ii. 2). No, we shall hear nothing from St Paul that is not in accord with the full stream of Christian theology. Only Divine truth is rich enough to admit of different angles of human approach. Grace does not destroy nature, it perfects nature; something of the human genius remains, and the pure gold of revelation is not always minted in the same work-shop. And St Paul's was no ordinary mind; sensitive, yet fearless, logical, yet poetic, infinitely tender with the scruples of others, yet unflinching in its honesty. A delicate instrument, it will interpret the melody of Christian thought in its own way. We must listen patiently, allowing him his own choice of language, not trying to fix on his words a meaning which has since become technical, not allowing our minds to be disturbed by the echoes of later controversy. You must come to St Paul with fresh eyes if you are to feel his magic.

ST PAUL AND THE OLD
TESTAMENT

All that is an allegory. The two women stand for the two dispensations; Agar stands for the old dispensation, which brings up children to bondage, the dispensation which comes to us from mount Sinai (Gal. iv. 24).

EVERY YEAR, on the fourth Sunday of Lent, the epistle at Mass consists of an elaborate allegory, in which St Paul contrasts Sara with Agar, Isaac with Ismael, something (it is not clear what) with mount Sinai, and the earthly with the heavenly Jerusalem. Every year, the faithful listen with an air of polite detachment, evidently feeling that they cannot be expected to understand what all this is about. It is this business of the overheard telephone conversation once more; the Galatians, no doubt, had a clue to St Paul's meaning which we haven't. . . . Yes, but, before you say that, think. Who were the Galatians? Heathens quite recently converted; it was only a year or two, perhaps only a month or two, since they had mistaken St Barnabas for Jupiter, and St Paul for Mercury. Now, Jewish missionaries were trying to persuade them that, in order to be good Christians, they must adopt the law of Moses. What an extraordinary thing that these people, quite stupid country people, Gentile by birth, heathen by education, should be expected to know all about Agar, all about mount Sinai, and not only to know about them, but to understand the mystical significance of them, when you and I can't make head or tail of it!

There is only one possible explanation of it; and that is that St Paul, when he instructed enquirers in the faith, told them a great deal about the Old Testament, or at least about the books of Genesis and Exodus. Even if they were Gentiles, to whom the sacred books of the Jews meant nothing, they had got to learn about the Old Dispensation first, before they could see the New Dispensation in its right context, against its right background. Poor stupid slaves from Galatia had got to be taken all through the family history of Abraham and the patriarchs before they got on to the part about Jesus Christ. That is perhaps why, in writing to these same Galatians, St Paul refers to the ordinances of the Jewish law as 'those old schoolroom tasks' (Gal. iv. 9) ; the Jewish background of the Christian revelation is something that must be laboriously learnt, like the Gender Rhymes, like the Rule of Three; it is a preliminary grind which you have got to get through before your education proper really begins. It might seem dull, but there was no help for it; you must be properly grounded before you could master your subject, and the groundwork of the Christian religion was the story of the Old Testament, which the poor Gentiles had never heard of.

How then does St Paul look back on it, the panorama

of history, and the pattern which his own race had woven through it? As a mirror, I think, which reflects the mysteries of the New Dispensation, but reflects them, you might almost say, back to front. Most of us, when we were younger, have tried to cheat the hours of some long railway journey by kneeling up on the seat and watching the scenery flash past, telegraph poles and fields and distant hills, in the looking-glass. Then, when you had got thoroughly accustomed to the rhythm of its movement, you would turn round suddenly and look out of the window at the real scenery, flashing past in the opposite direction. St Paul's view of history is rather like that; he looks back over history and sees the world not merely as bad but as going from bad to worse; that terrible passage in the first chapter of the Romans is meant, evidently, to be a picture of contemporary manners. And the coming of Christ meant, for him, that all that process had gone into reverse; with the coming of Christ, history was repeating itself, but repeating itself just the other way round.

He saw our Lord as the second Adam, the Adam who rose, the Adam who restored us, as contrasted with the Adam who fell, the Adam who ruined us. A familiar consideration; but how many times is it mentioned in the Gospels? There is no allusion, from end to end of the Gospels, to the Fall of Man. Adam is only twice mentioned in the New Testament, outside St Paul's epistles, and both times merely in passing. How much St Paul was following the lines of current Jewish interpretation, when he laid such stress on the Fall, we cannot be certain; but the references to it in the Old Testament, outside the second chapter of Genesis, are meagre and inconclusive. The tradition of the Church would beyond doubt have preserved for us, in any case, the doctrine of the Fall, and some account of how it dovetails in with the doctrine of our Redemption. But, so far as Scripture is concerned, you may say it was St Paul alone, under the prompting of the Holy Spirit, who gave the Fall of Adam the place it has in Christian theology.

St Paul saw the Old and New Testaments as a series of parallel columns; he tells us as much in that passage from the Galatians which I gave you as my text. And the list begins quite simply, 'Adam equals Christ'. We must see Adam as the head of the human race by physical descent, as summing up in his own person the whole experience of humanity; then we shall begin to understand how Christ is the head of the human race by spiritual adoption, and how he sums up in his own person the whole experience of his Church. Because Adam was the head of the human race, the guilt of his transgression transferred itself automatically to his descendants. Oh, no doubt they were sinners too; nobody was more certain than St Paul about the corruption of heathen humanity. But he does not think of them, in this connexion, as imitating and therefore sharing the sin of Adam. He is speaking of transgression; and where there is transgression, there must be a direct commandment to transgress; after the Fall, until the law of Moses came, there was no such direct law issued to mankind, and yet mankind had to bear Adam's punishment. Death reigned; physical death, at once the symbol and the sequel of spiritual inanition. The status of guilt incurred by Adam's transgression lived on in us, his descendants in the natural order (Rom. v. 12–14).

The obverse of that medal is not difficult to read. Sprung from Adam by physical descent, we acquire the status of guilty men; incorporated into Christ by spiritual adoption, we acquire the status of men reprieved; that is what it means, to be justified. And as it is not, primarily, anything we do that makes guilty men of us, but mere birth from Adam, so it is not anything we do that justifies us, but mere re-birth in Christ. To become the second Adam, it was only necessary for our Lord to come to earth as Man; he 'took birth from a woman, so as to make us sons by adoption' (Gal. iv. 4). It is in that sense, probably, that we should understand an obscure passage in the first epistle to Timothy, where St Paul, after alluding to the sin of Eve, tells us that 'woman will find her salvation in the child-bearing' (I Tim. ii. 15); almost certainly, our Lady's Child-bearing is meant. More commonly, it is our Lord's Death and Resurrection that are represented as the gate of the new life which comes to us; mystically associated with our Lord, we die with him and rise again with him. But always St Paul will keep to his chosen symbolism; baptism does not remind him, as it reminds St Peter, of Noe coming out of his ark to repeople the world, does not chiefly remind him, as it reminds the Church on Holy Saturday, of Moses crossing the Red Sea at the head of a redeemed people. No, mankind begins with Adam, who became, as Scripture tells us, a living soul; it is fulfilled in the Adam who has become a life-giving spirit. In a garden the second Adam, like the first, awakes to life.

Meanwhile, there is a gulf of history to be bridged, between man's fall and man's redemption. Something, surely, happened, something of far-reaching importance to mankind, when God gave his law to Moses on mount Sinai. We are accustomed to think of mount Sinai as a partial revelation, and perhaps St Paul might have used the same language; 'the Jews' he writes 'had the words of God entrusted to them' (Rom. iii. 2) although it is doubtful whether 'promises' would not be a better rendering than 'words'. But St Paul thinks in terms of redemption, not of revelation; and where redemption is concerned he will not allow the Mosaic covenant even the dignity of a half-way house. Ever since Adam's fall, the ambition of Man was to be justified; that is, to get rid of the sentence of outlawry imposed on him, and to be once more what Adam had been, a *persona grata* with God. Towards the achieving of that ambition, the law of Moses has not brought us one step nearer; not a single step.

No, if anything the law left us worse off than we were before. 'It was brought in,' St Paul tells the Galatians, 'to make room for transgression' (Gal. iii. 19). What does that mean? Why, surely this; that the sins committed between the time of Adam and the time of Moses were not, strictly speaking, transgressions, because (as we have seen) there was no direct law to transgress. With Moses, God's law was expressly promulgated to mankind, and every sin after that was a transgression; nobody could plead that he didn't know he was doing wrong, because here was God's law in black and white to tell him that he was doing wrong. God's purpose, as always, was beneficent; by thus throwing our sins into relief, he made us more eager than ever for the coming of our redemption. But the Law didn't help us to get nearer to God, because we all immediately started disobeying it, just as if it wasn't there. The Psalm describes Almighty God as looking down from heaven to see if he could find a single innocent man; but no, there is nobody who reflects, and searches for God, all alike are on the wrong course (Rom. iii. 11; Ps. xiii. 2) —it was a moral which you could illustrate abundantly, at every period, from the writings of the prophets. The Jews, who had received the law, were nevertheless continually disobeying it. That means, evidently, that the law shewed us what was the right thing to do, without bringing us the grace which would enable us to do it; revelation without illumination. To prove his point, St Paul gives you in the Romans that terrible chapter which describes the soul, unbefriended by grace, seeing at every turn what is the right thing to do, and doing just the opposite. 'The sense of sin, with the law's ban for its foot-hold, caught me unawares, and by that means killed me. . . . It is not the good my will prefers, but the evil my will disapproves, that I find myself doing. . . . Pitiable creature that I am, who is to set me free from a nature thus doomed to death' (Rom. vii. 11, 15, 24)? The law didn't justify us; it found us sinners, and left us not only sinners but transgressors; that is the long and short of it.

Not that there is anything wrong with the law; it is holy and just and good (Rom. vii. 12). Notice, once again, a difference between the gospels and the writings of St Paul. The Jews of our Lord's time had elaborated the law into a complicated system of taboos which made it unnecessarily burdensome; and our Lord denounced the Pharisees, in terms familiar to all of us, for the pedantry and the legalism of it. Nothing easier than for St Paul to have taken up the same point in writing to the Romans or to the Galatians. But he does not attempt to take any such advantage of his opponents; he will yield to none in his respect for the law, only—only the law was a temporary dispensation, meant to last until our redemption came, and no longer. By way of emphasizing the fact that it was only something temporary, something secondary, St Paul makes use of a tradition, evidently common among the Jews, although you find no trace of it in the Old Testament, that the law was given to Moses, not directly by God Himself, but by the holy angels, using one of their number as a spokesman (Gal. iii. 19). The law itself was not God's solemn covenant with man; it was only a sort of codicil, added afterwards to regulate the terms of it.

What, then, was God's solemn covenant with man? The promise made, long before, to Abraham. The prophets, when they appealed to the Divine fidelity, rested their claim chiefly on the promises made to king David; you will only find Abraham mentioned about seven times in the whole of their writings. But the older tradition survived; both in the Magnificat and in the Benedictus Abraham is the name of destiny. A series of prophecies had been made to him, of which the most far-reaching was, that in his posterity all the nations of the world should find a blessing. We must not lay too much stress on the actual form of the words. To say that all mankind will bless themselves in the name of Abraham's posterity does not mean more, necessarily, than that it will be used in formulas of benediction; 'May the Lord bless thee as he blessed the seed of Abraham'. But it was the tradition of the race that a more solemn assurance was involved; the remote issue of a homeless desert chief was, somehow, to acquire a world-significance. And had it, St Paul asks (Rom. iv. 14)? For a time it might have seemed as if the promise were being fulfilled, when Solomon's empire bridged the land-passage between east and west, receiving in its coffers the tribute of east and west alike. But all that was a thing of the remote past; the balance of the world had shifted, empires had changed hands, and the Jewish race was a despised, a scattered minority of mankind.

And now, with a stroke of the pen, St Paul sweeps away the whole edifice of Jewish privilege. Abraham believed God, and it was reckoned virtue in him; when was that? Before any law had been promulgated on Sinai, before the rite of circumcision had been enjoined, before the birth, even, of Isaac (Rom. iv. 10). It follows that the true descendants of Abraham are not those who claim his physical parentage, but those who share his faith. Carrying the war into the enemy's country, St Paul goes back to Ismael, the eldest son of Abraham, but born out of wedlock. And he allegorizes the whole story; Ismael, the natural son, serves for a type of physical descent, of outward observance, of the old covenant generally; Isaac, the child of promise, stands for a type of spiritual sonship, of interior religion, of the new covenant which was given to us in Jesus Christ (Gal. iv. 21 *sqq.*). St Paul has told us elsewhere that what is first in order of importance comes last in order of time (I Cor. xv. 46); man's body is created first, his soul afterwards. So it is here; Isaac, the late-born, who is despised by Ismael, and is none the less Abraham's heir—we are to see, in him, the image of the Christian Church, later in time than the synagogue, derided by the synagogue, and yet the final repository of God's mercies, the true explanation of his mysterious dealings with mankind, all those centuries ago.

And then, as if the lesson hadn't been made plain enough, the same situation repeats itself in Isaac's family as in Abraham's. Two brothers again; both, this time, born in wedlock; but Esau is the elder, Esau is his father's favourite. Esau is the world's choice, and Esau is rejected. How the Jews had relished that story, contrasting their own future greatness with the rude barbarism of their desert neighbours, the Edomites! But no, says St Paul, the contrast foreshadowed in the book of Genesis was not a contrast between two rival nations, both descended from Isaac. It was a contrast between two orders, the natural and the spiritual order; between those older things, the law of Moses, the pride of the Jews in their ancestry, and the newer thing that had come to pass, the birth of the Christian Church. Physically descended from Jacob, the Jewish people, like Esau, were being excluded from the promise of Divine mercy—or say, rather, they were excluding themselves from it, by their obstinate rejection of Christ (Rom. ix. 9 *sqq.*). Useless to ask, why God should allow such blindness to fall on them; you might as well ask why he allowed Pharaoh to harden his heart—indispensable prelude to the triumph of the Exodus. It is a mistake to read that ninth chapter of the Romans as if it were an essay on predestination and free will. St Paul is not thinking about all that; he is thinking about the rejection of the Jews, his fellow countrymen, so melancholy to witness, so difficult to understand (Rom. ix. 14 *sqq.*).

Always it is like that with St Paul; you cannot make any allusion to the Old Testament without his transposing it into a fresh key, restating it in terms of the New. Even the sins of Israel in the desert were recorded, he says, as a warning to us; to us, in whom history has reached its fulfilment (I Cor. x. 1 *sqq.*). Not a mirage, those old promises, but a mirror for Christian souls. I don't mean that St Paul had to invent all this for himself; our Lord during those forty days after his Resurrection, went back to Moses (we are told) and the whole line of prophets, interpreting the words used of himself by the scriptures. All I want to suggest is that St Paul fills in for us the outline which the gospels have left indistinct; what *did* it mean, in the long run, that Providential history of the Jewish people? St Paul can tell us; the Old Testament is a great overture, introducing beforehand all the motifs of the New.

ST PAUL AND CHRIST'S
DIVINITY

He is the true likeness of the God we cannot see; his is that first birth which precedes every act of creation (Col. i. 15).

WHEN A MAN gets hold of a new idea, or rather, is got hold of by a new idea, which throws him off his balance and reinterprets the world for him, it may have any one of three effects on his daily conversation, and on his published writings. He may keep silent about it, except when he is in specially congenial company; he may have the feeling that this idea is so much too big for him, he will only spoil it if he tries to put it into his own words; people will take it up wrong, and be offended by it, or people will misunderstand it, and exaggerate it, and vulgarize it; far best, when the general public is listening, to hush it up. Or the effect may be just the opposite; he may be so full of his subject that he cannot resist bringing it up on any and every occasion; always he is wanting to buttonhole people and tell them about it, argue about it. Or, finally, it may become, from the first, part of the background of his mind, something which he takes for granted, and takes it for granted that everybody else takes it for granted too. He does not drag it in, does not harp on it, it seems to crop up naturally; it makes itself known in casual allusions, in the unconscious overtones of his thought. Now, which of those three effects did his conversion have on St Paul?

Rather unexpectedly, neither the first nor the second, but the third. The more you read his epistles, the more (I think) you get the impression that the mysteries of Christian theology are neither a difficult topic which he is anxious to avoid, nor the professed subject of his teaching, but his whole mental background, which keeps on shewing whether he means it to or not.

It would have been so easy to understand, if St Paul, writing when he did, writing for the sort of people who were going to hear his letters read out, had felt inclined to soft-pedal the note of dogma. After all, who were these people? Mostly, you would imagine, rather stupid people, many of them slaves, nearly all of them pagans till yesterday. As pagans, they had worshipped a whole pantheon; it had been hard enough to make them believe there was only one God—wouldn't the doctrine of the Trinity be rather confusing to them? As pagans, they had offered incense to the memory of dead emperors, deified now, the neuropath Tiberius, the madman Caligula—would they be able to see the point of the Incarnation? Wouldn't it be safer to tell them stories about the life of Jesus? But no, St Paul would spare them nothing. Contrariwise, if you *were* going to mention dogma, you would be inclined to rub it in, with a lot of simplification and a lot of repetition: 'Remember, three Persons, the Father, the Son, and the Holy Ghost'—staccato echoes of the class-room. But no, that is not St Paul's method either. He treats his converts as if they had been instructed as well as you or I—better than some of us; he will refer to the august mysteries of the Faith in an almost casual way; as if everybody, naturally, would understand all about *that;* he alludes to these things not because the guttersnipes of Philippi will need to be told about them, but because they happen, for the moment, to throw light on his argument; a mere reference, a mere allusion, and he passes on to something else. How strange it seems to us! And perhaps rather humiliating.

The doctrine of the Trinity—how little your attention is drawn to it as you read through the first three gospels! Only at the last moment, when our Lord is making ready to ascend into heaven, does he explain to his apostles that they are to baptize in the name of the Father and of the Son and of the Holy Ghost. With St Paul it is quite otherwise; he doesn't insist on the doctrine, but it keeps on cropping up. It's not merely that he closes an epistle with a formula of blessing which includes the threefold invocation (II Cor. xiii. 13) . What is much more significant is the way his thought travels back, unbidden, to the subject we half expected him to avoid. He is telling the Corinthians that they ought not to quarrel about the importance of this or that spiritual endowment; after all, he says, all alike are the gift of the same Spirit. And then he adds, quite unnecessarily as it seems, 'just as there are different kinds of service, but it is the same Lord we serve, and different manifestations of power, though it is the same God who manifested his power everywhere in all of us' (I Cor. xii. 4, 5). He is not out to tell us anything about the Trinity, you see, but there is a kind of Trinitarian groove in his mind which carries it on from one Divine Person to another.

So it is when he has been talking to the Romans about the call of the Gentiles; he breaks out into praise of God's inscrutable wisdom, and once again there must be a threefold division; 'All things find in him their origin, their impulse, and their goal' (Rom. xi. 36). All things come *from* him; that is the turn of phrase St Paul regularly uses for God the Father. All things come *through* him; that is the turn of phrase St Paul regularly uses for the Divine Word. All things aspire *to* him; that is less natural and more difficult. But I think St Paul sees creation as an outward echo of that Divine Life which is shared by the three Persons of the Trinity. The Holy Spirit is that Love by which the cycle of the Divine Life returns upon itself; and the love which goes back to God from his creatures is therefore, as it were, his province; not because it is specially directed to him, but because he inspires and energizes it.

So it is again when St Paul is trying to promote a spirit of unity among his converts at Ephesus. You are one body, he writes, with a single Spirit, each of you, when he was called, called in a single hope; and then, after this threefold appeal to the Holy Spirit, there must be a threefold appeal to the Second Person of the Trinity, 'with the same Lord, the same faith, the same baptism'. And next, there ought to be a threefold appeal to God the Father; only St Paul is carried away, poetry as so often getting the better of logic, and finishes up with a fresh Trinitarian formula: 'who is above all, pervades all, and lives in all' (Eph. iv. 4 *sqq*.) . This time, we will not examine his choice of words; spend too much attention on the details of what St Paul says, and you get left behind; the majestic sweep of his argument has passed you by. Enough to have satisfied ourselves that the doctrine of the Blessed Trinity is always close to the surface of St Paul's thought. If for no other reason, because that is the starting-point from which he approaches the doctrine of the Incarnation.

I said just now that we are to think of God's creation as an echo, an extension (if that word may be cautiously used) of his own Divine Life. The eternal act of generation by which the Father begets the Divine Word is the model and as it were the impetus of that external activity by which he creates things outside himself. And so, even before we have begun to talk about the Incarnation at all, it is natural for us to think of the Divine Word as in some sense the medium by which we approach the Godhead. 'For us,' St Paul says, 'there is only one God, the Father who is the origin of all things, and the end of our being; only one Lord, Jesus Christ, the creator of all things, and our way to him' (1 Cor. viii. 6) . In the same sense, the epistle to the Hebrews tells us that it was through his Son God created this world of time; 'without him' adds St John 'nothing came that has come to be'.

Somehow, by some title we cannot hope to understand, the Divine Word is to be thought of as the link between God and his creatures.

That notion St Paul has worked out for us in one passage which startles us by its richness and firmness of expression; will startle us still more if we remember that the Christian religion was only about thirty years old—how rapidly its thought had crystallized! St Paul is writing to the Church at Colossae, threatened with an invasion of that heresy which afterwards gave the Church so much trouble under the name of Gnosticism. The starting-point of the Gnostic is this: The world we see about us is such a hotch-potch of good and evil, you cannot possibly attribute the creation of it to one God, and a God who is infinitely good. No, you can only account for the facts by supposing that a whole unseen world of angels exists, much higher than ourselves but not enjoying the perfections of Divine Wisdom; between them, as the resultant of ill-balanced forces, these must have produced the world as we know it. Easy to see that such a doctrine did not look altogether unlike Christian doctrine; easy to see that it had attractions for the mind of a Christian who, till yesterday, had worshipped a whole multitude of gods. In recalling the Colossians to the right tradition of theology, St Paul is concerned to point out that no responsibility for the act of creation can rest with any Being outside the Godhead itself. Angels and men and all the rest of creation are the direct work of God, and in some special sense of the Divine Word.

Among all the short-comings of the Gnostic system this especially challenges his attention; it denies the unique position of the Second Person of the Blessed Trinity as the sole intermediary between things human and things divine.

With that in view, St Paul gives us a well-known description of the Son of God, as he exists independently of his human nature, independently of the work of redemption. 'He is the true likeness of the God we cannot see; his is that first birth which precedes every act of creation. Yes, in him all created things took their being, heavenly and earthly, visible and invisible; what are thrones and dominions, what are princedoms and powers? They were all created in him and for him; he takes precedency of all, and in him all subsist' (Col. i. 15). He is the true likeness of the God we cannot see—the Epistle to the Hebrews puts that in another way by saying that he is 'the radiance of his Father's splendour, and the full expression of his being' (Heb. i. 3). Perhaps the least misleading of all the images by which we try to understand the Divine Nature is that of the artist. Every artist will tell you that he is trying to express himself, yet when he has done his best he will acknowledge that he has failed; he did not express himself fully. He tried to put himself into his work, but only a little of it, he feels, is really there. But God the Father, in the eternal generation of his Son, does express himself fully; for once, the likeness is adequate to the original, and is one with it. Of that eternal act, the creation of all things visible and invisible is only a kind of echo, only a kind of ripple; but to that tenuous extent it reflects the Divine Paternity. That is why, St Paul tells us, creation stands in a special relation, or rather in a special series of relations, to the eternal Son of God. It comes to be *through* him; he communicates to it the impulse which gives it birth. It exists *in* him; he is the medium which gives it coherency. It exists *for* him; he is the end towards which all its imperfect efforts aspire. He is, in a sense, the elder Brother of every created thing; not that he ranks with them in a series, but they lay claim like him, only under a very different title, to a Divine parentage. Even if we had never sinned, and needed no redemption, there would be something in our very position as creatures which would draw us closer to him.

Having said that, St Paul has said enough for his immediate purposes. He has warned the angel-worshippers at Colossae that they are cheating the Divine Word of the honour due to him, as being the sole intermediary (if such a word can be used) in the work of Creation. But when he has reached that point, he digresses; it would not be St Paul if he did not digress. He goes on at once from the work of Creation to the work of Redemption, and insists that the Divine Word himself is the sole intermediary between God and Man, here too. Only, this time, as Incarnate; a close parallel is drawn between Christ as Creator and Christ as Redeemer, with a repetition of the actual words used. 'He too is that head whose body is the Church; it begins with him, since his was the first birth out of death; thus in every way the primacy was to become his. It was God's good pleasure to let all completeness dwell in him, and through him to win back all things, whether on earth or in heaven, into union with himself' (Col. i. 18 *sqq.*). The eternal Generation of the Divine Word is the first echo, as it were, which breaks the mysterious silence of heaven. And the Resurrection of Jesus Christ is the first echo which breaks the silence after the long sleep of death which has gone on undisturbed since Adam fell. Christ as God stood in a vague relation to all his creatures as in some sense their elder Brother; Christ as Man stands in a definite relation to them as the Head, the Clan-Chief in whom and with whom the whole Clan is mystically united; all creation is summed up in him. Nothing henceforward is complete without him; everything is re-born, as it was born, through him; everything lives, with a new life now, in him; he, the Centre of their being, is now also the Magnet which draws them back towards him. To him, whether as God or as Man, both priority and primacy belong.

We sometimes wonder why a single Person of the Blessed Trinity, and the Second Person rather than the First or the Third, should have brought us salvation. St Paul, to be sure, has no doubt that this, like every other divine act, is fundamentally the act of all three Persons at once; 'God was in Christ, reconciling the world to himself' (II Cor. v. 19), and by 'God' St Paul evidently means God the Father, except where the context makes such in interpretation unnatural. But for St Paul, as for St John, there was a clear appropriateness about the redemptive mission of the Divine Word; he who had made should remake us. And he will not begin to tell us the story of Christmas Day by taking us to our Lady's home at Nazareth, or to the stable at Bethlehem. Like St John, he will begin at the other end; or rather, he will begin at the Beginning. Its starting-point shall be a prologue in heaven.

And then, from that height, he swoops down suddenly to earth. He has assessed for us the meaning of the Incarnation in a passage we all know almost by heart, a famous passage in his epistle to the Philippians, 'His nature is, from the first, divine, and yet he did not see, in the rank of Godhead, a prize to be coveted; he dispossessed himself, and took the nature of a slave, fashioned in the likeness of men, and presenting himself to us in human form' (Phil. ii. 6). There is metaphor, of course, in the terms St Paul uses; you cannot refer to such a subject without the use of metaphor. And I think you may say the picture St Paul has in his mind is that of a young prince who is determined to win the hearts of his subjects. Born in the purple, he is not dazzled by the pomp of royalty; he is prepared to lay all that aside. He cannot cease to be what he is, but he can voluntarily reduce himself to a condition in which the outward signs of royalty are foregone. And then the metaphor breaks down, as all metaphors must break down when you are referring to such a subject. The Divine Word really took upon himself the nature of Man, he, whose inalienable possession is the nature of God. If he came to us in human likeness, in human form, he was not practising a deception on our simplicity; he was Man.

So he came to us. We have seen what Man's position had been since Adam had fallen, how the fulfilment of the promises lingered, and the world seemed only to go from bad to worse; how the law was given, with no other result than to convict us more clearly of the guilt it could do nothing to remove. In that darkest hour the dawn came, as we are reminded in the thrilling epistle for the second Mass on Christmas Day: 'We, after all, were once like the rest of them, the dupes of error . . . our lives full of meanness and of envy, hateful, and hating one another. Then the kindness of God, our Saviour, dawned on us, his great love for man. He saved us, and it was not thanks to anything we had done for our own justification; in accordance with his own merciful design he saved us' (Tit. iii. 3 *sqq.*). All that happened in the interval had made no difference; we toiled away at our schoolroom tasks 'till the appointed time came. Then God sent out his Son on a mission to us. He took birth from a woman, took birth as a subject of the law, so as to ransom those who are subject to the law, and make us sons by adoption' (Gal. iv. 4). Born of a woman—yes, he was of our own flesh and blood, he had been through all the stages of human growth. Born under the law—yes, he had a historical context, belonged to a particular race, shared the culture of one particular country-side. St Paul knows how to come down to bedrock after all, to a particular cradle in a particular cave. But behind that, what a background of Providential design! He will not be satisfied until he has taken us back to the very origins.

ST PAUL AND CHRIST'S
HUMANITY

No question of it, it is a great mystery we worship
(I Tim. iii. 16).

WHEN WE talk about the life and death of our
Lord Jesus Christ, we are using words in a special
way. The word 'life-and-death' ought, if I may put it in
that way, to be connected by hyphens; the two facts are
intimately connected—indeed, you might almost say that
you have a single fact there, viewed under two different
aspects. Our Lord's death wasn't just the crown of his
life; it was the bud of his life bursting into flower. Let
me explain that phrase a little.

When somebody writes a book called 'The Life and
Death of Lord Nelson', he is writing about two separate
subjects. He is writing the life of a great admiral, who
saved England. He is also writing about the death of a
brave seaman who fell in battle. Oh, to be sure, Nelson's
end was an appropriate one, from the spectacular, from
the dramatic point of view. A poet could not have improved on the facts. But Nelson's life would have been
that of a great admiral, even if he had lived as long as the
Duke of Wellington. And Nelson's death would have
been that of a brave seaman, if he had been a simple
foremast hand. Whereas in our Lord's case we know

that he came to earth to die. Most of us have seen that
picture of Holman Hunt's, which represents our Lord
in the carpenter's shop at Nazareth, when some chance
arrangement of shadows has marked the wall behind
him, where he stands with outstretched arms, in the
figure of a cross. I don't know whether that picture is
good art, but it is good theology. Our Lord's whole life
is explained and is orientated by the death he foresees.

Because the two things are so closely connected, you
will find a certain difference, I will not say of opinion
but of emphasis, between Christian theologians. To
some, his atoning death is the only reason, as far as we
know, why he came into the world at all. The affront
which our sins offered to God was infinite, and if full
satisfaction was to be made for it, that could only be
done by a Divine Victim; so the second Person of the
Blessed Trinity became Man and suffered, in our stead,
the penalty we had deserved. That explains the Incarnation; what more could you want? Others have laid more
stress on Bethlehem, and less on Calvary; the mere fact
of God taking Manhood upon him was enough of itself
to heal and restore our fallen nature. They have considered it probable that there would have been an Incarnation, even if there had been no Fall.

Very roughly, you may say that the division is, as so
often, a division between east and west; that it is the
Latin Fathers who lay so much emphasis on the Atonement, the Greek Fathers who are more interested in the
Incarnation. Very roughly, you may say that the party of

the Atonement interprets the result of the Fall under a legal metaphor; the balance of the Divine Justice has been disturbed, and there must be compensation before it is adjusted. Whereas the party of the Incarnation interprets the result of the Fall in organic terms; human nature has been fatally wounded, and it can only be restored by being grafted somehow into the Divine Nature; it is something like a transfusion of blood. Very roughly, you may say that one party takes its cue from our Lord's own account of his mission, 'the Son of Man came to give his life as a ransom for the lives of many' (Matt. xx. 28) ; the other takes its cue from that other account which our Lord gave, 'I have come so that they may have life, and have it more abundantly' (John x. 10) .

So the stream of Christian tradition is divided, though only, as I say, as a matter of emphasis. On which side does St Paul come down? Which party claims his support?

It would be impossible to deny that St Paul describes the work of our salvation, sometimes, under legal metaphors. You cannot, after all, speak of redemption, as St Paul often does, without using a legal metaphor. In the Old Testament Almighty God is often described as redeeming his people, in a sense which generally passes over our heads. The Jewish law was very careful about hereditary titles to landed property, and if a piece of ground was up for sale, there was always somebody who had the first claim to be the purchaser, because he was the head of the family to which it originally belonged.

Only if he could not or would not buy it might it be sold to a stranger; you get that prominently mentioned in the Book of Ruth. In the mind of the Hebrew prophets, ever since their deliverance from Egypt, Israel belonged specially to God, by a kind of hereditary right; and when Israel was conquered by its enemies, when its people went into exile, it meant that God's ancient inheritance was (so to speak) up for sale. Surely then he, as having the first claim upon it, would buy in this precious possession of his, instead of letting it go to strangers! That sense of the word passes over into the New Testament, and when Zachary blesses the God of Israel for having visited his people and wrought their redemption, that sense will have been uppermost in his mind. And quite possibly St Paul, too, has it in mind when he writes to the Galatians about God sending his Son into the world to buy up those who were subject to the law (Gal. iv. 5); salvation was offered first to the Jews, because God had proprietary rights over them as his own people.

But it is not merely in this vague sense of proprietorship that Jesus Christ is said to redeem us. 'A great price was paid to ransom you,' St Paul writes to the Corinthians, and again, 'A price was paid to redeem you' (I Cor. vi. 20; vii. 23); here, perhaps, he is thinking of slaves being set at liberty, and drawing special attention to the fact that this can only be done by the payment of a ransom. What ransom it was that was paid to deliver us from the bondage of sin is a matter that admits of no doubt; the price paid for our liberty was a human life.

The idea of a life being given up by way of ransom was, of course, familiar to Jewish thought; it entered into the whole philosophy of sacrifice. Our Lord himself, as the first-born Son of his Mother, had to be redeemed by the slaughter of a turtle-dove, or two young pigeons. And he himself, as we saw just now, told us that the Son of Man came to give his life as a ransom for the lives of many—instead of many, if you insist on the full flavour of the word. St Paul does not imitate that turn of speech; he doesn't say that our Lord gave up his life in our stead, only that he gave it up on our behalf—perhaps a significant variation of language. We have reminded ourselves that, in St Paul's language, Christ Incarnate is the elder Brother of humanity; what a temptation for him to point to the position of the first-born in Jewish law! In theory, the first-born of every man or beast was forfeit as a sacrifice to Almighty God. In theory, then, you may say that the eldest son of a family gave up his life as a ransom for the lives of the rest; how apt a parallel that would have been! But nowhere does St Paul's language suggest it; he avoids, for the most part, the idea of a substituted Victim. Although he once refers to our Lord as a paschal Victim (I Cor. v. 7), offered on our behalf, he never uses the word 'lamb'; it is St John and St Peter who tell us about the Lamb of God. Why that is, perhaps we shall see later.

At the same time, you cannot deny that the Death of our Lord Jesus Christ is central to St Paul's theology. He is always for drawing attention to the Cross; he will make his boast of nothing else, however much the Jews shrink, however much the Gentiles mock, at the sight of its ignominy. Indeed, I think you can say that to St Paul the Cross suggested, not so much the idea of suffering, as the idea of publicity. He tells the Galatians that Christ has been advertised to them, hanging on a cross (Gal. iii. 1); and later in the same epistle he says that through it the world has been crucified to him, and he to the world (Gal. vi. 14); it was a kind of legal instrument, setting it on record that the world has nothing to do with Paul, that Paul has nothing to do with the world, in future. Yes, a legal instrument; St Paul is never afraid of talking lawyer's language. And above all the Cross is a document which sets on record the establishment of peace between God and man, like those old cairns and pillars which the patriarchs used to raise when they wanted to make a covenant. God's forgiveness means that he cancelled the deed which excluded us, the decree made to our prejudice, swept it out of the way, by nailing it to his cross (Col. ii. 14) —the cross, you see, is still the notice-board of the new covenant. A covenant of peace; it was through the cross that he abolished all feuds, including the old feud between Jew and Gentile; 'both sides, united in a single body, he would reconcile to God through his cross' (Eph. ii. 16). It was a legal instrument; you must not preach the gospel with devices of human rhetoric, for that would be cancelling—it is the plain meaning of the word—cancelling the cross of Christ (I Cor. i. 17).

That notion perhaps throws light on a very curious

phrase used in the epistle to the Colossians, about 'making peace through the blood of his cross' (Col. i. 20). It is all very well to say that it simply means 'his blood shed on the cross'; but if St Paul simply meant that, it would have been easy to say that. Surely he means us to have before our eyes the picture of a cross stained with blood; surely he means us to connect it with the picture you get in the epistle to the Hebrews, of Moses sprinkling the book with blood when he founded the old Covenant (Heb. ix. 19). Either testament was sealed with blood; the old, when Moses sprinkled the document which enshrined it, the new, when those red drops trickled down the upright wooden beam. The new covenant has the cross for its parchment, blood for its ink.

I don't mean to suggest that St Paul's thought was in any way out of harmony with our traditional Catholic doctrine of the Atonement; that he didn't look upon our Lord's death as the payment of a ransom; didn't see a foreshadowing of it in the Old Testament sacrifices. No, when Easter came round he would write to the Corinthians about Christ our paschal Victim (I Cor. v. 7), and in his farewell speech to the elders of Ephesus he would refer to the Church as that flock which God won for himself at the price of his own blood (Acts xx. 28). But that way of talking wasn't habitual with him; possibly because the old sacrifices always suggested to him the idea of substitution. Even when you offered sacrifice for a fault committed, and laid your hands on the head of the victim by way of transferring your guilt from yourself to it, that was only a kind of legal ceremony; the fact remained that you had committed a fault, and it was the goat, not you, that suffered for it. Now, we understand very little about the mystery of our redemption, and it isn't unnatural that we should represent it to ourselves as a transaction of that kind. God consented to treat our Lord's death as an expiation for our fault, although the suffering, and the acceptance of suffering, were not ours but his. The reason, I think, why St Paul didn't use that language was because it didn't match his outlook on the Incarnation. The Incarnation effected a mystical union between Christ and his Church which made it misleading to talk as if our Lord were one thing and his Church another. He didn't suffer instead of a guilty race; he identified himself, not by a legal fiction, but by a real (though mystical) union, with a guilty race, and suffered as its representative.

All through the epistle to the Galatians, especially, this idea seems to be pressing on the mind of the apostle, the identification of Christ with the Christian. He, Paul, has no longer any life of his own, it is Christ that lives in him; with Christ he hangs on the cross (Gal. ii. 20), so that the world is crucified to him, and he to the world (Gal. vi. 14); he bears on his body the scars of the Crucified (Gal. vi. 17). And this intimate indwelling is not for a privileged few, it is general to the Christian community; the apostle feels something like the pains of childbirth while he waits for Christ to be fully formed in his spiritual children (Gal. iv. 17). It is only a matter of development; already, it seems, they are Christ in embryo. 'All you who have been baptized in Christ's name have put on the person of Christ; no more Jew or Gentile, no more slave and freeman, no more male and female; you are all one person in Jesus Christ' (Gal. iii. 28).

Bethlehem means Christ born in Man, and Man reborn in Christ. Calvary means that Mankind has died in the person of Christ, it means also that Christ has died in the name of mankind; not instead of us, as our substitute, but in our name, as our representative. He identified himself with us; I do not know where you can get clearer evidence of St Paul's view in this matter than a passage in his second letter to the Corinthians, where he argues thus: 'If one man died on behalf of all, then all thereby became dead men' (II Cor. v. 14). If he had written 'instead of all', the argument would be nonsense; if one man dies instead of another, like Sidney Carton in the *Tale of Two Cities,* then we infer that the other man remains alive. But St Paul does not think of Christ as dying *for* us in that sense; rather as dying in the capacity of our representative, so that when he died we died with him. For St Paul, Christ did not die in order that we might live; he died in order that we might die. In what sense, we shall see in a moment.

It was not, then, by a kind of legal fiction that the sufferings of Jesus Christ, his, not ours, were allowed to count as reparation for our sins, ours, not his. It was in virtue of a mystical union with mankind that he was qualified to act as mankind's representative. And in this mystical sense you can even say that our guilt was transferred to him. At least, it is difficult to read any other meaning into that curious verse of the Galatian epistle, where St Paul writes: 'Those who take their stand on the law are all under a curse. . . . From this curse invoked by the law Christ has ransomed us, by himself becoming, for our sakes, an accursed thing' (Gal. iii. 10, 14). There is a rather far-fetched allusion, here, to a text in Deuteronomy: we need not go into the details of all that; the fact remains that St Paul is prepared to describe our Lord as becoming 'an accursed thing'. And in writing to the Corinthians he uses an even more startling phrase: 'Christ never knew sin, and God made him into sin for us, so that in him we might be turned into the holiness of God' (II Cor. v. 21). Christ never knew sin—oh, it is all right, St Paul is not being heretical. It was impossible that our Lord should feel, personally, the consciousness of guilt. Yet our Lord had so identified himself with us, that what hung on the Cross was, to the mystic's view, a load of guilt. To be sure, the Hebrew language made it easier for St Paul to talk like that; in Hebrew, the word for 'sin' can also be used to mean 'a victim for sin'. But the underlying sense of what St Paul says is plain enough; our Lord for our sakes became sin, so that through him we might become innocence. It is not enough to think of the Cross, like the hymn *Vexilla regis,* as a pair of scales with our sin on one side and our Lord's Sacrifice on the other. We are to think of the Cross as a pillory, upon which he who summed up the whole of humanity summed up the whole guilt of humanity, hung there as a kind of impersonation of guilt, and by the destruction of his body destroyed the body of our sin.

We think of our Lord's death as the meritorious cause of our deliverance from guilt; we say 'Christ died in order that we might arise again from the death of sin.' St Paul, usually though not always, thinks of Christ's death as the exemplary cause of our deliverance from guilt; he says 'Christ died, and with him and in him we died to our sins; Christ rose again, and with him and in him we rose again to a new life of innocence'. When he says 'We died to our sins', he is using language with which we are unfamiliar, but after all, as he points out, it is the language of common life. Death cancels all obligations; and we, who were debtors under the law, and bankrupt debtors, because we were bound to keep the law and we couldn't, escaped from our obligations by dying with Christ. We are dead, and our life is hidden with Christ in God; our creditor, the law of Moses, cannot get at us now.

Well, we haven't yet answered the question we set out to answer: Which school of Christian thinkers did St Paul belong to? Did he see the Incarnation as something important in itself, or as something important because of what it led up to—the Atonement? If you had put the question in that way, I don't think he would have known what to answer; because to him the Atonement was part of the Incarnation, one aspect of it, one mood of it, not to be isolated in contrast with the rest. 'All I know,' he would have told you, 'is that when Jesus Christ became Man, you and I were somehow mystically identified with him. His life, not just by the circumstances of it but by the whole purpose and dedication of it, led up to his death on the cross. And when he died, you and I, mystically identified with him, became dead to our old life of sin and disobedience; we were buried with him, and rose again with him into a new life, in which God is our sun and Christ is the air we breathe. Was it the Incarnation, or the Atonement, that did that? I cannot tell; all I know is that my life is the faith I have in the Son of God, who loved me, and gave himself for me' (Gal. ii. 20).

ST PAUL ON THE MYSTICAL BODY

May he be glorified in the Church, and in Christ Jesus (Eph. iii. 21).

THE WORDS I quoted to you at the end of my last sermon were a favourite text with the old-fashioned Evangelicals, 'the Son of God, who loved me and gave himself for me'. The reason is not far to seek; for the Evangelical, everything depends on an inner conviction that Jesus Christ has died for him personally, and this text was the ideal expression of it. What they omitted to tell us is that it stands alone in St Paul's writings; everywhere else, I think, he insists that Christ died for us, gave himself for us.

The point I am making is that St Paul is, if ever a man was, a churchman. St Peter, curiously, doesn't use the word 'church' in his epistles at all; St Paul uses it more than sixty times—in fact, if you are reading him in the Vulgate, you will find that the word occurs almost on every page. But it is not merely that he often has occasion to mention the Church; more than once he seems to mention it where you would have thought there was no occasion to do so at all. In those words, for example, which I gave you just now as my text, why was it neces-

49

sary for him, if he wanted to end up the chapter with a doxology, to phrase it in this extraordinary way? 'May he be glorified in the Church, and in Christ Jesus'—as if the Church took rank with her Incarnate Master as one of the organs of God's praise; nay, took first rank, with her Incarnate Master second? It bothered the copyists, and some of them left out the word 'and'. If you look in the Authorized Version you will find, 'to him be glory *in* the Church *by* Christ Jesus'—it has even altered the preposition. But there is no doubt that ours was the true reading, 'in the Church and in Christ Jesus'. St Paul's mind is so occupied with the thought of the Church, God's splendid tapestry of Jew and Gentile, that he can think of nothing else for the moment, and for once the Person of Jesus Christ comes in as a kind of after-thought.

Our Lord doesn't seem to have talked much about his Church; his favourite way of describing the Christian commonwealth was 'the kingdom of God' or 'the king-dom of heaven'. But on two occasions, at least, he did talk about the 'Church', and the memory it will have called up in the minds of his disciples was the assembly, the 'gathering together' of his ancient people the Jews, when he brought them out of Egypt into Chanaan. In old days, God had chosen a particular nation to be his Assembly; now he, Jesus Christ, would have an assembly of his own, no longer merely national in its membership. When the apostles took preaching the Gospel in Greek, they didn't call this new Assembly a 'gathering together', because that word 'synagogue', had already been appropriated by the Jews. They called it the ecclesia, the 'outcalling' of Christ. This was evidently, from the first, the technical way of describing the Christian body, and for the most part the New Testament authors use it in a severely technical sense. They don't seem to get excited about it; it is merely a convenient way of describing, either the total number of Christians in some particular area, or the total number of Christians in the world. Three times out of four, the word 'congregation' would answer just as well. Strange, that our Lord's defiant utterance, 'on this rock I will build my church', finds no echo, for example, in the Acts of the Apostles! No, I am wrong, there is one. 'Keep watch, then, over God's church, in which the Holy Spirit has made you bishops; you are to be the shepherds of that flock which he won for himself at the price of his own blood' (Acts xx. 28). But it comes in a speech reported verbatim, and the speaker is St Paul.

For St Paul, especially when he is writing to the Ephesians and to the Colossians, the Church is a mysterious entity with a life of its own, something much more than the sum of its members. He calls it, for example, the 'pillar and foundation upon which the truth rests' (Tim. iii. 15); already, in that dawn of believing, heresy begins to threaten, and the appeal from it is made, not precisely to the apostles who still lived, but to the *Ecclesia Docens,* human in her membership, and yet wiser than ourselves. But that is a solitary reference, late in his career. For the most part, he is lyrical about the Church not as the touchstone of truth, but as the focus of unity. We Christians are one in Christ, and the Church is both ideally the expression of that unity, and in practice the arena for realizing it.

Oh, I know, St Paul will talk to you about 'the churches' of Asia or 'the churches' of Macedonia, in a way that is apt to make you think of them as so many independent units, vaguely federated. But even as he does that, if you will look more closely at the context, St Paul is deliberately overriding these local boundaries. He is appealing to the various 'churches' to subscribe to a charity of his; a fund he is raising to help the impoverished 'church' at Jerusalem. And if you will read the eighth and ninth chapters of his second epistle to the Corinthians, you will see what importance he attached to it, and why. 'The administration of this public service', he says, 'does more than supply the needs of the saints; it yields, besides, a rich harvest of thanksgiving in the name of the Lord. . . . They will intercede, too, on your behalf, as the abundant measure of grace which God bestows on you warms their hearts towards you' (II Cor. ix. 12, 14). This very practical form of intercourse was the best way, he saw, of knitting together the hearts of Christian people who live remote from one another; he calls it 'the communion' (II Cor. viii. 4; ix. 13), calls it by that sacred name by which, already, men referred to participation in the Holy Eucharist. That was what St Paul thought of second collections.

For him, there was one Church, and its unity was diffused everywhere, like the air we breathe. He is not content to talk about 'the church' in this or that town; he will talk about 'the church' in so-and-so's household (e.g., Rom. xvi. 5) —the little group of Christian slaves, perhaps not always with a Christian master, who met to say their prayers together were a cross-section of Christendom, a little microcosm in which the Church was represented, as the sun may be reflected in a puddle. The Church itself was a glorious reconciliation of human differences; in it there was neither Jew nor Gentile, neither slave nor freeman, neither barbarian nor Scythian, neither male nor female, all were one person in Christ (Gal. iii. 28). And each family, in the same way, had its differences to be reconciled; 'I call upon thee, Euodia, and I call upon thee, Syntyche, to make common cause in the Lord' (Phil. iv. 2). Who were they? We don't know; we don't even know whether Euodia was male or female —perhaps St Paul didn't; but their bickerings were not to go on. And in the same way, he will put an end to rivalries in this or that congregation; everybody is to do his own job, and not be envious of the next man. How small-minded they were, even those first Christians! But St Paul is not discouraged by it; here is an excellent opportunity, he thinks, for realizing on a small scale the glorious comprehensiveness of Christ's Church.

How does he think of that Church, seen in its full extension? Three metaphors he has for it, all familiar enough, but all worth looking into. For him, it is the bride of Christ; it is the building of which Christ is corner-stone; it is the body of which Christ is head.

It is not a matter for surprise that St Paul should have pictured the relations between Christ and his Church under the image of man and wife. The Church was the people of Christ, exactly as the Synagogue was the people of God; and it is a commonplace, when you are reading the Old Testament prophets, to find Israel referred to as the bride of his youth, false to him now. 'And thou with many lovers hast played the wanton,' so runs the appeal of Jeremias, 'yet come back to me, the Lord says, and thou shalt find welcome' (Jer. iii. 1). No wonder that St Paul should employ the same kind of metaphor; 'My jealousy on your behalf is the jealousy of God himself; I have betrothed you to Christ, so that no other but he should claim you, his bride without spot; and now I am anxious about you' (II Cor. xi. 2). And so, in writing to the Ephesians, he represents our Lord himself as shewing his love for the Church by giving up his life for it, so that he might summon it into his presence, the Church in all its beauty; it was to be holy, it was to be spotless. All that we should expect; it is what follows, in this Ephesian passage, that makes us rub our eyes.

It is very characteristic of St Paul that he is not setting out to read the Ephesians a lesson in his doctrine of the Church. No, the Church comes in merely by way of illustration; what he is setting out to do is to make the husbands at Ephesus treat their wives less selfishly! But he is not content to say, 'Christ treated his bride the Church so lovingly, you men ought to treat your wives lovingly, in imitation of him'. He says, apparently, that a man ought to be a good husband merely from self-interest; after all, the wife is part of her husband just as the Church is part of Christ. 'That is how a man ought to love his wife, as if she were his own body; in loving his wife, a man is but loving himself. And so it is with Christ and his Church; we are limbs of his body, flesh and bone, we belong to him. That is why a man will leave his father and mother and will cling to his wife, and the two will become one flesh. Yes, those words are a high mystery, and I am applying them here to Christ and his Church' (Eph. v. 28, 29, 33).

Useless, perhaps, to ask St Paul which is the premiss from which he starts, which is the conclusion he reaches. Is he telling us that man and wife are one thing, therefore Christ and his Church are one thing? Or is he telling us that Christ and his Church are one thing, therefore man and wife ought to be one thing? I doubt if you can hold St Paul down to a syllogism like that. Rather, he sees the two truths simultaneously, either mirrored in the other. Either truth is mystical, although in the case of the husband there is a moral application; the grace of the sacrament, here as elsewhere, has to be lived up to. What concerns us, is that our mystical union with Christ is essentially a corporate one; St Paul has betrothed the Corinthians to Christ not as so many brides (the language of a later mysticism) but as a single bride; it is in and through our identification with the Church that we are identified with Christ.

The point is still more clearly emphasized by an alternative image which the Apostle gives us in this same letter to the Ephesians, that of a spiritual building. 'Apostles and prophets are the foundation on which you were built, and the chief corner-stone of it is Jesus Christ himself. In him the whole fabric is bound together, as it grows into a temple, dedicated to the Lord; in him you too are being built in with the rest, so that God may find in you a dwelling-place for his Spirit' (Eph. ii. 20–22) . Two minor difficulties occur to the reader, neither of which has great importance for our present purposes. Are the prophets in question the prophets of the Old Testament? More probably those of the New; not in the sense that they were ever recognized as taking rank, merely as prophets, in the hierarchy of the Church, but in their capacity as preachers; 'he who prophesies', we are told elsewhere, 'builds up the church' (I Cor. xiv. 4) . Again, does 'the foundation of the apostles' mean a foundation consisting of the apostles, or a foundation which the apostles lay, as in the third chapter of the first Corinthian letter (I Cor. iii. 10) ? I doubt very much if St Paul stopped to ask himself which of the two he meant.

The metaphor is a common one; St Peter uses it (I Pet. ii. 4) , perhaps with some memory of Caesarea Philippi. St Paul, in writing to the Ephesians, has a particular application for it; he has been talking, all through the chapter, about the vocation of the Gentiles, and he represents Christ as the corner-stone, *lapis angularis qui facis utraque unum;* in him Jew and Gentile, hitherto distinct, meet and are bound into one. The key-word of the passage is a word which only occurs in one other place in Greek literature; 'the whole fabric is bound together'—perhaps we ought to say 'is dove-tailed together', if we want a vivid translation. The apparently ill-assorted people fitting in together after all—that was how St. Paul saw the ideal Christian congregation, each man following his own aptitudes and doing his own job without, somehow, feeling inclined to criticize the way the other man was doing his. And so it is here, on a larger scale; Jew and Gentile, why shouldn't they mix, in Christ? Why shouldn't different nations, different cultures, each have their own contribution to make, for the perfecting of Christ's building? All that, perhaps, St Paul would have developed; even, perhaps, developed the other side of it, as it is developed in the hymn *Caelestis urbs;* the shaping, the fashioning of each stone, *fabri polita malleo,* which has to be done before it fits into its right niche, the retrenchment of personality which we call mortification. . . . But he doesn't develop all that; and if he doesn't, I think it is because he didn't like taking his metaphor from stones and mortar; they were dead things merely superimposed on one another, and St Paul liked to think of Christian people as living things, growing out of one another.

Living things, growing out of one another—so, in his epistle to the Romans, he compares the fusion of Jew and Gentile in the Church not to a feat of architecture, but to a feat of gardening. They are not two walls,

meeting at a common angle, they are two growths of
olive, one wild, one fruit-bearing, and the wild growth
of the Gentiles is grafted into the fruitful Jewish stock
(Rom. xi. 17 *sqq.*). That was well enough, but he would
go deeper yet. I said just now that the word which I translated 'dove-tailed' only occurs twice in Greek literature. It
does; once in Ephesians ii. 21, and once in Ephesians iv.
16. In this latter passage he takes the same word and
deliberately grafts it on to an organic metaphor. It is as
if he were saying 'Dove-tailed, yes; I told you just now
that we were dove-tailed into one another like different
parts of a building. But really it is a closer union than
that; we are dove-tailed into one another like different
parts of the human body'. So it is that you get the mag-
nificent passage in which he tells us that we are to grow
up, through charity, into a due proportion with Christ,
who is our head. How good his metaphors are! Because
of course a child's head is out of proportion, it is waiting
for the rest of the body to grow up and match it; so
Christ and we. 'On him all the body depends; it is or-
ganized and unified by each contact with the source
which supplies it; and thus, each limb receiving the
active power it needs, it achieves its natural growth,
building itself up (he is betrayed into the old, discarded
image again) —building itself up through charity.'

He is not really happy, you see, about his doctrine of
the Church until he has expressed it in terms of the Mystical Body. As our Lord had a natural body, which must
be swaddled and suckled by our Lady at Bethlehem, so

he has a mystical body which must take shape and receive nourishment and so grow up into the perfect thing he wants it to be. This image is the same, yet not the same, as our Lord's own image of the True Vine (John xv. 1–6). The same, because there too you get the sense of an intimate connexion; the branch does not depend upon its parent stock more wholly than we depend on our incorporation into Christ; does not perish more surely if it is lopped off than we do if, most miserably, we allow ourselves to be separated from him. And yet not the same, for our Lord is thinking only of our relations with him, not of our relations with one another. Each of the people to whom he is speaking—and they, remember, were the great princes of his Church—is only a twig, you can hardly call it a branch, of the one Vine; the Vine, all of it except the twigs, is himself. All that tells you the truth about our union with Christ; it does not tell you the full truth about our union in Christ. For St Paul, Christ is the head, and we are members of the body, depending not only upon him but upon one another, as the members of a human body do. 'The body, after all, consists not of one organ but of many; if the foot should say, I am not the hand, and therefore I do not belong to the body, does it belong to the body any the less for that? There was to be no want of unity in the body; all the different parts of it were to make each other's welfare their common care. If one part is suffering, all the rest suffer with it; if one part is treated with honour, all the rest find pleasure in it. And you are

Christ's body, organs of it depending on each other' (I Cor. xii. 14 *sqq.*). One with Christ, and one in Christ; the doctrine of the Mystical Body will not be summed up under any formula which falls short of that.

We have said that Christ grows in his Mystical Body; no need, then, to suppose that all these high-sounding phrases which St Paul uses about the Church refer to a collection of Saints already made perfect. To be sure, he calls all Christian folk 'saints'; it is his way; he sees us not as we are but as we ought to be. These 'saints' had to be warned against fornication, against thieving, against bitter schisms; it is the Church we know. We are not impeccable, not confirmed in grace, he tells us, any more than the Jewish people, God's church in the desert (I Cor. x. 12). But we are Christ's Bride; shall we mar that beauty? We are Christ's body; shall that unity go for nothing?

ST PAUL ON THE RISEN LIFE
OF THE CHRISTIAN

You, by baptism, have been united with his burial; united, too, with his resurrection, through your faith in that exercise of power by which God raised him from the dead (Col. ii. 12).

WE HAVE SEEN how St Paul loves to dwell on the union, the self-identification, of Christ with his Church. The Church is his body, 'the completion of him who everywhere and in all things is complete' (Eph. i. 23) —nothing less than that paradox will content St Paul. The Humanity of our Blessed Lord is the most absolute achievement in God's creation; you cannot think of it but as a thing utterly complete in itself. And yet, if you look at the whole question from another angle, the Sacred Humanity would be incomplete without us; it was for our sakes he came down from heaven, and if, *per impossibile,* nobody from our Blessed Lady downwards had believed in him or accepted the gift of salvation from him, the purpose of the Incarnation would have remained unrealized. St Paul is very fond of this word 'completion', and it may be true that he was using, in an orthodox sense, the language of those heretics whose false teaching was a danger to the Church at Colossae. But I sometimes wonder whether it may not have suggested to him, besides, a familiar image. St Paul came from Tarsus, a place of ships and seamen; less than a century before, it had been the great center of piracy in the Mediterranean. And the Greeks talked about 'completing' a ship where we should talk of 'manning' a ship; described the crew of a ship as its 'completion'. Did he, perhaps, at the back of his mind, think of the Sacred Humanity as a ship, an Ark, which would have meant nothing if there had been no crew to sail it?

On the other side, hard as it may be to think of ourselves as the completing of Christ's nature, there is no difficulty whatever in realizing that he is the completion of ours. 'In Christ,' says the Apostle, 'the whole plenitude of Deity is embodied, and in him you find your completion. . . . You, by baptism, have been united to his burial, united, too, with his resurrection' (Col. ii. 10, 12). Man's nature, ever since the Fall, incapable of achieving his clear destiny, conscious, however dimly, of the desire to please God, yet with no apparatus for doing it—how could anything be so manifestly incomplete? Compare him, if you will, to a ship bound for some distant port, with no complement of sailors to man her. . . . You would almost expect to find St Paul comparing Christian baptism with the rescue of Noe and his sons in the ark. But he doesn't; it is St Peter who does that (I Pet. iii. 20). For St Paul, the type of baptism is the people of Israel, led out from its Egyptian bondage through the Red Sea.

That analogy will have been in the minds of Christian

people from the first; it could hardly be otherwise. Our Lord suffered death at the time of the great Jewish feast; evidently he meant us to understand that he was being sacrificed for us as our Paschal Victim, meant us to understand that the escape of Israel from Egypt by way of the Red Sea was a type of Christian baptism, cutting us off, as if by a wall of water, from our dead past. The hymn *Exultet,* which we sing on Holy Saturday, a hymn that in its whole inspiration takes you right back to the very beginnings of Christendom, is full of that imagery. 'This night, long ago, thou didst rescue the sons of Israel, our fathers, out of Egypt, over the Red Sea bidding them pass dry-shod; none but this, with pillar of cloud to enlighten it, shadow of man's sin could purge away.' So we bless the candle that is the type of our Lord himself, that will be dipped into the new Font, and make it pregnant with the power of spiritual re-birth. All that, or at least the doctrinal kernel of all that, St Paul knew about; we learn as much from a casual reference, a single word of one of his letters—how prodigal he is of unexploited allusion, throwing out a significant word to us, and passing on!

He is warning the Corinthians that it is a fatal error to presume on one's grace; you must co-operate with it energetically; he who thinks he stands firmly should beware of a fall. And he illustrates that by recalling the infidelities of the Jewish people in the wilderness; they (he says) could sin and did sin in spite of the great graces bestowed on them. Had they not been saved from the pursuit of their enemies by the cloud that overhung their camp, by the waters of the Red Sea which closed behind them? Only he does not use that phrase, 'Saved from the pursuit of their enemies'; his words are, 'All alike, in the cloud and in the sea, were baptized into Moses' fellowship' (I Cor. x. 2). What he means, evidently, is that Christian baptism, intimately connected with our Lord's Resurrection and with the feast of our Lord's Resurrection, is the fulfilment of a type; it puts a distance between us and our sins, isolates us in the close unity of Christian fellowship; we too are like men who have escaped from bondage, rallied now under a divine leadership. On all that background of his thought the Apostle just lifts, as it were, the corner of a curtain when, almost absent-mindedly, he calls the crossing of the Red Sea a baptism.

But of course, from his point of view, the type is only a feeble image, it doesn't do justice to the situation. The Israelites, when they escaped from Egypt, escaped with their lives; it is not so with Christian baptism. To be baptized is to undergo a mystical death, in union with our Lord's death on the cross, a mystical burial in union with his burial, a mystical resurrection in union with his resurrection. We have been taken up into Christ's death, in our baptism, we have been buried with him, died like him, that so, just as Christ was raised up by his Father's power from the dead, we too might live and move in a new kind of existence'. We are grafted into a new stock; 'our former nature has been crucified with him, and the living power of our guilt destroyed, so that we are the slaves of sin no longer. Guilt makes no more claim on a man who is dead' (Rom. vi. 4). Do not ask St Paul whether this mystical death sets us free from the old law, or sets us free from guilt; it is the same process—the burden we carried when we were still unregenerate was that of an obligation we could not meet; the law and our sinfulness played into one another's hands, were the upper and nether millstone which ground us between them. Now it is all right; we are dead, and death cancels all obligations. Elsewhere, pressing his imagery still more boldly, he tells us that we are dead, and our life is hidden away with Christ in God (Col. iii. 3) ; we take refuge from our pursuers, and our hiding-place is a tomb.

Not that St Paul is unacquainted with that other and more familiar imagery which describes baptism as washing us clean from our sins; 'he saved us with the cleansing power which gives us new birth' (Tit. iii. 5). But that is not his favourite way of talking; and, I think, for two reasons. Washing is something external to ourselves, we get rid of something on the surface that was never really part of us: whereas the grace of baptism goes down to the very roots of our nature, restores us to a new kind of existence. And washing is a process we may repeat as often as we will; baptism is not like that, it is a single, crucial moment, like the moment of death. Dead, buried, and risen with Christ, that is our state, when we have been baptized. We must not imagine, when St Paul uses a legal metaphor about death cancelling all claims, that he looks on this baptism-death as a mere legal fiction. No, we must think of ourselves as dead to sin, and alive with a life that looks towards God (Rom. vi. 11). New life, for St Paul, does not mean merely new habits of living, turning over a new leaf. It means that a new principle of life altogether has been implanted in us; it is as if God were repeating that act by which he breathed life into the dumb clay of his creature Adam, long ago in Paradise.

There are passages in which you will find the apostle pressing this notion still further, as if the change which takes place in us at baptism were something more, even, than a death and a rising again; as if it involved the annihilation of the thing we once were, and the creation of a fresh human being altogether. 'Circumcision means nothing,' he tells the Galatians, 'and the want of it means nothing; when a man is in Christ Jesus, there has been a new creation' (Gal. vi. 15). And so, in a passage I have already quoted, he insists that our old self has been crucified with Christ (Rom. vi. 6). Of course, by a metaphor, you may talk of a man's old self and his new self when he has undergone any considerable change of heart. But St Paul seems to mean more than that; does he mean (we are tempted to ask) that the regeneration which comes to us with baptism undoes all the effects of the Fall, that we no longer feel the sting of concupiscence, that we are sealed, irresistibly and automatically, for heaven? But no, that is not what he is telling us. On the contrary, in these very passages where he insists so strongly on the catastrophic effects of the new birth, he is pleading with us to live up to it and be worthy of it. 'You must be quit, now, of the old self whose way of life you remember, the self that wasted its aim on false dreams. . . . You must be quit of the old self, and the habits that went with it; you must be clothed in the new self, that is being refitted all the time for closer knowledge, so that the image of the God who created it is its pattern' (Eph. iv. 22; Col. iii. 9). He tells us that we have got to get rid of the old self, not that we are rid of it. The doctrine of the new birth is not an All-clear signal to tell us that the struggle with sin is all over. It is a call to arms, bidding us enter on the struggle, because at last we have a chance of victory. 'You must not make your bodily powers over to sin. . . . Sin will not be able to play the master over you any longer; you serve grace now, not the law' (Rom. vi. 13, 14).

You serve grace now, not the law—that means, evidently and most importantly, a better chance in the struggle; the law does but set before us a high standard, which we despair of achieving, grace enables us. But something else, I think, is implied. When you serve the law, you serve it, inevitably, in a legal spirit, unwillingly, grudgingly, according to the letter. When you serve free grace, you serve it in a spirit of freedom; you enter (as we say) into the spirit of it, cooperate, gladly and generously, with its designs for you. That contrast between doing God's will because you have got to and doing God's will because you want to is more explicitly set forth elsewhere. When the Jews were rescued from their bondage in Egypt, they emerged (you might almost say) from one bondage into another; they were God's slaves now instead of Pharao's, obeying him, if they obeyed him at all, blindly, unquestioningly, as they obeyed Pharao. But when the grace of Jesus Christ came to us, it was no longer, this time, a mere change of masters. 'The spirit you have now received is not, as of old, a spirit of slavery, to govern you by fear; it is the spirit of adoption, which makes us cry out Abba, Father!' (Rom. viii. 15). It is the same principle which our Lord himself had taught, though with a slightly different emphasis, when he told his apostles, 'I do not speak of you now as my servants; a servant is one who does not understand what his master is about, whereas I have made known to you all that my Father has told me, and so I have called you my friends' (John xv. 15). If the practice of the Christian religion seems to you and me something uncommonly like drudgery, that is our fault; it was not meant to be. The only really Christian attitude is to obey God with the dutifulness of loving sons, is to follow Christ with the loyalty of devoted friends.

With baptism, we escape from the sense of mere law-abidingness which afflicted us under the Old Covenant, a dull, negative thing, and become conscious of an active principle working in us instead. What is this active principle? Nothing other than the Holy Spirit; where the Lord's Spirit is, there is liberty (II Cor. iii. 17). We have not, after all, finished the story when we have reminded ourselves that Christ died and was buried, and rose again from the dead. The natural corollary of our Lord's rising from the dead is his Ascension. He went down to the lower regions of earth; and he who so went down is no other than he who has gone up, high above all the heavens, to fill creation wth his presence. He has given gifts to men—so one of the psalms had prophesied, in the version of it which St Paul knew; Pentecost, in its turn, is the corollary of the Ascension (Eph. iv. 8–10). And now he, who fills all things with his presence, has poured out the love of God in our hearts by the Holy Spirit, whom we have received. Confirmation, in those days when so many catechumens were grown men, followed close on baptism, just as Pentecost followed close on the Resurrection. 'We too, all of us, have been baptized into a single body by the power of a single Spirit, . . . we have all been given to drink at a single source, the one Spirit'—you have two processes there, but they are complementary; how should a body exist without breath in it? We are to live by the spirit as naturally (I had almost said, as unconsciously) as our physical bodies live by the breath we breathe.

To live by the Spirit, as, in ideal at least, Christians should, is sometimes referred to as 'walking about in the Spirit' (Gal. v. 16); strolling about at our pleasure (that is the notion of the Hebrew metaphor), taking our ease, 'finding ourselves' in that element. Sometimes it is referred to as being 'led about' by the Spirit, as if the responsibility for every decision was taken out of our hands, so instinctively do we respond to the least touch of the divine guidance (Rom. viii. 14) . That is why, as we were reminding ourselves just now, the new covenant of grace is a covenant of freedom. The life of the spirit, St Paul tells us, has appetites of its own, diametrically opposed to the appetites of unregenerate nature and therefore, ideally, excluding them (Gal. v. 18 *sqq.*) . A combat the Christian life may be at any level; if we find it a conflict, that is because it is being lived at a low level—the reign of the Spirit in us is incomplete.

I say, ideally; it is quite evident that even in St Paul's day there could be, and there was, maladjustment in Christian lives. All through his letters to the Corinthians, that is his chief anxiety; the exceptional gifts of the Holy Spirit—less exceptional then than now—such as prophecy, healing of sickness, speaking with unknown tongues, abounded at Corinth; but where were those other qualities, gifts of the Holy Spirit no less, that made for the building up of the Church, the spirit of discipline, the spirit of humility, above all, the spirit of charity (I Cor. xii. 31) ? This doubt on the apostle's part will account for the way in which he always includes in his list of spiritual gifts various aptitudes which have nothing of the abnormal, nothing of the sensational about them; there is a charisma of preaching the word, a charisma of teaching, a charisma, even, of financial administration (I Cor. xii. 28; Eph. iv. 11) . Any quality, he insists, which makes us useful members of the Church is bestowed upon us by that same Spirit who enables us to prophesy, to speak with tongues. The craving for powers which are unusual, which are apparently supernatural, is for St Paul a kind of vulgarity.

It is perhaps possible to trace the same warning when he tells us that 'the Spirit comes to the aid of our weakness; when we do not know what prayer to offer, to pray as we ought, the Spirit himself intercedes for us, with groans beyond all utterance' (Rom. viii. 26). He does not mean that the groans are indescribable, but that they find no outlet in words. More impressive, to him, than all the outcry of prophet and glossolalist was that inner, silent experience of the mystic who feels that the business of prayer is being taken out of his own hands, that the Holy Spirit is praying in him.

'Abba, Father'—why does St Paul say that? Why does he give you the title first in Aramaic and then in Greek? He does it twice over; the Galatians, too, are reminded that God has sent out the Spirit of his Son into our hearts, crying out in us, Abba, Father (Rom. viii. 15; Gal. iv. 6). Is he consciously quoting from St Mark's account of Gethsemani, where alone (perhaps by way of an editorial note) the Aramaic word is given and then translated? If so, it is the only verbal quotation from the Gospels in St Paul's writings. Or is it possible that the first two words of the Paternoster were pronounced, in the first age of the Church, bilingually, just as we still talk Greek and then translate it into Latin when we recite the Reproaches on Good Friday? Nobody can tell you. But when St Paul uses little touches like that, one thing emerges about him clearly, the very thing I have been trying to emphasize all through this course of sermons—that he is an authentic, independent witness, agreeing always with the Gospels, yet never quoting the Gospels or referring to the Gospels. He has preserved for us, concurrently with them yet independently of them, the same tradition of Christian teaching which has come down across all these centuries to you and me; only, he tapped it at the source. When he wrote, Christian theology had not been standardized in technical terms; consequently, the presentation of it you get in St Paul's writings has something individual about it, something of himself in it; and the same can be said of the images which are his favourite images. But always, as he told the Corinthians, the message he hands on to us is the message which was handed on to him (Cor. xv. 3). Original, if ever a human mind was, the mind of Paul has been surrendered to Christ's service.